Southern Renascence

The Literature of the Modern South

SOUTHERN RENASCENCE

The Literature of the Modern South

Edited by

LOUIS D. RUBIN, JR.

and

ROBERT D. JACOBS

Baltimore : The Johns Hopkins Press

for

ELLIOTT COLEMAN

© 1953 by The Johns Hopkins Press, Baltimore, Md. 21218
Printed in the United States of America
Library of Congress Catalog Card No. 53–11174
Distributed in Great Britain by Oxford University Press

Originally published, 1953
Second printing, 1954
Third printing, 1961
Fourth printing, 1966

Johns Hopkins Paperbacks edition, 1966

Preface

The idea for the present volume was conceived two years ago on a moderate enough scale. The editors, who were also the editors of The Hopkins Review, planned for that magazine a series of perhaps three essays in which the more obvious characteristics of the host of modern Southern writers might be touched on. The response to the project, however, was so overwhelming, and so encouraging, that it was realized just how widespread was the latent interest in Southern writing, and how potentially important a thoroughgoing survey and analysis of the literature of the modern South might be. Accordingly, plans were expanded tenfold, and the present volume is the result.

Almost all of the essays in this volume were originally published in The Hopkins Review. Two kinds of essays were sought: those which would present a detailed analysis of a single author, and those which would work across the field in an attempt to delineate common themes. No single critical outlook, no one critical approach is embodied in this volume. Persons of varying tastes and interests were intentionally selected as contributors. Nor have the editors intended that the views embodied in the essays coincide with their own views.

The editors hope that the volume provides the first reasonably thorough treatment of the literature of the modern South. They are aware that gaps exist in the presentation. They were unable, for example, to secure a competent study of the many obvious relationships between the Southern Agrarian critics of the 1930s on the one hand, and the increased emphasis upon traditional religious values evidenced throughout the western world during the past two decades on the other. There seemed to be a strong tie implicit there. Neither was it possible to secure a general overall treatment of the modern Southern poets.

The editors wish to make the following acknowledgments. Mr. Donald Davidson, of Vanderbilt University, both contributed an

essay and provided suggestions for several contributors. Mr. Cleanth
Brooks, of Yale University, was likewise most helpful in suggesting
contributors. Among others to whom any achievement in this under-
taking must be in large measure ascribed are Professors C. Vann
Woodward, Leo Spitzer, Charles R. Anderson, Georges Poulet, N.
Bryllion Fagin, and George Boas, of the faculty of The Johns Hopkins
University; Dr. Francis J. Thompson, of the faculty of Rollins College,
Winter Park, Florida; Mr. A. D. Emmart, of the editorial staff of
The Evening Sun, Baltimore, Maryland; Mr. John Edward Hardy, Miss
Emily F. Greenslet, Mrs. B. Bernei Burgunder, and Mr. John G.
Koenig, Jr., of Baltimore; Mr. Robert Hazel, of New York City; and,
for their patience and their assistance, Eva Redfield Rubin and Mildred
S. Jacobs.

The essay " The Irony of Southern History," by C. Vann Woodward, was originally delivered as Dr. Woodward's presidential address
to the Southern Historical Association, and is reproduced in the present
volume through courtesy of the Journal of Southern History, in which
it originally appeared.

The material contained in the essay " Theme and Method In *So
Red The Rose*," by Donald Davidson, is presented in enlarged form
in Mr. Davidson's introduction to the Modern Standard Authors edi-
tion of *So Red The Rose* (Charles Scribner's Sons, 1953) and is used
by permission of Charles Scribner's Sons. Portions of the essay " The
Poetry of John Peale Bishop," by Robert W. Stallman, originally
appeared in an essay on Bishop by Mr. Stallman in The Western
Review. Several passages in the essay " The Conservatism of Caroline
Gordon," by Vivienne Koch, are taken from other articles on Miss
Gordon's work by Miss Koch in the Briarcliff Quarterly and the
Sewanee Review. Permission to use the material listed above is grate-
fully acknowledged.

Finally, we wish to list here some of the books from which quotations are presented in the present volume, and to make proper and
grateful acknowledgment to the author and publisher in each instance:

Caroline Gordon and Allen Tate, eds., *The House of Fiction* (Charles
Scribner's Sons, 1951).

Caroline Gordon, *Alec Maury, Sportsman* (Charles Scribner's Sons, 1934).

Caroline Gordon, *The Garden Of Adonis* (Charles Scribner's Sons, 1937).

Caroline Gordon, *Penhally* (Charles Scribner's Sons, 1931).

John Crowe Ransom, *Selected Poems* (Alfred A. Knopf, 1945).

Allen Tate, *Collected Poems* (Charles Scribner's Sons, 1947).

T. S. Eliot, *Notes Toward A Definition Of Culture* (Harcourt, Brace, 1949).

William Faulkner, *Light In August* (New Directions, 1932).

William Faulkner, *Absalom, Absalom!* (Random House, 1936).

William Faulkner, *Collected Stories* (Random House, 1950).

William Faulkner, *The Wild Palms* (Random House, 1939).

William Faulkner, *Requiem For A Nun* (Random House, 1951).

William Faulkner, *The Unvanquished* (Random House, 1938).

Ellen Glasgow, *The Sheltered Life* (Doubleday and Co., 1932).

Ellen Glasgow, *Barren Ground* (Doubleday and Co., 1925).

Paul Green, *Salvation On A String* (Harper and Bros., 1946).

Marjorie Kinnan Rawlings, *When The Whipporwill . . .* (Charles Scribner's Sons, 1940).

Norman Mailer, *The Naked And The Dead* (Rinehart and Co., 1948).

James Branch Cabell, *Beyond Life* (Robert M. McBride and Co., 1919).

James Branch Cabell, *Cream Of The Jest* (Robert M. McBride and Co., 1921).

James Branch Cabell, *The Way Of Echen* (Robert M. McBride and Co., 1929).

Donald Davidson, *The Attack On Leviathan* (Chapel Hill, 1938).

Donald Davidson, *Lee In The Mountains* (Charles Scribner's Sons, 1949).

Robert Penn Warren, *World Enough And Time* (Harcourt, Brace, 1951).

Thomas Wolfe, *The Web And The Rock* (Harper and Bros., 1939).

Thomas Wolfe, *Look Homeward, Angel* (Charles Scribner's Sons, 1929).

Stark Young, *So Red The Rose* (Charles Scribner's Sons, 1934).

John Peale Bishop, *Collected Poems* (Charles Scribner's Sons, 1948).

LOUIS D. RUBIN, JR.
The Johns Hopkins University

ROBERT D. JACOBS
The University of Kentucky

Baltimore, Maryland
July 1, 1953

Preface to the Paperback Edition

That *Southern Renascence,* almost fifteen years after its inception and twelve since its first publication, should be going into a new, paperback edition, is, for its editors at least, a quite astounding phenomenon. Five years or so ago we thought it was dead. We even edited another collection which we thought handled the matter in question—the whys and wherefores of modern Southern literature—more comprehensively. Yet to our surprise, not only did the appearance of the newer book *not* finish off *Southern Renascence,* but the earlier volume continued right on its way and even outdistanced the newer one. So that now it proceeds, on the strength of a twelve-year published life, into paperback.

What we did in 1953 was to publish the first attempt at an inclusive examination of the literature of the modern South. It began as a symposium in the magazine we both edited, the late and lamented *Hopkins Review.* We were able to pay our contributors not a cent for their essays. We proceeded despite assurances from some who, by their rank and dignity, should have known that there was no such thing as *Southern* literature; and when the book appeared, one young man, now a distinguished critic and editor, informed us in the pages of a noted quarterly that our subject didn't even exist and that the whole project was silly.

There have been a number of books about modern Southern literature since 1953—some of them, no doubt, better than this one. Possibly a good bit of what was said in this book will now appear dated and occasionally, be it said, even chauvinistic. But *Southern Renascence* was the first of the sort and some of its essays are of the kind that endure. We would be less than candid if we did not admit to a distinct satisfaction that, considering the way it was put together, it stands up as well as it does twelve years after it first appeared.

Southern Renascence was dedicated to Elliott Coleman, then as now chairman of the Writing Seminars of The Johns Hopkins University. Never was a dedication more deserved, for the very existence of the book was a result of the editors' having been able to be part of that marvelously creative academic operation going on in the basement of Gilman Hall of The Johns Hopkins University. That it still goes on in 1965 as in 1953 is Elliott Coleman's doing, not as contributor to this book, but as primary agent in creating conditions in which young men are encouraged to write and think about the literature of their own time, what it means and how it came to be. We should like once again to express our thanks to Elliott Coleman, to Emily Greenslet, to our contributors, and to all who took part in the various creative endeavors that made the Writing Seminars of The Johns Hopkins University the most privileged experience that those associated with it have ever enjoyed, before or since.

LOUIS D. RUBIN, JR.
Hollins College, Virginia

ROBERT D. JACOBS
The University of Kentucky

July 31, 1965

Table of Contents

IV. THE POETRY OF THE SOUTH

I. The Mind Of The South

ROBERT B. HEILMAN

The Southern Temper

The Southern temper is marked by the coincidence of a sense of the concrete, a sense of the elemental, a sense of the ornamental, a sense of the representative, and a sense of totality. No one of these endowments is unshared; but their concurrency is not frequent. This concurrency is *a* condition of major art and mature thought. The endowments, like most endowments, are not possessed in entire freedom, without price. If you buy an endowment, you don't buy something else. To live with an endowment runs risks, and even the concurrency of several endowments does not guarantee a funding of the counter-deficiency which may accompany the possession of any single one.

The Southern temper is not the temper of all Southerners, who, for all of the predeterminations of Northerners from Portland, Maine, to Portland, Oregon, are as various as dwellers in other regions. The South generally—the politico-economic-social South, the problem South, the South in need of precept and reprimand—is not my business. It is after all so much like so much of the rest of the country that there is not much to say. The temper I will try to describe is that of certain novelists, poets, and critics who have now, for some twenty or twenty-five years, been at least in the corner of the literate public's eye.

The sense of the concrete, as an attribute of the fiction writer, is so emphatically apparent in Faulkner, Warren, and Wolfe, so subtly and variously apparent in Porter, Welty, and Gordon, and so flamboyantly so in someone like Capote (who hardly belongs here at all) that everybody knows it's there. It is there, too, in the poetry of Ransom, Tate, and Warren. In fact, the lesson that fiction and poetry must be grounded in the sensory world, and the dramatic situation, has been learned very thoroughly in our day; everybody—even the

3

students in writing courses whose goal is an abstraction, the omnipurchasing formula—knows how to go out and record the broken eggshells on the pavement, the smell of armpits and violets, the feel of chewing gum, the sound and fury, the synesthetic confluences. Most experts in sensography do not know what to do with their bursting haul, for they have not inherited or been provided with an adequate way of thinking about it or with it, and hence are likely to stop short with a record as lush as a seed catalogue, as miscellaneously hard as hooves on concrete, and as variously pungent as a city market toward the end of the day. In the transcendence of aesthetic audio-visual aids, as we shall see, the Southerners are better off.

In criticism, the Southern sense of the concrete takes the form of a preoccupation with the individual work and the precise means by which its author goes about his business. Eliot, Richards, and Empson were predecessors in this critical mode; in America, Burke has long been working in it; and many successors have learned it, even to providing, at times, an embarrassment of explicatory riches. But in neither country is there any other group which, whatever its differences in opinion, can, because of its common background and its shared allegiances, be thought of as a group and which has so much sheer talent in all its parts as Ransom, Tate, Brooks, and Warren. Instinctively they move always to the individual poem; in answering challenges they incline not to linger in the realm of theory as such but to hurry on to the exemplary case. The concretist method extends over into their textbooks and is perhaps more conspicuous there than anywhere else. In the vast influence of these textbooks, imitated almost as widely as they are used (an influence gloomily and often suspiciously complained of), we see the spontaneous welcome of a method of literary study which has put adequate substance where not enough of it had been before. The critical analysis of concrete works by first-rate minds has been the chief influence in getting literary study out of the doldrums of the first three decades of the century, in giving it intellectual respectability, and in making it as attractive to gifted students as physics, mathematics, and medicine. The older schools of literary study gravely lacked intellectual distinction; the neo-humanists, while at least they did offer the excitement of ideas and therefore some maturity of appeal, were deficient in the reading of the concrete work; but the literary historians, interested neither in ideas nor in the concrete work, lavished an essentially clerical perseverance and ingenuity upon matters in the main external to literature. As students of literature, they too often chose the realm of the "pseudo concrete."

In one direction the more recent type of literary study, to which the chief impetus in this country has been given by Southerners, has tended to create a new order of teacher-critics; in another direction it has tended to create—a fact not yet noted, I believe—a more competent general reader. In this respect these critics, sometimes called "reactionary," have done a considerable service to democracy. The older historical mode of study had little to offer the general reader except occasional dashes of extra-curricular enthusiasm but of its nature was concerned largely with training a rather narrow professional class—a technocracy of the humanities. Often the literature was forgotten entirely, with serious loss to the community.

The extraordinary competence in dealing with the concrete work is not matched at the level of theory; on the whole I suspect—and this may seem disputable—that Southern critics have not found the most effective theoretical formulations for their insights. Perhaps I should say "have not yet found"; or perhaps they have a deep suspiciousness of abstraction which inhibits the formulatory aspect of thought. In contrast with their enormous influence in focussing attention upon the individual work and its organic relations and in gaining adherents for the single theoretical position implied in their practice, namely that the individual work and its structure are the ultimate concern of literary study, the Southerners have had relatively little influence in other matters of theory—concepts of genre, stylistic and structural modes, etc. This is perhaps less true of Tate, though his intellectual impact is more marked in nonliterary matters. The Southerners have broken trail for Wellek and Warren, and for some very effective generalizations by Wimsatt. But in the specifications of literary form and function, in the extension of theory into new domains and problems, they have been much less influential, say, than Burke. Yet the true counterpoint to the Southerners is not Burke but the Chicagoans, elaborating dogmatic theory, providing a valuable center of speculation but living predeterminedly, monastically, away from the concrete work, remaining therefore almost without influence, seeming content to issue caveats and Everlasting No's and to ambush those who are affirming the living literature and enlarging its status. If their peculiarly arid rationalist plateau could be irrigated by a fresh flow of the literary works themselves, freely submitted to and spontaneously experienced, they might find a more fruitful role than that of erecting such inexorable proofs and carrying so little conviction. In their high abstractionism they are at the opposite extreme from the pseudo concretism of the old-line scholars.

In their social criticism the Southerners are led, by their sense of the concrete, to suspect the fashionable abstraction, the clichés and slogans, which to the unperceiving may seem the very embodiment of truth but which on inspection are found to ignore many realities of the actual human being. Progress? The concrete evidence of the human being is that he does not change much, that he may actually be harmed by the material phenomena usually implied by *progress*, and that in any case his liability to moral difficulty remains constant. The mechanized life? The concrete evidence is that man is up to it only within limits, that its exactions are more damaging than those of a slower and more laborious mode of life, that he needs regular work in an individualized context, and that few human beings are capable of making leisure fruitful rather than destructive. Political utopias? Man is perfectly capable of making certain improvements in social and political order, but to assume that the millennium is here or will ever come is to ignore the concrete facts of the nature of man. In such realizations the Southerners are by no means alone. Yet it is worth while rehearsing such points, though they are neither unique nor unfamiliar, to suggest the relationship between the creative writing, the criticism, and the social thought, and to call attention to the extreme concreteness of the regionalist and agrarian aspects of Southern thought, which have been felt to be very unfashionable and "unpractical." What about the American ideal of the "practical"? May not practicality itself be, paradoxically, an abstraction from reality, that is, another instance of the "pseudo concrete"? This is certainly what is implied in Warren's persistent concern, from his own fiction to his essay on Conrad, with the problem of the "idea" (or even the "illusion")—the ideal or meaning or value which establishes the quality of the deed or "redeems" it. In terms of man's need for spiritual grounding we have "the idea as concrete." This rejection of a moral positivism implies a similar objection to philosophical positivism as another mode of addiction to the pseudo concrete. But that attitude, which is expressed recurrently by Tate, carries us into another aspect of the Southern temper, with which we must deal later.

The sense of the elemental and the sense of the ornamental are roughly complementary phases of the Southern temper—complementary at least to the extent that in our historical context an awareness of the elements is likely to lead to a rejection of ornament, and a devotion to ornament may make the elements seem unacknowledgeable. Fifty years ago, of course, ornament was in the lead, whereas now—not always without self-deception—we tender greater devotion to the elements. In architecture the shift from Victorian Gothic to "modern," with its utilitarian aesthetics, is one symbol of the change in emphasis. But the dramatic version of the element is still a pretty polite thing, and the mid-century modernist is often left very uncomfortable by the amount of violence in Faulkner and Warren, by their sense of the furious drives that contort and distort men, by the crazy transformations of personality in people under stress, by the unornamented varieties of sex, by all the passions unamenable to sentimentalizing diminuendo. And equally, we should add, by the juxtaposing of life and death in Porter, the insistent awareness of death in Porter and Gordon, and by a certain mystery of being inseparable from the closest factuality in Elizabeth Madox Roberts and Welty. These are only for the mature. For the others, there will be satisfaction with Wolfe, with whom the elemental is not very much more than an orchestral wind soughing through the pines with a kind of calculated unhappiness (there are occasional such accents in Randall Jarrell, too)—an enchanting tune for young men, who thus, with little imaginative commitment or risk, are permitted to enjoy the sensation of being torn by force and sorrow. For the others, also, there is Caldwell, who does not disturb but reassures by selecting materials which elevate almost any reader to an Olympian eminence. But his appropriate marriage of the libidinous and the farcical reduces the elemental to the elementary. Another way of saying this is that he is not sufficiently concrete; just as one may be concrete without being elemental—as in the standard "realistic" novel, or in the work of a satirist like Mary McCarthy—so one may strive for the elements and end in an abstraction: with Caldwell, lust is almost a paradigm or an idea, withdrawn from a concrete human complexness. For these others, who like the elements easy, there will be difficulty in the conception of man as linked to nature, in Ransom's idea that man must make peace with nature. This kind of elementalism is hardly welcome to an age given to two other forms of naturalism—the literary sort in which man is a victim of nature and nature-like forces and can feel sorry for himself, and the scientific sort in which man is a victor over nature and can feel proud of himself. The man of the age who may be puzzled by Ransom may find it easier going with Hemingway, who is inclined to view nature as conquerable, and who, furthermore, for all of his feeling for death and deathliness, is hampered—and not quite willingly—by a fastidiousness that constricts his presentation of the elemental.

As a society we oscillate uneasily between bareness and overstuffed elegance; Hollywood plays it stark one minute, lush the next. Either extreme is hostile to true grace, social or spiritual. If we are uncomfortable with the elemental, we also shy at the true ornament, that of manner and mind (though we are rather tolerant of the spurious kinds). For that reason, the Southern sense of both is distinctive. To speak of the Southern sense of the ornamental is in one way rather startling, for the literary criticism of Southerners has been marked by the severity of its functionalism (with some exceptions, perhaps, for Ransom); yet I am by no means sure that the formal perfection which is the implied standard of judgment in many of Southerners' literary analyses is not itself the essence of ornament. For by ornament I do not mean superfluous or distracting embellishment; rather I mean nonutilitarian values; whatever comes from the feeling for rhythm, the sense of the incantatory, the awareness of style as integral in all kinds of communication; the intangible goods that lie beyond necessity; grace. A political reflection of the sense of the ornamental is "Southern oratory"—in most of its present manifestations debased, parodistic, really pseudo-ornamental. A social reflection is "Southern manners," a reality which has virtually been blotted out by promotional facsimiles —the unhappy fate of any virtue that is popularized and made the object of public self-congratulation. Something more than a social reflection appears in contemporary Southerners' assertions of the grace of ante-bellum life; the very assertion attests to the sense of which I speak. These assertions, which are a way of affirming a value, raise an important issue— the counter-attack charges that the social cost of the achievement was prohibitive. Though we may acknowledge that the cost was too high, we must also face the counter-problem of the cost of doing without the value—a problem of which the Southerners at least serve to remind us. To return to literature: the critical manner of the Southerners, even in vigorous controversy, is on the whole urbane, indeed strikingly so compared with such others as the scholarly cumbersome style, the *Partisan* truculent, and the Chicago opaque. The sense of nuance, refinement, the special communication by tone and color, is conspicuously acute. Finally, the sense of ornament appears in the rhetorical bent of Warren and Faulkner—not that with either of them style itself is a subject, amenable to decorative arrangement on the surface of another subject (characters, ideas, etc.), but that there is a special awareness of the verbal medium, a disposition to elaborate and amplify as a fundamental mode of communication, a willingness to utilize the rich and the rhythmical, an instinctive exploration of the stylistic instrument to the ultimate point at which one senses something of the supererogatory but not yet the excessive or obtrusive. At least in its application to Faulkner, this statement will run into objections. But even in most cases where Faulkner apparently lays himself open to the charge of mannerism or sheer lack of control I believe it demonstrable that his main devices—length of sentence and frequency of parenthesis—are meaningful as formal equivalents of a central imaginative impulse: to view experience as inclusively as possible, to mould-together-into-one, to secure a godlike view of present and past as one. But this brings us to a point for which we are not yet ready—the Southern sense of totality.

If the sense of the ornamental and the sense of the elemental at least in part complement each other, so the sense of the concrete and the sense of the representative may interact fruitfully. To have, as a writer, a sense of the concrete but not a sense of the representative is to exemplify in one way the modern dilemma—to have the concrete world, apparently controlled more or less, at one's finger tips and not to know what it means. To have a sense of the representative alone is to be in danger of falling into hollow allegory. The Southerners, we have seen, always cling to the concrete—in fiction and poetry, in literary and social criticism—but they are not chained to the concrete. The best fictional characters are always individuals, but something more than individuals too: Willie Stark is Willie Stark, but his career adumbrates a philosophical issue; the Snopeses are so representative as to have become a by-word; in Welty's work we see Everyman as salesman, in Gordon's as sportsman, in Porter's as a soul lost in the currents of time. Warren and Faulkner both dig into the past, not for the past's sake, but because of a sense of the immanence of past in present, and for the sake of finding or creating tales of mythic value. It is presumably for some success in this endeavor that the Southerners

have won a substantial audience. They certainly cannot appeal either
to hunters of the trivial exotic or to the devotees of the stereotype or
"pseudo representative"—that product of an imagination weak at the
general or universal (and for that matter, at the concrete, too). Under
sense of the representative we can include Warren's preoccupation with
the "idea"—a significant reaction against American anti-Platonism.
Again, if Southern criticism is marked by its devotion to the concrete
work and to the concrete structural elements, it is equally marked by
a sensitivity to the symbolic, to the work as symbolic of the writer, or
more particularly to the meanings and values symbolically present.
It boldly assumes as axiomatic the symbolic quality of all works, and
finds in the explication of the symbolic content a basic means of distinguishing the trivial and the important. And to give one final instance of the sense of the representative, this one from the social
criticism: if regionalism is on the one hand marked by a sense of
the concrete necessities of immediate living and has emphasized the
specificities of local place and manner, it is also true that regionalism
has been said to provide a sound base for internationalism. From this
point of view regionalism has not been a vain separatism or a sterile
cult of uniqueness, but at once a rejection of the abstract "different-
ness" implied by nationalism and a search for a mode of embodying
the representative human values on which both individual life and a
sound internationalism must rest.

Finally, the sense of totality: it is a sense of time, of the extent
of human need and possibility, of world and of spirit. It appears in
Faulkner's style; in the critical focussing on the organic whole; in the
anti-nominalism which has been most explicitly formulated by Richard
Weaver; in Tate's emphasis on mythic or non-scientific values; in the
conjunction, in numerous pieces of fiction, of violence and spiritual
awareness—a conjunction disturbing to readers who are used to taking
one part of the whole at a time; in the penumbra of mystery—a
mystery to be accepted, not solved—always bordering the clean light
of Welty's characters and scenes; in the nostalgia, so frequent in
Porter, for the reality felt behind the stage of action; in the questioning of nostrum and panaceas which can exist only by treating a part
of human truth as if it were the whole; in suspecting our inclination
to separate the present from all the rest of time, to exhaust all devotion
in the religion of humanity, and to consider scientific inquiry as the
only avenue to truth.

Whereas Hemingway's most reliable talent is that for seizing upon the lyric moment, Warren's enveloping mind can hardly go in short stories but needs all the room to be found in the novel (or the long poem); Faulkner is impelled to invent whole sagas; Gordon's stories expand into the myth of a recurrent character. In their instinct for inclusiveness, these and others, in both fiction and social criticism, dig into and rely upon the past. For the past is in the present; we do not live alone in time, thrust into eminence, and into finality, by what went before, servile and unentangling. With their sense of the whole, the Southerners keep reminding us that we are not altogether free agents in the here and now, and that the past is part master. The past also provides allegiance and perspective—not as an object of sentimental devotion but as a storehouse of values which may be seen in perspective and at the same time may permit an entirely necessary perspective on our own times. Through a sense of the past we may escape provincialism in time, which is one mark of the failure of a sense of totality.

With a comparable unwillingness to be uncritically content inside fashionable limits, the Southerners apparently find the religion of humanity inadequate. Not that any of them do not value the human; the question is whether the obligation to be humane can be secured by a secular religion, and whether humanity alone can adequately engage the religious imagination. Inclined to question whether suffering is totally eliminatable or univocally evil, the Southerners are most aware that, as Tate has put it, man is incurably religious and that the critical problem is not one of skeptically analyzing the religious impulse or of thinking as if religion did not exist for a mature individual and culture, but of distinguishing the real thing and the surrogates. They have a large enough sense of reality not to exclude all enlightenment that is not laboratory-tested. For them, totality is more than the sum of the sensory and the rational. The invention of gods is a mark, not of a passion for unreality, but of a high sense of reality; is not a regrettable flight from science, but perhaps a closer approach to the problem of being. The Southerners utilize and invoke reason no less than, let us say, any follower of John Dewey; but also they suspect an excessive rationalism which mistakes the ailerons for the power-plant and fosters the illusion that all non-rationalities have been, or can be, discarded.

This kind of evidence of the sense of totality is plain enough in Southern criticism and the fiction (though the latter, as yet, has difficulty in finding a dramatic form for the sense). I am inclined to add that the whole man is really not very fashionable right now, and that the sense of totality is likely to get one into disrepute as a kind of will-ful and fanciful archaist, for we are supposed to have got man properly trimmed down to a true, i.e., naturalistic dimension. Aside from this intellectual majority-pressure, there is another difficulty in that insti-tutions that historically stand for the sense of totality have suffered from loss of belief in their role and from an addiction to organiza-tional politics, so that to be believed to be unreservedly en rapport with them may lead to misconceptions of one's role. But the Southern-ers have been content to take their chances, with very little effort at self-protection by evasive movement.

The Southerners, indeed, have a surprisingly "liberal" com-plexion; they are in the classical American tradition of "protest." Their agrarianism could be read as a protest against both capitalist giantism and Marxism, their regionalism as a protest against abstract nationalism and uniformitarianism, their essential critical habits as a protest against the relativist antiquarianism of literary study (their fondness for "paradox" a protest against an exaggerated view of the straightforwardness of literature; for symbolism, a protest against the hampering limitations of realism, which had assumed a normative role). And their sense of totality, we have seen, leads to overt or implied protests against the restrictions of secular rationalism. There is, of course, protest and protest. In its most familiar manifestations, protest is topical; a social or political injustice brings it forth, often in a historical context that may require great bravery and sacrifice of the protestant,—and is alleviated. Yet this context may so mould the style of the liberal protestantism that it may go on like a habit, the old slogans becoming platitudes, the old courage replaced by fluency and complacency, the old vitality declining into sheer forgetfulness of the calendar. Thus standard liberalism of the 1950's seems at times to be still living in the 1920's. Then there is another protest, the pro-test exemplified by the Southerners—what I should call a radical pro-testantism because it is rooted in the sense of totality. It is a philo-sophical protest against lack of wholeness, against exclusions that re-strict human potentiality, against the naturalist closure of other avenues to wisdom. Though it is nowadays a minority operation, we may perhaps risk calling it, according to its actual nature, catholic. If Mr. Tate, who has exhibited it with particular force, becomes, as we must expect, the most protestant of Catholics, his fellow-Southerners, we may predict, will become no less catholic in their protestantism.

I want to re-emphasize my earlier statement that it is the strength and the *combination* of the qualities enumerated that the Southern temper is distinctive. No trait is distinctively Southern, of course, and all of them may be found to some extent in other American literature and thought, i.e., in the American temper. As a people we doubtless have a considerable sense for the concrete yet we often take up with abstractions that will not bear much critical inspection—e.g., freedom as an absolute. We like to be at once "down to earth" and up to the amenities, but we are perhaps too Victorian to feel at ease with the elemental, and too anti-Victorian to trust the ornamental. As for a sense of the representative: we have produced Hawthorne and Melville and James, though it is only lately that we have begun to estimate them seriously; and we are inclined to take a rather particularistic view of ourselves. We have enjoyed special immunities, and they tend to seem an inalienable grace. And though we like the phrase "the whole man," it is perhaps the sense of totality which is least widely possessed among us. On the philosophical side, it is our bent to take the naturalist part for the whole; and since those who would argue for a larger view seem contrary, out of line, unwilling to "advance" with the rest, and even prone to the last sin against the times—invoking the past—we are honestly ready to regard them as in headlong retreat. This view must often have tried the Southern temper, and have seemed to invite a reply in the words of Agatha in *Family Reunion*:

> In a world of fugitives
> The person taking the opposite direction
> Will appear to run away.

RICHARD M. WEAVER

Aspects of the Southern Philosophy

One of the significant aspects of Southern literature is that it does not contain a corpus of purely philosophical writing. It contains some of the best political commentary written in America, and Southern theologians were debating points of doctrine with a seventeenth-century seriousness some while after their contemporaries in other sections had turned to applied religion. But generally over the years, the phrase "camp and senate" fixed the poles of Southern creative activity, and the senate did not produce philosophy of the kind which deals with ultimate questions. With the exception of the recent Fugitive-Agrarian movement, there has been no systematic attempt in the South to articulate a theory of the world or a philosophy of life. Consequently one who writes of the Southern philosophy has little opportunity to speak from texts. What he says must be inferred, partly from the unexpressed postulates of a way of life, and partly from the tendencies of a non-philosophical literature.

We may find a clue to this literary fact by looking at the Southerner as we find him today and examining the points of belief in which he most strongly contrasts with the dominant American type, which may still with reasonable accuracy be called the Yankee. A comparison of the two minds leaves one first impressed with the high resistance which the Southerner shows to the idea and practice of analysis. Probably there are few types of minds in the world today so little given to the analytical approach. This characteristic can be seen in the policies of Southern statesmen, in the intellectual processes of Southern college students, and in the household and financial management of the average small citizen. So opposed is the Southerner to the method of analysis that he seems to regard it as a treasonable activity, and I raise the question of whether this may not give us a better insight into his essential mentality than the explanations which are commonly put forward. Sometimes it is said that he does not analyze because he will not make the exertion; some-times it is said that his education has not brought him up to the level of analysis, and both of these have a degree of plausibility. Yet I feel that both miss the true factor, which is that the Southerner rebels against the idea of analysis because his philosophy or his intellectual tradition, however transmitted down the years, tells him that this is not the way to arrive at the kind of truth he is interested in. It is his habit to see things as forms or large configurations, and he senses that the process of breaking these down (which is nearly always carried on for some practical purpose) somehow proves fatal to the truth of the whole. In fine, analysis is destructive of the kind of reality which he most wishes to preserve.

It is a general rule that analytic procedures issue in one kind of activity and synthetic procedures in another; and it so happens that the analytical successes are the ones upon which the modern world sets a premium. The Southerner is consequently reproached for this incapacity, which has indeed left him a laggard in many of the modern world's competitions. Yet it is possible to take a different view of his condition, for it must be borne in mind that if an extreme development of the analytical faculty suits a man for one type of work — or for one kind of life — it unsuits him for another. We have only to recall that in the achievements of the world's cultures, the work of analysis is fairly late and is somehow specialized. The form in which the messages of the great religions come, for example, is seldom if ever analytical. Such creations are synthetic; they appear to us in large groupings or visualizations which are vitiated by the operation of analysis. That is to say, if one tries to take them apart piece by piece the genius of the message vanishes. They are wholes, like stories, and we have to grasp them with a single act of the mind, as it were. The evidence seems overwhelming that synthesis is the way of religion and art and that analysis is the way of science and business, and this distinction underlies a wide range of Southern attitudes and choices. The typical Southerner is an authentically religious being if one means by religion not a neat set of moralities but a deep and even frightening intuition of man's radical dependence in this world. That awareness is something which has to be achieved immediately rather than mediately, and I suggest that the Southerner's practice of viewing the world in this way is the postulate of all his thinking, and that it causes him to demur at the analysis of life, or love, or war, or any other large subject. What he wants is a picture of it, in which the whole is somehow greater than the analyzable parts.

Naturally this distrust of analysis has kept the traditional Southerner at loggerheads with progressive elements, both those from within his own borders and those from other sections. Again and again the North, or groups representing its prevailing opinion, have presented the South with statistics showing its miserable condition. The South looks at the statistics and doesn't believe them. How can it ignore them? Well, statistics are, after all, the most abstract form of analysis, and what do they tell about an organic whole? The Southerner prefers to take in this whole through a kind of vision, in which the dominant features are a land and sky of high color, a lush climate, a spiritual community, a people inclined to be good humored even in the face of their eternal "problems" and to adapt themselves to the broad rhythms of nature. A Kentuckian of my acquaintance once described the feeling: "Statistics show that Kentucky is next to the bottom in educational facilities. But just take a ride from Lexington to Winchester. Isn't it beautiful!" It is a unitary pattern, and the attempt to segment any part of it with the aim of some practical application violates his notion of the due regard for things. There is likely some obscure connection between this feeling and those religious taboos which forbid the counting of things and especially the taking of census.

For even a threshold understanding of the Southern mind, one must recognize that the South's intractability in the face of statistics proceeds from a positive and not a negative factor, as has been more commonly supposed.

There appears to exist, furthermore, an essential linkage between this virtual defiance of analysis and the South's cultivation of legend and anecdote. No other section compares with it in fecundity of stories of all kinds; and it is almost the rule for an untutored Southerner to be adept at the telling of tales. But always for him the point of the story is in the story, and he is stopped and confused when a single statement is extracted from it for sociological or political analysis. Thus a story about mountaineers or sharecroppers will not be about the sociological status of mountaineers or sharecroppers, but about the dramatic point of the story. In such resistance to the sociological construing of the drama of his life he shows most frankly his antiscientific bias. And so in regard to his humanism, for man is something that can be perceived as a whole too; and it is a prevailing antipathy toward the specialist or the man of unshapely development which has kept the South humanistic in comparison with those sections which have followed the route of analysis and science. We may understand by the same principle why the South insists on putting forward as political leaders highly symbolic personalities rather than the colorless successes with efficient habits and the mentality of book-keepers which moneyed urban areas prefer. With these examples in mind I wish to turn to a more widely diffused expression of the same tendency.

When we look over the roster of Southerners who have won distinction in the history of the nation we discover that virtually all of them, with the single exception of the soldiers, have been workers in the realm of words. The South has produced no scientists of front rank, few if any creative geniuses in business, no men of any real importance who have been manipulators of things rather than of words. But its manipulators of words have been in the front rank from the beginning, not omitting the most depressed periods of Southern history. As I perceive this characteristic of the Southern mind, it is no accident that the two greatest rhetoricians to occupy the White House, Abraham Lincoln and Woodrow Wilson, were men of Southern nurture. Lincoln early nourished his mind upon that exquisite rhetor "Parson" Weems and upon the frontier anecdote; later he sought to model himself upon Henry Clay. Wilson grew up in close contact with Southern theological rhetoric, of which his father was a professor. If we regard Jefferson as of equal rank, we can raise the number to three. And it seems to be Patrick Henry rather than Daniel Webster who survives in the popular mind as the nation's orator. In the department of utterance, then, the South has made its deepest mark, and we can see that with some changes in form of expression and subject matter, the tradition continues strong today.

An impressive evidence appears in the contemporary school of Southern literary criticism. It is a lamentable fact but a true one that Southern institutions of higher learning have produced nothing of sufficient merit to be followed by the nation as a whole except this literary movement. About 1920 a group of brilliant individuals, drawn together more or less by a conscious Southern heritage, began a new approach to the interpretation of literature. Within less than two decades, they succeeded in putting literary criticism in this country upon a new basis, and so completely that almost any literary critic beginning today has to take up where they are. This they were able to do without the aid of institutional prestige; indeed, one might say that they did it despite the handicap of poor institutional rating. A peculiar qualification for using the word, and for criticizing the use of the word, thus enabled them to make the single contribution of the South to contemporary American intellectual history. Then there comes as culminating evidence the fact that the only Southerner to win a Nobel prize is a literary figure and one, furthermore, whose writing has notable rhetorical qualities. In the background of these exceptional performances is the conspicuous role that Southern drama and fiction have enjoyed on the literary scene at every level of sophistication. But always, work with the word.

The explanation of so consistent a success, contrasting with the barest poverty in other fields of activity, must somehow concern the word itself. The most probable answer is that the word is a synthesizing instrumentality. It can, of course, be used for analysis, as in dialectic; but in rhetoric words make use of things already dialectically determined in a further and final expression which has to do with matters of policy and value. In this further operation the typical Southerner feels as much at home as he feels lost in the activity of rational or piecemeal inquiry, for he is made a rhetorician by the nature of the society in which he grows up. The very stability of its institutions makes possible a vocabulary which does not exist, or exists with much less authority, where things are characterized by distracting change. There are decisive advantages to the rhetorician, and along with him to the man of letters, in a vocabulary whose acceptance does not have to be called into question. Its very settledness gives him a range of opportunities — including that of meaningful deviation — which a vocabulary challenged or in flux cannot give. He enjoys something comparable to what the lawyers call "the right of assumption"; and working from these advanced positions he can accomplish things which would be far harder or impossible if he had to go back and shore up the assumptions underlying every predication.

When a culture and a vocabulary thus settle down together as correlates, there develops a natural tendency to assume that a mastery of the word is equivalent to a mastery of the institutions, and this development can reach an unhealthy extreme. On the whole, the

Southerner has perhaps been too credulous about language. His responsiveness sometimes leads him to the belief that if a man can make a good speech, all other things should be credited to him. By this we may account for the great prestige which the orator has traditionally enjoyed in the South, and not merely by those who have encountered Cicero and Quintilian in their education, but also by the masses. The kind of political folk hero who has proved incomprehensible to the remainder of the nation finds the greatest source of his power in a widespread admiration of confidence and even *bravura* in the use of language. When the pistol-toting henchman of Willie Stark in Warren's *All the King's Men* tries to explain why he so admired Stark, he comes out with an answer which would satisfy an average Southern audience: "Couldn't nobody talk like him."

Yet on the other hand, if this reverence for the word can run into liability, it can also constitute an asset of a singularly important kind. For the same set of facts will explain why the South remains the stronghold of religious and perhaps also of ethical fundamentalism. Verbal skepticism is the beginning of moral nihilism; and it is just this belief that words are among the fixed things which has kept the South conservative in regard to those forces which are liquidating values. Just as soon as men begin to point out that the word is one entity and the object it represents is another, there sets in a temptation to do one thing with the word and another or different thing with the object it is supposed to represent; and here begins that relativism which by now is visibly affecting those institutions which depend for their very existence upon our ability to use language as a permanent binder. With all due recognition of semantic analysis, this distinction is one of the most perilous morally that can be made. It seems to open a hitherto excluded middle between the word and the thing signified, where every sort of relativistic dodge becomes possible. I have come to abominate the expression "Southern gentleman" because it is used presumptuously, yet there must be some connection between the old concept of "the word of a gentleman" and this view of language as having fixed pertinence.

The South is often described as differing from the rest of the nation through a disproportionate amount of piety, but it is easy to fall into an erroneous impression here. For a long while I labored under the illusion that the South is peculiarly the pious section and that the North, as its democratic professions would lead one to imagine, is opposed on principle to the idea of reverence. But years of residence in the North have convinced me that such is not true. Northerners have their piety too, as probably every people does; but Northern and Southern piety differ in a way to produce even more mischievous disagreements than the condition I had supposed to exist. I would define piety as an attitude of reverence or acceptance toward some overruling order or some deeply founded institution which the mere individual is not to tamper with. Ultimately perhaps it is religious, but immediate religious associations are not essential to it; it may manifest itself toward various objects as what Matthew Arnold called "the discipline of respect." There would in fact be some advantage in changing the term to "pieties," for the attitude sometimes shows itself in seemingly unrelated responses. In any case, the Northerner is as reverential towards his sanctioned order or objects as the Southerner is towards his, but the two orders are not the same.

Southern piety is basically an acceptance of the inscrutability of nature. Under its impulse the individual Southerner feels that nature is not something which he is to make over or change; it is rather something for him to come to terms with. The world is God-given; its mysteries are not supposed to be fully revealed; and the only possible course in the long run is to accommodate oneself to its vast pulsations. Thus nature is seen as providential, and even its harsher aspects must be regarded as having ends that we do not fully comprehend. In a word, the Southerner reveres original creation. His willingness to accept some conditions that his more energetic Northern cousin will not put up with is not purely temperamental or climatic; it is religious or philosophical insofar as it stems from this world view. Often the Yankee's effort to become complete master of his environment appears to the Southerner an effrontery against an order which is divinely provided and which, in the total outcome, is not going to be improved by busy human schemes. It never occurs to the typical Northerner, for example, to ask whether it is right to move a mountain or alter the course of a river; but it may occur to this fundamentalist Southerner, and some degree of this feeling will be encountered in every level of the population.

Northern piety, on the other hand, finds its objects in things of human creation. It shows itself primarily through attitudes toward education and learning and the kinds of conventions erected upon these. Perhaps it could be most generally described as a respect for ideas. Essentially the Northerner is a child of the Enlightenment; and his theology is very much like Tom Paine's; that is, his religion is to do good, and his own mind is his church. It is in tendency a strongly Protestant mentality which insists on judging a thing by its works.

Consequently one coming to the North from a Southern background is forcibly impressed by the Northerner's willingness to receive any good idea, regardless of its provenance. The Northerner considers irrelevant any question as to whether the bearer of the idea has family or position or current recognition; if the idea is cogent, that is enough. For him, it is only necessary that a thought be able to give a good account of itself dialectically. The North has never had much democracy of condition, especially when judged by its own slogans; but it has enjoyed this democracy of thoughts, which has undeniably served as a fountainhead of enterprise and resourcefulness. It makes for a much greater viability of ideas and for tolerance of criticism, since no person is impelled to feel that his status or his character is being assailed when his idea is being criticized.

In the South the bearer of an idea must come vouchsafed and certified. He must be of a good family or hold some public position or represent some important element before he can get a hearing. Who is he to have an important thought? To put the matter in another way, the Southerner expects the idea to come with what the old writers on rhetoric used to call "ethical proof." That is to say, he frankly evaluates the idea against the background of its origin. I scarcely need add that in most situations the "proof" is not ethical at all, but political or worse, since it attempts to rate thought according to some notion of social prestige. This habit has been one of the stifling influences in Southern culture and more than one otherwise loyal son has complained of it.[1]

However, if the South loses in some respects through this providential view of nature and through this unwillingness to judge by abstract determinations, it gains what many would regard as an important compensation. For one of the most noticeable qualities of the Southern people today is the comparative absence of that modern

---

[1] George W. Cable, writing to a friend in the North who had offered to get some publicity for his early work, felt impelled to say: "if you love me don't offer *anything* that I *ever* do to *anybody* except on its intrinsic merits. You will excuse me for appearing to suspect such a thing; it's such a common occurrence down here, and therefore — besides all the better reasons — because I am a Southerner — I would like the handful of people that make up my little world to be assured I am nobody's widow."

spirit of envy which has so unsettled things in other parts of the world. Of all the peoples of the Western world, probably only the peasant populations of Europe are so little affected by this increasing distemper. And since the absence of envy produces a kind of character not much seen since the decay of the feudal order, some account of it may here be in order.

When I affirm that the average Southerner of traditional mentality does not envy, I do not mean that he will not take a better job if it is offered him, or that he will pass up a chance to make a quick fortune, or that he will not admire material success. He will do all these things, and without apology. What I do affirm is that it is not in his character to hate another man because that man has a great deal more of the world's goods than he himself has or is ever likely to have. He is not now and never has been a leveller. The fact that three fourths of the soldiers in Confederate armies owned no slaves and never expected to own any is part of this pattern. If the principle of envy I have mentioned had been abroad, these armies would have dissolved in a matter of months. But the historical fact is that the Confederate armies possessed one of the toughest morales in modern history, a morale which is studied by war colleges today in an effort to learn what made it so impervious to cracking. Something of the pattern endures today. If a rich man lives in a Southern community, he will be a subject of talk, as he would be anywhere, but he will not be an object of envious hatred because fortune has dealt lavishly with him and sparingly with his neighbors. Much contemporary political and economic thought carries the implication that we should pull down our neighbor's house if we cannot have a house at least as fine; but the average Southern proletarian, urban or rural, has never been penetrated with this notion. The poor success of trade unionism in the South is one of the concrete evidences. Trade unionism runs up against both the distrust of analysis and this hesitancy about tampering with a prevailing dispensation. Whereas modern social doctrine encourages a man to question the whole order of society if he does not have as much as somebody else, the typical Southern farmer or millhand tends to regard fortune, like nature, as providential. From his point of view there is nothing written in the original bill of things which says that the substance of the world must be distributed equally. Nor was there anything, before modern advertisers availed themselves of the press and radio, to tell him that he is entitled to the best of everything. That some should have more and others less is, in his view, part of the inscrutable provision. This modern impulse which elevates envy into a principle of social action and which animates much of the class struggle in regions supposedly more advanced is thus completely foreign to his tradition, though now and then he has struck back politically when he felt that he was the victim of sectional political exploitation. For the failure of collectivist doctrine to penetrate the South the Southern Chambers of Commerce may not claim the slightest credit. That opposition was determined long ago, and at a level far deeper than such organizations can reach.

The factors considered thus far go back to the beginnings of Southern history, but it cannot be overlooked that an important part of the Southern philosophy is a philosophy of the South's place in the nation since the Civil War. Southerners have undergone some peculiar experiences which have left them a highly conscious minority within the nation. Everyone remarks the surface manifestations of this status, the self-awareness, defense-mindedness, over-assertiveness, and occasional bad manners. But I feel the need here to push below these surface displays and look at some of the ways in which special conditions have affected profoundly the Southern intellectual and cultural outlook. They have had the effect of giving the Southerner a point of view and a set of values which the remainder of the nation is highly curious about but which he has difficulty in explaining because of the lack of common denominators. A detached account of how he came to his present state may provide some basis of communication.

There occurs in Walter Hines Page's *The Autobiography of Nicholas Worth* a striking figure in which the surviving Confederate brigadiers are likened to ghosts in a stage play. The point of the comparison is that although they have only a ghostly being, they succeed, like a stage ghost, in monopolizing the attention of the audience. What will it do next? what will it say? are the questions it provokes in the minds of the onlookers. Since the Civil War the South as a whole has played this kind of role in the American drama and has held a comparable degree of attention. And it has succeeded in doing this for the same reason as the ghost, if we grant that it possesses a different kind of being from the other actors. That difference of being can be explained through reference to its special history.

If we look at the typical American against the background of his experience, his folklore, and his social aspirations, we are forced to admit that he represents, more than any other type in the world, victorious man. He has surpassed the people of every other country in amassing wealth, in rearing institutions, and in getting his values recognized, for better or for worse, throughout the world. While he is often chided for his complacent belief in progress, it must be confessed that events have conspired to encourage that belief, and to make progress appear the central theme of his history. In all sorts of senses he has never ceased to go forward; and to much of the world America has come to symbolize that future in which man will be invariably successful both in combat with nature and in his struggle with the problems of human organization. This adds up to saying that in the eyes of the world as well as in his own eyes the typical American stands for success unlimited.

But this is the point at which the Southerner ceases to be classifiable as American. He has had to taste a bitter cup which no American is supposed to know anything about, the cup of defeat. Thus in a world where the American is supposed to be uniformly successful, he exists as an anomalous American. Much of the Southerner's nonconformity and intransigence results from the real difficulty of adjusting a psychology which has been nourished upon this experience to the predominating national psychology, which has been nourished upon uninterrupted success.

The effects of this adverse history upon the Southern mentality have never been candidly appraised. For example, it cannot be without significance that the Southerner today is the only involuntary tenant of the American Union. I am not suggesting that there exists at present a mass feeling in favor of political independence, as there did at one time; but the record of American history, which he has to read along with his Northern brother, says that he is where he is as the result of a settlement of force against him. To argue that the resulting condition is economically or otherwise to his advantage is beside this point; the book continues to say that a supreme act of his will was frustrated, and that as a consequence of that defeat he had to accommodate himself to an unwanted circumstance. And that, of course, is the meaning of failure. Therefore in the national legend the typical American owes his position to a virtuous and effective act of his will; but the Southerner owes his to the fact that his will was denied; and this leaves a kind of inequality which no amount of political blandishment can remove entirely. Although there appears today no lively awareness of this frustration, it none the less lies deep in his psychology, a subdued but ingrown reminder that at one time his all was not enough — a reminder, furthermore, that Americans too can fail. Probably this explains why his presence sometimes irks his fellow Americans. He cannot sit in conclave with their unspoiled innocence, for he brings, along with a certain outward exuberance, these sardonic memories.

The comparative poverty which has existed in the South for nearly a hundred years is directly connected with this circumstance; for when the states composing the Confederacy lost the independence which they had asserted, they lost also a large measure of their ability to recover from physical destruction. When a nation is defeated in international war, its opportunities for recovery are enhanced many times if it can only hang on to its political autonomy. It may have to cede territory, to pay indemnity, and to make other sacrifices to expiate its misfortune; but as long as it remains a self-governing unit, it can adapt its internal and external economy to the necessities of the situation. In other words, it can prescribe the medicine that it needs and take it; and it can choose the best conditions for its convalescence. A good example is France after her defeat by Prussia in 1871. But when a nation loses its independence along with the war, its people have to recover on terms set entirely by the enemy, and these will seldom if ever be generous in the sense of promoting a real revival of strength. The South is a clear example of the second situation. After 1865 it not only had to undertake a great task of physical restoration but it also had to undertake this without any real freedom of initiative. It was reduced to being part of a far larger and generally unsympathetic unit called the Union, whose will prevailed in all major policies. The way in which the South was systematically bled in the decades following the war has been set forth by Southern historians, and there is no need to enter into it here. It is enough to point out that a recovery which under favorable conditions might have required ten or fifteen years required more than fifty and actually cannot be regarded as complete yet.

This is substantially what I mean by saying that the South has a different kind of being from the other sections, which gives it something of the interest of the ghost in the play, or something of the ominous presence of the suppliant in a Greek tragedy.

History indeed, as Eliot reminds us in a poem, has many cunningly contrived corridors, and if we will follow this one of defeat and impoverishment, we shall arrive at a view which is better suggested by the ghost or the suppliant in the tragedy than by the studies of sociologists. Let us begin with the touchy matter of education. It has been for many decades a widely received belief that the South is the least educated of the sections; yet there is a true and most important sense in which it is the best or the "most" educated section. I refer here to an education in tragedy, which is the profoundest education of man. The South, as has already been shown, is the only section of the United States which knows through poignant experience that defeat is possible. The ancient states knew it and their sages expressed the truth in memorable sayings; the medieval states knew it, and their writers spoke of the Wheel of Fortune; every state of modern Europe has had to taste some measure of it. Only the victorious American of the North and West has it yet to learn. He may imagine that he knows it from copybook maxims, but that is not knowing it. One must have been through the humiliation and despair, must have felt the impossibility of vindicating oneself before any earthly tribunal to savor the real essence of it. Defeat in war is an unpleasant thing, but truly it is "one of those experiences nobody should be without." Nothing else can bring home so forcibly the truth of the proverb that time and chance happen to us all. The imprint of it upon the mind and character of the South has proved lasting. It is out of this ancestral memory that the South has remained the most militarily inclined of the sections. (To say that defeat in war teaches a people that "force never pays" is fatuous. What it does teach is that "too little force never pays.") It was out of this that its representatives in Congress swung the vote for renewal of conscription in 1941. It is out of this generally that the South serves as a flywheel to the nation as a whole, often slowing down the work of those who would perfect society overnight, yet speeding up those policies which its harder experience has taught it to accept. In this respect the average Southerner may be said to have "a European education." He knows that every great success is poised right on the brink of tragedy; and he knows that those forces which have molded the lives of men for five thousand years cannot be simply waved into abeyance. It may be that his peculiar pride is a perverse outgrowth of this knowledge. He has had to face what the existentialists call "ultimate situations" and he has come through, and it is very difficult to convince him by educators' statistics that he doesn't know anything. Indeed, one of the unfortunate results of this circumstance is a certain contumaciousness toward Northern-endorsed book learning.

This cunningly contrived corridor issues also in the blessing that the South has never had much money. At the risk of presuming on a controversial point, I call this a blessing for the plain reason that it has retarded the spoiling of the South. Everyone recognizes that the possession of wealth, especially if it is long continued, causes men to set their expectations at too high a level. They tend to forget what went into the creation of that wealth; and they begin to assume that this world is naturally a world of comfort and even of surfeit, which is one of the saddest of all distortions of reality. Of course the Southerner has no greater natural immunity to his weakness than any other American; but the situation being what it was, he had to continue working for a living; more than that, he had to work as a primary producer since his only capital (to amount to anything) was the land. From this combination of causes the people of the South have remained predominantly a rural working people. North Carolina, which now stands tenth among the states in total population, stands first in farm population, and other Southern states will show comparable figures. This phase of the South's misfortunes, then, has kept from the Southern people the peculiar degenerative effects of the possession of wealth, and it has kept them in close contact with the natural environment, which can itself be a profound instructor. There is no more eloquent sectional contrast than the fact that whereas the South has the farms, New England has the insurance companies. It has not helped New England to have the insurance companies, except to grow rich; and it has helped the South to have the farms, as can be shown by its biological and imaginative fertility, and by the fortitude of its people. On this last point there is an oblique but interesting commentary in Norman Mailer's *The Naked and the Dead*. General Cummings is addressing Lieutenant Hearn in one of their conversations.

"After a couple of years of war, there are only two considerations that make a good army: a superior material force
and a poor standard of living. Why do you think that a
regiment of Southerners is worth two regiments of
Easterners?"
"I don't think they are."
"Well, it happens to be true. . . . I'm not peddling theories.
And the conclusions leave me, as a general officer, in a poor
position. We have the highest standard of living in the
world and, as one would expect, the worst individual fighting
soldiers of any big power. Or at least in their natural state
they are. They're comparatively wealthy, they're spoiled,
and as Americans they share most of them the peculiar manifestations of our democracy. They have an exaggerated idea
of the rights due themselves and no idea at all of the rights
due others. It's the reverse of the peasant, and I'll tell you
right now it's the peasant who makes the soldier."

Today Southern boys fill up our volunteer armies as the rustics of
the Italian peninsula filled up the legions in the days of the Republic.

If the time ever comes to write the definitive history of the
Southern people, it may prove impossible to find a better epigraph
than the line from *Gerontion*: "Virtues are forced upon us by our
impudent crimes."

Before closing this topic of the Southerner's place within the
nation I should like to point out a poorly understood source of Southern
grievance. This is, more specifically, a circumstance which has kept
the North from understanding the South and has kept the South from
understanding the North's misunderstanding. The fact is simply
that for the North the South is too theatrical to be wholly real; therefore it is "history" and not "real life." The South appears to the
North a kind of tableau. It is interesting, even fascinating, to look
upon, with its survivals of medievalism, its manners that recall vanished eras, its stark social cleavages, its lost cause, its ballads and sentimental songs. But the very presence of these causes the typical
American to view it with the same dubious credulity that one shows
toward the exhibit in the glass case of a museum. It is so strange
that one cannot conquer the feeling that it must be in some degree
fictionized. For this reason mainly the North has never been able
to credit the actual suffering which has been a part of the South's

story. The tendency is to think that characters so theatrical cannot have suffered any more than the actors who have just presented a stage tragedy. Northerners of the present generation appear to believe, as Warren once put it, that the blood which was shed at Gettysburg and Chickamauga was not real blood at all; it was only tomato ketchup used to make the scene look realistic. That attitude leads to a systematic if unconscious discounting of the facts which make the South what it is today, physically and spiritually.

The Southerner naturally knows that life in his region is quite authentic and has been so from the start, despite certain aspects of pageantry. It may seem picturesque in comparison with lives lived in other regions, but it is paid for in most of the same pains, with a few special ones occasioned by its climate and situation. To work on the land where the temperature reaches 90 degrees in the shade fifty days out of the year, to wrest a living from a soil which was not very fertile to begin with and which has been abused in cultivation, and to move amid the tensions of an almost irremediable race situation do not make a purely idyllic life, whatever the traditional songs of the South may suggest. Temperamentally the Southerner is disinclined to feel sorry for himself; but he is irked to have the solid facts of his history treated as if they were something out of a Gilbert and Sullivan opera; and I believe that the attitude of belligerence which others sometimes sense in him stems from this situation more than from any other.

It should be a welcome sign that contemporary literature, including that written on both sides of the Mason-Dixon line, is doing something to correct this focus. I once heard a Southerner long resident in the Northeast say that he was delighted with "The Little Foxes" because it showed that the South too can have a first-class murderess. The tremendous impression which Miss Mitchell's Scarlett O'Hara made upon the Northern audience is owing to the fact that Scarlett is a type of ruthless entrepreneur which Northerners have met in their own life and can therefore understand and credit. And the dimensions of Mr. Faulkner's world are so unyielding that they have compelled assent in the most reluctant quarters.

If the world continues its present drift toward tension and violence, it is probable that the characteristic Southern qualities will command an increasing premium. While this country was amassing its great wealth, those qualities were in comparative eclipse; but the virtues needed to amass wealth are not the virtues needed to defend it. Such is our ambiguous position today that the possession of the greatest wealth in the world is going to require an amplitude of those qualities developed in the school of poverty and deprivation, and in that of rural living. Important among these "enforced" virtues are fortitude and the ability to do without. But perhaps most important of all is the Southerner's discipline in tragedy. Belief in tragedy is essentially un-American; it is in fact one of the heresies against Americanism; but in the world as a whole this heresy is more widely received than the dogma and is more regularly taught by experience. Just as certainly as the United States grows older, it will have to find accommodation for this ineluctable notion; it is even now embarked upon policies with tremendous possibilities if not promises of tragedy. If we are in for a time of darkness and trouble, the Southern philosophy, because it is not based upon optimism, will have better power to console than the national dogmas.

It will do good to heart and head
When your soul is in my soul's stead.

ANDREW NELSON LYTLE

How Many Miles To Babylon

It is not given to a man to know midways of the journey how many are the miles, their quality and meaning. I take it the three score miles and ten is a disguise, as is the habit of riddles, for the Biblical number of allotted time; and a warning not to take the measure too soon. But this warning is a further disguise to hide the actual meaning from the pragmatism of the materialist, that ultimate poverty of the spirit Christ said we would always have with us. (I am assuming certain nursery rhymes are fragments of older forms of meaning metamorphosed by time or Christianity.) In one sense Babylon is the acceptance of matter as the only meaning, the source of the mystery. That man could accept the shell for total meaning, that his vanity could lead him to believe a probing into can control matter and hence life, is the ultimate folly which brings on the confusion of tongues: that is, the failure of communication which returns society to the wilderness, the untended garden. Babylon was sometimes called Babel and always understood in the Bible as confusion. In the New Testament it meant Rome and hence the symbol of its day for all world cities which grow like a boil on the landscape; or they are like a disorder in nature, the head instead of ruling feeding on the body politic until it bursts, too, from surfeit. Babylon sprawled for two hundred square miles on both sides the Euphrates, but who knows how far it made itself felt as the dominant presence? Because of the size of this country and other reasons New York is the best image of such a city. It stands in only one relationship to the hinterland. At least London and Rome retain long memories of themselves as capitals, with physical and metaphysical relationships to the surrounding land. But any one of them focuses the modern predicament. The Agrarians might be said, by exposing the synthetic mythology behind Industrialism, to warn that Babylon has returned. Twenty years is a short time as history goes, but I see no reason to withdraw the assumptions upon which the Agrarians based their warning. There has been a change but only of degree. It is apparent that the confusion of tongues is immeasurably increased. The pace of history varies. As it approaches crises, it goes very fast.

If this insight of twenty years back still seems valid, what of Calhoun's a hundred years ago? His term for totalitarianism, or Babylon, was the Rule of the Numerical Majority: that amorphous majority controlled by the small irresponsible minority, which in turn responds to variable pressure, and all deluded by the fiction of representation. Betrayal always comes about in the guise of the thing betrayed. The very meaning of language, that men and nations mean what they say (that is, words), was undone by the deliberate distortion which preceded the last war. Its after-effects are more dangerous than the threats of any atomic explosion, for even if the world blows up, each man dies by himself, which he is going to do anyway. But the confusion of tongues will destroy a civilization. This Calhoun foresaw, and how quickly his words showed their prophetic truth. The Constitutional Union came to an end at the hands of those who said they were fighting to preserve it.

The world Calhoun lived in was relatively stable. There was little of the confusion we know to point to. His wisdom diminishes that of all his disciples, and I take it the Agrarians were pretty much that. All he had to go on was his imagination and a care for the public thing, that final protection of private life; but he did know that ideas do have consequences, and he knew the meaning implicit in action as well. Before the clarity of his mind how glib now seems Webster's rhetoric, and one wonders how disingenuous it was. Webster is dead, along with Calhoun, but the rhetoric is not. It is the long undertone of history, rising like static when the will fails. It was first heard in the Garden. It is whispered by the mouths of present-day liberalism. It is the old evangelical tongue that renews its skin with the season. It is the tongue that was heard in the corridors when Hiss was on trial. It says publicly that property rights are hostile to human rights, as if one of the human rights, in American belief, is not the right to own property. It has many skins but one body. It casts off Abolitionism to take on humanitarianism. It is the lips of the man who says the idle pleasant word. It is the gift which costs the giver nothing. It is the largesse of spending another's money. Pierre Bezukhov practices it when he gave orders to improve his peasants' lot only to increase their sorrows. It is the fairweather friend. It undertakes the act but refuses the responsibility for it. It says in the nature of things all men are created free and equal. It is always assuming the prerogatives of the godhead and ends up cutting the Gordion knot. Perhaps as rhetoric its harm would pass, but somewhere behind there is always the box of Beecher's bibles. It is finally dangerous because it is in every man. It is compassion for man's lot, but it is also sloth and therefore self-betrayal. It wants the body of the world without the pain and effort of earning it, or caring for it. Babylon is its reward and its doom.

"Can I get there by candle light? Aye, and back again."

This question and answer exposes the other attitude towards man's predicament. Candle light is metaphorically the Agrarian admonition. The body of the world will remain mysterious and fearful, no blaring searchlights to make it seem immediate and reducible to man's will, for beyond the glare lies the dark velvet of space, which the great light barely pricks. The body is frail, the mystery irreducible; therefore the feet must be nimble and quick as well. This is the riddle, old when it was first made, older now. It makes a more modest assumption about man's capacity, but the man it considers is more of man. He is both good and evil, and he has a soul to win or lose. The defense against the evil within and without begins in a structure of a stable society. He must have location, which means property, which means the family and the communion of families which is the state. Otherwise, as now, the individual is at the mercy of his ego. He understands that awareness of limitations is as near as he can come to freedom. Without control of space he is lost in time. The discrete objects of nature make a treadmill. Lest he mount it again he must engage and restrain himself by ritual, manners, conventions, institutions (as opposed to organizations). He may explore and enjoy but at his peril possess beyond the flare of the candle light. An all enveloping institution, some Church, should guide and contain and suffuse the various divisions of society. But there is no need to walk over the tracks of twenty years ago, except to add one thing that seems clearer now than then. The South may well become the salvation of this country yet, both at home and abroad. Private property, controlled by the proprietor, may be the only restraining influence to remind us that the great corporate business has something private about it. The time will come, otherwise, when it will seem more efficient for the state to take over. In this sense there will be the change of tactics from twenty years ago: the enemy will become an ally of a sort.

And then we must remember that the South is the only section of this country that knows the meaning of defeat, that is, the nature of the world. Everywhere else there has been nothing but a rising triumph, a pyramiding of success upon success. It is a perilous condition. Here Babylon mounts to Babel.

ROBERT D. JACOBS

Poe and the Agrarian Critics

There is sufficient reason why some of the Southern Agrarians who have become identified as New Critics have not been particularly anxious to recognize Edgar Allan Poe as a worthy ancestor. Neither his poetry nor his prose stands up well under the explicatory attack (I refer especially to the Brooks-Warren analysis of "Ulalume" in *Understanding Poetry* and the equally devastating commentary on "The Fall of the House of Usher" in *Understanding Fiction*); and his patent defection to the Romantics would void the claim to attention made by his Aristotelian criticism. However, the Romanticism in Poe's theory is more patent than real. If we examine the total mass of his achievement, we find a startling resemblance between his social and political ideas and those of *I'll Take My Stand*. If we look closely, we shall also find implicit within the body of his criticism an essentially classic world view which affirms the limitation of man and the supremacy of nature. We shall find, too, a trace of speculative thought which, in spite of many seeming blind alleys and unwarranted detours, never strays far from one central idea—that the universe is for the artist the immutable order whose perfection lies before him as an everlasting analogical model.

It was more than two decades ago that twelve Southerners published *I'll Take My Stand*. In this volume the most cogent attack of our time upon technology and the doctrine of Progress was mustered. In it Andrew Nelson Lytle wrote that today there is "a war to the death between technology and the ordinary functions of living." John Crowe Ransom was equally outspoken: Progressivism was "a principle of boundless aggression against nature." Industrialism was a "program under which men, using the latest scientific paraphernalia, sacrificed comfort, leisure, and the enjoyment of life to win Pyrrhic victories from Nature at points of no strategic importance."

One has little difficulty in locating Poe's affirmation, nearly a
century earlier, of the same positions.   In *The Colloquy of Monos and
Una* he uses a futuristic fantasy as vehicle for an attack on precisely
the same evils that the Agrarians saw in modern civilization.   Monos,
Poe's spokesman, tells of the final refutation of the argument for
Progress.   For centuries the world had "progressed" toward spiritual
ruin, but occasionally some vigorous intellect would emerge as critic,
"boldly contending for those principles . . . which should have taught
our race to submit to the guidance of natural laws rather than attempt
their control.   At long intervals some master-minds appeared, looking
upon each advance in practical science as a retro-gradation in the true
utility."   Monos goes on to make a specific connection between abstract theories of social betterment (theoretical equalitarianism) and
industrialism, classifying them both as an assault on Nature:

> Man, because he could not but acknowledge the majesty of
> Nature, fell into childish exultation at his acquired and still
> increasing dominion over her elements. . . . He grew infected
> with system and with abstraction.   He enwrapped himself in
> generalities.   Among other odd ideas, that of universal
> equality gained ground; and in the face of analogy and of
> God—in despite of the loud warning voice of the laws of
> *gradation* so visibly pervading all things in earth and Heaven
> —wild attempts at an omni-prevalent Democracy were made.
> . . . Meantime huge, smoking cities arose, innumerable.
> Green leaves shrank before the hot breath of furnaces.   The
> fair face of Nature was deformed as with the ravages of
> some loathsome disease.

We can also make an easy comparison of these views of science
with those recently expressed by Mr. Allen Tate, one of the original
twelve Agrarians, in a lecture, "To Whom is the Poet Responsible?"
(*The Hudson Review,* Autumn, 1951).   More modestly and ironically held open to question in Mr. Tate's words than in Poe's is the
scientist's "myth of omnipotent rationality which has worked certain
wonders; but perhaps a little too rapidly."   Like Poe, Tate distrusts
system and abstraction: The "Nazi and Stalinist unities," operating
at a high level of abstraction, "for some reason took little account of
human nature."   With really outstanding support from the events of
recent world history, Mr. Tate goes on to question the validity of the
rationalistic idea of human perfectibility: "Reason—in the sense of

moderate unbelief in difficult truths about human nature—and belief in the perfectibility of man-in-the-gross, were the great liberal dogmas which underlay much of our present trouble." Poe's own denial of perfectibility can be deduced from his frequently stated opinion that merely human effort could neither change the scheme of things nor alter human nature for the better. His view of human nature as fixed in the Divine Plan, unaltered and unalterable within time (as man experiences it), precluded any intellectual traffic with the idea of achieving perfection by means of environmental improvement. Moreover, he specifically denied the validity of the idea in a letter to James Russell Lowell:

> I have no faith in human perfectibility. I think that human exertion will have no appreciable effect upon humanity. Man is now only more active—not more happy—nor more wise, than he was 6000 years ago. The result will never vary—and to suppose that it will, is to suppose that the foregone man has lived in vain . . . (July 2, 1844).

There would be little purpose to this essay, however, if there were no further connection between Poe and the Agrarians than the similarity of their social and political ideas. Even the most sanguine of the Agrarians can hardly expect that his criticisms, however intelligently conceived or piercingly expressed, can penetrate the armor of Science, forged and buckled on by the Positivists. Although Agrarianism as a social philosophy or a mode of political action has had little force in the last two decades, as the ideological basis for aesthetic doctrine it has been the most vital and enduring belief our century has yet seen. Perhaps Agrarianism's validity in the aesthetic realm comes as an actual consequence of its present inutility in political action; certainly Mr. Tate and his fellow Southerners deny the role of agitator to the artist as artist. It is, then, within the world of art that we must expect to find the most significant accomplishment of the Agrarians, most of whom are artists; and certainly therein lies the real achievement of Edgar Allan Poe as well.

Robert Wooster Stallman, in an essay ("The New Criticism and the Southern Critics," *A Southern Vanguard*, 1947) clarifying the position of the Southern critics, states that there has been one basic theme in their work: "the dislocation of modern sensibility—the issue of our glorification of the scientific vision at the expense of the aesthetic vision." Donald Davidson, writing in *I'll Take My Stand*, found the dislocation becoming apparent in the Age of Johnson:

> Eighteenth century society, which pretended to classicism artistically and maintained a kind of feudalism politically, was, with all of its defects, a fairly harmonious society in which the artist was not yet out of place, although he was beginning to be. But in the middle of the eighteenth century democracy and the industrial revolution got under way simultaneously. The rise of the middle classes to power, through commercial prosperity, prepared the way for the one; scientific discovery, backed by eighteenth century rationalism, prepared the way for the other, and society speedily fell into a disharmony, where it has remained.

The eighteenth century then, under this scrutiny, becomes the breeding time of revolutions, the birth-century of the rights of man, the spawning period of the doctrine of progress (in the modern sense). But it was also the era of a great attempt to preserve harmony between the subjective and the objective worlds, the world of values and the world of measurement. It is in the work of the scriptural apologists of the eighteenth century that we can see the attempt most clearly. Harried divines like Bishop Butler, forced to acknowledge the invasion of science, tried to contain the enemy by seeking "analogies" between the Word of God and the Newtonian universe. The attempt was doomed, of course, a last ditch stand. Sin and evil could not properly subsist in the best of all possible worlds which operated with the mechanical precision described by Newton. How far the imagination failed in the attempt to accommodate itself to the new view can be seen in the bathos of a commonly used metaphor: the world was a precise mechanical instrument, a watch; God was the great watchmaker.

However, the attempt becomes extremely interesting in relation to the work of Edgar Allan Poe. Seeing with surprising clarity the predicament of the poet, cut off from a harmonious society, "living and perishing among the utilitarians," he made his own effort to contain the enemy in much the same way as did the eighteenth century divines. Again we may go to the *Colloquy of Monos and Una* to find a convenient summary of his beliefs. Key words representing his controlling concepts are (1) *Gradation*, as the scheme of things, and (2) *Analogy*, as the mode of apprehension by which the physical universe is understood in qualitative terms, a mode of apprehension which finds truth when abstract logic fails:

> . . . those truths which to us were of the most enduring importance could only be reached by that *analogy* which speaks in proof-tones to the in..agination alone, and to the unaided reason bears no weight . . . (Monos, in *The Colloquy*).

The word *gradation* leads us at once to the concept of the Great Chain of Being, that idea which was explored with such fullness by Professor A. O. Lovejoy in his book of the same name. The concept, in brief, was this: God in His infinite wisdom created the best of all possible systems, which embodied the principles of both plenitude and continuity. The principle of plenitude was that all possibles were realized in the utmost fullness of creation. The principle of continuity was that from the lowest form of life to God was an unbroken chain of being, that there was a continuum of forms from the lowest to the highest. This was the concept in Pope's *Essay on Man* when he wrote of a

> Vast chain of being! which from God began,
> Natures aethereal, human, angel, man,
> Beast, bird, fish, insect, What no eye can see,
> No glass can reach; from Infinite to thee,
> From thee to nothing.—On superior pow'rs
> Were we to press, inferior might on ours;
> Or in the full creation leave a void,
> Where, one step broken, the great scale's destroy'd;
> From Nature's chain whatever link you strike,
> Tenth, or ten thousandth, breaks the chain alike.

We see now the ideological background of Poe's statement in *The Colloquy* that democratic equalitarianism was "in the face of analogy and of God—in despite of the loud warning voice of the laws of *gradation* so visibly pervading all things in earth and Heaven."

Professor Lovejoy explains the social application of the concept most clearly:

> The universe, it was assumed, is the best of systems; any other system is good only in so far as it is constructed upon the same principles; and the object of the infinite Wisdom which had fashioned it was to attain the maximum of variety by means of inequality. Clearly then, human society is well

constituted only if, within its own limits, it tends to the realization of the same desiderata. . . . To seek to leave one's place in society is also 'To invert the laws of Order.' Any demand for equality, in short, is 'contrary to nature.' (*The Great Chain of Being,* pp. 205-6)

To work against the laws of gradation was a sin against God; and men who would rise above the limitations placed upon them by Nature were guilty of Pride. As Poe wrote in *The Colloquy*: "Man, having gained dominion over nature, stalked a God in his own fancy."

A further consequence of the idea of gradation was a certain humility. Man, in his middle position in the chain, was a creature of limitations. He was as far below God as the worm was below him. Accordingly he should avoid all ambitious intellectual projects which were purely rational in nature; in his merely human state he was not fitted to carry them out. This particular attitude we can also find exemplified in Poe. His fictional heroes who attempt to shun reality and live in the world of sheer intellectual absorption usually suffer disaster. Usher, severed from life and lost in idea, perishes deplorably. William Wilson, although participating in life, pursues a course of purposeless evil like the rational villain of the Renaissance. In killing his conscience (the *moral sense*) he destroys himself. The unnamed narrator of "Morella," poring over "forbidden pages" with his erudite wife, loses his love for her. She is woman enough to pine away in sorrow, but he, "with the heart of a fiend," longs for her decease. On her death bed she pronounces sentence: "Thou shalt no longer, then, play the Teian with time, but, being ignorant of the myrtle and the vine, thou shalt bear about with thee thy shroud on the earth. . . ." Losing the real world of love (the myrtle, sacred to Venus) and natural creativity (the vine, bearing fruit), he suffers psychic death in life.

We remember also that Poe had the greatest contempt for transcendentalism, for systems and abstractions not grounded in human nature. Once he even accused his favorite critical philosopher, Coleridge, of an "anomalous metaphysicianism." Finally, in *Eureka,* where his own pride in intellect seemingly gets the better of him, he "religiously abstains" from investigating the principle of repulsion, because of an "intuitive conviction that it lies involved in a consideration of what now—in our human state—is not to be considered—in a consideration of Spirit in itself."

This belief in the limitations of man, due to his position in nature, is, I believe, responsible for Poe's anti-rationalism; and his acceptance of the postulate that the universe (which he called a "plot of God") was perfect, rendered absurd to his mind all attempts based upon pure theory to alter the scheme of things by political or social revolution. A great many of the attitudes which bespeak the eighteenth century cosmic Toryism are implicit in Poe's idea of gradation; and it was these attitudes which were responsible for his contempt of what he called the "modern reformist Philosophy." "The fact is," Poe wrote in the *Marginalia,* "that in efforts to soar above our nature, we invariably fall below it. Your reformist demigods are merely devils turned inside out."

More than one agrarian in *I'll Take My Stand* demanded the same humility as did Poe. Andrew Nelson Lytle proposed as ideal a society which "recognizes the supremacy of nature and man's frailty." Mr. Ransom again makes a more sweeping assertion: there is "no deep sense of beauty, no sublimity of religion, no heroism, not informed by the humble sense of man's precarious position in the universe." Mr. Tate's dim view of perfectibility (the *possibility* of man as opposed to his *limitations*) has already been indicated. This unity of opinion we may assume as characteristic. The important question is its aesthetic implications. In Poe's work as well as that of the Agrarians, they are far-reaching: since it is specifically the rational aspect of man that is the object of distrust, it follows that those modes of knowledge which are qualitative receive emphasis.

It has already been noted that an attempt to adjust revealed religion to the new science was made in the eighteenth century. The method used was that of analogy: the Bible was to the Newtonian world something like metaphor to the objects of experience. Although the aim of the method was frequently to find analogical resemblance between natural and revealed religion, it was also used to interpret the relationship between the physical and moral worlds, between nature and man. As Poe expressed it, the "poetic intellect" found those truths which could only be reached by analogy. Consequently it follows that nothing could be more "noble" than a poem, the product of the poetic intellect. It was as a poem that Poe wished *Eureka* to be regarded. He maintained that his road to truth was *intuition,* not induction and deduction, those "two narrow and crooked paths—the one of creeping and the other of crawling—to which, in their ignorant perversity, they have dared to confine the Soul. . . ." If we attempt to disengage Poe's thought from its welter of grandiose and inaccurate terminology, sometimes Platonic, sometimes phrenological, and occasionally incomprehensible, we discover what he is really saying is that poetry is "an independent form of knowledge, a kind of cognition equal to the knowledge of the sciences at least, perhaps superior." This is the position of Tate and Ransom (I am using Mr. Stallman's essay here), and also, I judge, that of Cleanth Brooks and Robert Penn Warren.

As a special form of knowledge, a poem does not need an "ulterior motive." Poe writes, "the simple fact is that would we but permit ourselves to look into our own souls we should immediately there discover that . . . there neither exists nor *can* exist any work more thoroughly dignified . . . than . . . this poem *per se*, . . . which is a poem and nothing more, . . . written solely for the poem's sake" ("The Poetic Principle").

Poe, like the Southern critics, denies the hortatory function of poetry, but he does not forbid the poet to treat of evil in his own way: "taste [the poetic sense] contents herself with . . . waging war with vice merely on the ground of its inconsistency with fitness, harmony, proportion—" (Review of Longfellow's "Ballads"). Again Poe's idea seems to be that the poet's job is to write poetry, that he is concerned with moral or political questions only as they happen to fall within the periphery of his special vision (Mr. Tate expresses it, "the poet has a great responsibility of his own: it is the responsibility to be a poet, to write poems . . ."). And the ultimate worth of the poet's vision is that it enables him, laboring among "the things and thoughts of Time," to anticipate the beauty of the absolute.

According to Mr. Stallman's essay, it is Allen Tate's belief that poetry "springs from the irresistible need of the mind for absolute experience, a need which cannot be adequately satisfied in ordinary experience nor in an absolute metaphysics which classifies this ordinary experience into moral states and defines it intellectually." So far we seem to have a precise stating of Poe's own position. The poet who writes of ordinary experience, Poe says ("the sights and sounds which greet him in common with all mankind"), fails to satisfy the need for poetry. "There is still a thirst unquenchable. . . This burning thirst belongs to the immortal essence of man's nature. . . . It is a passion to be satiated by no sublunary sights, or sounds, or sentiments, and the soul thus athirst strives to allay its fever in futile efforts at creation."

The first significant difference between Poe's theory and Mr. Tate's may be found in this quotation. They seem to have fitted nicely together so far. Both deny to the poet any responsibility other than being a poet. Both hold the purely rational, the purely abstract world view in question, and both of them oppose utilitarianism in art. More important, both of them find an "irresistible need" in the mind for absolute experience which poetry attempts to satisfy. But in Mr. Tate's theory the need may be satisfied "in the absolute which poetry constructs in its 'portrait of reality' rather than in the absolute which philosophy constructs" (Stallman). Poe's absolute is the absolute of the philosopher; it is the Platonist's beauty of reality that lies beyond appearances, never to be achieved by human effort but always existing as the immutable order which lies beyond "the things and thoughts of time." This is the most significant deviation of Poe's theory from the operative aesthetics of the Southern Critics. It is, of course, a serious difference, because it denies to the poet the "coherent reality" that may be realized by his artistic ordering of experience. It leaves him in mortal discontent, ever yearning for a divinity that he cannot possess in the world of time, measuring his human artistry against the perfection of the eternal model. Consequently, in despair at the narrowness of his boundaries, the poet finds himself in a state of everlasting grief concerning the human predicament, at his "inability to grasp *now*, wholly, here on earth, at once and forever, those divine and rapturous joys of which, *through* the poem, . . . we attain to but brief and indeterminate glimpses" ("The Poetic Principle").

The vagueness to which Messrs. Brooks and Warren object in Poe's poetry grows out of this Platonic concern with the beauty of the reality beyond appearances and the human inability to grasp it. It most emphatically does not spring from the confusion of poetry with painting which they imply by quoting a letter written by Poe in 1831, before his theory was fully developed (See *Understanding Poetry*, rev. ed., 1950, p. 199). Shunning the quantitative world far more assiduously than Mr. Tate and Mr. Ransom, Poe would forego objective reality almost completely, showing it only "through the veil of the soul." Consequently his poetry lacks those concrete particulars which the Southern critics have found necessary to the total experience given by poetry. Leaving the world of spatial perception Poe would make poetry approach the condition of music. It becomes an ordering of time only, and as such lacks what Mr. Tate calls "tension," which is the synthesis between the abstract and concrete that every good poem possesses. Mr. Tate once stated that the "Ode to the Confederate Dead" had only one spatial image, that of the blind crab ("Narcissus as Narcissus," *Va. Quarterly Review,* XIV: 108-122); but no one would be likely to criticize the poem for lacking particularity.

Another and somewhat curious difference between the critical theory of Poe and that of the Southern critics is his defection to science, which he attacks when it appears in the practical form of industry or in the philosophical form of utilitarianism. Poe had no quarrel with science when it investigated physical nature (astronomy, physics, etc.) or even when it examined human nature (psychology). Considered as a follower of Coleridge, it is not surprising that he should be concerned with the psychology of art; but actually it is likely that Poe would have arrived at the same position without Coleridge. As a youth he lived in a society (Richmond) where the name of Thomas Jefferson was still held in respect, even though some of his ideas were beginning to be questioned. Poe's only formal advanced schooling was at Jefferson's University of Virginia; his approach to the psychology of art was mainly through channels discoverable in the Scottish group of psychologists, rhetoricians, and philosophers recommended by Jefferson (mainly Kames, Blair, and Dugald Stewart). Even the first patron that Poe sought was William Wirt, who belonged to the Jefferson circle. Jefferson, according to Mr. Tate, was the only Southerner in whom the scientific mind really operated (*I'll Take My Stand,* p. 173), and his intellectual influence during Poe's day was still strong in the University of Virginia. There in the library Poe could have found the criticism of Lord Kames, whose "principles," along with those of Blair and Johnson, would not fail, according to Poe, "until Nature herself expires." Kames was really a psychological critic. The first half of his *Elements of Criticism* was devoted to analyzing the mind. There in the library Poe could have found also the works of Gall and Spurzheim, the originators of the "science" of phrenology. Poe used, among other works of this nature, the phrenology of George Combe, who claimed to have engrafted this new science upon the philosophy of the Scotsmen, Hutcheson, Smith, Reid, Stewart, and Brown (Preface, *The Constitution of Man considered in Relation to External Objects,* Boston, 1845). Thus for Poe the faculty psychology of the Scots, who following Hutcheson had had marked aesthetic leanings, was made scientific and brought up to date by the phrenologists. The new science gave him hope that the inner sense, *taste,* located in the brain and analyzed scientifically, would at last yield up its "natural" principles. He stated his hope confidently:

> Not the least important service which, hereafter, mankind will owe to *Phrenology*, may perhaps be recognized in an analysis of the real principles, and a digest of the resulting laws of taste. These principles are as clearly traceable, and these laws as really susceptible of system as are any whatever (*Complete Works*, ed. Harrison, XI, 65).

No more than the Southern critics did Poe believe that one could rely on the judgment of taste; but somewhat like the early I. A. Richards or Kenneth Burke he expected to arrive at a sound judgment by psychological analysis of the *effect* of a work of art, whereas Mr. Tate, who investigates the poem as poem, holds that the psychological approach leads us only to the poet's mind, an interesting form of investigation but not criticism.

Another effect of psychology upon Poe's theory, of course, was his strict limitation of the length of a poem by what he considered the duration of attention. His great error, which sometimes science makes itself, was in considering as fixed in nature, invariable and unalterable, the imperfect "laws" discovered by an infant science. Nevertheless, the ideological basis of Poe's defection into science was that same neo-classic conservatism which lay behind his social and political views. Part of it was the idea that human nature is forever the same. Poe wrote,

> That a criticism 'now' should be different in spirit . . . from a criticism of any previous period, is to insinuate a charge of variability in laws which cannot vary—the laws of man's heart and intellect—for these are the sole basis upon which the true critical art is established ("Exordium," *Works*, XI, 5).

This idea of unchanging human nature was the keynote of the neo-classical criticism which held that Homer was the everlasting model, simply because he had endured, pleasing human nature for more than a score of centuries, proving that his work was, in the words of Poe's contemporary Hugh Swinton Legaré, "the natural, the universal, the unchangeable—*quod semper, quod ubique, quod ab omnibus.*" Poe, however, given by science the hope of a more available test than the long march of the centuries, looked for the eventual solution to the problem of judgment in psychology.

All this was as yet theory. When Poe came to the practice of criticism, he found that the "laws of taste" were not yet fully available to him; and his actual method turns out to be strikingly like that of the New Critics. For he wished to "limit literary criticism to comment upon *Art*."

> Criticism is thus no 'test of opinion.' For this test the work, divested of its pretensions as an *art-product*, is turned over for discussion to the world at large—and first, to that class which is especially addresses. . . In this, the only true and intelligible sense, it will be seen that criticism, the test or analysis of *Art*, (not of opinion,) is only properly employed upon productions which have their basis in art itself . . . ("Exordium").

Thus we see the wheel come full circle. Poe, starting from the same classical world view as the Southern Agrarian critics, maintaining the supremacy of nature and the limitations of man, exalting the qualitative mode of knowledge and deprecating that which is merely quantitative, deviates first into romanticism in his Platonic yearning for the absolute beyond appearances and then into science by his desire to find permanent, objective standards of judgment. Consequently his artistry is invalidated (at least to the most determinedly analytic of the Southern critics, Cleanth Brooks and Robert Penn Warren) by the first defection, and his critical theory vitiated by the second. Yet in his actual criticism he comes back into his own, limiting himself to technical analysis of the poem itself and boldly maintaining that the special form of knowledge which is poetry is not simply equal but is superior to the knowledge obtained by science or logic. Perhaps it is the long-range similarity of his ideological commitments to those of the Southern Agrarians which has motivated Mr. Allen Tate's enduring interest in Poe; possibly it is the close-up resemblance of his critical method to that of the New Critics. Whatever it is, if Mr. Tate ever prepares a full length study of Poe as critic and poet, we may expect it to be the most interesting analysis that the much abused Southern poet and critic has ever received.

WADE DONAHOE

Allen Tate And The Idea Of Culture

I.

There are no doubt various means of approaching the formulation of a system of values for one's profession or livelihood. The pursuit of abstract philosophical principles and concrete experience of the social order through the agency of professional problems combine to require a peculiar professional order in accordance with one's personal needs. That order is one's private political integrity; but in the process of recognizing and providing for the minimum of private honesty, one is obliged to recognize that other individuals are apt to have other needs, and the occasional public association of private virtue does not make automatically for a public virtue. When this state of affairs is seen, the organization of public values that will include what is constant in human nature becomes the duty of the citizen toward his society. Such duty, though it may vary in societies possessed of different degrees of harmony, is by no means evident only when a society labors in some extremity. Every order degenerates when its individuals have nothing better to do; but the duty bears differently on different capacities. One person may formulate the idea of a desirable society, bring his practice into conformity with that ideal, and attempt to persuade his actual society to join in achieving it. Another may express his or her sense of values only by containing his or her activities within its limits. Another may act contrary to belief and live by a faithlessness at once anxious and shot through with hypocrisy. I of course speak only of those who are conscious of need for objective values through the exigencies of a profession.

Mr. Tate arrives at his idea of cultural unity by three actions. He acts in his art on the values which he thinks privately and publicly desirable; he defends the objectivity of art works, political forms,

economic customs, and religious orders; and he attacks the cultural
results of "positivism." During the defense of culture and the attack
on positivism, he gives a running account of history, as a specific relation of concretions. The idea of a desirable system of relations
among the various terms of culture emerges from these actions and
is pitted against various specific disorders in education, the arts, the
sciences, manners, customs, etc. The attack on adverse cultural
phenomena is used mainly in his prose opinions; but the sense of
"a deep illness of the modern mind" informs the poems, where it
is played against a scarcely visible better order of things in our Christian past. I cannot recall a single poem of his that has not at its basis
the idea of culture. His only novel, *The Fathers,* is constructed around
the mysterious conduct of one of the principal characters who cannot
either contain himself in a real tradition or submit to picturesque
imitations of the surface of tradition. It is difficult to determine what
such use of an idea means. In the prose opinions it means that everything is controversy and polemic, though it does not mean that the
controversialist did not learn "how to write for an occasion without
being submerged in it." Its use in the creative arts is still more difficult
to evaluate. I don't know whether or not such use may be said to be
a form of didacticism, a doctrinaire procedure, or rationalism in poetry.
If one is permissible, the value of the distinction also remains impossible to fix. I do not believe it is necessarily the sole means of
fulfilling one's duty to contain one's practice within one's system of
values, nor the sole method for persuading one's society to join in the
imitation of one's idea of a desirable society.

According to Mr. Tate, the "positivist" is marked by the "naturalistic repudiation of the moral obligation to judge." He uses abstraction to avoid experience of specific form; he replaces rootedness with
internationalism or nationalism, being totally ignorant of the regionalism of the great historic moments, such as the period of the Greek
city-state, or the Elizabethan era. He continually forces on the mind
the impossible task of knowing everything before it can know anything. He is an enumerator who dissolves the valuable object into
the welter of its background, influences, and sources. He takes
literature to be "merely one among many forms of social and political
expression." He substitutes method for intelligence in everything, and
his activities are everywhere marked by the "vulgarity of the utilitarian
attitude."

The principal action of positivism is "pragmatic reduction" of whatever is encountered, combined with an apparent seriousness in the detailing of attendant circumstances. Behind this defection of intelligence from the main to the incidental object lies an assumption that "all experience can be ordered scientifically," which assumption has "logically reduced the spiritual realm to irresponsible emotion," since that realm continually overflows the limits set by positivist logic. What does not fit in must be reduced to an abstraction that will fit in. If the particular is intractable, it is held to be the conveyor of the universal class it implies, not an embodiment, and the universal is appealed to as a means of disregarding the particular. Life then becomes a mere technique (mechanics), which is either servant to its abstract meaning, or else an end in itself—for in certain instances the particular is allowed to obviate the universal. Living becomes a "situation" which governs its terms, not embodied minds in a natural setting.

The results of positivism as personal and public attitude are to be seen in various professions, but the thing goes deeper than the mere externals of culture; "historicism, scientism, psychologism, biologism, in general the confident use of the scientific vocabularies in the spiritual realm, has created or at any rate is the expression of a spiritual disorder." Its effects on certain liberties are equally disastrous; for "when you lose the moral and religious authority the military authority stands ready to supervene. Professor Dewey's social integration does not intervene." Thus it subordinates "our spiritual life and our material satisfactions to the single purpose of gaining superior material satisfaction in the future, which will be a materialistic Utopia of mindless hygiene and Tom Swift's gadgets."

One is occasionally puzzled by Mr. Tate's isolation of the term "positivism". The readiness he describes to relate the art work, or the specific form of anything, to particulars, and the subsequent abandonment of the formed whole for the discovered relation to nature has been dealt with for centuries under the general head of Nominalism. The abandonment of the specific form to its abstraction is quite as well treated. New names, accepted from their purveyors or imposed, obscure the well-known limitations and purposes of a historical movement, and in part absolve them from previous history, a thing which Mr. Tate of all people does not want to do. The positivist as historical scholar, or as literary critic, or as novelist or educator, only succumbs to his prurient and destructive curiosity about specific forms and to the collation of irrelevant knowledge when he has nothing better to do. Which, along with some valuable interests in actuality, is one of the known issues of Nominalism.

As I understand Mr. Tate's account of positivism, the positivist in his dealings with objective forms seeks to verify the relevance of the form to nature in his particular system. His reasons for doing so seem sufficient to him. He has nothing left to believe in but a limited range of facts, limited in meaning though not in number. His own relation to history (though perhaps not to a particular history) seems factual. The schemata of sociological, psychological, or "historical" disciplines seem to furnish objective referents, and they are indeed objectified within their several systems of discourse. He knows that forms had better be relevant to some actuality, but since the world seems unreal to him except as schematized in his favorite system, the nature of the relevance escapes him. The form is adjudged a failure: it is not true, or it does not exhibit the correct principles. He becomes lost in the details of the form, or in the details of the form's relations to the system of nature to which he is subjecting it. His job, as Mr. Tate has repeatedly demonstrated, is too large, and its largeness comes of misuse of instruments and of the resultant cultural confusion. He is removed from history, "so that he cannot participate as a living imagination in a great work of literature." The remark refers to a professional historian, but we are all historians.

It doesn't matter, but it is apparent that the exigencies of controversy led Mr. Tate to invent a figure who never was and to belabor him as a representative of various practices that are indubitably confused and confusing, but never wholly represented in any one system of attitudes or opinions. The social theories Mr. Tate has exemplified, however, arise out of an account of recent history, and it is in the account, not in the points at which the blame is laid, that we must expect instruction. The social theories imply that those values which man has long placed at the center of his highest and deepest efforts, that is, those values which lie beyond expediency and are the points at which man's daily needs are justified, have been displaced in modern society. Men no longer do whatever they do of good and evil for the glory of God. Nor are their symbols of connection with reality the works of art and philosophy and religion they once were. God has become the object of week-end and emergency sentiment; and art is popularly made the object of relaxation and a beneficent self-deceit. Philosophy, caught up in such progress, becomes the servant of the sciences. If Mr. Tate's account is largely true, I don't know what it implies except barbarism, either a temporary barbarism, or one likely to extend over several centuries.

Our trouble derives immediately, according to Mr. Tate, from "finance-capitalism and its creature, machine production," made possible by specialized science and technology. "For the social structure depends on the economic structure, and economic conviction is still, in spite of the belief of economists from Adam Smith to Marx, the secular image of religion." Machine production, money-standards, and the specialized sciences furnish the gadgets, but the incarnation of the machine and its logic goes further back. He cites several examples of the change. One is in the fact that men of letters now have no public that will support them without sweating them. Another lies in the position of the clergy. We consult various specialists; but we do not readily turn to the priesthood for expert advice on moral and spiritual problems. We do not because the priest carries with him the burden or stay of our past. We prefer to reduce the moral and spiritual problems to problems in social adjustment and self-expression. But "the concrete forms of the social and religious life are the assimilating structure of society." The absence of customary support of activities which are meeting places for our temporary concerns means the loss of justification—in the psychologist's sense of the term, if you will. The absence of an informed and "technical" religion means not that we have no religion, but that we have a scattering of temporary, disconnected, and culturally unworkable ones.

The separation of the various human disciplines from the community of tradition is the work of the state of mind that Mr. Tate calls positivism, a term we will stick to for this essay. On the political plane it is evident that positivism thrives not only in such States as Soviet Russia, where its orientation is obvious, if the logic is a little subject to State dogmas. Positivism also thrives under the tutelage of liberalism. The reasons for this are not immediately apparent, but unquestionably the attitudes of positivism have made radical changes in the practice of the expanding society during the present century.

Apparently the juncture of positivism and liberalism is made feasible by the peculiar disabilities of the liberal mind. That mind depends on faith in its own honesty and on a tolerance which assumes it includes everything good. Tolerance as a political theme is greatly enhanced, when entertained by the morally naive, by the pleasant feeling of being virtuous which it bestows. Such a state of mind suffers the illusion of belonging to a virtuous minority in its political aspect, though one that would include the human race, if it would only follow its real nature. It is psychologically rather feminine in its receptivity, and its corruption takes the form of admiration of hardness, technical skill, in short, the machine.

The philosophy of liberalism issues in the belief in natural man's inevitable success when he is freed from past mistakes—what the liberal desires above everything is a fresh beginning—severity, and commitment to fixed positions (other than those in the dogmas of Freedom). The sense of tolerance implies that the tolerant mind occupies no position, that it occupies all positions at once, like God. Unfortunately, these god-like attributes do not prevent the liberal mind from being at a serious disadvantage before disaster and the progress of public evil. Since men have wicked tastes, which are natural, they must be curbed by law. But the tolerant mind that is also a relativist mind cannot justify its judgments. It knows that men ought to be progressive, that the world's future will some day be perfected for man, that for the doubtful present men ought not to deprive each other of their rights. When someone asks, What rights? the liberal mind is unable to establish its answer. The opportunist who creates or takes advantage of mass hysteria (among those trained by liberalism) to promote his own position, and fixes the attention of the electorate on a bogus or real enemy while he builds a reputation for patriotism and candor, is indulging in a taste for power. The liberal mind cannot combat him except by trying to outshout him, a task for which it is not fitted.

A relative position continually deteriorates with its changing relations to the other elements of the moving stream. It naturally seeks a technique for fixing its position or for describing its flux. Psychologically it develops a soft center in its holders; and the liberal ends by inviting the ruthless chase so that as he is being mauled he may feel the extremity of his virtue. If he can discover some ruthless men on his side, he will take them, providing their disguises are at all acceptable. At this point the positivist Mr. Tate has described enters the scene and becomes an integral part of liberalism.

The bankrupt liberal changes imperceptibly into the opposite of his intent; from a political point of view it is in this change that the liberal attitude is most defective. If the liberal is sensitive he will be increasingly oppressed by an unformulated sense of the liberal-humanist stasis of our era. It is under such weight that he becomes an emperialist, without knowing it, without intending it, and indeed in the pursuit of virtuous ends. He begins to vie with the more fixed political attitudes for power, and his debased liberalism begins to show its lack of center in larger configurations than his mere familial, professional, and recreational conduct. He delays recognition of his bankrupt state by extending his efforts to save erring man. Involved in a world-wide action, he requires a technical jargon, an abstract description of his world problems, which positivism stands ready to furnish. He becomes so busy himself that he no longer needs to examine his private mind, and his virtue is thus made secure in the complexity of his activity. The distractions of complexity may overwhelm him, and he may at this point turn to some dogmatic system for a safe enclosure; but even there, he will be that socially most unbearable of men, the convert who is determined to make amends for his misguided past. Usually no such melodramatic change occurs; he will go on taking whatever tolerant views are popular in his set; he will increase his alignment with abstract systems that engage his tasks. There will be wicked men, whom he can quietly oppose, who wait to drive their fangs into his flesh; and the tolerance and the innocence will be too heady a habit to abandon.

I exaggerate; but the absurd account is not without relevance to the mechanical relations of Mr. Tate's positivist and current liberalism. Without some such exaggeration it is difficult to explain how positivism, which is a specialized genius for elaborate logical patterns, could have become a fixture of such a domain of the amateur as liberalism has hitherto been. Mr. Tate defines provincialism as the condition of "being committed to the immediate interest." A culture such as the liberal desired could hardly fail to permit the various cultural regions to lapse into provincialism; but through the aid of positivism liberalism is given another reprieve. When the world is made politically one world, without a "non-political or super-political culture such as held Europe together for six hundred years and kept war to the 'limited objective,'" we shall have world provincialism.

II.

Western culture was once a loose classical-Christian unity. Now all that remains is a measure of individual resistance to chaos, which stubborn freedom of will cultural conditions can never entirely overcome. "The individual human being will probably have in the future as in the past a natural economy to which he can occasionally return, if he is not meddled with too much by power at a distance."

> This natural economy cannot be an effective check upon the standardizing forces of the outside world without the protection of the regional consciousness. For regionalism is that consciousness or that habit of men in a given locality which influences them to certain patterns of thought and conduct handed to them by their ancestors. Regionalism is thus limited in space but not in time.
>
> The provincial attitude is limited in time but not in space. When the regional man . . . extends his own immediate necessities into the world and assumes that the present moment is unique, he becomes the provincial man. He cuts himself off from the past, and . . . . approaches the simplest problems of life as if nobody had ever heard of them before. A society without arts, said Plato, lives by chance. The provincial man, locked in the present, lives by chance.

And, one might add, lives in readiness to be included in a more authoritative cultural unit than the one he occupies, providing the authority can, given sufficient motivation, penetrate his preoccupations in an effective guise.

Mr. Tate looks at the region from without. It remains undefined, and the "solution" to the world decline seems a trifle thin when compared to the grandiose schemes of the internationalist. The vast Utopian blunder (not Mr. Tate's intelligently modest proposal for the restitution of the regional economy), hopeful and expansive, not guarded or desperate, has the better chance of being adopted.

He reminds us that we must be "realistic" about tradition, for "to revive something is to hasten its destruction—if it is only picturesquely and not sufficiently revived." Nonetheless, we have no choice but to try, for only by resisting cultural disintegration may we hope to retain civilization. In the era of cultural integrity "man belonged to his village, valley, mountain, or sea-coast; but wherever he was he was a Christian whose Hebraic discipline had tempered his tribal savagery and whose classical humanism had moderated the literal imperative of his Christianity to suicidal other-worldliness." When the Christian complex broke down, we were "left with our diverse regionalisms." But the "myth of science which undermined this culture and created the modern economic man rooted out the regional economies and is now creating a world regional economy." This will have all the defects of provincialism without the advantages of continuity and intimate knowledge inherent in a regional economy.

Mr. Tate occasionally makes a reading of history in which, through a typical contrast of now and then, he perhaps argues the case too well for the past. It seems to me that the best that can be said for the past is that it was a nightmare, like the present, but that men were not obliged to contemplate the nightmare all the time; they had the privilege of contemplating an ideal order which seemed to be feasible and possible. It is doubtful if the amount of specific evil in the world was thereby lessened, that it was less than it now is, or that it ever will be less than it now is. But it is a question of the relation to evil that Mr. Tate comments upon, with a view to an organization of values in society that will ameliorate the inescapable condition of living with conscience: the consciousness of the disparity between perfection and practice. An area of agreement among the terms of culture provides a cushion against the unmitigated imposition of the ideals of perfection for those who are not equipped to bear that weight, which is all of us; and it is for that that those who entertain the idea of cultural order work.

Consider, Mr. Tate asks us, "two worlds: the provincial world of the present, which sees in material welfare and legal justice the whole solution to the human problem; and the classical-Christian world, based upon the regional consciousness, which held that honor, truth, imagination, human dignity, and limited acquisitiveness, could alone justify a social order however rich and efficient it may be." That classical-Christian universalism through regionalism "could do much to redeem an order dilapidated and corrupt . . . if a few people passionately hold those beliefs." He adds, however, that since we are at present committed to the provincial attitude, it is better to have good-will toward even the Four Freedoms and such like abstract monstrosities, than to hold ill-will toward them.

He again defines the past through his famous contrast of the major myth of the religious imagination with the minor myth of the historical imagination. The description was offered not as "history," but as a "chart."

> First, there is the religious imagination, which can mythologize indiscriminately history, legend, trees, the sea, animals, all being humanly dramatized, somehow converted to the nature of man. Secondly, there is the historical imagination, which is the religious imagination *manque*— an exercise of the myth-making propensity of man within the restricted realm of historical event. Men see themselves in the stern light of the character of Cato, but they can no longer see themselves under the control of a tutelary deity. Cato actually lived; Apollo was merely far-darting.

He is dealing with the popular idea of truth in our age, when we are deprived of both those ways of looking at the world. Now, instead of "so workable a makeshift as the historical imagination," we have only "plain everyday history." To describe such history, which is not the interaction of prejudiced minds with each other in nature, the positivist introduces the idea of method. The method writes history for us; but "scientific method is itself not attached to anything. It is just abstract method—from which plain, abstract, inhuman history differs not by a hair . . . The historical method then may be briefly described . . . as the way of discovering historical 'truths' that are true in some other world than that inhabited by the historian and his fellow men: truths . . . that are true for the historical method."

The method is a pattern of abstraction at one with the abstractness of finance-capitalism and the future-mongering and one-worldism of the liberal idea. These deprive society of the continuity of specific knowledge furnished by tradition. The "untraditional society does not permit its members to pass on to the next generation what it re-

ceived from its immediate past." Now man's "human nature demands
a homogeneous pattern of behavior that his economic life will not
give him." The traditional man "dominated the means of life, he
was not dominated by it," and in that lies "the distinguishing feature
of a traditional society . . . traditional men . . . are making their
living all the time, and affirming their humanity all the time."

If one asks what is traditional about such an order of society,
the answer is "that if such a society could come into being now, and
had no past whatever, it would be traditional because it would hand
something on." Under finance-capitalism, men are removed "from the
responsible control of the means of livelihood," and the system is
"necessarily hostile to the development of a moral nature." Ultimately,
"the economic basis of life is the soil out of which all the forms, good
or bad, of our experience must come"; abstraction used to displace
concrete experience is a rock on which no seed grows.

The prevalence of money standards and other standards based on
secularized power is a symptom of our loss of the sense of history,
including history as religious experience. Religion has been reduced,
adulterated, fragmented, and otherwise removed from necessary participation in daily life. As it receded other forms of secular power
filled up the gap, each form a fragment of the whole. Religion, however, is concerned with the whole man, whereas pseudo-religions arising in the absence of a mature religion are symbols of preoccupation
with isolated activities and problems. For example, the modern mind
is abnormally concerned with man-power, and invents machines representing the power-mania as proof that it has no respect for the whole
man. Two of these half-religions that grew out of the absence of a
whole religion continually present themselves. One is "a religion
concerning how things work," the other "asserts that nothing works."
The one is the religion of the positivist; the other "is the religion of
the symbolist poets and of M. Henri Bergson."

The half-religion of works asserts that the whole nature of man
can be "subsumed under a concept of logical necessity." This gives
it the appearance of facing up to the harder sorts of truth, but in
practice it can predict for man only a vague future success for which
the present is to be sacrificed. A whole religion "takes account of the
failures . . . It is a mature religion, and it is not likely to suffer disillusion and collapse. Here it is very unlike the half-religion of works

which has a short memory of failure; the half-religion can ignore its failures to a certain saturation point, beyond which they will be overwhelming, and the society living under it is riding for a crushing fall." As soon, of course, as it ceases to have something engrossing to do which permits or helps to maintain the sense of community, at which point it may turn to the half-religion that holds that nothing works.

Man's relation to history is the subject, considered as a complex of events in any time. If we think of history as an image, it "reduces to a vast clutter of particular images" from which "we are able each of us to take our choice; we may reconstruct this scene or that period." Some persons prefer the Renaissance, some the age of Pericles; "or perhaps they concentrate their loyalty to a special kind of life in a particular document of an age or a people . . . These sad, more concrete minds . . . look at their history . . . as a concrete series that has taken place in a very real time . . . as full of sensation, and as replete with accident and uncertainty as the time they themselves are living in, moment by moment."

The alternative to thinking of history as a series of concrete images is to take it as an abstraction. If it is so conceived, you can ignore "the rival merits of the Greek and Roman cultures; they were both 'ideas' comprehensible after some study under a single concept which their chief business is now to illustrate . . . the particular instance fades away into a realm of phenomena related as cause and effect . . . There is ideally no accident or contingency; for accident and contingency are names for our insufficient information . . . The illusion of contingency that harassed the past . . . is dissolved by the Long View . . . For this Long View history becomes an abstract series opposed to the concrete series of the Short View."

For those who take the Long View past history occurred "without sensation, accident, or contingency . . . for the Short View, history is the specific account of the doings of specific men who acted their parts in a rich and contemporaneous setting which bewildered them. In their bewilderment they invented, or preserved even older, simple stories with a moral." The Long View which reduces the events of history "to identity of natural law gives to us the privilege of choosing between them; for assuming even that we are the offshoot of one of them, there is yet no reason why we cannot take up the other . . . But the Short View holds that the whole Christ and the whole Adonis are sufficiently differentiated in their respective qualities (details) and that our tradition compels us to choose more than that half of Christ which is Adonis and to take the whole, separate and unique Christ."

This distinction of the specific form from the mass of its background, origins, likenesses, and its resultant meanings is of course performed by Mr. Tate for poetry in a manner similar to the above argument for the specific quality of a historical configuration. It is interesting to note in a given mind the extensions of a discovery to orders other than that from which it issued first—I assume that what Mr. Tate knows has come through the development of his professional capacities. This is one of the distinctive qualities of Mr. Tate's mind, the clarity in which he sets whatever objects he contemplates—it is a quality especially to be appreciated in some of his poems—and the distinction of the specific form of culture is the point at which Mr. Tate's thesis is most severely tested. When we have "reconstructed" a historical period out of which some valuable elements of what we now are have come, the question arises as to the nature of the "loyalty" we owe to our source. The source is not the specific results of our living, whatever of its forms we may still contain and whatever abstract analogues exist in our own specific modes of life. What commands our loyalty, the specific form of our present (including whatever it does include of its past) or the specific forms of our past as those once were? If there is any virtue to such loyalty to a historical configuration as it is involved in our present forms, we owe our loyalty to the good of our whole condition. That condition is, as Mr. Tate indicates, full of contingency; its character is one of continuous transcendence of its origins, according to the laws of growth. There are no doubt occasions when, through ignorance or conflict of equally valuable courses, we cannot choose to continue the specific forms of the past as they have been. In seeking to make our present forms justly related to their origins, the original forms can be distinguished coldly as they were, perhaps, and as they bear on our present; but all this amounts to playing at games of identity and likeness, unless our purpose is to support only what is good, true, and beautiful—through whatever specific forms we can have intimate, whole knowledge of.

The remark quoted above, that "our tradition compels us to choose more than that half of Christ which is Adonis and to take the whole, separate and unique Christ" raises a difficult question. "Why

should our tradition compel us to choose anything?" He replies that
it cannot, that "tradition must . . . be automatically operative before
it can be called tradition." Even the defense of cultural loyalty by
rational argument is itself irrational. Why, then, talk about the matter
at all? The answer is that that is the way the Western mind works.
We have always vacillated "between a self-destroying naturalism and
practicality, on the one hand, and a self-destroying mysticism, on the
other . . . thus we have a special notion of tradition—a notion that
tradition is not simply a fact, but is a fact that must be constantly
defended."

The qualitative half of the whole man (Mr. Tate uses a horse,
which I've turned out to pasture during the season of this resume
of his arguments), "his image, must be defended against pure practicality, or his abstraction. His defense with us is abstraction itself. For
the only defense we know is rational and scientific, and it is thus
evident that dogma is not a personal property of religion, but is a
mere instrument. And it is an act of sheer generosity when this instrument sets about the defense of its natural enemy, the qualitative
view of experience. But, in the Middle Ages, it was so enamored of
this enemy that it could not be brought to destroy him, even if dogma
as rationality is a half-religion and is on the way to becoming science
or practicality."

Scholasticism tried to make rational the "spirits and myths and
symbols" of Christianity, and "it was only a step from natural
phenomena to supernatural noumena." "By making reason, science,
or nature an instrument of defense for the protection of the other
than reasonable, the other than scientific, the other than natural," the
Church achieved "a tremendous feat of spiritual unity. It is the only
kind of unity that the Western mind is capable of." The Eastern
Church never had "to construct a plausible rationality round the supernatural to make it acceptable; it has never had a philosophy, nor a
dogma in our sense; it never needed one."

The Western Church made reason the servant of the qualitative
view of experience. Reason developed its powers; "nature began to
see the practical possibilities of knowing herself. For reason and
nature are one, and that is the meaning of naturalism. The symbol
and the myth meant that the external world was largely an inviolable
whole; once the symbol and the myth were proved to be not natural

acts but unnatural fictions that fitted into no logical series tolerable
to the rational mind, nature became simply a workable half."

These passages of great interest were written in 1930; possibly
Mr. Tate would not now agree with his earlier views. Whether or
not he would, the metaphor of the integration of history, and of the
spiritual world as organism, is essential to the idea of culture which
he has advanced. If the world of man is an organic whole, the individual will exists in the enormous provision of spiritual being. It
either remains freely obedient to that whole, or it becomes an agent
of disease if it revolts. This view provides for a complete orthodoxy,
the state spiritually analogous to that of the beast in the forest. The
beast feels its own presence as a part of the world. It senses the
specific elements of its world, but it lives below thought, deep in its
own nature, totally immersed in time. The idea of cultural integrity
derived from the anthropologist is of primitive society. There the
act of intelligence, while it is ordinarily genuine and necessary, and
is as capable as any civilized act, remain in conformity with the community sensibility (which is itself whole and the parts congruous in
their relations), though it is not enslaved by that unity as, for example, are the members of a mob in their responses to mass hysteria
actors in our present society.

Given the theory of cultural integrity—which must not be taken
too literally—it is reasonable to interpret the modern advance of
various activities as ends in themselves as steps in the disintegration
of our culture. For as those activities attained virtually the status of
ends in themselves during their provision for the sensual man, they
became fascinating as symbols of power; preoccupied with them, we
now lose the symbols, the practical machinery, of our cultural order
through disuse. But "we do nothing without symbols and we cannot
do the right thing with the wrong symbol."

We must defend our culture, and that means a defense of tradition, particularly our religious tradition. The nature of Western
unity requires a philosophical defense; but the philosophy must be
kept in hand.

Since there is, in the Western mind, a radical division
between the religious, the contemplative, the qualitative, on
the one hand, and the scientific, the natural, the practical, on
the other, the scientific mind always plays havoc with the

spiritual life when it is not powerfully enlisted in its cause; it cannot be permitted to operate alone.

One wonders who will bell that particular cat.

Mr. Tate has asked how one can take hold of tradition in society whose economic, intellectual, and religious structure do n work together to furnish the free mind with a unified culture. H answer is that we can take hold of tradition only by "violence"; v must bore from without. "This method is political, active, and, the nature of the case, violent and revolutionary. Reaction is th most radical of programs; it aims at cutting away the overgrow and getting back to the roots. A forward-looking radicalism is contradiction; it aims at rearranging the foliage." We "must u an instrument which is political, and so unrealistic and pretentiou that we can scarcely bear it, "to reestablish a private, self-containe and essentially spiritual life."

Whether Mr. Tate's view of culture will assist in accomplishin that future depends upon the genesis of public attitudes; but as a instrument for dramatizing the present it has already been eminent successful. Men require whole images of the world; such images a always temporary and perilously selective. Like works of art the need not include every possibility the world holds out.

C. VANN WOODWARD

The Irony Of Southern History

In a time when nationalism sweeps everything else before it, as it does at present, the regional historian is likely to be oppressed by a sense of his unimportance.[1] America is the all-important subject, and national ideas, national institutions, and national policies are the themes that compel attention. Foreign peoples, eager to know what this New World colossus means to them and their immediate future, are impatient with details of regional variations, and Americans, intent on the need for national unity, tend to minimize their importance. New England, the West, and other regions are occasionally permitted to speak for the nation. But the South is thought to be hedged about with peculiarities that set it apart as unique. As a standpoint from which to write American history it is regarded as eccentric and as a background for a historian something of a handicap to be overcome.

Of the eccentric position of the South in the nation there are admittedly many remaining indications. I do not think, however, that this eccentricity need be regarded as entirely a handicap. In fact, I think that it could possibly be turned to advantage by the southern historian both in understanding American history and in interpreting it to non-Americans. For from a broader point of view it is not the South but America that is unique among the peoples of the world. This eccentricity arises out of the American legend of success and victory, a legend that is not shared by any other people of the civilized world. The collective will of this country has simply never known what it means to be confronted by complete frustration. Whether by

[1] This paper was presented as the presidential address before the Southern Historical Association at Knoxville, Tennessee, on November 7, 1952.

luck, by abundant resources, by ingenuity, by technology, by organizing cleverness, or by sheer force of arms America has been able to overcome every major historic crisis—economic, political, or foreign—with which it has had to cope. This remarkable record has naturally left a deep imprint upon the American mind. It explains in large part the national faith in unlimited progress, in the efficacy of material means, in the importance of mass and speed, the worship of success, and the unquestioning belief in the invincibility of American arms.

The legend has been supported by an unbroken succession of victorious wars. Battles have been lost, and whole campaigns —but not wars. In the course of their national history the Americans, who have been called a bellicose though unmartial people, have fought eight wars. And among them there has not been so much as one South African fiasco such as England encountered in the heyday of her power. This unique good fortune has isolated America, I think rather dangerously, from the common experience of the rest of mankind, all the great peoples of which have without exception known the bitter taste of defeat and humiliation. It has fostered the tacit conviction that American ideals, values, and principles inevitably prevail in the end. That conviction has never received a name, nor even so much explicit formulation as the old concept of Manifest Destiny. It is assumed, not discussed. And the assumption exposes us to the temptation of believing that we are somehow immune from the forces of history.

The country that has come nearest to approximating the American legend of success and victory is England. The nearness of continental rivals and the precariousness of the balance of power, however, bred in the English an historical sophistication that prevented the legend from flourishing as luxuriantly as it has in the American climate. Only briefly toward the end of the Victorian period did the legend threaten to get out of hand in England. Arnold J. Toynbee has recalled those piping days in a reminiscent passage. "I remember watching the Diamond Jubilee procession myself as a small boy," he writes. "I remember the atmosphere. It was: well, here we are on the top of the world, and we have arrived at this peak to stay there —forever! There is, of course, a thing called history, but history is something unpleasant that happens to other people. We are comfortably outside all that. I am sure, if I had been a small boy in New York in 1897 I should have felt the same. Of course, if I had been a small boy in 1897 in the Southern part of the United States, I should not have felt the same; I should then have known from my parents that history had happened to my people in my part of the world."

The South has had its full share of illusions, fantasies, and pretensions, and it has continued to cling to some of them with an astonishing tenacity that defies explanation. But the illusion that "history is something unpleasant that happens to other people" is certainly not one of them—not in the face of accumulated evidence and memory to the contrary. It is true that there have been many southern converts to the gospel of progress and success, and there was even a period following Reconstruction when it seemed possible that these converts might carry a reluctant region with them. But the conversion was never anywhere near complete. Full participation in the legend of irresistible progress, success, and victory could, after all, only be vicarious at best. For the inescapable facts of history were that the South had repeatedly met with frustration and failure. It had learned what it was to be faced with economic, social, and political problems that refused to yield to all the ingenuity, patience, and intelligence that a people could bring to bear upon them. It had learned to accommodate itself to conditions that it swore it would never accept and it had learned the taste left in the mouth by the swallowing of one's own words. It had learned to live for long decades in quite un-American poverty, and it had learned the equally un-American lesson of submission. For the South had undergone an experience that it could share with no other part of America—though it is shared by nearly all the peoples of Europe and Asia—the experience of military defeat, occupation, and reconstruction. Nothing about this history was conducive to the theory that the South was the darling of divine providence.

II

In his recent book, *The Irony of American History*, Reinhold Niebuhr conducts an astute analysis of national character and destiny that emphasizes another set of American pretensions which he calls the illusions of innocence and virtue. These illusions have their origins in both North and South, though at a period before there was any distinct regional consciousness. They were fostered by the two great moral traditions of early national life, New England Calvinism and Virginia humanism of the Jeffersonian school. While they differed upon theology, theocrats and humanists were agreed that their country was "God's American Israel," called out of a wicked and corrupt Old World and set apart by providence to create a new humanity and restore man's lost innocence. I believe that Niebuhr would agree that what I have described as the American legend of success and victory has assisted in fostering and perpetuating these illusions of innocence and virtue. At any rate he demonstrates that these illusions have been preserved past infancy and into national adulthood. Arriving at man's estate, we have suddenly found ourselves in possession of immense and undreamed of power and compelled to use this power in ways that are not innocent and that cover us with guilt. In clinging to our infant illusions of innocence along with our new power, writes the theologian, we are "involved in ironic perils which compound the experiences of Babylon and Israel"—the perils of overweening power and overweening virtue.

Our opposite numbers in the world crisis, the Russian Communists, are bred on illusions that parallel our own with ironic fidelity, even though they are of very different origin and have been used to disguise (perhaps even from themselves) what seems to us much greater guilt of oppression and cruelty. They combine these illusions with Messianic passions that find a paler reflection in one layer of American conscience. Looking upon their own nation as the embodiment of innocence and justice, the Russians take it for granted that America is the symbol of the worst form of capitalistic injustice. Both America and Russia find it almost impossible to believe that anyone could think ill of them and are persuaded that only malice could prompt suspicions of motives so obviously virtuous. Each tends to regard the other as the only force willfully thwarting its dream of bringing happiness to all mankind.

There are many perils, both for our nation and for the world, inherent in this situation—and they do not all come from abroad. We are exasperated by the ironic incongruities of our position. Having more power than ever before, America enjoys less security than in the days of her weakness. Convinced of her virtue, she finds that even her allies accuse her of domestic vices invented by her enemies. The liberated prove ungrateful for their liberation, the reconstructed for their reconstruction, and the late colonial peoples vent their resentment upon our nation —the most innocent, we believe, of the imperial powers. Driven by these provocations and frustrations, there is the danger that America may be tempted to exert all the terrible power she possesses to compel history to conform to her own illusions. The extreme, but by no means the only expression, would be the so-called preventive war. This would be to commit the worst impiety of the Marxists, with whom it is dogma that they can compel history to conform to the pattern of their dreams by the ruthless use of force.

To save ourselves from these moral perils, Dr. Niebuhr adjures us to disavow the pretensions and illusions of innocence derived from our national childhood, along with all self-righteousness, complacency, and humorless idealism. If we would understand our plight and prepare for the role we must play, we must grasp the ironic implications of our history. I realize that Niebuhr's view of human strivings is based on theology, a subject definitely beyond my province. Whatever its theological implications—and I have frankly never explored them—the view has a validity apart from them that appeals to the historian. Yet the ironic interpretation of history is rare and difficult. In the nature of things the participants in an ironic situation are rarely conscious of the irony: else they would not become its victims. Awareness must ordinarily be contributed by an observer, a nonparticipant. And the observer must have an unusual combination of detachment and sympathy. He must be able to appreciate both elements in the incongruity that go to make up the ironic situation, both the virtue and the vice to which pretensions of virtue lead. He must not be so hostile as to deny the element of virtue or strength on the one side, nor so sympathetic as to ignore the vanity and weakness to which the virtue and strength have contributed. Obviously the qualifications of the ironic historian are pretty hard to come by.

III

Now the South is deeply involved at present in the ironic plight of our country as a full-fledged participant. In fact the headlong precipitancy with which the South has responded to the slogans of nationalism in recent world crises has often exceeded that of other sections of the country. Mass response sometimes suggests the zeal of recent converts. Yet there are aspects of its history and experience that make the South an observer as well as a participant, which set it apart in certain ways from the experience of the rest of the country, and which constitute a somewhat detached point of view. From that vantage point I believe it is possible for the southern historian, and indeed all those absorbed in the study of southern history, to make a special contribution to the understanding of the irony of American history, as well as that of the South's history.

The ironic implications of southern history are not concealed by any legend of success and victory, nor by the romantic legend of the Lost Cause. To savor the full irony of the confident and towering ante-bellum dream of a Greek Democracy for the New World one has only to recall the words of a speech that Robert Barnwell Rhett made when South Carolina seceded. The orator was picturing the historian of 2000 A.D. writing this passage: "And extending their empire across this continent to the Pacific, and down through Mexico to the other side of the great gulf, and over the isles of the sea, they established an empire and wrought out a civilization which has never been equalled or surpassed—a civilization teeming with orators, poets, philosophers, statesmen, and historians equal to those of Greece and Rome—and presented to the world the glorious spectacle of a free, prosperous, and illustrious people." As a matter of fact, in the eyes of the true believer the coming of the Golden Age did not have to await the year 2000. It had already arrived, full blown, here and now. For as Charles Sydnor has observed, "the affirmation of Southern perfection" meant just that. Blind to evils and imperfections all around them, Southerners described what they saw as the ultimate in social perfection. "Fighting to defend their way of life," says Sydnor, "they had taken refuge in a dream world, and they insisted that others accept their castle in the sky as an accurate description of conditions in the South."

The shattering of this dream and the harsh education that followed has not made the South the home of a race of philosophers. Nor does it seem to have made Southerners any wiser than their fellow countrymen. But it has provided them with a different point of view from which they might, if they will, judge and understand their own history and American history, and from which to view the ironic plight of modern America.

The meaning of the contrast between the 1930's and the 1940's is a case in point. This transformation took place too recently for anyone to have forgotten, though many seem to have forgotten it entirely. In the thirties and well into the following decade there occurred the most thoroughgoing inquest of self-criticism that our national economy has ever undergone—not even excepting that of the muckraking and progressive era. No corner nor aspect nor relationship of American capitalism was overlooked, and no shibboleth of free enterprise went unchallenged. The prying and probing went on at every level from the sharecroppers to holding companies and international cartels. Subpoenas brought mighty bankers and public utility empire-builders to the witness stand. Nor was this activity merely the work of the wild-eyed and the woolly-haired, nor the exclusive concern of one of the major parties. It was a popular theme of the radio, the press, the screen, the theater, and even the pulpit. Some churches took up the theme and incorporated it into their programs. Universities hummed and throbbed with it. And in 1940 the former president of a public utility holding company, then candidate for President of the United States on the Republican ticket, made the theme a part of his campaign. Some of the outpouring of criticism in the thirties and forties was misdirected, some was perhaps a bit silly. But the electorate repeatedly endorsed with large majorities the party that was the more closely identified with the movement. On the whole the people regarded it as productive of good. It was at least indicative of a healthy and self-confident society, uninhibited by fear.

Then in the mid-forties something happened. It happened rather suddenly. The floodstream of criticism dwindled to a trickle and very nearly ceased altogether. It was as if some giant sluice gate had been firmly shut. The silence that followed was soon filled with the clamor of voices lifted in accusation, denial, or recantation. No reputation was now secure from the charges of the heresy hunters, the loyalty investigators, and the various committees on public orthodoxy and conformity. Choruses were lifted in rapturous praise of the very institutions that had been so recently the objects of attack. And the choruses were joined by many of the former critics.

Surveying this remarkable transformation, the historian of the South can hardly escape the feeling that all this has happened before—or something strongly suggestive of it: that what happened in the 1940's had its counterpart in the 1830's. The earlier development was on a smaller scale, to be sure, and there were certain other obvious discrepancies to be taken into account. The dangers inherent in any such comparison between historical epochs are numerous and forbidding, for certainly no analogy is perfect since no two eras, movements, or events are entirely alike. To suggest that modern capitalism is comparable to slavery as a system of labor would be to indulge in the loose and irresponsible language of polemics and propaganda. With due precaution and full awareness of the risks, however, one may venture a comparison not between the two institutions but between the public attitudes toward them and the transformations that took place in those attitudes.

What happened in the South during the 1830's is too familiar a story to require elaboration here. Before it happened, however, we know that the Jeffersonian tradition protected and fostered a vigorous school of antislavery thought in the South. The great Virginians of the revolutionary generation, nearly all of whom were on record for emancipation, lent their prestige to the movement. Critics of slavery spared no aspect of the peculiar institution. They spoke out against the effect upon the master as well as upon the slave; they exposed the harm done the manners and morals of the South as well as its economy and society. Nor were the critics mere misfits and radicals. They included men of influence and standing: politicians, editors, professors, and clergymen. Antislavery thought appeared in respectable newspapers and infiltrated evangelical sects of the upper South particularly. In the 1820's the slave states contained a great many more antislavery societies than the free states and furnished leadership for the movement in the country. It would be false to suggest that slavery was on the way out, or, in spite of some amelioration, that the reformers made any very substantial alterations. But it is not too much to say that this was a society unafraid of facing its own evils. The movement, you will recall, reached a brilliant climax in the free and full debates over emancipation in the Virginia legislature during the session of 1831-1832. The effort to abolish slavery failed there as elsewhere. But as Joseph Robert writes, "The institution was denounced as never before; it was condemned wholesale fashion by legal representatives of a slave-holding people. The vigor and breadth of the assault provide the debate with its most obvious distinction."

In spite of the vigor of the movement and the depth of its roots in southern tradition, it withered away to almost nothing in a very brief period during the middle thirties. By 1837 there was not one antislavery society remaining in the whole South. Of the thousands of voices that had been raised in outspoken protest a short while before there were to be heard only a few whispers. Opponents changed their opinions or held their tongues. Loyalty to the South came to be defined in terms of conformity of thought regarding one of its institutions. Past records and associates were scrutinized closely, and the recency with which one had denounced northern abolitionism became a matter of public concern. The South concentrated its energies upon the repression of heresy and raised intellectual barricades against the ideas of a critical and unfriendly world. The institution that had so recently been blamed for a multitude of the region's ills was now pictured as the secret of its superiority and the reason for its fancied perfection.

IV

The causes behind the transformation of attitudes in the South were numerous and complex. So are the reasons behind the transformation that has taken place in the attitudes of contemporary America. Broadly speaking, however, both of these revolutions in public attitudes were reactions to contests for power in which the two societies found themselves involved. These great struggles included many clashes of interest and issues quite apart from those concerning morals and contrasting labor systems. Even in the absence of ideological differences the strains of conflict would have been severe in each case. In the 1850's as in the 1950's, however, the crisis tended to be increasingly dramatized as a clash between different systems of labor: as slave labor versus free labor. In both the nineteenth-century war of words and the twentieth-century cold war each party to the conflict, of course, contended that the other practiced the more immoral, wicked, and shameless type of exploitation, and that its own system was benevolent, idealistic, and sound. Our own opinions as to which of the parties in each crisis was the more deluded or disingenuous in its contentions are likely to be pretty firmly fixed already, and the problem is such that it need not detain us.

The point is that there exists, in spite of obvious differences, a disquieting suggestion of similarity between the two crises and the pattern of their development. The mistakes of the South, some of which have already been suggested, are readily apparent and their meaning open to all who would read and understand. In the first place the South permitted the opposition to define the issue, and naturally the issue was not defined to the South's advantage. In the second place the South assumed the moral burden of proof. Because the attack centered upon slavery the defense rallied around that point. And as the clamor increased and the emotional pitch of the dispute intensified, the South heedlessly allowed its whole cause, its way of life, its traditional values, and its valid claims in numerous nonmoral disputes with the North to be identified with one institution. And that was an institution of which the South itself had furnished some of the most intelligent critics. It was a system known to have reached the natural limits of its expansion in this country already and one which was far gone on its way to abandonment abroad. Yet in its quest for friends and allies the South made the mistake of competing with the North for the favor of the West by insisting upon the acceptance of a system totally unadapted to the conditions and needs of the territories and often offensive to their moral sensibilities. And in looking to Europe for support from England and France, powers that might reasonably have been expected to be drawn to its cause for reasons of self-interest, the South encountered difficulties from the start. Some, though certainly not all, of these difficulties were due to the fact that those countries had already repudiated the system upon which the South had elected to stand or fall.

The knowledge that it was rapidly being isolated in the world community as the last champion of an outmoded system under concerted moral attack contributed to the South's feeling of insecurity and its conviction that it was being encircled and menaced from all sides. In place of its old eagerness for new ideas and its outgoing communicativeness the South developed a suspicious inhospitality toward the new and the foreign, a tendency to withdraw from what it felt to be a critical world. Because it identified the internal security of the whole society with the security of its labor system, it refused to permit criticism of that system. To guarantee conformity of thought it abandoned its tradition of tolerance and resorted to repression of dissent within its borders and to forceful exclusion of criticism from outside. And finally it set about to celebrate, glorify, and render all but sacrosanct with praise the very institution that was under attack and that was responsible for the isolation and insecurity of the South.

Modern America is more fortunate than the ante-bellum South in having an economic system which, though threatened with abandonment by other countries, has shown few of the serious weaknesses and is covered with little of the moral obloquy from which slavery suffered. And in spite of verbal orthodoxy regarding the doctrine of capitalistic free enterprise, the American political genius has shown willingness to experiment extensively with heterodox cures for ills of the orthodox system. This experimentation has, of course, been accompanied by loud protests of loyalty to the true faith. Again, modern America is not handicapped in the struggle against its powerful antagonist by the economic and military weaknesses that helped to doom the South to defeat.

There is, however, no cause for complacency in this good fortune. Nor does it rule out entirely the analogy that is here suggested. We should not deceive ourselves about the opinions of other peoples. While we see ourselves as morally sound and regard our prosperity as the natural and just reward of our soundness, these views are not shared by large numbers of people in many parts of the world. They look upon our great wealth not as the reward of our virtue but as proof of our wickedness—as evidence of the ruthless exploitation, not only of our own working people but of themselves. For great masses of people who live in abject poverty and know nothing firsthand of our system or of industrialism of any kind are easily persuaded that their misery is due to capitalist exploitation rather than to the shortcomings of their own economies. Hundreds of millions of these people are taught to believe that we are as arrogant, brutal, immoral, ruthless, and wicked as ever the South was pictured in an earlier war of words. And among their leaders are extremists ready with the conclusion that people so wicked do not deserve to live and that any means whatever used to destroy their system is justified by the end. One of these means is the subversive indoctrination of our labor force for insurrection. The malevolent caricature of our society contrasts so glaringly with what we believe to be the demonstrable facts—not to mention the contrast with our traditional illusions of virtue and innocence—that we are driven to indignation. And when we hear faint echoes of the same propaganda from our own allies, who no longer share our dedication to capitalism, our indignation turns into a sense of outrage.

Fortunately modern America has not yet followed the course of the South between 1830 and 1860, but the pattern of response evoked by these exasperations is not a wholly unfamiliar one. There are some unhappy similarities. Threatened with isolation as the last important defender of an economic system that has been abandoned or rejected without a trial by most of the world and is under constant moral attack from several quarters, we have rallied to the point of attack. We have shown a tendency to allow our whole cause, our traditional values, and our way of life to be identified with one economic institution. Some of us have also tended to identify the security of the country with the security of that institution. We have swiftly turned from a mood of criticism to one of glorifying the institution as the secret of our superiority. We have shown a strong disposition to suppress criticism and repel outside ideas. We have been tempted to define loyalty as conformity of thought, and to run grave risk of moral and intellectual stultification.

Opposing each of these dangerous tendencies there is still healthy and wholesome resistance struggling to reassert our ancient tradition of tolerance and free criticism, to maintain balance and a sense of humor, to repel the temptation of · self-righteousness and complacency, and to reject the fallacy that the whole American cause and tradition must stand or fall with one economic dogma. But it is too early to say that on any one of these points the healthy resistance is certain of triumph. In fact the fight is uphill and in many instances the issue is doubtful. I am not contending that successful resistance to all the tendencies I have deplored will guarantee peace and solve the problems of the 1950's, any more than I am sure that the same course would have resulted as happily in the 1850's. But I believe I am safe in contending that in view of the South's experience each of these tendencies should be the subject of gravest concern.

V

In the field of diplomacy and foreign relations modern America suffers from a divided mind, torn between one policy that is reminiscent of the way of the South and another more suggestive of the way of the North in the Civil War crisis. On the one hand are those who would meet the foreign challenge by withdrawing from a critical community of nations teeming with heresies and, by erecting an impregnable barricade, forcibly keep out all alien ways, influences, and ideas.[2] Another modern group that has a counterpart in at least one school of Southerners in the 1850's are those who in the 1950's, heedless of world opinion, would brook no opposition, would not co-operate with, nor consult other people's views, but insist that America must be strong enough to carry her way by economic coercion or by force. Suggestive also of the southern way are those who, in

[2] Recent examples are the admission of the Post Office Department that it is burning tracts mailed from the Iron Curtain countries, and the action of port authorities in excluding alien seamen for political reasons in enforcing new immigration laws. Both instances, of course, suggest ante-bellum counterparts.

competing with our opponents for the favor of uncommitted peoples, would urge upon them institutions and abstract ideas of our own that have little or no relevance to their real needs and circumstances. And there are those also who resent as evidence of disloyalty any defection on the part of our allies from the particular economic faith upon which we have decided to take our stand.

More reminiscent of the way of the North, on the other hand, are those who hold that this is an irrepressible conflict, that a world divided against itself cannot stand, that the issue is essentially a moral one, that we are morally obligated to liberate the enslaved peoples of the earth, punish the wicked oppressors, and convert the liberated peoples to our way of thought. The true American mission, according to those who support this view, is a moral crusade on a world-wide scale. Such people are likely to concede no validity whatever and grant no hearing to the opposing point of view, and to appeal to a higher law to justify bloody and revolting means in the name of a noble end. For what end could be nobler, they ask, than the liberation of man? Fortunately wiser counsel prevails at the moment,[3] counsel which charts a course of foreign policy between the perilous extremes of isolationism and world crusade. But each of the extreme courses still has powerful advocates and neither can yet be regarded as a dead issue.

We have been admonished lately to heed the ironic consequences of the characteristic American approach to international affairs since the beginning of the present century. The main deficiencies of our policy of the last fifty years, we are told, are our legalistic and moralistic approaches to foreign relations. It is possible and even desirable, I believe, to accept the validity of this critical insight without embracing the strictly amoral, pragmatic, power-conscious policy of national self-interest that has been proposed as an alternative by those who criticize the moralistic approach. It is all too apparent that the association of the legalistic with the moralistic concept results in a torrent of indignation and bitterness against the lawbreaker and a blinding conviction of moral superiority to the enemy. Expressed in

[3] This was written in October, 1952.

military policy and war aims these passions overwhelm reason and find no bounds short of the complete submission, unconditional surrender, and total domination of the defeated people. The irony of the moralistic approach, when exploited by nationalism, is that the high motive to end injustice and immorality actually results in making war more amoral and horrible than ever and in shattering the foundations of the political and moral order upon which peace has to be built.

Those who trace our moralistic aberrations back to the American crusade to liberate Cuba have, I believe, overlooked remoter origins. For there would appear to be valid grounds for seeking these origins in the period of the Civil War. While both sides to that dispute indulged in legalistic as well as moralistic pretensions, it was the South that was predominantly legalistic and the North that was overwhelmingly moralistic in its approach. Although southern historians have made important contributions to the understanding of that crisis, it is doubtful whether anyone has stated more aptly the ironic consequence of the moralistic approach than a northern historian in a recent book called *And the War Came*. "Yankees went to war," writes Kenneth Stampp, "animated by the highest ideals of the nineteenth-century middle classes. . . . But what the Yankees achieved—for their generation at least—was a triumph not of middle-class ideals but of middle-class vices. The most striking products of their crusade were the shoddy aristocracy of the North and the ragged children of the South. Among the masses of Americans there were no victors, only the vanquished."

Ironic contrasts between noble purposes and sordid results, between idealistic aims and pragmatic consequences are characteristic of reconstruction periods as well as war crises. This is nowhere more readily apparent than in the postwar period through which we are now living and with the problems of which we are still struggling. It is especially in such times that moralistic approaches and high-minded war aims come home to roost. As usual, it is only after the zeal of wartime idealism has spent itself that the opportunity is gained for realizing the ideals for which the war has been fought. When the idealistic aims are then found to be in conflict with selfish and pragmatic ends, it is the ideals that are likely to be sacrificed. The probability of moral confusion in reconstruction policy is increased when a nation finds itself called upon to gird for a new world moral crusade before the reconstruction consequent upon the last is fairly launched. Opportunities for moral confusion are still further multiplied when the new crusade promises to be fought in alliance with the public enemies of the previous moral crusade and when the new public enemy happens to have been an ally in the previous crusade.

Americans have in common the memories of an earlier experiment with reconstruction and are generally conscious of some of the shortcomings of that effort. But again, the South experienced that same historic episode from a somewhat different point of view. Once southern historians have purged their minds of rancor and awakened out of a narrow parochialism they should be in a singularly strategic position to teach their fellow countrymen something of the pitfalls of radical reconstruction: of the disfranchisement of old ruling classes and the indoctrination of liberated peoples, of the occupation of conquered territory and the eradication of racial dogma, of the problems of reunion and the hazards of reaction. They should at least have a special awareness of the ironic incongruities between moral purpose and pragmatic result, of the way in which laudable aims of idealists can be perverted to sordid purposes, and of the readiness with which high-minded ideals can be forgotten.

With all her terrible power and new responsibilities combined with her illusions of innocence and her legends of immunity from frustration and defeat, America stands in greater need than she ever did of understanding her own history. Our European friends, appalled by the impetuosity and naïveté of some of our deeds and assumptions, have attributed our lack of historical sophistication to our lack of a history—in their sense of the word. America's apparent immunity to the tragic and ironic aspects of man's fate—that charmed and fabled immunity that once made America the Utopia of both the common men and the philosophers of Europe—has come to be pictured as Europe's curse. For the fear that haunts Europeans is the fear that America's lack of a common basis of experience and suffering will blind her to the true nature of their dilemmas and end by plunging them into catastrophe. But the Europeans are not entirely right. America has a history. It is only that the tragic aspects and the ironic implications of that history have been obscured by the national legend of success and victory and by the perpetuation of infant illusions of innocence and virtue.

America has had cynical disparagement of her ideals from foreign, unfriendly, or hostile critics. But she desperately needs criticism from historians of her own who can penetrate the legend without destroying the ideal, who can dispel the illusion of pretended virtue without denying the genuine virtues. Such historians must have learned that virtue has never been defined by national or regional boundaries, and that morality and rectitude are not the monopolies of factions or parties. They must reveal the fallacy of a diplomacy based on moral bigotry, as well as the fallacy of one that relies upon economic coercion through the fancied indispensability of favored products. Their studies would show the futility of erecting intellectual barricades against unpopular ideas, of employing censorship and repression against social criticism, and of imposing the ideas of the conqueror upon defeated peoples by force of arms. Such historians would teach that economic systems, whatever their age, their respectability, or their apparent stability, are transitory, and that any nation that elects to stand or fall upon one ephemeral institution has already determined its fate. The history they write would also constitute a warning that an overwhelming conviction in the righteousness of a cause is no guarantee of its ultimate triumph, and that the policy that takes into account the possibility of defeat is more realistic than one that assumes the inevitability of victory.

Such historians must have a rare combination of detachment and sympathy, and they must have established some measure of immunity from the fevers and prejudices of their own times, particularly those bred of nationalism with all its myths and pretensions, and those born of hysteria that closes the mind to new ideas of all kinds. America might find such historians anywhere within her borders, North as well as South. But surely some of them might reasonably be expected to rise from that region where it is a matter of common knowledge that history has happened to our people in our part of the world.

II. The Themes Of Southern Literature

HOWARD W. ODUM and JOHN MACLACHLAN

Literature In The South: an exchange of views

EDITOR'S NOTE

In a recent talk on "Why the Modern South Has a Great Literature," Mr. Donald Davidson made the following statement:

> . . . I turn to sociology and ask whether it can account for the appearance in Mississippi, of all places, of William Faulkner, in the three decades between 1920 and 1950. My question has a corollary which I believe I am entitled to state: Can sociology also explain why William Faulkner, or some novelist of comparative stature, did *not* appear, during this period, somewhere north of the Ohio — say, in Massachusetts or Wisconsin?*

In the opinion of the editors, Mr. Davidson in so doing asked a root question, one which must be thoroughly considered in any serious attempt to understand the modern literature produced by Southerners. Mr. Davidson, the editors felt, was asking the sociologists to account for the seeming paradox that the South, which by so many of the standards of sociological measurement was the most backward, the least "progressive" region in the United States, was also the region in which American literature seemed best to flourish.

Accordingly, the editors agreed to invite two eminent sociologists to comment on the problem, taking as their theme the paragraph from Mr. Davidson's address quoted above. Their conclusions are herewith presented.

---

* — delivered at Mississippi State College, April 21, 1950, and reprinted in Vanderbilt Studies In The Humanities, I, Nashville, 1951, pp. 1-17.

1. ON SOUTHERN LITERATURE AND SOUTHERN CULTURE

Howard W. Odum

The sources of American ideals, the regional quality of American letters, and the genesis of Southern writing have long constituted major themes for students of American culture and literature. Although it must be clear that it is not possible to oversimplify causal factors or to identify complete characterizations or distinctive qualities of writing as related to either regions or authors, nevertheless few themes appear to be more persistently popular in the search for satisfying answers. In the case of Southern writing there are several factors which accentuate the timeliness of questions that are often asked concerning the sources and nature of Southern literature. In addition to the general assumption that American literature has been preeminently regional, the South has itself contributed more than a proportionate share of the nation's literary output during the first half of the 20th century. So, too, since the South has been more thoroughly documented and written about, both by Southern and national authors, than any other region, it has constituted a sort of perennial theme for public appraisal. Then, within more recent years the widespread critical discussions of William Faulkner and Thomas Wolfe, to mention only two, have focused new critical queries as to the genesis and nature of Southern writing.

This paper, by request of the editor, has to do with two aspects of these queries, namely the possible relation of general socio-economic factors and cultural backgrounds to Southern literature and the specific question raised by Donald Davidson and others as to why William Faulkner should be the product of Mississippi and the South rather than of Massachusetts and New England.

Donald Davidson's question as to whether sociology can explain why William Faulkner, or some novelist of comparable stature, did *not* appear, during the first half of the 20th century in the United States somewhere north of the Ohio—say, in Massachusetts or Wisconsin?,[1] offers a fair setting for a reasonable discussion of the genesis

---

[1] Donald Davidson, "Why the Modern South Has a Great Literature," *Vanderbilt Studies in the Humanities*, I (Nashville: Vanderbilt University Press, 1951), p. 3.

and development of regional literature. Moreover, his question is a sort of specific corollary to a broader question as to why the contemporary South has produced great literature when its general socio-economic culture reflects statistical ratings in the lower quartiles as compared to the other regions of the United States.

These questions are apparently based on a general misunderstanding of sociology and the facile assumption that the sociologist would always look for a great literature in an advanced society with a high index of gadget civilization, advanced achievements in the arts and sciences, and in the setting of intellectualism and cultural specialization. Nor would he, by the same token, appraise a great literature as exclusively the highest achievement of culture. On the contrary, culture for the sociologist is identified with the sum-total of all the cumulative processes and products of societal achievement, rather than any one or two intellectual or technical specializations.

Nevertheless Davidson's specific insistence upon exploring the reasons why William Faulkner, coming from Mississippi, the lowest indexed state, should not have been produced in Massachusetts, the highest indexed state, affords a setting for the answer to his more relevant general question as to why the South, rather than, let us say, New England has excelled in its recent general literary writing. For, during the first fifty years of the twentieth century the South has contributed no less than five-thousand titles to the full-sized-book literature of the nation as measured by standard catalogues and major publishers.[2] Of these approximately one half may be classified as "literature" in the traditional sense, with 1000 volumes of fiction, 500 biography, 400 poetry and 125 drama. The total "writing" contributions, however, include something like 800 volumes on History, 800 on Negro Life, 400 on Nature and the Folk, more than a hundred each on Socio-economic Studies, Nature and Resources, Travel and Description. So far as our inquiries go none of the other regions, the Northeast, the Middle States, the Northwest, or the Far West approximate this quantitative measurement of achievements.

To limit our inquiry to fiction, in which William Faulkner is the representative and Nobel Prize winner, and toward which Davidson has directed his inquiry, the qualitative measure of Southern writing is indicated by the fact that there have been no less then eight

---

[2] See Anna Greene Smith's forthcoming volume *Fifty Years of Southern Writing*.

Pulitzer Awards to Southern novelists and perhaps one hundred
Southern best sellers, as compiled by *The Publishers' Weekly* ratings
of each year's ten top best selling books. In addition to Pulitzer
Awards in fiction, and exclusive of journalistic awards, there have
also been three in drama, three in biography and three in poetry.[3]
In all the categories, Pulitzer Awards have been made to Southern
authors in more than half of the years since the first awards in 1917.

Of the eleven best sellers that have exceeded or approximated
a million copies, ten were by Southern authors. An examination of
the titles of the Pulitzer Prize winners and best sellers will indicate
the closely related themes of most of these volumes to Faulkner's
own major contributions, so that the answer to Davidson's specific
question about Faulkner and Mississippi will surely throw some light
on the more general inquiry about the South's total literature.

Davidson's oversimplified assumptions with reference to the sociologists' analysis of interacting causal factors in societal development
may be found in a number of quotations. First, Davidson asks,

> Now in the formative period of William Faulkner—
> and, if you wish, of his contemporaries—what cultural factors,
> exactly, were at work in the Southern scene?[4]

He then answers,

> I am very sorry to have to report to you that during
> William Faulkner's formative period the cultural factors
> were extremely forbidding in the State of Mississippi. I can
> hardly see how Mr. Faulkner survived, much less wrote
> novels. On the evidence of Mr. Odum's tables, culture was
> at a very low ebb in Mississippi—so low that, if I had only
> these tables to depend upon, I would confidently assert, as
> a devoted follower of sociology, that a William Faulkner
> in Mississippi would be a theoretical impossibility; and that

---

[3] The Pulitzer Awards are: Julia Peterkin's *Scarlet Sister Mary;* Oliver La .Farge's
Laughing Boy; T. E. Stribling's *The Store;* Caroline Miller's *Lamb in His Bosom;*
Margaret Mitchell's *Gone With the Wind;* Marjorie Kinnan Rawlings' *The Yearling;*
Ellen Glasgow's *In This Our Life;* Robert Penn Warren's *All the King's Men;* Hatcher
Hughes' *Hell-Bent for Heaven;* Paul Green's *In Abraham's Bosom;* Marc Connelly's
utilization of Roark Bradford's *Ol' Man Adam and His Chillun* in *The Green Pastures;*
Marquis James' *The Raven;* Douglas Southall Freeman's *R. E. Lee;* Marquis James'
Andrew Jackson; Conrad Aiken's *Selected Poems;* George Dillon's *The Flowering Stone*
and John Gould Fletcher's *Selected Poems.*

[4] Davidson, *op. cit., p.* 4.

if he emerged at all, he would have to originate in say, Massachusetts, where the cultural factors were favorable to literary interests.[5]

Davidson continues by asserting that "The cultural factors described by Mr. Odum either had a causal influence on William Faulkner or they did not."[6]

If they did have a causal influence, we must, under the rigorous impulsion of sociology, reach an astonishing conclusion: namely, that the way for a society to produce a William Faulkner is to have him born in a thoroughly backward state like Mississippi, of a chivalrously inclined, feudal-minded, landed Southern family that was ruined by the Civil War and later dipped, not very successfully, into modern business. In other words, a prevalence of rural society, devoted to cotton-growing, afflicted by sharecropping, rather poverty-stricken, conservative in religion and politics, prone to love the past rather than the future, chockful of all the prejudices and customs of the South—that is what it takes to produce a William Faulkner.

Contrarily, a prevalence of material progress, great wealth, modern institutions such as libraries and art museums, factories, industrial gimcracks, liberalism, science, political radicalism— that is the way *not* to produce a William Faulkner. If it were otherwise, Massachusetts and Wisconsin by this time would have produced not one but a couple of dozen William Faulkners.[7]

As a matter of fact, Davidson's assumption that William Faulkner would be an impossibility in any complex cultural setting negates the authentic findings of historical and sociological study, as do his assumptions as to the nature of cultural factors which are "favorable to literary interests." For the sociologist, if he is scientific, like the historian of great literatures and the biographers of great writers must understand and portray the total configuration of culture, with all of its interrelationships and interaction with the heritage and behavior of the individual as well as the interlocking causal factors that have made him what he is. On these assumptions the sociologist

---

[5] *Ibid.*
[6] Davidson, *op. cit.*, p. 7.
[7] Davidson, *op. cit.*, pp. 7-8.

would predict a Faulkner from Mississippi rather than look to Massachusetts for some or many expected greats.

More important for the question at hand, Davidson queries the sociologist only in terms of the partial socio-economic measures, not in terms of the folk-regional analysis of a relatively unified and dynamic culture. The socio-economic statistics which Davidson cites do indeed present a partial picture of the South in relation to the total nation. This relative picture was drawn in order to have realistic, attainable goals for future development, in the normal and traditional American custom of "state of the union" stock-taking.[8] More fundamentally, however, the vigorous development of the Southern people within the last generations has so clearly demonstrated that these attainable goals are an integral part of Southern aspirations, even as defiance toward total conformity is shouted from the platforms of national political conventions. So that any analysis of the regional culture that does not have a place for this dynamic is bound to be progressively tangential.

But even so these technical goals are but frames upon which rest all the other cultural conditioning forces, the backgrounds of causal factors, the present social structure of the South, and the possible facets of future development. For, as I have pointed out often in many places,

> the way of the South has been and is the way of the folk, symbolic of what the people feel, think, and do as conditioned by their cultural heritage and the land which Nature has given them. The culture of the South is the culture of the folk often in contradistinction to the civilization at its flood tide of urbanism, technology, intellectualism, and totalitarianism. This folk culture is deeply bottomed in the realities of Nature and the frontier struggle, in the heritage of multiple migrant people, in the rise and fall of the upper-folk aristocracy, and in a later powerful race and regional conflict. This is an elemental reality definitive of most of the South's culture and economy. The folk society of the South is well-nigh all-inclusive and is reflected on many levels of

---

[8] See: Howard W. Odum's *Southern Regions of the United States* (Chapel Hill: University of North Carolina Press, 1936), *American Regionalism* (New York: Henry Holt and Company, 1938), *The Way of the South* (New York: The Macmillan Company, 1947), and *An American Epoch* (New York: Henry Holt and Company, 1930).

time and class and in the organic nature of the folk-regional
society as definitive of how all societies are formed and
grow up.

The elementary sources of this powerful folk society are
reflected in a fourfold heritage. There are the growing up
of the earlier frontier folk in their struggles with Nature and
the Indian alongside the earlier folk culture which was of
the vintage of Virginia and the planter aristocracy. Then for
a time nearly all of the South consisted of the rural folk with
their rugged individualism and their struggle with land and
climate, with victory or defeat or harvest time in their blood.
And there were the remnants of frontier folk symbolic of
mountain culture or flatwood frustration or swamp and
bayou levels of living in the out-of-way places throughout
the Deep South. And finally there was the powerful folk
society of the Negroes themselves as both apart from and a
part of the dominant white folk.

*   *   *   *   *   *

In reality the vigorous and lusty South that was growing
up in the way of Nature and the frontier, of race and the
folk, could be understood only through a knowledge of the
way of all culture as it develops from the earlier folk stages
on through various maturing levels until it flowers in civilization.[9]

About this South as a nursery for the conditioning and nurturing
of writers and for stimulating them, we have pointed out something
of the conflicts, frustrations and intellectual and emotional tensions
which were basic to any creative contributions that Southerners would
be making.

So came the challenge to critics, North and South, in
America and Europe, who saw the South capable of contributing powerfully to the greater American epoch of the
twentieth century. Whatever contributions the South had
made, whatever forms and patterns had evolved in the past,
had grown out of realities, now springing from soil rich in

[9] Howard W. Odum, *The Way of the South* (New York: The Macmillan Company,
1947), pp. 61-62; also Chapter V, "The Way of Culture and History"; *In Search of
the Regional Balance of America* (Chapel Hill: University of North Carolina Press,
1945), p. 25; "The American Blend," *The Saturday Review of Literature*, Aug. 6, 1949.

romance and large undertaking, now from poverty and hardships, now sinking back into the sources from which they came. These sources remained in perpetuity and awaited the full development of a well-balanced civilization. To the pictures of the Old South and the New South of 1930, therefore, must be added still other pictures of the South of a New American Epoch built upon the Old. And whatever the distance backward or forward, the measures of resurrection or resurgence or of new trail-blazing were to be found in the vigor of the common-place, in the power of new biological and cultural combinations, in the social potentiality of these four generations of Southerners, and in the happy blending of these elements with the other essential elements of the nation and of the times.[10]

There was no doubt about the power of the old tradition in conflict with the new, nor the struggles for survival alongside the stubborn allegiance to the departed glory.

An era had ended. An era had begun. Old golden pages of history, shining parchment records of culture, then yellow and faded, scorched and seared with years of embattled conflict, and epic struggle . . . Gallant figures on black horses and white . . . and crude, simple folk, sore with the footfall of time, passing across an epoch which was to be destroyed by physical and cultural conflagration and to rise up again in another American Epoch strangely different and vivid and powerful. Cultures in the making, social processes at work, portraiture descriptive of how civilizations grow. All the South's yesterdays, with their brilliant episodes and with their sordid pictures receding, giving way to the South's tomorrows, through a sweeping American development of universal culture.

Both the old and the new culture abounded in sharp contrasts and logical paradoxes. There were many Souths yet *the* South. It was preëminently national in backgrounds, yet provincial in its processes. There were remnants of European culture framed in intolerant Americanism. There were romance, beauty, glamor, gayety, comedy, gentleness,

---

[10] Howard W. Odum, *An American Epoch* (New York: Henry Holt Company, 1930), p. 333.

and there were sordidness, ugliness, dullness, sorrow, tragedy, cruelty. There were wealth, culture, education, generosity, chivalry, manners, courage, nobility, and there were poverty, crudeness, ignorance, narrowness, brutality, cowardice, depravity. The South was American and un-American, righteous and wicked, Christian and barbaric. It was a South getting better, a South getting worse. It was strong and it was weak, it was white and it was black, it was rich and it was poor. There were great white mansions on hilltops among the trees, and there were unpainted houses perched on pillars along hillside gullies or lowland marshes. From high estate came low attainment, and from the dark places came flashing gleams of noble personality. There were strong men and women vibrant with the spontaneity of living, and there were pale, tired folk, full of the dullness of life. There were crusaders resplendent with some perpetual equivalent of war, and there were lovers of peace in the market place. There were freshness and vivacity as of a rippling green-white rivulet, and there were depth and hidden power as of gleaming dark water beneath an arched bridge.[11]

Now it is exactly in this framework of the folk-regional society of the South that the sociologist finds his testing ground for understanding and exploring much of the behavior and achievements of the Southern people. For it is his assumption, based upon adequate source materials, documented by students of many disciplines, and reinforced by his own historical and empirical studies, that all societies grow up and mature in a continuum from the folk culture to the state civilization, the one coinciding with growth, development and creativeness and the other with maturity, standardization and decay. The Massachusetts and New York of Mr. Davidson's premises reflect the most advanced state of civilization that has yet appeared on this earth and is in somewhat opposite polarity from the main folk culture pattern of Mississippi and the old and recent South. The sociologist, in this case, points out that

This complex society of the world we live in may best be characterized by the term *state civilization,* as comprehending the total traits of the most advanced technological and

---

[11] *Ibid.,* pp. 330-331.

organizational society in a continuum which has its genesis
and constant growth and survival processes in the contrasting
folk culture, symbol also of the close knit societal integration
of all growing civilizations. The state civilization, symbolizing the secularization of the folk culture, is fabricated of five
main threads so thoroughly interwoven in warp and woof
as to make a clearly defined and powerful pattern of human
relationships. The first is *science, invention, and technology*.
The second is *industrialization and urbanization*. The third is
intellectualism and cultural specialization. The fourth is
centralization and power. The fifth is *totalitarianism and the
super-state society*. Each of these is fabricated of still other
weavings of multiple minor designs.

Interwoven with science, invention and technology are
unprecedented achievement, with speed, technics, standardization. Interwoven with industry and urbanism are the
machine economy, the assembly line, stratification, a new
way of community living, an extraordinary high standard of
living, and great concentrations of art, drama, and wealth.
Interwoven with intellectualism and cultural specialization
are scientific humanism, the concept that the intellect is the
supreme guide for living, the standard of living as a chief
index of social values, and undreamed of contributions in
creative art and literature, science for science's sake. Interwoven with centralization and power are bigness, concentration, corpocracy, organization, limitless production, efficiency
like a miracle. Interwoven with totalitarianism and the
superstate are coercion, regulation and secularization with
ruthless power more relevant than human liberty and with
force as a living ideal. Needless to say, all these are in-
separably related in an indescribably rich fabric of human
achievement beyond the dreams of men and constituting a
continuum of interaction processes in the loom of societal
development.

The *state civilization* is sequel to and an extension of
the universal *folk culture,* the two constituting the main currents and levels of cultural development in the universal
societal continuum from early folk society to late state
society. The folk culture is also fabricated of a number of
threads with their multiple qualities of interaction between
the folk and nature, between the folk and their own cultural

environment, and between the folk of one culture and of other cultures. First, the folk culture is identified with nature with reference to natural laws, time, climate, geographic environment, close to the soil. Folk culture is further characterized by primary relationships and institutions, kith and kin in ethnic relationships, and primary occupations. The folk culture conforms essentially to rural and religious institutional character reflecting primarily the solidarity of a moral order. It is essentially institutional, deriving its social character from societies that are small, isolated, reflecting love of liberty, loyalties, homogeneities of structure. The folk culture is closely knit, cohesive, nonorganizational, with behavior primarily spontaneous, personal, traditional, yet strongly integrated through its community of growth and moral order. The folk society is thus essentially in contrast to the state society, the one geared to nature and to ethnic and moral structure and the other to technology and to civil organization and specialized structure.

*   *   *   *   *   *

Such a state civilization, flowering into its complex attainment of technology, industrialization, urbanization, intellectualism, cultural specialization, organization, centralization and power, tends to assume the nature of a *technological order* rather than a *human society* or a *moral order* such as has been assumed as the universal constant in all growing human societies. Inherent in such a technological order could be not only such complexity as to accelerate antagonisms, conflict, derangement, breakdown and disintegration, but the capacity to weaken or destroy human society, through decay from non-use of cultural processes, from the exhausting and destructive power of science and technology, and from the literal capacity of atomic science to destroy; or from the assumption by the totalitarian state of the functions of all the other institutions which are the creators and creatures of the total healthy societal system.[12]

So much for the general reference to the sociologists' conceptualization of cultural development as it might be utilized to ex-

[12] See also Odum's *Understanding Society* (New York: The Macmillan Company, 1947), Chapters, 5, 7, 11, 12, 14, 15, 19, 20, 29, 35.

plain Faulkner's Southern origin and achievement. Logically this
would place him in a favorable position on two counts. In the first
place he has been contemporaneous with the growth stage of a folk-
regional culture. In the second place in identifying him with the folk
culture of the South we identify him with struggle and travail, in
conflict with race, nation, and powerful tradition, fighting for survival
for itself and its people. This might very well be illustrated by a
sort of analogy between William Faukner's contribution to the stream
of American literature and that of the Elder Dumas to France. For
I have pointed out how

> This Southern picture was, for instance, in many ways
> reminiscent of the century-old picture of an incredible, bushy-
> headed, country bumpkin come to Paris, destined to usher
> in a new romanticism and to divert 'the stream of French
> letters from its narrow channel into a wide and rushing
> river.' In the development of his career and the reshaping
> of a literature were present to a remarkable degree the ele-
> mentary forces whose blending creates new cultures and
> challenges human vitality, tested in a social crucible white
> hot with the stirrings of physical power, emotional conflict,
> and intellectual striving. There was a heritage, on the one
> side, of maturity, experience, prestige, glory, and aristocracy;
> and, on the other, of primitive folk-stock and fresh blood,
> rough hewn pillars and strong foundation fabric for some
> noble superstructure. There were youth and strength and
> temper. There were ability, temperament, and genius. There
> were trial and error, successes and failures; and again failures
> and successes. There were time and unforeseen resistless
> incidence. There were social conflct and revolution, fire and
> sword, death and exile. There were old and new epochs wit-
> nessing the rise and fall of new leaders and followers. And
> there was the flowing stream of social process, now suddenly
> shallow and sluggish, now bursting forth in full volume and
> power.[13]

Or, it might not be amiss to refer to an abundance of illustrations
from Davidson's beloved classical literature to indicate that "a native
central in the shaping of ancient fiction was the desire to defend and

---

[13] Odum, *An American Epoch*, p. 328.

perpetuate cultural values which were in danger of being lost."[14] Certainly the analogy would not be inappropriate to the Davidson query as to why Tennessee, with its low socio-economic cultural index, produced the Agrarians and the Fugitive group of poets reflecting "the expressions of a minority's will to cultural survival" and so eloquently striving to glorify a Southern tradition and echoing the sentiment that "a subject people can have no glories but departed ones." But, to return to Hadas' citations relevant to cultural survival:

> In Asia Minor the conquest of the Persians made Ionian Greeks look back wistfully upon their past glories and their departed heroes . . . . A subject people can have no glories but departed ones, and when epic is dangerous or ludicrous, prose chronicles take its place. Herodotus . . . states specifically that the object of his book is to keep alive the memory of the great deeds of the Greeks and non-Greeks . . . . among the ancient peoples on the eastern periphery of the Greek world the break with the past was catastrophic, and here we have evidence of a remarkable proliferation of books which dealt somehow with national traditions and glorified ancient national heroes . . . . in all the books of this class the vanished grandeur, military and social, of depressed minorities was glorified . . . . Of all such literary efforts calculated to insure the cultural survival of depressed minorities in the Hellenistic world we have most extensive remains and are best informed concerning those produced by the Jews especially by the Jewish community of Alexandria. From the time of Ptolemy Philadelphus onwards, Alexandrian Jews devoted themselves to producing a body of apologetic literature . . . calculated to demonstrate the antiquity and high merits of the Jewish tradition.[15]

Returning now to Faulkner's own writings and whatever of his works may reflect the power of Southern creativeness we note that Malcolm Cowley has estimated that three major themes have dominated Faulkner's work. The first of these is "The Southern Tradition," meaning the South's historic cause. The second is "The Contemporary Chaos" which is Faulkner's "anatomy of the present

---

[14] Moses Hadas, "Cultural Survival and the Origin of Fiction," *The South Atlantic Quarterly*, LI (April, 1952), 253.
[15] *Ibid.*, pp. 254-256.

world, its nihilism, violence, and horror." The third is "Man's Future" in which "man's hope lies in the reversion to a simpler life with its concomitant virtues of stoicism, simplicity, and decency."[16]

In the light of our present inquiry we need to add to these at least three corollaries, if not major themes. One of these is the power of the historic evolutionary past of mankind so often implied in Faulkner's themes of contemporary chaos and man's future. One aspect of this is the powerful sensing of the merging of the early past in America and its European heritage with the frontier and its ruthlessness, the rich details reflecting the transfer of culture from aristocracy, pseudo-aristocracy and power, from the coastal states to new southern and western frontiers. This is, of course, a main pattern in the expansion, south and west, of the Southern States that later came to be "aristocratic," and subsequently a basic pattern of the Southern way of life defended by the Agrarians and others. This is essentially also, on the upper levels, the same pattern that made Mark Twain "descended from a miscellany including rifle-toting trail-blazers, pious Quakers, and hard-working Southern yeoman, with haughty but dubious claims to aristocratic ancestry in England and Virginia."[17]

Perhaps the most powerful of these corollaries is Faulkner's sensing of the deep stream of consciousness in the human mind evolving and struggling for survival and salvation as well as his mastery of many of the newer psychological and psychopathological techniques. Perhaps no one has succeeded so well in running the gamut of the human mind between and among the facets of brilliance in waking hours, dreams in sleeping tempo and near-derangement in mental pathology, of the stream of consciousness that pervades every mentality sometime, somewhere, somehow; or in merging in some sort of continuity the awakening processes of youth with vigor, physical power, and limitless aspiration; or mental degradation with the revivification of the creative mind and body in maturity and old age. Certainly no one has succeeded so powerfully in portraying the irresistible tropism of woman, in the lower and higher brackets, to-

---

[16] Malcolm Cowley, "The Portable Faulkner," *William Faulkner: Two Decades of Criticism*, eds. Frederick J. Hoffman and Olga W. Vickery, (East Lansing: Michigan State College Press, 1951), p. 63. See also Harry Modean Campbell and Ruel E. Foster *William Faulkner: A Critical Appraisal*, (Norman: University of Oklahoma Press, 1951) p. 12.

[17] Walter Blair, "Last of the Jongeurs," *The Saturday Review of Literature*, (August 30, 1952), 9.

ward, doing what she aims to do and what she is driven to do, as reflected in the multiple folk conflicts of a South in travail.

A third corollary must surely be found in the major theme of the Negro with his tragic evolutionary background, his stranger-than-fiction Southern story, and his modern unprecedented quick entrance into the total consciousness of a nation. One cannot imagine a Massachusetts author with so compelling and frustrating environmental pressure as an upsurging source of power as is reflected in a Faulkner page-after-page long sentence reflecting a powerful sympathy, a bitter satire upon the South and the white man, and an eloquent and logical defense of the Southern doctrine, rationalized for the good of the Negro. Yet this, stewed in an inchoate mass of Southern mixtry, inseparable from subliminal psychology and sex, in perpetual conflict with unfathomable subconsciousness, provides a powerful genesis for mastery in literature, scarcely found anywhere else.

Finally there is another unequaled combination of blending what is usually called an "imaginary locale" with a powerful reality of situation. For, I myself have known Yoknapatawpha and it is no purely imaginary fantasy. Once when a son of the first and noblest families of "Jefferson," weakened by frustration and conflict between aspiration and reality, had gone off the deep end, I remember riding an unbroken colt from Toccopola to Pontotoc, to Tupelo to New Albany in and out across swollen streams and backwoods and pine hills, often reflecting physical reality stranger than fiction. I have been close enough to Faulkner's quicksands to sense something of its terrors and have often imagined, behind the cedars and columned houses, that anything could happen there. Faulkner's Yoknapatawpha was symbol of frontier, a frontier echoing both primitive and civilized heritage; of Mowrer's three men of civilization, one savage and ruthless, one soft and civilized, and one hoped for, balancing the qualities of the folk and civilization.[18] Suppose there *is* a barbaric past, merged with a "flowed and cherished past melting into one desolation, one hopelessness," so what? In the light of these and other overpowering evidences, Donald Davidson's query as to why Massachusetts did not produce one Faulkner or many Faulkners appears to be little more than rhetorical.

---

[18] Edgar Ansel Mowrer, "The Third Man," *The Saturday Review of Literature*, (July 5, 1952), 6-8.

But, returning again to possible interacting causal factors responsible for the conditioning of Southern authors and the quality of Southern writings we need to note a number of situations other than the general socio-economic and cultural-historic backgrounds. First of all we must emphasize the futility of attempting to isolate a single "cause and effect" relationship. Rather we must undertake to analyze the total configuration of complex environmental factors playing within the framework of universals, and especially of the changing structure of society and its institutions in relation to the conditioning of the individual and the psychological aspects of his behavior. Here, as may be seen from our previous diagnoses, the South has proved to be rich soil for the growing of varied cultural crops, sometime thin and sparse on eroded lands, sometimes rank and luxurious and often untilled fields of mixtures of weeds and grain with now and then rare specimens to be selected, replanted and multiplied.

Another fundamental causal factor, the most important of all, is the individual, with his inherited endowment even though he is inseparable from the society which produced him. In the South, no less than anywhere else, the natural answer to oversimplified questions of environmental factors would be to ask why, if Faulkner was produced exclusively by Mississippi, there was only one Faulkner or why would Stark Young, born and raised in the same town of Oxford, turn out to produce such distinctively different literature as reflected in *So Red the Rose* and in his many years of literary criticism. At the time Faulkner was growing up in Oxford and before the University of Mississippi had its chance at him, why would the influence of the University at Oxford reflect such different conditioning on the three new instructors that came to the university at that time, namely Stark Young, Dudley Howe Miles, Howard W. Odum, respectively nurtured in Mississippi, Texas, and Georgia? Or, more profoundly, did the endowment of the individual have the definitive answer as to why there was one Ellen Glasgow in Virginia, one William Hines Page in North Carolina, one Julia Peterkin in South Carolina, one Margaret Mitchell in Georgia, one Marjorie Rawlings in Florida, one Robert Penn Warren in Kentucky and Louisiana? Or again, why only one Emerson or one Walt Whitman, or Mark Twain? Why would the same environment produce one William James the psychologist and one Henry James the novelist? Or was it the environment mainly that produced an Amy Lowell or Gertrude Stein?

In addition, however, to these fundamental factors of environmental conditioning, individual heritage, and the complex setting of universal humanity and cultural struggle, there have been at least two major external factors responsible for much of the flowering of Southern writing. The first of these was the extraordinary prolific writing of, for, by, and about the South at the turn of the century and during the first quarter of the 20th century. Illustrative would be the greater part of such a body of writing as found in the national magazines: the *American Mercury, Atlantic Monthly, Century, North American Review, Harpers, Review of Reviews, Scribners,* and *World's Work.*[19] For instance, we have catalogued a varied exhibit of titles ranging all the way from specialized literary criticism and writing to specialized research and social interpretation. In the *American Mercury,* samplings of no less than 25 articles; in the *Atlantic Monthly,* 32; *Century,* 23; *Harpers,* 18; *North American Review,* 26; *Review of Reviews,* 42; *Scribners,* 25; and *World's Work,* 54.

The other major influence, stemming partly from this featuring of the South by national magazines and others, was the specific influence and cooperation of many national publishers, national foundations, and distinguished literary leaders, especially H. L. Mencken, who was both symbol and reality of outside goading and encouragement of Southern writers. Refering again to similar influences which molded Dumas in France, we have pointed out that there were

> . . . five friendly influences which were to span the distance between bumptious youth and brilliant Frenchman. These influences were four friends and a notable company, the arsenal. One friend was forever impressing upon the youth the shame of his abysmal ignorance. Another was ever opening the doors of living literature. A third relentlessly spurred him on to constant achievement. A fourth assured him resources, time, and leisure. And a fifth provided him with a finishing school for his artistry. And in the final picture the backgrounds and forces were transcended by form and line and pattern and brilliance.[20]

H. L. Mencken, the bad boy of Baltimore, not only did "The Sahara of the Bozart" but went out of his way to stimulate, to encourage,

---

[19] Odum, *An American Epoch,* pp. 346-356.
[20] *Ibid.,* p. 329.

and to give special priorities to Southern writers. And there were others, none like him, but in the same category of favoring the South and of soon discovering that it was a very profitable business, even at that. A single publisher such as Alfred Knopf, Bobbs-Merrill, Doubleday, Page and the others were very real decisive factors in the bringing to light and rewarding the creative work of Southern writers. Many of the national foundations and awards were constantly underwriting and endowing situations from which a new generation of the South, even as Dumas, were assured resources, time and leisure.

Among the criticisms that have been leveled at Faulkner was that he has not had the benefit of association with the literary elite and the constant fellowship of those who excelled in the literary techniques of fiction writing and new forms. Three considerations perhaps here are relevant. The first is that even the critics sometimes admitted that Faulkner may have profited from his isolation and concentration over and above the benefits he might have received from the technicians. Next, we may well note that of the 446 U. S. members of P. E. N., the supreme international organization for authors, all but 42 are from the Northeast, while New York has 296 of the total and Mississippi has just one member. On the basis of technical advantages would New York be expected to produce many equivalents of Faulkner? The third consideration may be found in the reference to the literary refugees of the United States who "escaped" America in the 1920's to concentrate for great production in the setting of fellowship and leisure abroad but who, as pointed out by Malcolm Cowley, not only lost their own feelings, beliefs and integrity but found no substitute for them and created little as the price of their sojourn. And many promising authors who migrated from the hinterlands from which they gave such promise to urban centers where they were expected to excel, found more intellectual and literary fellowship, more autograph parties, more cocktail parties and talk but less writing. And even the "great ones" could not "come back," loosed from the moorings of the cumulative incentives and power of their cultural milieu.

William Faulkner is a "natural" from Mississippi and not Massachusetts, yes?

2. NO FAULKNER IN METROPOLIS

John Maclachlan

I

More often than not the major novelists of modern Europe have been city born and city reared. Yet with very few exceptions the metropolitan regions of the United States have failed to produce novelists of any stature. When one pauses to reflect, it becomes startling how little New York, Chicago, Philadelphia and the rest have done towards filling out the list of consequential modern American writers of the novel, and how much, relatively, has been done by the far provinces of the nation.

The question as to why this should be the case has been raised by Donald Davidson, and is the point of departure here. The matter might be tested variously; by a statistical survey, by a tabulation from Harry Warfel's compendium of American writers, or inversely by answering a question once posed by Howard Washington Odum in another connection—not "Is it true?", but "If it were true, why would it be true?" or, in other words, what factors make it seem likely or plausible?

At first glance this is perplexing. In the great cities the higher reaches of the culture flourish, and one would suppose accordingly that they would be the apexes, the towering heights, from which the novelist might get the widest perspectives of contemporary life. There are the libraries, the museums, the art centers, the printeries and binderies, the markets for the finished literary product, the specialization and efficiency to provide time for the derived productivity of the artist. There are the teeming crowds and the focal points of the lore and happenings of the earth.

There too are the tools and instruments of a giant technology, overt compelling evidence of the power of science, example supreme of man's quest and conquest in the world of physical being. Finally, there are collected by batallion and regiment the highly intelligent, the highly trained, the mature and sophisticated minds of the age, since the city is the best market, paying the highest price, for the kinds of work they do.

101

Yet by and large the creative writer in America has gone to the city only to turn back to Oxford or to Asheville or to the western heartland. Else, in going to the city he has taken and kept with him the Carolina hills or the undulating clay slopes of Mississippi. Then he has gone home again, or he has never left home. Sometimes, of course, he has disappeared into the ranks of the lesser figures who turn out the scripts, scenarios, anonymous or pedestrian or pathetic manuscripts, the nothings or almost-nothings of commerce.

American city life has been a refuge in which the creative writer has found passing sanctuary and a market for his wares, and no more. It has been more often the graveyard than the spawning ground of literary talent. The bright young man, the sentient young woman, who might have been creative artists become there something less.

Two things about this are sad. One is that, as cultures do, our metropolitan culture gives rewards which make its victims comfortable, because having become what they turn into they establish themselves as standards, norms, their own ways and foibles as the symbols of success, so that they value the lesser gain above the greater loss. The other sad thing is that they forget what might have been, what it is to live at one's highest level of insight and talent, seeking one's own creative utmost. It becomes amusing to them to recall that once they had the innocent temerity to hope for greatness, to seek within themselves the greater rewards of living, that they saw and felt writing as an end in itself, as a moral responsibility and an ultimate good.

There is thus far no William Faulkner in Megalopolis. We know that there are, among the hundred million more or less who live within and around the American metropolis hundreds of thousands, if not millions, who have the inherent stuff of genius, 'top percentile' intelligence and its correlates. But no Faulkner. His sense of the final in the immediate and the universal in the particular, of the fire and drama and worthiness of the human struggle, has found no voice among them. Such sensitivity and sensibility seem to come to metropolitan minds *ex post facto*: reading it they grasp it, only to forget it straightway again; the grasp is half-handed, 'intellectual', unfelt, lacking that strength which goes with a sense of elemental reality . . . . .

II

It requires much to unravel such a riddle. No small answer will solve it, no easy explanation the problem it poses. A simple reason may suffice for one unrealized genius but multiple and comprehensive cause must lie behind so large a matter as this. One can understand so large an issue only by seeing what is common to the experience of the sentient in the metropolis, not by seeking serially and separately what is unique to each of them.

An answer, then, may lie in the distinctive culture of metropolitan America, in the patterns, complexes and traits, the molds and structures of role and status, which that culture fixes upon the men and women who might, who could, write at the uppermost level. This answer is in the opportunity and lack of opportunity, the avenues and the *culs-de-sac* of expression and activity, around the potential novelists of the urban regions of the land.

A culture has its overall being, and within that its component parts. In its largest aspect is the *ethos,* the all-pervading, distinctive way of life and of looking at life which marks it off from all others, explicit in its science and religion and philosophy and art, implicit in its lesser parts. Within the *ethos* are the swirling, constantly changing major patterns of living, of values and concepts relevant to getting born, getting a living, dealing with the immanent and imminent crises of life and death. Within the *ethos* and the distinctive patterns of the culture, again, are the more restricted, more readily definable and visible ways of doing and being through which the customary clusters of folk get along. It is within these tangible complexes that the innumerable separate traits of the culture have direct meaning, and that the experience of the individual is worked out.

The prose writer in our metropolitan culture encounters at least two such complexes which are especially disastrous. One of these is the 'formula', the other 'the line'. They are alike in their constricting effect upon his mind, different in the means through which they bind it up, and both are expectable cultural resultants of forces which are indigenous to the cities.

The 'formula' complex is an aspect, at the literary level, of metropolitan commercialism. It is as powerful as it is, and as destructive in its power, because it envisions the novel as a commodity to be manufactured, processed, graded, stored and sold when the market is ready. Many of its most gifted victims are "staff" writers, persons of conspicuously reliable talent who can produce, and do produce, specified weight and count of words of predetermined, fixed and limited quality. They produce for a clientele, not for a market in the wide sense, but for a known number of listed readers, purchasers who must get in November of 1952 the same proportionate amounts of the same materials they received in November of 1948 and will get in that month of 1958.

These are the arrivees of the formula, the fortunate talented who have in hand the precise technique, the exact vocabulary, the properly varied but essentially changeless plot. Their work is not, need not be, hack in the poorest sense; but it is work, it is repetition, it is chained to the typewriter and the bank account, the retainer and the contract. It will produce in November after November, in June and April after June and April, what it has brought forth before and will bring forth again.

Far more minds are caught in another phase of the 'formula' complex. These are the young men and women, the housewives and students and clerks, who think of writing as a means to extra income, to a modicum of status as 'a writer', and seek success through becoming 'market conscious'. They buy and read treatises on 'what will sell', surveys of the thousands of outlets large and small through which typed pages may be turned into publishers' checks. They write and rewrite, labor and struggle to fit or better to force themselves into the formula, the accepted pattern, the specifications of the familiar and clearly priceable commodity.

All this is as it may be. One does not "blame" the staff writer for his suburban comfort, for his knowing accomplishment of a saleable trifle, or the part-time writer for his anxiety to be published at all. For that matter, it is not the business of the observer of a culture to praise or condemn it, since in doing so he ceases to be an observer. In the meantime 'the formula' leaves little time for experiment, little room for individuality, and less of both for daring and disturbing insight.

In quite a different way the 'line' complex arrives at the same end, substituting another gain and satisfaction for that of literary creation. Whereas the 'formula' complex clusters around the economic value of writing technique, fitting words and sense to the limits of a commercial enterprise, the 'line' is manifestly of an ideological order. It produces a school or a party or a coterie of interchangeable intellects, all seeing man's fate from the same viewpoint, all explaining that fate through the same syllogism. It shows itself in the parade of intellectual fads and fashions, in the cults and esoteric or exoteric movements that eddy about in the metropolitan swarm, in the flow and play of the cross-currents of interest groups and pressure groups.

Thus we have had a clinical-psychiatric line, a line of economic determinism, a Freudian line, these and others within our time. Like the 'party line' in politics, these modes and movements in literary life put a premium upon conformity. To them the supreme intellectual virtue is conformity, deviation the great sin. The follower has only to follow, once the line has been determined, to achieve virtue and excellence. But let him doubt or wonder, and he is lost. Let him consider that there may still be a mystery in the universe, a limbo out of and into which we move, an unknowable or even an unknown facet of life, a retrievable freedom of the human spirit, and he is not only lost but damned and destroyed. For it is universally true that each 'line' contains a prescribed determinism, an inexorable pattern of description and interpretation whose violation is anathema.

Once again, the observation is not one of blame or judgment. The follower of the intellectual-literary 'line' of the time, ironically, embraces the line with a sense of liberation and fulfillment. The ready-made *weltanschauung*, besides being emotionally warming, is a quick and reliable substitute for ratiocination. It is in a chaotic world a clear and perfect guide. It has the quality of bringing intellectual strength, or a seeming of such strength, through an act of faith, and if that act descends into the *auto da fe* the descent is, to its possessor, no more than regrettable. If it makes the follower a zealot, seeing good in his kind and evil in all else, it still confirms in him a sense of wholeness, rightness, wisdom. If it blinds him to reality, if it makes him forget that individuality is possible, if it conceals from him that man's unaided mind can apprehend only the semblances of things, these are unnoticed items in his account with the universe.

There is likely to be a measure of correctness within the syllogism of any literary 'line'. There is a struggle for survival in nature, but it may be that the separate individual is not the unit of that struggle. The sex urge is potent in man but it may be, as indeed Freud himself would have insisted, infinitely more complicated than a mere urge to sexual expression. Personality distortion produces tragedy, but tragedy may be deeper and more meaningful without that distortion. Class conflict has been and is a phenomenon of modern life, but it may well spring from and result in other than crudely economic forces and issues . . .

The point here has to do not with the truth or falsity in 'lines', but with their strait-jacket effect, which operates in a dual fashion. On one hand it fits the writer into a mold, a range and limit of subject matter and a predetermined pattern of thinking. On the other it leads him to see man as a mannikin, a passive creature wholly driven by forces beyond himself; his plot becomes a didactic demonstration of revealed truth, his whole effort a self-conscious aping of the stereotyped mean, median, mode, of his 'line'. Thus he cannot grow, for growth is change, rejection, deviation. He cannot experiment, because experiment is challenge. He cannot wonder or doubt, because these affirm independence of thought and spirit.

Although these two complexes express essentials of the metropolitan situation, there remain other matters. One of these is physical in the plainest sense. In the metropolis the realities of life are too much shut up, closed away, put behind walls and barriers. Birth and death occur in remote, aseptic caves. The earth is captive beneath pavement, behind rails and hedges, regimented and disciplined in parks and subdivisions. The seasons of the year are hid behind heating systems and cooling vents, the sun and rain above roofs and canopies. Time and space are man's toys, his pawns. Man, the automaton of the 'line', is master of a mechanized and docile universe. In all this fear and pain are vassals, the pangs of the individual human being are microcosmic and trivial, the essences of life are the roar of traffic, the surge of crowds, the rhythm of the great urban machine.

Finally, less in a sense but not less in any reality, is the endless pattering about, the busy-work, with which the lives of sensitive folk must be filled when there is nothing else to fill them. The appointment, the 'date', the cocktail party, the tea, the commuting, the conversation piece, the arbitrary and artificial deadlines and commitments and potherings, which urban congestion, urban distances, urban schedules, the very compacting of great numbers of likeminded folk beget; these and things like them round out the score, give the riddle sense and meaning and a possible answer.

III

Over and above all, sentient man in the metropolis is a willing prisoner of his culture, because of the prestige it enjoys, the accolade bestowed upon it by one and all. If it be acknowledged that here culture is at its perihelion, then man here must be at his zenith. If it be the nearest approach to perfection, then one has only to conform to share in its quality. In consequence there is no difference made between the good and the less than good attributes of the culture of the great city, no challenge and no urge to find another way.

Faulkner's Yoknapatawpha County is a far place. There is nothing between its folk and the elemental forces of the universe, no canopies, walls, clinics, ranks of professionals and bureaucrats to stand between them and life and death. There is no segmentation, segregation, of caste, class, sex, of age from youth or male from female or white from black, to prevent a whole view of life as a whole.

There is no formula, no line, because the cultural forces which beget them are not there. There is no overwhelming manmade technology, because the doings of man are dwarfed, as are his machines, by the immensities around them. They are dwarfed, let it be said, in a different fashion from the minuscule of the city. Here a man, one man, stands alone in a field, and has it out with the elements. Here the child sees death, and the elder sees birth. Here is the original of man's experience down the ages, the general, the broad contact of psyche and universality.

Jefferson is a hub of the universe. It is a small town, a village, but it is more. Center and turning point of its surrounding countryside it is, like any point in an infinity of time and space, a place of departure equidistant from all others. Moreover it is a community of no secrets. Each knows all that is true, and much that is not, about each. Not a man's own life alone is known, but the life of the father and the grandfather as well, and that of the son. Something done or said on an occasion fifty years ago may well come into the talk of explaining what happened, what was done and said, last Saturday night.

Much that is true of Jefferson is also true of all provinces, of all clusters of folk in agricultural regions. Much, however, is unique to Jefferson or at least to the culture area for which Jefferson stands as an instance, a symbol. Much might be inserted at this juncture about local history, about the insulation and isolation which breed cultural distinctiveness, about the crosscurrents of religiosity and sensuality, of puritanism and liberalism, about the tradition of violence and that of hospitality, about the rise and surge of new rulers in the land, the decline of elder patterns.

But on reflection all these things seem to be secondary. Essential to Jefferson but not to all cultural provinces is an ethistical factor. That is, that in the *ethos* of Jefferson and Yoknapatawpha, the essence of man lies in being, not in having or doing. Metropolitan men are judged and judge themselves on performance, on externals, on what they possess or what they have accomplished. In Jefferson possession and accomplishment are taken for granted, seen as inevitable outcomes of being. Being, that is, a male, a white, a Sartoris — or else a Snopes; being, in terms of attributes which other cultures may regard as mere products of experience — brave, cowardly, honest, dishonest; being in terms of inherent nature, unchanging and unchangeable; being in terms of foreordination, in terms of absolutes . . .

Thus seen, man the individual becomes a force rather than a product of force, the active agent of his own fate rather than the wondering victim of the *deus ex machina*. He is what Spengler called Faustian man, engaged in eternal struggle against an unfriendly universe. The struggle is foreordained, however, because of the urge within man himself and not because of some external determinism.

That this should be true rests upon many considerations. It is a facet of puritan protestantism, with its doctrine of perfectionism, i. e., that to avoid eternal damnation one must never sin during this life, but that the drive to sin, 'the Old Adam' is inborn. It is implicit in the ancient planter-small farmer dichotomy of the society, that affirmation of aristocracy in the folk culture which accepts the fact even if condemning it. It is insistent in the biracial caste pattern that differences, not merely of ability, but of essentials of the spirit as well, are inherent in the two races and in conflict, rather than merged or averaged off, in the crossbreed. It is even explicit in the traditional equation of the sexes, which sets sharply different roles, personalities, even vocabularies, for male and female in every social class, and assumes that the resulting divergencies are expressions of male-being on one hand, female-being on the other.

In all of these, the human being must do, and does do, what is done because of his being. And not, be it said, his biological, physiological being, but the eternal spirit within him.

What has been said above is not said about Faulkner, the novelist, or about his philosophy. It is said about the culture within which he has lived, the unselfconscious folk world around him. It is said, moreover, out of a lifetime of living through the same culture elements and twenty years of study and research in the region. Oxford is not Jefferson, except as Holly Springs, Columbus, Natchez, Grenada, and towns throughout the plantation south and the upland small-farm south are Jefferson. Nor is Lafayette County Yoknapatawpha County, except as the hill counties of Tippah and Tishomingo are, or as Washington and Leflore in the Delta or Lowndes in Alabama or Mississippi, are Yoknapatawpha.

In a word, Faulkner's town and county wring out the inner realities of Southerns agrarian culture. That they could do so, that he could reach as deeply into the matters below the surface, is explained in part at least by a final advantage the sensitive mind in the provinces has over its counterpart in the metropolis.

That advantage, easier to apprehend than to define, is simply that there is no regularly assigned status or role for the writer in the folk culture. Born and bred within its domain, he still becomes exterior to it as soon as he develops the alien concern with creative writing. He is forced into the role of a participant observer, knowing and feeling its essences as no outlander ever could, but still seeing it from without, in a detachment not of his own seeking.

The real community of Oxford, unlike Jefferson, has a full share of the literate and informed, of persons who are sophisticated in the sense that they are aware of and influenced by the culture of the world beyond their region. That they are almost wholly excluded from Jefferson is readily understandable, since they would confuse the issue, divert attention from the main theme, even change the entire preoccupation of the novelist.

But there is a more substantial reason than this. It is that the formative years, the childhood and adolescence and the young manhood, of the novelist were spent in closer communication and association with the folk. The child in the Southern community like Oxford, at least up to a quarter of a century or more ago, lived close to every kind and level of the people. He was intimate, whether on friendly terms or not, with Negroes of all ages and both sexes, with 'redneck' boys and the sons of the squires. He ran headlong and pellmell into dealings with adults, too, of every description. Errands took him into the homes of the washerwoman and the carpenter, the judge and the doctor. He roamed the community at will, up and down all its alleys and avenues. He heard and saw all that could be seen and heard and, like children everywhere, he stored up lore, questions and answers, gossip and knowledge, fortuitous ignorances and gratuitous wisdoms, against the coming of his adult years.

If he happened to have the sensitivity which would make an artist, that extra awareness, he would absorb more, question more, react more strongly, than his fellows. He would revolt more against the rule of the folkways, respond more intensely to the forces of growth and decay around him, prepare himself more strenuously for a later evocation of what he had seen and heard and felt. He would carry into manhood the full panorama, the total sense, of the culture and of the personalities and the crises which typify and dramatize it.

This explains in a sense the superlative opportunity that the province offers, over the city in which social classes have less interaction, in which whole square miles may be inhabited by a single kind of folk, in which the growing child, the developing mind, sees and hears and feels only a fraction of the culture around about. It does not, and cannot, explain genius.

But there does appear one clue even in this direction. The prescient youth, growing up in metropolis, discovers that he too can be fully a member of a group, a tribe, of his own kind. Even in junior high school he can take a course in creative writing, join the literary society, enjoy the approbation of his fellows, fit comfortably into a coterie who seek derived learning, secondary experience. But in the small provincial town of a generation ago in the deep South this was hardly true. There conformity was in the occupations established by tradition, in the modes and forms of acceptance, uncritical acceptance, of the whole culture. Deviation, dissidence, were punishable, as they are in the metropolis of 'line' and 'formula', into which the junior high school prodigy above will graduate.

Here, however, in the Jefferson which was an aspect of the small towns of the rural south, the dissidence of genius would naturally take the form of an independent, highly individual critique of Jefferson itself, the deviation the form of a strong drive to succeed, not financially but intellectually, to justify one's calling by attaining its heights. Jefferson (one does not anywhere here mean Oxford) at best could see writing as an amusement, an avocation, a polite adornment of gentility; and at worst, when writing interfered with stoking the furnace or sorting the mail, would see it as a pernicious activity, an even criminal waste of time and energy and ability. Thus it would resist rather than encourage the embryo writer.

Small talents, lesser drives to expression, wilt and turn away. The larger talent which might in metropolis have grown comfortable and fat and conformable, however, cannot do so. *Ad astra per aspera.*

WALTER SULLIVAN

Southern Novelists and the Civil War

It is a fact that since 1865 Southern novelists have simply not been able to leave the Civil War alone. Certainly, John Esten Cooke must have planned the opening chapters of *Surrey of Eagles Nest* before the surrender at Appomatox, and I am told that a dissertation recently submitted to the history department of the University of North Carolina enumerated not less than five hundred novels with Civil War backgrounds, all of which were of Southern origin. In the past twenty years Stark Young, Allen Tate, Andrew Lytle, Caroline Gordon, and William Faulkner have written Civil War books, and other writers, such as Robert Penn Warren, have made extensive use of the War without devoting an entire novel to it. Indeed, Southern War novels have become so plentiful that many citizens of the North have now come to suspect the Rebels of continuing with their pens a conflict they lost to the sword. Why do they write about the War at all, the Yankee asks, if not to vilify the ghost of General Sherman? One answer is that novels are not, strictly speaking, written *about* wars, but this is an evasion of the issue. The problem of why the War should exist so prominently in Southern fiction is one that deserves consideration. The solution must be found, I believe, in terms of the novelist and what we generally refer to as his world.

Since the time of Sydney, certainly since the days of Samuel Johnson, it has not been necessary for the artist to defend himself against any criticism based on the fact that the writer's world does not approximate in every detail the empirical world of the reader. The truth of fiction, as everyone knows, exists on another level, and we need not dwell upon this point. But in formulating his world, the writer does not execute an act of pure creation. He does not build a *Kosmos* out of chaos. Rather, he begins with what is near at hand, a contemporary or an historical moment, and his art is one of selection and emphasis, of perceiving and bringing into focus that which already exists. Indeed, the initial problem of the novelist may be more specifically defined. Every time and place, every potential setting for a story, contains in itself an aggregation of simple, indisputable fact—the empirical truth of the "real" world at a given instant in time. These are not the writer's ultimate truths, the "old verities" which William Faulkner refers to. But they are part of the vehicle, they furnish the detail and sometimes they become symbols. In the important novels, the empirical world is discovered to be a kind of moral fabric, the relatively stable ethical framework within which subtler values are disclosed by means of character and plot. Therefore, one of the novelist's first tasks is that of determining the when and the where, the particular part of the actual world on which his own world will be founded. The reason that so many Southern novelists have chosen to make use of the Civil War is perhaps most readily seen in *The Fathers* by Allen Tate.

It is perhaps easiest to begin with Mr. Tate's book because of all modern Civil War novelists he is the only one who completely defined his position on the South and the Civil War some years before he sat down to write his novel. I do not mean to imply by this that *The Fathers* is in any way redundant. The values of Mr. Tate's novel are not precisely those found in "Ode to the Confederate Dead," and the book has its meanings beyond those which are stated in "Religion in the Old South." But in 1938, when the book was published—or for that matter in any subsequent year—a great many readers must have approached *The Fathers* with some rather definite notions concerning Mr. Tate's view of the South. One should have known, for example, that Mr. Tate deplored slavery on the ground that the Negroes did not function as a proper peasant class, which in turn is the *sine qua non* of a great culture. He should have remembered what he had been told in one of the essays: that the Southern God was a spurious God, an alien borrowed from sixteenth century merchants. He should have recalled Mr. Tate's contention that the plutocracy of the North and the aristocracy of the South were similar in their essential qualities. But most of all he should have kept in mind the essayist's distinction between the Long View and the Short View of history. For the Long View is "the religion of the half horse," and only the Short View—that way of seeing history as an image or a number of images—can provide the artist with a foundation on which to build his world.

To the Southern writer who would deal with the past, the Civil War is the most significant image of all. For, if I may borrow a term from the spatial arts, the War is the pregnant moment in Southern history, that instant which contains within its own limits a summation of all that has gone before, an adumbration of the future. To put it another way, the war is important not merely in itself, but in what it implies; for at the hands of a skillful artist, the single image may be made to convey an entire civilization and the moral code on which that civilization was constructed. Indeed, in many Civil War novels the actual conflict exists only as a background against which certain ramifications of the traditional Southern code are developed.

Shortly after *The Fathers* first appeared, it was reviewed in one of the quarterlies by Lionel Trilling. Now, I have no quarrel with Mr. Trilling, whose work I respect almost as much as I respect that of Mr. Tate, but it seems to me that Mr. Trilling's remarks are an excellent example of the sort of misunderstanding that results from the use of the Long View of history as a critical principle. Mr. Trilling took Major Buchan to be a representative of the old order, and he saw Major Buchan's limited, Virginia world as a microcosmic manifestation of the traditional society of the South. George Posey, he understood as a symbol of Northern industrialism, and the conflict of the novel was joined with the meeting of these two forces. This is, as far as it goes, a legitimate reading of *The Fathers,* but Mr. Trilling had one complaint to make. He could not see that Mr. Tate had *logically proved* the superiority of the traditional society over the culture that Posey represented. There was, he said, only Mr. Tate's fine and sensitive writing about the Buchans, which was, ultimately, no kind of proof at all. In other words, the novel contained no abstract theory, but merely a grand image. Mr. Tate had taken the Short View.

The central image of *The Fathers* is the Buchan family group including on one hand a dead grandfather and on the other the in-law, George Posey, and from beginning to end, the essential qualities of the image do not vary. I do not mean by this simply that the closing events of the book are prepared for in the opening pages.

Certainly, this is true. But of more importance is the fact that the destructive element, that weakness of the Southern culture which leads toward doom is visibly present with the ordered precincts of the family. The reader's progress through the novel, the way of the book, itself, is that of discovery; we are allowed to see, one after another, the various faces of the image, and we come to understand the profound truth of it in the end.

The critic's first task, then, is to ascertain the exact dimensions of the image, and this done, to probe for its meaning. I have no desire to re-examine ground that has already been covered by reviews of *The Fathers* which were written almost fifteen years ago, but it is necessary to point out that Posey is not only a part of the central image but also a manifestation of a rudimentary weakness in the culture of the South. If he seems out of place in the Southern tradition, he does so simply because we have come erroneously to believe that Henry Grady was the first traitor to the agrarian ideal. For the reasons that Mr. Tate has given us, we should know better.

Grandfather Buchan, the dead ancestor who comes to life in the final pages of the novel, points out that Posey could not have existed in his, the grandfather's, eighteenth century world. "The only expectancy that he shares with humanity is the pursuing grave," the old man says, "and the thought of extinction overwhelms him because he is entirely alone. My son, in my day we were never alone." But Grandfather Buchan goes further. He tells the story of Jason and the Golden Fleece, not only more clearly to define the nature of Posey's defection, but to show as well that evil breeds without fail in any vacuum that is created by the absence of good. Posey's intention is morally neutral. The intention of the *ante-bellum* society was good. But there were rents in its armor, gaps in the philosophy on which it was built. This is evident at the beginning of the novel.

When we see Major Buchan and Posey together for the first time, they are locked in battle and the issue is resolved in Posey's favor. Posey wins because he will not abide by the rules, he will not conduct himself in accordance with inherited standards. This reading of Southern literature as the story of traditional men who must either violate their own code or suffer defeat is one that has been suggested many times before. It has been developed, for example, by Malcolm Cowley in his excellent essay on Faulkner. But not enough attention has been given to the underlying reason for the failure of the traditional Southern culture. We cannot believe, of course, that in this world victory is always with the right, but neither are we justified in assuming that the warrior unrestrained by rules will always overcome the man who fights by an ethical code. Grandfather Buchan's society was as ordered as that of the major; its code was as strict. But the culture of late eighteenth century Virginia was powerful enough to hold in abeyance the spirit that motivated Posey. This was so because the Southern weakness of believing that the highest good of man is the good of politics had not, before 1861, developed to its destructive logical conclusion.

Major Buchan was a religious man and on the eve of the Civil War he read in his morning prayer the alternative version of the Episcopal service which was provided in the book for use when calamity threatened the family. But this final decision to cast his lot with the Union was a moral judgment made according to political theory rather than Christian theology. That is to say, he looked to Thomas Jefferson to find out what was right and then prayed God to strengthen his resolution. He was doomed in the end to be defeated by Posey and all that Posey represented not because he lived by traditional rules, but because the tradition itself was founded on a political and not a religious ethic.

As the narrator, Lacy Buchan, puts it, "I cannot to this day decide just how papa looked at it: whether in his mind the domestic trials, growing out of my mother's death, were one thing, and the public crisis another. Nor can I decide in my own mind whether it was possible to distinguish the two—they worked together for a single evil, and I think the evil was the more overwhelming among us because of the way men had of seeing themselves at that time: as in all highly developed societies the line marking off the domestic from the public life was indistinct." In the final analysis, what Mr. Tate is telling us is this: the War must be understood as the climax of Southern culture, the last moment of order in a traditional society. Before 1861, the inherited code of the South remained an adequate guide for ethical conduct—the existence of all the George Posey notwithstanding. After 1865, the old morality was no longer sufficient to serve as a valid standard of behavior. Therefore, the War, taken alone without reference to the tradition, is meaningless. It function in the Southern novel as a dramatic symbol; in a sense, it is the catastrophe at the end of the play. For the character of the *antebellum* South was essentially that of the conventional tragic hero. It was strong and great and good, but it had a flaw.

There is a great deal more that can and certainly ought to be said about this excellent novel, but a complete study of *The Fathers* is beyond the scope of this paper. We must turn to other writers and among the best of the modern Southern novelists is Andrew Lytle. Mr. Lytle's *The Long Night* appeared in 1936, two years before Mr. Tate's book was published. It is a first novel, written with amazing skill and constructed with a great deal of subtlety. The main character of *The Long Night* is a young man named Pleasant McIvor and the story divides itself into two, almost equal parts.

The initial half of Mr. Lytle's book is concerned with McIvor's quest for revenge. Aided occasionally by relatives, but operating mostly alone, Pleasant sets out to kill every member of a large band of speculators who have previously murdered his father. There follows a series of climaxes as Mr. Lytle brings to full development one after another of a list of characters and allows each in turn to fall victim to McIvor's steadfast purpose. But at the final moment, when Pleasant has his gun levelled at the leader of the thieves, the direction of the novel suddenly changes. The Civil War has been declared, and on hearing this McIvor leaves the chief villain alive, swears to kill him at some future time and goes off to join the Confederate Army. From here on the emphasis of the story is shifted. There are further murders by Pleasant, it is true, but very quickly the cause of revenge is superseded by the greater purpose of the War until the two themes are brought together again in the final pages of the novel.

I have recapitulated this rather familiar material in order to show that the unfying element of the novel is its thematic structure. For if one examines the book with a view that does not see beyond the plot, he will discover certain frailties, certain breaks in continuity and shifts in intention that appear on the surface to be flaws. The single motive of the story seems to dissipate in the last half of the novel, a new set of characters is introduced, a whole new world is drawn. Any proper reading of *The Long Night* demands that we recognize the breadth of Mr. Lytle's talents. They encompass both war and peace.

In the early sections of *The Long Night* there are two important images: the McIvor family and the band of speculators headed by Tyson Lovell. The image of the family is central to the novel and it is one which Mr. Lytle has very carefully unified. Certainly, the meeting of the McIvor clan is one of the finest scenes in the novel; it is the sort of thing that Mr. Lytle does with inimitable skill. But its primary purpose is to establish the integrity of the family, to show the group itself as a moral force. There is an overall harmony of feeling among those at the gathering which transcends individual differences concerning the proper method for obtaining justice.

When the meeting is ended and Pleasant, with help from an uncle and a cousin, starts on his work of vengeance, he is acting in accordance with the general will of the family. That is to say, he is fulfilling a domestic, a private obligation. Further, the family duty, as the McIvors see it, coincides precisely with the public responsibility —that of ridding the community of murderers and thieves. Even the method, execution, is the same. All of this changes abruptly, however, when we are introduced to the Civil War, the third and final image of the book. In the first chapter which deals directly with the Confederate Army, Pleasant kills four of his ancient enemies, but the consequences of his act, under the new war conditions, become immediately apparent. He must pretend that his comrades were victims of the Yankees and thereby give false intelligence to his commanders. The War develops; we are treated to a magnificent handling of the Battle of Shiloh; and with each page the breach between public and private duty widens. The old ethic, based on political considerations, is inadequate to cope with this new, unforseen moral situation. Armistead McIvor, Pleasant's cousin, recognizes this, and advises the boy to forget about his revenge. But Pleasant clings to his purpose, and the novel moves on to its conclusion.

In one of the last scenes of the book, Pleasant neglects his responsibility as a scout in order to attempt another of his acts of retribution. He moves close to one of his enemies, raises his pistol, and finds that he cannot shoot. He has come to knowledge; he has discovered the significance of the War and the imperfection of his moral position. But he sees, too, that his understanding has come too late. Pleasant's military defection is the direct cause of Ellis Roswell's death. Adherence to private duty has damaged both the public and the private good. The end is renunciation: of the living and the dead, of war and vegeance, of the old, traditional order by which he had lived.

Caroline Gordon's *None Shall Look Back*, which was published in 1941, is perhaps of all Southern novels the sternest and most un-relenting in its treatment of the Civil War. For at the conclusion of the book, every single character who has remained constant to the Southern ethic has either been killed or sadly broken. Rives Allard, George Rowan and Spencer Rowe are dead; Ned's health is permantly impaired by months of prison life; Fountain Allard has lost his reason as the result of a severe stroke. Except in the cases of Belle Allard and Love Minor, there is nothing but bereavement and a kind of hopeless bitterness among the women. Of all the immediate Allard connection, only Jim, who represents the spirit of commerce, is seen to thrive in the end.

It would be superfluous to do more than point out the fact that here again the principal image is the family and that the public and private moralities coincide until the *status quo* is ruptured by the War. Fountain Allard knows that what is good for the land is good for his own children and his own slaves and for all the community at large. This is superbly conveyed in the chapters that deal with his morning ride over the plantation at Brackets and his investigation of the overseer's cruelty at Cabin Row. But of more importance to the success of Miss Gordon's novel is the superb development of the character, Rives Allard. He refuses to live beyond the failure of his inherited moral code.

Andrew Lytle, in his essay on Miss Gordon's work, finds that the main theme of *None Shall Look Back* is the young man's pursuit of death. There is much in the text of the novel to substantiate this view, and early in the story the careful reader must certainly be aware that Rives will not survive the War. When he is leaving Donelson with Forrest's cavalry, riding past the wounded over the frozen ground, his eye is caught by one of the injured and a moment later he pre-dicts his own end. "The dark glance had been enigmatic but there had been in it a flicker of hostility which men look on at unbearable suffering. It was as if the man dying in the circle of the firelight could not endure the spectacle of the living, who were only riding toward death." This is not mere foreshadowing, a device to prepare the reader for the denouement of the book. It is rather the first in a series of incidents which plainly demonstrate that Lucy and Rives, himself, participate in the knowledge of his ultimate doom.

The sense of mortality is developed through the consciousness of Lucy. It is she who compares the walls of the bridal chamber to the sloping sides of a casket. She feels the chill of death on the ground where recently Rives has lain; and when a strange Confederate captain dies at the Allard home, Lucy weeps not for him but for her husband. These are a few examples of the novel's constant concern with death. There are others of increasing intensity, all of which lead to the final scene between man and wife, the last evening that Lucy and Rives are together. In bed with him and wakeful during the night, Lucy has studied his face. "The light coming in at the window illuminated his features: the high, aquiline nose, the eyes set in their deep hollows, the stern mouth. In the moonlight they were like marble. The kind of face that might be carved on a tomb. She drew a quick breath, sank down beside him, after a little reached over and laid her fingers on his nerveless hand. It comforted her to find it warm." Death has begun to take him already. It is as if the chemistry of Rives' body has already submitted to a fate it does not wish to avoid.

This brings us, I think, to the proper center of the novel. Rives knows as well as Lucy does that he is going to die and until the very end he is free to save himself. Late in 1864, even the Negroes knew that the War was lost, and a Confederate soldier who was at home on leave might have stayed forever with no fear of being molested by his officers. Rives rejects his chance to live, not because he loves death but because he is devoted to the civilization which he is defending. In so far as she was immediately concerned with the War, *per se*, Miss Gordon was content to build her image and then to enhance its value by allowing a strong man to die for it. Indeed, much of the strength of the image is personified in the man, and among views of history, Miss Gordon's is perhaps the shortest one of all.

A novel that is quite different in technique from *None Shall Look Back* is *So Red the Rose* by Stark Young. This is a loose, sprawling sort of book which deals with the grand houses and the large slaveholders in and around Natchez, Mississippi. On the basis of a first reading, one has a strong inclination to dismiss Mr. Young's novel as another moonlight and magnolia romance, a tale built on the crumbs of history, the anecdotes about famous men which have drifted down from the past. But such a view of *So Red the Rose* is less than just. For in spite of the efforts of recent Southern writers and historians to minimize the role of the rich planter in the over-all pattern of Southern culture, the great plantations did exist. They were a part of the South, and they will serve as the stuff for an image.

As is the case in Mr. Young's *Heaven Trees*, everybody in *So Red the Rose* seems to be related to everybody else by some ramification of blood or marriage. The family is the image, and whatever is good or evil in the Southern culture must be found in the glories and failures of the Mississippi clans. There is much talk in the novel about politics. Jefferson Davis, himself, is one of the minor characters. But the talk is superficial; Davis is poorly drawn. Mr. Young fails ever to examine the political ethic of the South. For this reason, the image of *So Red the Rose* is more strictly limited than that of any other noteworthy Civil War novel. The book succeeds because the reader is made to understand the full implications of Southern ancestor worship.

Late in the novel, when the War is over and Mississippi is in the hands of the carpetbaggers, Hugh McGehee remembers a story he used to tell to Edward, his son who died at Shiloh. It is an account of the death of the Earl of Montrose. The Scottish peer had been a Presbyterian, and he was betrayed and captured while fighting for Charles II.

He was to be walked by the bailiffs all along Prince Street to the Mercat Cross, where the gallows was. Instead of his rags, friends had sent him a suit of fine black cloth, a black beaver hat with a silver band, a scarlet cloak richly laced to the knee; his stockings were carnation silk. He had also, with these, fine white gloves on his hands and ribbons to his shoes. The mobs had been hired to mock and howl at him, but when they saw him, he was so beautiful and grave, there was not a sound, except for their low prayers and tears. He was denied the privilege always granted, even to common criminals, of speaking to the crowd. But to those

near the scaffold he spoke a moment, and a boy named
Gordon took it down. ". . . . . . drawing near to God. If
He enable me to embrace it even in its most ugly shape, let
God be glorified in me, though it were my damnation."

Hugh saw a little boy listening to this. "So when he
walked along the street like that, Father, there wasn't a
sound," Edward used to say. "No, Buddie," said Lucy, "not
a sound, he was so beautiful. Papa's told you that." "And
we fought for him," Edward said.

The McGehees fought for him, and every McGehee that came
after, down to Edward who died and Lucy who lived through the
travesty of Reconstruction, carried forever in his mind's eye an image
of the Earl of Montrose's beauty. "But what they would do better
to speak of," Hugh McGehee says later, referring to the people of the
South, "would be not what they have but what they have loved."
Their devotion to a concrete image of the past, their fidelity to a traditional ethic.

This is Mr. Young's thesis, and the method of his novel is to
develop first the code of morality that has been inherited, and second,
the love of family and respect for the past which give the code its
practical strength. Therefore, much is made in this book of old
portraits and heirloom jewels and stories that have been handed down
from father to son. The conduct of the living Bedfords and McGehees
is made significant by Mr. Young's careful attention to the past from
which they sprung.

Thomas Sutpen, the main character in William Faulkner's
Absalom, Absalom!, is as far removed from Hugh McGehee in background and feeling as Jefferson, the county seat of Mr. Faulkner's
Yoknapatawpha, is different from Natchez and the grand establish-
ments that overlooked the river. Whether or not he was of Scotch
descent, Sutpen himself could not say, and the only past that he loved
was the past that he expected to create for all the other Sutpens who
would come after him. He was born in the hills of Western Virginia,
and he turned up in Jefferson in the eighteen thirties, having already
abandoned his wife and child and a prosperous establishment in
Haiti. He had left his family, because the woman he had married
was part Negro, and he was determined to make of himself a Southern gentleman, and to create a line, a dynasty of Sutpens who would

rule in Mississippi as the Tidewater aristocrats held sway in his native Virginia. He was, in the end, defeated by the son he had rejected, by his own innocence, by the scope of his own ambitions.

In the final analysis, the War had very little to do with the frustration of Sutpen's design; indeed, the conflict was probably responsible for prolonging his hopes four or five years until the business with the Yankees could be attended to. But Sutpen has a place in this discussion for at least two reasons: he may be compared with the McGehees and the Buchans, the Allards and the McIvors, to demonstrate the barren quality of the Southern code when it is assumed and not inherited, when it is regarded outside its context, without benefit of the Short View of history. And in the second place, Sutpen's situation in 1861 was in some respects similar to that of the South as a whole; the rules by which he had guided his life had at last proved less than adequate.

"Sutpen's trouble," Quentin Compson remarked, "was innocence." This is a theme that has been developed at some length by Cleanth Brooks, and I do not need to discuss it fully here. But it should be understood that one of the forms which Sutpen's innocence took was a misunderstanding of spiritual values as material ends. He wanted a family, or, specifically, a son, to carry on the Sutpen name, and it is true that he conceived of his grand design in terms of Sutpens of the past and of the future. But what he knew of the family was simply that every aristocrat had one—ancestors fondly remembered and children nurtured with pride. Of love and duty and fidelity among those who share the same blood, he understood nothing. So Bon, the son of his first marriage, waited four years in vain, for some sign, some word spoken, some touch of the flesh. It did not come. Sutpen, who saw the importance of a family to his great scheme, failed to see what Stark Young's Hugh McGehee understood so perfectly: that the Southern culture, the traditional code of ethics was to a certain extent a projection of family devotion, and once stripped of its basis in human affection it became worthless as a standard by which to live. Henry killed Bon, and Sutpen was deprived of his heir.

There is another book by Mr. Faulkner which demands consideration in any study of Civil War fiction. I refer to *The Unvanquished* which appeared in 1938. The main characters are the Sartorises, the point of view is that of Bayard, and the central theme, which receives partial development in each of the individual stories, is one of moral redemption through a modification of the inherited ethical order. As long as the formal conflict is in progress, the traditional Southern morality is a responsible standard of conduct. It will serve to condone Granny's behavior when she steals the Yankee mules, for she is working still for the public good, distributing money and stock to the poor. And it is sufficient, too, at the very end of the War, to suggest to Bayard and Ringo not only a general course of action, but also the specific *modus operandi* by which they track down and kill the bushwacker, Grumby. It remains perhaps a valid code even as late as 1866, when John Sartoris enters the polling booth with his derringer in his sleeve and shoots the two carpetbaggers named Burden. But from this point on the code is doomed to fail; it will no longer furnish the basis for moral action. Once more the military defeat of the South coincides in time with a significant defection of the traditional ethic.

The old code is no longer adequate, because the time has finally come when even Southern aristocrats like John Sartoris are no longer willing to live within the limits of the tradition. Sartoris builds a railroad. He launches his enterprise in partnership with Ben Redmond, and to the world of commerce, he brings his fierce agrarian pride, his planter's code of honor. He must badger Redmond, abuse him, not because Redmond has been guilty of any breach of conduct, but because he, Sartoris, has attempted to operate in a strange world without altering the old ethic. Belatedly, he realizes his mistake, but by then, he must kill Redmond, who participates in the Southern tradition too, or he must, as happens, be killed by him. The responsibility for action is bequeathed to Bayard.

On the night of John Sartoris's murder, when Ringo is waiting to start the long ride back to Jefferson, Bayard pauses at the door to shake hands with Professor Wilkens.

> I knew he believed he was touching flesh which might not be alive tomorrow night and I thought for a second how if I told him what I was going to do, since we had talked about it, about how if there was anything at all in the Book, anything of hope and peace for His blind and bewildered spawn which He had chosen above all others to offer immortality, *Thou shalt not kill* must be it, since maybe he

even believed that he had taught it to me except that he had not, nobody had, not even myself since it went further than just having been learned. But I did not tell him. He was too old to be forced so, to condone even in principle such a decision; he was too old to have to stick to principle in the face of blood and raising and background, to be faced without warning and made to deliver like by a highwayman out of the dark: only the young could do that—one still young enough to have his youth supplied him gratis as a reason (not an excuse) for cowardice.

Bayard finds an answer. He does not reject the traditional morality: he modifies it, amalgamates it with the principles of Christianity.

Late in 1864, when the War is almost over, Charles Bon of *Absalom, Absalom!* speaks to Henry Sutpen. "Not God; evidently we have done without him for four years . . . and so if you don't have God you don't need food and clothes and shelter, there isn't anything for honor and pride to climb on and hold to and flourish. And if you haven't got honor and pride, then nothing matters."

Whether or not we have been doing without God ever since the War, I cannot say with any certainty. But even the spurious God, of whom Mr. Tate speaks, that deity fashioned by the sixteenth century merchants, must have been sufficient for a while. Because in the Old South the honor and the pride were there, not as individual virtues in isolated men, but as a part of the public consciousness, the moral basis on which the culture was constructed. This is the reason that the War has been used so often by so many Southern writers. It is the grand image for the novelist, the period when the "ultimate truths," with which Mr. Faulkner says the writer must deal, existed as commonly recognized values within a social framework. It is the only moment in American history when a completely developed national ethic was brought to a dramatic crisis.

H. BLAIR ROUSE

Time And Place In Southern Fiction

Southern time and place—Southern setting—have functioned with varying significance in Southern stories.[1] Fictional setting primarily comprises time and place. Certain other elements, such as minor characters and local mores, may be included as parts of setting.

Time may figure with relative simplicity as a period of greater or less duration in human history; it may be indicated with very slight emphasis on the relation of the story to the period, or with an overwhelming emphasis on the significance of the particular time to the story and the lives of the characters. Many Civil War novels stress both time and place, specifying the particular day and hour of events or referring to well known, definitely recorded historical occurrences as a means of bringing out the relation of the time to the story and the characters. DuBose Heyward's *Peter Ashley* is a good example of a novel in which a particular historical period functions in such a way that all the action and the atmosphere is constantly related to the tense period of late 1860 and early 1861 when the Southern states were seceding and the Confederacy was rising. The place is Charleston, but it is decidedly Charleston of a particular moment. The concern is concentrated upon the occurrence of certain events and the passage of the tense days of early 1861 in the lives of Peter Ashley and his uncle, Pierre Chardon, and what these times mean for them. Indeed, the treatment of the days and their passage is of far more im-

---

[1] Material for illustrative analysis has been drawn largely from the works of Erskine Caldwell, Ellen Glasgow, Paul Green, DuBose Heyward, Julia Peterkin, Marjorie Kinnan Rawlings, Elizabeth Madox Roberts, and T. S. Stribling. The work of these authors has been used because of its especial pertinence to the purposes of this essay and because these authors seemingly would not be considered extensively elsewhere in this symposium. Of course, this latter point will not apply to all of these writers. Moreover, for reasons sufficiently apparent, there is some discussion of the work of William Faulkner, Robert Penn Warren, and Thomas Wolfe in its relation to the subject of this essay.

portance for the story than is any treatment of place or character. This is a novel of tense and decisive *days* and *hours* rather than of character or narrative.

In some Southern novels, time as a clearly defined period of weeks, months or years in human history may be scarcely noticeable. Indeed, the author seems purposely to have avoided any reference to recorded events or to other facts by which the particular time of the book may be identified. Sometimes in certain of Elizabeth Madox Roberts' works or in some of the writings of Julia Peterkin and Paul Green, the authors appear to have de-emphasized the time of the action so far as it pointed to a particular period in history so as to give an effect of timelessness, so that one may feel that he is reading of "old forgotten far-off things and battles long ago." These writings, as well as those of Marjorie Kinnan Rawlings, are not entirely lacking in historical references, but these are not especially noticeable. Indeed, they may not appear until well along in the book, when a reference to some recorded event reminds the reader that these things did occur at such and such a time. One is not especially conscious of historical time in Marjorie Kinnan Rawlings' *Golden Apples* until the Big Freeze occurs; this event serves as a hitching post for history. Yet so slightly does historical time concern the reader of this novel, that even this reference is likely to receive little notice. One is aware, likewise, that the events of Julia Peterkin's *Black April* occur after the Civil War; later, one receives definite assurance that this is so. Yet historical time seems of slight importance to these Negroes in their sea island plantation home. That these are post-bellum years is important in this book for at least one reason: although slavery no longer exists, these Negroes on Blue Run plantation have a relation to the white owners which is very near that of feudal serfs if not that of slaves. This is clearly evident; but beyond this fact, historical time has little importance. Time here is almost entirely in terms of the passage of the seasons and the passage of months and years in the lives of the Negro characters, of the turning earth on the plantation and of the running sands of time in the years of Big Sue, April, and Breeze, the small Negro boy.

The treatment of time which may be of least aesthetic consequence is a simple *statement* of the passage from one point of time to another, either in recorded history or in the lives of the fictional characters. In this treatment, the reader is *told* that time has passed, but he is not *shown* that it has passed; he is not really made *aware* of its passing. This treatment is likely to occur in those novels in which the author has undertaken to tell of the lives of several generations in a family or group. In Marjorie Kinnan Rawlings' *South Moon Under,* one is *told* of the passage of the years in the life of Piety, the central character, from childhood to old age. Yet the story seems to move in jerks and starts, and the reader may not always be *aware* of this passage of the years in the life of Piety and her family. This is rather unfortunate in this book, for there was an opportunity here to treat time more significantly, an opportunity either overlooked or muffed.

Ideally, a work of fiction should *show* the passage of time, should give the reader an understanding of the duration of time, and should present, significantly, the *effect* of time's passing upon the human beings concerned. A number of the more important Southern novelists have been aware of this need and have given much care to the interpretation of time's duration. Thomas Wolfe's whole great work, of which the separately published novels are parts, is principally concerned with the passage of time, with time's erosion of humanity. William Faulkner has given most careful attention to this aspect of his fiction. Indeed, such novels as *The Sound and the Fury, Absalom, Absalom!,* and *Light in August* are chiefly concerned with what the passing years have done to these human lives as they have swept over and around them.

This effect of time as erosion or as attrition—the wearing away of life—figures importantly in the novels of several Southern writers, but with greatly varying effectiveness. Marjorie Kinnan Rawlings, in *South Moon Under,* apparently sought to reveal what life has done to Piety, the central character in the book. Mrs. Rawlings does tell us what Piety's life is, in terms of certain events and changes such as growth to maturity, marriage, births, deaths, middle age and old age. Yet because time's grinding effect is *told* rather than completely *shown,* the reader may not be entirely convinced that change has actually taken place, that the elderly woman in the cabin at the end of the book is not simply the child, Piety, of the earlier chapters masquerading as an old mother. This failure—if it be such—may result from the inadequate indication of time's passage and even more from the author's relying too much on an external narration, on a *telling about* the life of Piety rather than a revealing of the erosion of time from within and almost wholly from Piety's viewpoint.

Elizabeth Madox Roberts is concerned with this problem of time erosion in two of her novels, *The Time of Man* and *My Heart and My Flesh;* it figures, of course, in some of her other works, such as *The Great Meadow*. Though the effect of time's passing on Ellen Chesser, the central figure of *The Time of Man,* is evidently important to the author's purposes, her treatment of this element is not successful in the latter chapters of the novel. There is a suggestion of haste, of a hurry to finish the story, in those chapters which deal with Ellen's maturity. Ellen's childhood and youth, her life as the child of poor tenant farm people, what it was for her to grow up as one of this class and this outlook, are *shown* with great care; yet one is *told,* with rather unseemly haste, of Ellen's life after her marriage. Miss Roberts may have intended the latter chapters to give the effect of the rapid and relatively eventless passage of Ellen's mature years, to show how like the life of her parents, of her people for many generations, was the life of Ellen Chesser Kent. If this was the author's intention, something of the desired effect is achieved. One realizes the similarity of Ellen's lot to that of her people before her, how harsh it is and yet how rewarding in many ways. However, the attrition of time, to which attention is certainly drawn, is more effectively revealed in the life stories of Ellen's parents than in her own. The apparent haste of the latter chapters of the novel, the rapid glimpses of events in Ellen's married existence and then the quick skipping of several years to another event, suggest a motion picture film run through a projector at the wrong speed. There is distortion; everything moves unnaturally and too rapidly. Of course, this defect in the novel should not cause one to overlook the book's other and very real merits which far outweigh this weakness.

In *My Heart and My Flesh* Miss Roberts was more successful in handling this effect of the erosion of time, possibly because the novel does not cover so long a period as does *The Time of Man*. Moreover the revelation of time's passing for Theodosia, the central character, is far more subjective; time becomes, for her, very nearly an embodied character, a friend or an enemy in its varied manifestations. The attrition of the years, concentrated within a shorte space, is more vividly and dramatically projected through the events and situations which most closely touch Theodosia as she grows into youth and maturity from her relatively sheltered childhood; as she is brought into the experience of death, betrayal, hate and love, want, and, ultimately, relative peace with her world. Certainly here the more concentrated and dramatic presentation of time's wearing away of life is more successful than the narrative method of *The Time of Man*. Moreover, the preservation of point of view has much to do with this increased effectiveness. In the latter portion of the book, when Miss Roberts has clearly blocked in her characters' lives and their situations in time and place, the concentration upon the inner struggles of Theodosia is often so intense as to be painful.

In Paul Green's *The Laughing Pioneer* and in DuBose Heyward's *Lost Morning* there are situations involving characters who have experienced the wearing effect of time's passing; in both the reader is *told* that this is so rather than shown how and why. Indeed, in *The Laughing Pioneer* it seems that the author's handling of time actually works at cross purposes. This story of country folk in the North Carolina Piedmont is told in such a manner that the reader may feel that almost everything that happens is relatively timeless, that Danny Lawton and the other characters in the Little Bethel country dwell in a kind of never-never land, or that the tale is akin to the *maerchen* or an old ballad of days long dead. Yet there are other figures in the pattern, certain harsh realities with which the reader is frequently confronted, such as a rival lover who clerks in a country store, the cruel beating of Danny by a masked mob, and the very struggle of the farm work in heat and cold. Especially is there the fact of Miss Alice's existence. Miss Alice experiences the passing of time and the destruction of her hope for happiness. In the life of this woman the reader might have found more concern with the erosion of time, but it is not there. Indeed Miss Alice seems to have suffered life without actually experiencing it. The indignities, the disappointments, the degradation, the poverty, the loss of all that might make her life worthwhile pass over Miss Alice without clearly affecting her. Of course one is *told* otherwise, but one is not *shown*. Just as Miss Alice kept the world at a distance from her, so the author kept the reader at too great a distance.

Felix Hollister in DuBose Heyward's *Lost Morning* is one who has felt the grinding of the wheels of time, or so one is informed. Yet, here again, the author failed to show, failed to make the reader see with his mind's eye and with his heart how the years wore away the life of this artist until there was little remaining but a shell. Because one is told too much and shown too little about the effect of time's passing upon the central character of this novel, the ultimate effect is that of a contrived tale.

Ellen Glasgow was much concerned with the erosion of time in such novels as *Virginia, The Sheltered Life,* and *Vein of Iron. Virginia* is mainly concerned with the life of a Virginia *lady,* Virginia Pendleton Treadwell, who cannot adapt herself to changing ways and circumstances in the lives of those about her, whose temperament, training and traditions as a Southern lady have a paralyzing effect upon her. Yet even for Virginia, who could not change her ways of thinking, acting and feeling, the passage of the years made great differences. Although she cannot actually comprehend why such things should be, Virginia knows that she who once was happy is miserable, that she who once was filled with hope and desire is destitute of all hope and all desire. Time and marriage, combined with an unthinking inability to adapt herself to change, have worn away Virginia's beauty and her joy in life although they have not entirely destroyed the inner core of her character, that inner strength which is both her sustenance of spirit and, by its very unbending and unadaptable nature, is also the cause of her disaster.

In *The Sheltered Life* Miss Glasgow gave much more attention to the attrition of time, as it could be shown in the lives of old General Archbald and Eva Birdsong. Throughout the book are reminders that the years have ground cruelly the lives of these people. Disappointment, frustration, the repeated denial of his hopes and aspirations, the repeated demands that he do that which is repellent and not do that which is desirable—all this has acted with abrasive power upon General Archbald yet has not destroyed him. For he is one of Miss Glasgow's civilized Southerners, and within him is an inner fiber which may be cruelly worn yet not destroyed. Eva Birdsong also experiences the erosion of time as she sees the years pass over her, bringing betrayal by husband and friend, loss of beauty and loss of health, and ultimately complete disaster for herself and all those around her. Her downfall is apparently complete, for her beauty and her belief in the ideal of beauty have been very nearly her whole soul's sustenance; when these are lost, Eva is destitute.

In *Vein of Iron,* as well as in her last published novel, *In This Our Life,* Miss Glasgow portrayed several characters who experienced time's erosive effects yet who possessed their means of resistance. In both of these novels the reader is clearly shown, as well as told, what

time has meant in its passing for these people: Ada Fincastle, to
whom the years bring frustration and disappointment but not defeat,
John Fincastle, her father, whom opposition and worldly rejection bend
but cannot crush, and especially Grandmother Fincastle, whose stern
Calvinist heart sustains her in the face of poverty, disappointment, her
son's religious defection, and what she believes to be her granddaughter's disgrace.   There is a comparable treatment of the effects
of time on character in *In This Our Life* where one again is *shown*
how Asa Timberlake, apparently a failure by the world's standards,
has resisted the grinding of the years with their disappointments and
frustrations so that he and his daughter, Roy, who is much like him,
seem the only ones in this Virginia family able to retain a modicum
of decency and self-respect when disaster strikes them.

When time is treated subjectively, the passage of minutes, hours,
days, months and years blends with place and action in such a manner
that all these factors are interwoven into the life pattern of the characters. In some instances time may be so treated that past, present and
future become very nearly one, and time itself seems to constitute a
dimension. Of course, recent Southern novelists hold no patent on
such fictional presentation of time. Novelists of the eighteenth and
nineteenth centuries such as Sterne and Dickens, were interested in
such means of greater effectiveness in their character revelation. More
recently, James Joyce and Virginia Woolf were particularly successful
in their subjective handling of time.

Many Southern novels are deeply concerned with the meaning of
the past for the characters or with the pastness in the very present
existence of a central figure or group. With those novels and novelists
which are most characteristically Southern, time as the essence of all
that has happened in the Southern past becomes the factor of greatest
importance in the fiction and may control the shaping of the narrative,
the character development, indeed, the patterns of the work. Time is
handled subjectively and with considerable aesthetic effectiveness in
Faulkner's *The Sound and the Fury,* where the very structural organization and the style of the novel are involved in this projection; where,
indeed, the interweaving of the South's past and present and the past
and present of the Compsons becomes so involved that the uninitiated
reader encounters some difficulty in plumbing the depths of meaning.
In the writing of Thomas Wolfe time is a potent factor in the presentation of all the meaning of the lives of the characters; the past

merges with the present and projects into the future. It is no accident that one of Wolfe's novels is called *Of Time and the River*. Robert Penn Warren made most effective use of time as a subjective factor in *All the King's Men*. There is little use of complicated or unusual techniques in this novel. Warren succeeded admirably in making time an ever-powerful force in the lives of his characters and especially in the life of his narrator, Jack Burden; for in this book it is Jack Burden's life and point of view rather than that of the political dictator, Willie Stark, which is of the greatest importance. Moreover, this very time-awareness in Jack Burden and the lack of any feeling for time, tradition, or the past in the present in Willie Stark, make Jack Burden's narrations of his own life and that of Willie meaningful in their contrasts and conflicts, perhaps desperately tragic in their import. The Cass Mastern passage in *All the King's Men* is meaningful only as a factor in the subjective time treatment of the whole novel. Through Jack Burden's exploration of the life of Cass Mastern, Warren projected with dramatic vividness the past into the present tormented existence of his narrator.

In *The Sheltered Life*, by Ellen Glasgow, in the section called "The Deep Past," there is the meditation of old General Archbald. Here the novelist succeeded in bringing together in relatively brief compass the meaning of history in the South for civilized people in that land. The section is too long to quote in its entirety, but a few passages reveal something of Miss Glasgow's treatment:

> Suddenly, while he meditated, it seemed to him that the shape of the external world, this world of brick and asphalt, of men and women and machines moving, broke apart and dissolved from blown dust into thought. Until this moment he had remembered with the skin of his mind, not with the arteries; but now, when the concrete world disappeared, he plunged downward through a dim vista of time, where scattered scenes from the past flickered and died and flickered again. At eighty-three, the past was always like this. Never the whole of it. Fragments, and then more fragments. No single part, not even an episode, complete as it had happened.
>
> In each hour, when he had lived it, life had seemed important to him; but now he saw that it was composed of things that were all little things in themselves, of mere frac-

tions of time, of activities so insignificant that they had
passed away with the moment in which they had quivered
and vanished. How could any one, he asked, resting there
alone at the end, find a meaning, a pattern? Yet, though his
mind rambled now, he had walked in beaten tracks in his
maturity. His soul, it is true, had been a rebel; but he had
given lip-homage, like other men all over the world, to
creeds that were husks. Like other men all over the world,
he had sacrificed to gods as fragile as the bloom of light on
the tulip tree. And what was time itself but the bloom, the
sheath enfolding experience? Within time, and within time
alone, there was life—the gleam, the quiver, the heartbeat,
the immeasurable joy and anguish of being. . . .

The trail plunged straight and deep into the November
forest. There was the tang of woodsmoke far off in a clearing. Frost was spun over the ground. The trees were brilliant with the yellow of hickory, the scarlet of sweet gum, the
wine-red of oaks.

Why was he here? How had he come? Was he awake or
asleep? Ah, he knew the place now. A forest trail at Stillwater. But they had left Stillwater fifty years ago. Well,
no matter. No matter that he was a boy and an old man together, or that the boy wanted to be a poet. It was all the
same life. A solitary fragment, but the same fragment of
time. Time was stranger than money. Stranger than his
roaming again through this old forest, with his snack and a
thin volume of Byron tucked away in his pocket. Here was
the place he had stopped to eat his snack, while his pointer
puppies, Pat and Tom, started game in the underbrush.

. . . .

. . . Well, the past was woven of contradictions. For eighty-
three years he had lived two lives, and between these two
different lives, which corresponded only in time, he could
trace no connection. What he had wanted, he never had;
what he had wished to do, he had never done. . . . . (*The
Sheltered Life,* pp. 147-149, 152.)

In this section of *The Sheltered Life* and in the meditation of
Grandmother Fincastle in *Vein of Iron,* Ellen Glasgow succeeded in

treating time as an extra fictional dimension suggestive of such treatment as that of Proust in *A la Recherche du Temps Perdu*.

Place, as an element of fictional setting, functions with possibly even greater variety of degree and manner and perhaps greater differences in effectiveness than does time. In the practice of some novelists time and place are so closely involved, so integrated in their functions, as to be very nearly indistinguishable. At its simplest and probably least important, place, as the physical surroundings in which the lives are lived and the action of the fiction occurs, may appear to the reader as little more than a backdrop, an exterior rural or urban scene or an interior that is where the events of the story happen—nothing more. When this is the case, the location of the story is actually of relatively small importance so far as the work is concerned, whether as art or as simple entertainment. Place, when it is simply outdoors or indoors, Virginia or Texas, a sign indicating a location, when it does not participate, when it does not have any real involvement in the structure and meaning of the work, does little more than mislead readers. This is likely to be true in works largely dependent upon odd or exciting situations or upon the exploitation of eccentric characteristics concerning the persons involved—in other words, humorous or supposedly comic farces which concern actuality or ideality to a very slight degree. Probably more Southern fiction than is generally realized is "placed" in the South in this sense. The reader learns that the story "takes place" in Georgia or Tennessee or wherever, and that is just about the end of the author's—and the reader's—concern with the whereabouts of the story. Of course, from time to time the author may drop little hints as to place, but rarely in such writing will these allusions to location actually involve the life of the characters in such a way that the reader comes to understand these people as living in a physical world possessing specific characteristics and a true and actual location. Dubose Heyward's *Lost Morning* is laid in Piedmont Carolina; or so the reader is told. Beyond this telling, the reader has no more concern for the specific place where most of the events of the story occur. As Mr. Heyward was a resident of South Carolina, one may suppose that is the state referred to; later when tobacco factories are mentioned, one may suppose that it is North Carolina. The reader is not likely to be greatly bothered about the precise place involved in this novel even though the location actually is of considerable importance in the lives of its people, or so one is led to understand. Yet, in actuality, because so much is simply told yet not completely revealed concerning place and the people in their setting, one is likely to feel that the author might well have said that the events occurred in Colorado or Connecticut and have been equally convincing. This is the story of a once poor artist who sells his soul for the comforts and luxuries of a country club existence which his Babbitty wife makes him believe are imperative; actually the story has little relation to its setting beyond the fact that it is somewhere in the United States of America. *Lost Morning* is a novel nominally occurring in the South, but that is about all that is Southern about it. There are references to features of Southern scenery now and then or to factories common in the Piedmont of both Carolinas, but such scenic "props" are just that and nothing more.

Probably most readers of Erskine Caldwell's fiction, after swearing with anger or admiration, would readily assert that his stories are placed in the South. If they recalled that Georgia is specifically mentioned in some of them, these readers would also insist that these are stories with a Georgia location. Yet, with slight qualification, it may with equal validity be asserted that place is actually of little importance in most of Caldwell's tales. About twenty years ago, when *Tobacco Road* in its stage metamorphosis was enjoying its long run, Mr. Caldwell was reported to have said that his book, its characters and events were not essentially Georgian or even Southern, that comparable situations might be found and portrayed in other parts of the country. This statement did little, presumably, to calm congressmen and others who believed that their state and region had been traduced. Yet place in Caldwell's fiction is really little more than a set of "props" and painted cloths. This may be less the case with *Tobacco Road* and *God's Little Acre* than it is with Caldwell's more recent work. It may be conceded that in the earlier fiction there seems to be some attempt to treat place significantly, but there is little more than a glance of the author in this direction. Augusta is mentioned with some frequency in *Tobacco Road,* and there is the reported love of Jeeter Lester for the land; there are even a few upper class Southerners as "props" now and then. Yet actually place is of little importance in this story. Change the names about a bit and say that these people lived in a rural area or a small town slum in California; the average reader would have little quarrel so far as the actual story and its characters are concerned. As a novel of sensational situation and character exploitation, it was tremendously effective; but place was really quite unimportant in the book.

In *God's Little Acre* the author seemed to give more attention to place and the significance of the actual location of his story. Here the land and the relation of the people to it are more closely presented. Moreover, in those portions of the book which concern the mill town, the life of the town and its people is more vividly concerned with the actual location. Yet even in this novel, place and time are relatively incidental matters in a story that is primarily one of eccentricity and violence. In most of Mr. Caldwell's subsequent tales, place has been treated with a greater or less degree of casualness. Some houses along a village street exist as the background for the hilarious antics or the dull villainy of the eccentrics, or "humor" figures, with which the author and presumably the reader are to be concerned. This is evidently so, no matter how much pretense there may be of a concern with reform, and with pointing to evils with horror. Such attitudes are clearly little more than pretenses in such novels as *A House in the Uplands, Place Called Estherville* or *Episode in Palmetto*. The old estate, in the first of these, is a backdrop for the usual story the author has to tell, his tale of degradation, miscegenation, violence and general unpleasantness not too cleverly mixed together and liberally spiced. *Place Called Estherville* may actually seem to emphasize place, to promise an evocation of its scene, but neither this novel nor *Episode in Palmetto* actually use the Southern village scene for anything more serious than as a backdrop for the author's customary brand of lechery, lust, and general human cussedness stewed together into a pretended tract for the times and warning to sinners.

It would be foolish to suggest that Mr. Heyward and Mr. Caldwell are the only Southern authors who have used place insignificantly. Many so-called Southern novels have actually been very little concerned with the Southernness of their physical backgrounds. For instance, T. S. Stribling's *Teeftallow* purports to be a story about hill country folk in Tennessee. There is a hill village and a county seat in the hill and mountain country; the novel concerns the people of this region. Yet, actually the setting is of slight importance. Essentially this novel is one of violent situation, comic or otherwise, rather than character revelation and interpretation. These hill folk are cousins of the cartoon characters, Kennesaw and the mountain boys of the *Esquire* cartoons, except that most of Stribling's hill people in *Teeftallow* do wear shoes. The countryside and the villages are scenes for violence or farce comedy.

Place may be treated so that its function is more significant for the final effect of the whole work aesthetically. Three separate aspects of the treatment of place may actually be varying degrees of a single approach to the projection of meaning for a fictional scene. Thus, the physical surroundings of an action may serve to induce a certain mood or to produce a desired atmosphere which the author believes essential for the total effect of his work. In such a treatment, scene is still relatively an external matter so far as one understands the inner lives of the characters; place is a matter of interior or exterior sights and sounds which still function in much the same way as stage scenery, props and noises. Yet when used with some skill and some awareness of aesthetic possibilities and needs, such treatment of scene may be highly effective in so far as it serves to suggest atmosphere or mood.

Another, perhaps more desirable, approach to the treatment of place is that in which physical surroundings are used so that they constitute the "room" in which the characters have their worldly and, to a certain extent, their spiritual beings. When place is so used, it becomes to some extent an essential factor in the development and interpretation of character and in the actual structure of the novel.

Still another use of place is that in which the physical setting very nearly assumes the function of another character in the story, becomes an *actor* in the structure of the work. Of course there is always the danger that when place is so treated the author will slip into the sin of the pathetic fallacy. Yet if he can avoid the pathetically fallacious treatment of nature, the author may achieve the finest artistic success in bringing his characters' physical surroundings into so close a relation to their lives and actions that the scene of the novel may veritably be endowed with a kind of spiritual significance; that the scene may, for those moments of highest intensity, actually seem to possess soul. Obviously, such treatment of scene is not frequently encountered; too often the author who attempts it only falls into the trap of the pathetic fallacy.

Several elements in Southern novels may actually function as parts of the physical surroundings of the main characters and their actions. Minor characters sometimes serve as a part of the scene and may induce atmosphere or act simply as parts of the "background" against which the more important characters of the story live their lives. Usually when characters function in this way, they remain "flat" and may be little more than stereotype figures; more effectively used, such characters achieve the stature of living human beings and are realized as such. Yet they blend into the place and time of the action and serve as part of the surroundings of the story. Frequently human beings are presented in such a way that they lose individuality and are realized only as mobs, crowds, or armies. The mass may function as a background against which the action takes place, even though such action may also involve the mob and be involved with it. Or the crowd may actually function as a single character as in scenes of riot or other such action.

Another set of elements which may function as scene comprises the habits and customs of a character or set of characters. In some works it may be difficult to distinguish such use of peculiar ways and manners from their use for character presentation and development. Yet there are books in which the beliefs and attitudes of a group of people, their manners and their ways of doing or not doing things, are as thoroughly involved in the scene, atmosphere, and mood of the novel as are those parts of the scene which are more evidently the physical surroundings.

These different approaches to the treatment of setting are rarely so clearly and separately evident as I may have made them appear in these descriptive statements. More often an author's procedure with respect to place and his treatment of scene vary within a single novel or even within a single short story; the emphasis and care in the treatment of setting may vary considerably in degree in a single work. Perhaps the ideal treatment of setting is that in which both time and place, especially place, are so presented that they are completely integrated factors in the inner artistic structure of the work; so that setting functions as time, as physical surroundings, and yet very nearly as character in its involvement in action. In such instances, setting is so completely embodied in the very fabric of the work that if it were removed the whole structure would collapse and the novel would cease to exist.

DuBose Heyward, in *Mamba's Daughters*, treats place effectively in so far as he gives a sense of actuality to his Charleston scenes and to the phosphate mines where much of the action takes place. Indeed, the Charleston of *Mamba's Daughters* and of *Porgy* is far more significantly involved in the lives of the fictional characters and projected as a part of those lives than is the Charleston of the firing on Fort Sumter and the founding of the Confederacy which serves as the scene of *Peter Ashley*. In the latter novel, one is likely to see and believe in the Secession Charleston with very little more sense of its reality and involvement in human life than for the sets of a musical comedy. On the other hand, both the slum Charleston and the well-to-do Charleston of *Mamba's Daughters* and of *Porgy* do serve as the essential "room" of the central figures of the books.

In Julia Peterkin's *Black April*, setting, in terms of physical surroundings, of habits and customs, seems to have taken over the book to such an extent that the story is very nearly swallowed up in mood, atmosphere, and folk lore. Indeed, the reader almost loses sight of narrative entirely and may realize the central characters, the Negroes of the Blue Run plantation on the South Carolina coast, Big Sue, Breeze, and April, only as clusters of attitudes, customs, superstitions, religious peculiarities, and folkways in the natural surroundings of fields, woods, and marshes, and in the cabins of the quarters. Here setting very nearly becomes the whole work; character and action are almost incidental.

In some of his Little Bethel stories, Paul Green uses place with some success as a means of inducing a mood or the desired atmosphere. Though the location of Little Bethel is definitely indicated, there is not too much insistence on concrete realities and geographical specificity. Indeed, in many of these tales of country white folks and Negroes in North Carolina, although one is given particular towns and rivers to steer by, one may still feel that he is reading of a land and a people who have their origin and their habitation very largely in the country of the author's mind. Scene is more often a matter of atmosphere and of mood in these tales of country ways and rural happenings. Indeed, there is a curious combination of effects or mingling of moods in Paul Green's fiction. The treatment of character and the use of action in stories that are essentially anecdotal may suggest something of the Rabelaisian, humorous quality of Caldwell or Stribling. There is also a suggestion of the sociological inquiry which one finds in those authors. Yet such an estimate of Green's fiction falls short of the truth if left at that point. For there is also an emphasis on the poetry of human existence which is lacking in most socio-realistic Southern fiction. In many of the tales in *Salvation on a String and Other Tales of the South* the characters which may be little more than light sketches and the stories which may be relatively slim anecdotes are clothed in a spirit of comedy or tragedy or both, as in a light and darkness lifting them above and beyond the solid realities in which they are involved. They take on something of the qualities of the old folk ballads, full of the joy and the terror of life, with the breath of a faery world surrounding them. Of course, Paul Green's prose style and handling of narrative have much to do with the effect of sustained song which carries these tales along. Yet the treatment of scene is also important in this connection. For instance, this paragraph from the title story of the collection, *Salvation on a String*, may suggest something of the way in which Paul Green treats the physical surroundings in which his tales occur:

> The valley was a great turpentine country then, and vast thundering forests stretched from here to the foothills farther west. The long-leaf pines stood a hundred feet high, and night and day the sound of the boxing blade and the hanh-hanh of the scraper were heard. And every few miles the smoke of a turpentine still showed itself like a swirling fog among the underbrush. The slaves, fat and greasy as butterballs, were working like bees around the boiling vats, hacking and making staves for barrels, gashing the trees, and rolling the barrels of rosin and spirits down to the landing on the river there. And the river itself was a great watery highway of trade. Steamboats and flatboats came up as far as Fayetteville from Wilmington, and some of them even as far as Smiley's Falls. And schooners and square-riggers from the North and from the South, from the West Indies and even from Europe itself came pushing up the river to anchor at Wilmington, waiting for their loads from the smaller boats above. (*Salvation on a String and Other Tales of the South*, p. 1.)

Here the long past scene is vividly present in all its sights, sounds and smells, with its varied implications for the whites and Negroes who lived there. Though Green does not always evoke the very spirit of place, he does so often enough to merit the reader's and the critic's attention.

Thomas Wolfe, Robert Penn Warren, and William Faulkner have given great care in their fiction to the treatment of place. Wolfe's presentation of the North Carolina mountains which lie about Asheville is suggestive rather than explicitly detailed. One may not get the impression that Wolfe deeply loved nature as he observed it in the woods and fields about his Southern small-town home. He seemed more concerned with the overall influence of the mountains upon the people who dwell among them, with their isolating effect rather than with their beauty which a real love for such things might have led him to express. On the other hand, he gave the small Southern town a most detailed study so as to make it amazingly and even painfully present for the reader. Wolfe's evocation of his Southern urban existence is matched only by his handling of scenes in the large Northern metropolis.

William Faulkner's treatment of scene is a subject for an essay in itself. In his Mississippi stories he has created a whole world which is both a real and concrete place of human existence while at the same time it is a country of the imagination. Jefferson and Yoknopatawpha constitute one of the most remarkable evocations of the spirit and meaning of a part of the South that one may discover; yet, while this Southern world, lying along the border of the hills and the low grounds in northern Mississippi, is so patently a land of the author's and the reader's imagination and idealization, it is also a country of the most material and utterly factual actuality. It is this unusual and even shocking blending of the ideal with the material which gives Faulkner's treatment of scene its powerful effect. In Faulkner's South, time and place, present and past, what once was and what now is, indeed, what will surely come, all are brought together and imaginatively possessed by the reader's understanding, as violently and as meaningfully as they are by Faulkner himself. As he wrote in *Intruder in the Dust,* it is always, for him and for such readers, as for the comprehending characters in his fiction, not yet two o'clock on that afternoon in July, 1863, when Pickett awaited the signal from Longstreet. Or it is now and always will be the Jefferson houses and streets and the Yoknopatawpha hills, forests and fields of the Indian, slave, pioneer, and planter, as well as the Confederate soldier, the freed Negro, the "poor white," and the fallen aristocrat. It is important to realize that while Faulkner has imagined the physical surroundings of his stories with vigor and has projected them into his printed pages with technical skill, his use of place and time is clearly in relation to their meaning for his characters. The woodland of "The Bear" and the great beast himself are significant because they are meaningful for the human beings with whom they are involved; thus they assume spiritual stature and a significance far greater than as simple elements of an action or a scene. Rarely are natural surroundings used perfunctorily in Faulkner's writing. He wishes his readers to know clearly, with a depth of understanding beyond that involved in the reading of most fiction, just what was the physical world of his people and what it meant to them, how it affected them and how it was affected by them. Indeed, Faulkner's insistence on the involvement of his people in their particular world has resulted in a body of fiction which may be difficult for the reader unaware or stubbornly superficial. The author's refusal to write so that the reader finds everything plainly laid out in neat rows upon a level surface undoubtedly has resulted in failure to understand. For one must keep aware of the natural surroundings as well as the man made world of these stories, in all times and in all their varied metamorphoses, and in all possible relationships to the human lives lived there. If there is a key to any supposed mysteries needed for such works as *The Sound and the Fury, Absalom, Absalom!,* or *As I Lay Dying,* then the author's handling of time and place and their meaning may well be that key.

Robert Penn Warren has treated place, as well as time, with purposes not unlike Faulkner's, though perhaps not always with the intensity and the evocation of the very spirit of the South which Faulkner achieves. In *All the King's Men,* however, Warren certainly brings out the meaning of the Deep South surroundings of his people and the events of their lives to such a degree that place becomes completely integrated into the very structure of the work and is clearly so necessary an element for comprehending all that one must know and realize about the characters, that place in this novel is truly an "actor" in the drama. Indeed, one may recall, this novel was first written as a play and produced several times by amateur and semi-professional groups. *All the King's Men* in stage form was not too successful as a work of art. One thing which may have made the play far less effective than the novel is that the sense of place and time, especially of place, was very slightly projected into the awareness of the audience. Warren may have been so concerned with the abstract philosophical meanings which he wished to bring out strongly in the relatively brief moment of a stage production that he either overlooked or neglected the setting of his drama. Indeed, some measure of this abstraction may be indicated by the fact that this play, in at least one production, was rather effectively produced with a highly abstract stage setting. Yet the story of the characters actually demands that the people be shown in clear relation to a material world in which other lives have been lived, where suffering and joy have occurred in times gone by. When he rewrote the play as a novel, Warren seems to have realized the need for a clearer and more powerful treatment of scene. At any rate, he does make the South of Jack Burden, Willie Stark and all the others so vitally involved and insistent a factor that without a clear understanding of this South as a pattern of times and places, of history, topography, climate, politics, society and all the rest, the lives of these people and their tragedy cannot be read with any degree of comprehension. Indeed, one may wonder whether the difficulty experienced by some readers of this novel did not grow out of failure to give sufficient attention to Warren's treatment of time and place. This is not a novel in which the "background" can be neglected by the reader, for here the "background" is in the very foreground of the story and constitutes an essential element of the work.

Marjorie Kinnan Rawlings, Elizabeth Madox Roberts, and Ellen Glasgow all at some time wrote about people of the lower classes in the South. Some of their people might correctly be classed as "poor whites" or even "poor white trash"; more often they are poorer small farmers, tenant farmers, backwoods hunters and trappers—people of limited education and straitened economic status, yet people possessing their own customs and codes of living. Sociologically and economically, the characters in stories by these authors have a similar classification with those of a number of other Southern novelists. Yet the casual reader—or even the more careful critic—might find it difficult to realize that many of the people in the works of Glasgow, Rawlings and Roberts were the neighbors and the cousins of Caldwell's *Tobacco Road* degenerates or of Stribling's hill folk. One of the essential differences in the portrayal of the poorer white people of the South by various writers of fiction lies in their treatment of the physical surroundings and the historical traditions of these people. Too often, especially in the more sensational and violent Southern stories, the people seem to exist in a vacuum. It is difficult to see Caldwell's people as human beings or to think of them with any sympathy because they appear to have so little connection with any actual world of humanity. On the other hand, Glasgow, Rawlings, and Roberts made place and time of the utmost significance. The lives of their people and the reader's experience are enriched because of this. Nor was this done at the expense of reality. These Southern authors have proved that poor folk, even those degraded and evil, can be shown with understanding and appreciation for what their lives actually mean for them in their daily and yearly surroundings, generation after generation. They have shown that the fact that backwoods, hill country, and tenant farming people live in a different way and perhaps farther from the authors or the readers is not a reason for treating them as peculiar specimens under a microscope, to be examined, marveled at, and regarded with scorn, laughter, or horror. They have seen poor people in their own environment, in all senses of that word, and have sought to portray their lives in all the manifold significance and in all the involvement with time and place. Hence the lower class characters in the stories of Miss Roberts, Mrs. Rawlings, and Miss Glasgow almost inevitably possess a rounded reality, an individuality and an appeal to the understanding of the reader, which are largely lacking when such people are portrayed as though they existed only as statistical items or subjects for raw anecdotes. In other words, their people are persons rather than monsters.

Of these three writers, Mrs. Rawlings probably gives more completely detailed descriptions of the physical environment of her backwoods people who live in the scrub country of Florida. She tells of everything which affects the lives of the characters, as well as that which had been the experience of these people's ancestors. So completely are Mrs. Rawlings characters involved in their surroundings and their environment in them that it is difficult to imagine their living elsewhere or, indeed, to imagine them other than as they are shown and where they are shown. The treatment of the Baxters, the central characters in Mrs. Rawlings' most popular work, *The Yearling*, is significant in these respects. The Baxters are very poor people of the Florida backwoods; they live from the slim proceeds of the little they can raise on their small clearing or from trapping and hunting. Yet because they are shown in such close relation to their environment, one comes to understand and appreciate the richness of their lives despite the difficulties, deprivations and harshness which they experience. Even the Baxters' neighbors, the Forresters, with all their slovenliness and downright orneriness, their occasional resemblance to caricatures of backwoodsmen or to the exaggerated woods people of some of the old Southwest humor, never actually lose their humanity nor the reader's sympathy. Though they seem a bit less civilized than the Baxters, a little wilder, they so clearly belong to their place and so completely fit into the life of the woods and swamps that one understands them even though he may find them unpleasant. Obviously, this close integration of time, place, and character in a work of fiction is very largely a matter of the overall treatment of these elements throughout a story, with constant care and understanding of their significance for the work as a whole. Something of Mrs. Rawlings' more explicit treatment of setting may be evident in the following passage from "A Crop of Beans":

> When a stranger—a Georgia truck driver or a platform buyer—asked Lige his business, he answered with a mustered defiance:
> "I'm a bean man!"
> It was true. The long hours he gave to the Widow Sellers' rich farms had no meaning beyond their moment. In mid-afternoon he hurried off to his own field, sweaty and excited to turn furrows, to plant, to cultivate, to hoe, to harvest.
> The quick growth of the crop stirred him. One week, the sandy loam lay golden, its expanse passive for the reception of the seed. The next week, the clearing in the hammock was covered with cotyledons, pale-green and pushing, like twin sails dotting a tawny sea. In forty-eight days the first crop was ready for picking. The emerald bushes crowded one another in the straight rows. The long beans hung like pendants, butter-yellow if they were wax, jade green if Giant Stringless or Red Valentine.
> The earth responded to him. When he and the soil were not interfered with, they made beans as fine as old man Tainter, who kept a wagon-load of niggers and bought fertilizer by the carload.
> He was betrayed constantly by elements beyond his control. He fared no worse than the other growers, but the common misfortunes struck more implacably. Men who could borrow money for seed and fertilizer and rations, who were free to do other farming or stock raising, made out more or less comfortably until the inevitable time when a good crop sold on a high market. There was a finality about his loss of a crop. (*When the Whippoorwill—*, pp. 7-8.)

All the elements of Lige's environment, his life in his time and place, are here revealed in their full significance, yet with evident economy. Lige belongs as much to his fields and his bean crops as they do to him; indeed, he is more truly possessed by his environment and used by it than otherwise.

Elizabeth Madox Roberts used place, as she did time, in such a way that the physical world of her characters assumes almost an extra dimension, a spiritual atmosphere and air of being carried above and beyond ordinary, mundane affairs. This might seem to mean that Miss Roberts treated scene so that it assumed a mysterious air of unreality that would disqualify the settings and the stories from any comparison with fiction of an evidently realistic sort. Yet her stories tell of probable, even commonplace, events in the lives of plain, though certainly not uninteresting, farm people; the action of these stories takes place, for the most part, in the hills and valleys of mid-Kentucky in recent times. A reader familiar with that state might be able to identify the precise location of these farms, streams and villages; he is not invited to do so. Rather there is an evocation of the country scene in which these lives pass so that the woods, fields, roads, and streams acquire a special quality all their own, breathe their own air, and shine with their own peculiar light. Miss Roberts exercises a fictional magic of a sort that seems to throw an enchantment about her stories of country folk, these store-keepers, millers, farmers, kind and cruel, calm and violent. This enchantment suggests most nearly the world of the folk songs, a world in which ordinary people and the things of their lives take on a magic glow without being any the less real, any the less material. Isolated quotations will scarcely illustrate this treatment of time and place, for it is involved in the whole work of art in such of Miss Roberts' novels as *A Buried Treasure, The Time of Man,* and *Black Is My True-love's Hair* (where the ballad reference is directly suggested by the title). In these and other stories the novelist seems to have set before herself the problem of taking the most ordinary, the most humble folk in the Kentucky farm country and of telling stories of their lives which never violate the concrete, everyday probabilities, yet in which these people, their daily actions, and the very land on which they live should take on something of "the light that never was on land or sea." These people and their country, so treated, acquire a spiritual stature that carries them into the realm of high poetry. This may be both the clue and the description of Miss

Roberts' achievement: that she has worked with the sustained creative imagination of the poet to create novels having a lyric quality, an atmosphere of ideal beauty enveloping them, yet never lacking the solid reality, the motion, the dynamic aliveness of dramatic scene, narrative sweep, and vivid character portrayal necessary for successful fiction. Miss Roberts' secret may have been in her ability to awaken the land to consciousness while stimulating her readers to a realization of the deep and inmost meanings of time and place in the lives of the people who inhabited that land.

Southern fiction of the highest artistic distinction gives the reader a vivid, intense awareness of human life. The best Southern novels are those that are quick in every element that has entered into their creation. The scene breathes the very air of those who walk the land, step along the streets, or move through the rooms of the houses. In the best of her novels Ellen Glasgow achieved such integration of place and people. It is evident in the worn-out fields of *The Voice of the People* as well as in the sleepy village of that novel, in the tobacco growing and the bleak dwelling place of the Blakes in *The Deliverance,* in the old streets of a once fashionable neighborhood in *The Sheltered Life,* now deserted by most of the "good families" and cursed by the miasma of industrial intrusion, and it is notably evident in the pages of Miss Glasgow's most widely read novel, *Barren Ground.* It must be emphasized once more that this treatment of place is almost inevitably a matter of the whole conception of the work and the over-all projection of the meaning of the setting into the lives of the characters. This passage, however, may suggest Miss Glasgow's understanding of this problem and her successful evocation of the meaning of her setting:

> Bare, starved, desolate, the country closed in about her. The last train of the day had gone by without stopping, and the station of Pedlar's Mill was as lonely as the abandoned fields by the track. From the bleak horizon, where the flatness created an illusion of immensity, the broomsedge was spreading in a smothered fire over the melancholy brown of the landscape. Under the falling snow, which melted as soon as it touched the earth, the colour was veiled and dim; but when the sky changed the broomsedge changed with it. On clear mornings the waste places were cinnamon-red in the sunshine. Beneath scudding clouds the plumes of the bent

grasses faded to ivory. During the long spring rains, a film of yellow-green stole over the burned ground. At autumn sunsets, when the red light searched the country, the broom-sedge caught fire from the afterglow and blazed out in a splendour of colour. Then the meeting of earth and sky dissolved in the flaming mist of the horizon.

At these quiet seasons, the dwellers near Pedlar's Mill felt scarcely more than a tremor on the surface of life. But on stormy days, when the wind plunged like a hawk from the swollen clouds, there was a quivering in the broomsedge, as if coveys of frightened partridges were flying from the pursuer. Then the quivering would become a ripple and the ripple would swell presently into rolling waves. The straw would darken as the gust swooped down, and brighten as it sped on to the shelter of scrub pine and sassafras bushes. And while the wind bewitched the solitude, a vague restlessness would stir in the hearts of living things on the farms, of men, women, and animals. "Broomsedge ain't jest wild stuff. It's a kind of fate," old Matthew Fairlamb used to say. (*Barren Ground*, pp. 3-4.)

Here, as so often elsewhere, the physical world of these Virginia farmers and village people in Ellen Glasgow's fiction has been subjected to the transforming touch of the artist's imagination. Here, as was her custom, she enabled the reader to see the beauty even in the bleakness of a land dull to the blinded eyes of minds shackled by unawakened souls. Yet her treatment of scene was never that of another sort of blindness, the willful idealism that evades all realities which violate the pleasant aspects of life. Miss Glasgow succeeded, rather, in enabling readers to comprehend the meaning of time and place for all people who are truly alive, to understand the life-in-death that must result for all those who have lost the life-giving connection with their environment, to realize the possibilities of a mental and spiritual quickness through an intense awareness of people in their relation to the realities and the idealities of their place and time.

Southern authors of fiction in this century have written of greatly varying lives and of people of highly disparate interests. The South has been little more than a name for some of these writers, and their fiction has little concern with either an actual or an imagined country. For others the South has been so utterly a world of their imagination that their setting has slight relation to any South of factual realities. For still others the South has meant very largely the reality of a statistical report; flat characters have been twitched about a flat and unmoving setting. The true artists among Southern writers of fiction, however, have realized the meaning of Southern time and place for the people in their stories, have blended the elements of setting with character, have realized that for human beings time and place are significant, and have evoked that significance for their readers.

III. The Novelists Of The South

WILLIAM VAN O'CONNOR

Protestantism in Yoknapatawpha County

Once having recognized that Faulkner is concerned with the spirit of Protestantism as a part of the Southern mores, one is surprised at the frequency with which he examines it. Sometimes it is the key to a short story, sometimes it clarifies the motivation of a type of Southern character, sometimes it is an incidental sentence that contributes to a description of a town or country landscape, and on two important occasions it is the thematic center of whole novels. Faulkner does not treat the Protestant spirit, of course, as a simple, readily characterizable factor in the Southern mores. His view of it and the tone he evokes depend upon the context, the specific character and subject. He is prepared to find virtues in the Protestant tradition, but he is also willing to be harshly critical of it, or parts of it.

A humorous treatment is "Uncle Willy," [1] a story, told by a fourteen-year-old boy, of righteous church people who decide to cure the likeable and orderly but ineffectual old druggist of his forty-year habit of taking dope:

> But they made him quit. It didn't take them long. It began one Sunday morning and it was finished by the next Friday; we had just sat down in our class and Mr. Barbour had just begun, when all of a sudden Reverend Schultz, the minister, was there, leaning over Uncle Willy and already hauling him out of his seat when we looked around, hauling him up and saying in that tone in which preachers speak to fourteen-year-old boys that I don't believe even pansy boys

[1] *American Mercury*, XXXVI (October, 1935), 156-68. Reprinted in *Collected Stories*, 1951.

like: "Now, Brother Christian, I know you will hate to leave
Brother Barbour's class, but let's you and I go in and join
Brother Miller and the men and hear what he can tell us on
this beautiful and heartwarming text," and Uncle Willy still
trying to hold back and looking around at us with his run-
together eyes blinking and saying plainer than if he had
spoke it: "What's this? What's this, fellows? What are
they fixing to do to me?"

And a paragraph later:

Then Sunday school was over and we went out to wait
for him, to go to the store and eat the ice cream. And he
didn't come out. He didn't come out until church was over
too, the first time that he had ever stayed for church that any
of us knew of — that anybody knew of, papa told me later
— coming out with Mrs. Merridew on one side of him and
Reverend Schultz on the other still holding him by the arm
and he looking around at us again with his eyes saying again,
only desperate now: "Fellows, what's this? What's this,
fellows?" and Reverend Schultz shoving him into Mrs.
Merridew's car and Mrs. Merridew saying, loud, like she was
in the pulpit: "Now, Mr. Christian, I'm going to take you
right out to my house and I'm going to fix you a nice glass of
cool lemonade and then we will have a nice chicken dinner
and then you are going to take a nice nap in my hammock
and then Brother and Sister Schultz are coming out and we
will have some nice ice cream," and Uncle Willy saying,
"No. Wait, ma'am, wait! Wait! I got to go to the store
and fill a prescription I promised this morning —"

Faulkner's sympathies are with Uncle Willy and obviously he finds
sanctimoniousness extremely offensive.

Preacher Whitfield of *As I Lay Dying* holds a high place among
the despicable creatures Faulkner has created. He is treated in a
passage taut with contempt, not because he has sinned with Addie
Bundren, another man's wife, but because he is so quick to allow his
rhetorical gifts to create for himself the role of a prodigal son and
to glory in it, until he learns that, Addie dead, no one knows of his
sin. God, he says, has already forgiven him, so there is no need for
public confession. Cora Tull, a comic figure in the same story, has a
somewhat similar genius for rationalizing her actions and her fre-

quently madly reasoned opinions. But as a simpleton she is free from the kind of irony which Faulkner brings to bear on Whitfield. One has no difficulty accepting the report from Oxford, Mississippi, that at the time Faulkner was scoutmaster, "hard shell Baptist opinion considered him unfit for the post." [2]

Faulkner is troubled by the cruelty that frequently accompanies righteousness, the willing persecution of those who seem or are unrighteous. In *The Wild Palms* there are a doctor and his wife who act partly out of a sense of human decency but also out of a grim and perversely enjoyed righteousness. The following is a description of their watching the young couple who have rented the cottage next to them:

> She [the doctor's wife] did not say "They are not married" though it was in both their minds. They both knew that, once it was said aloud between them, he would turn the renters out. Yet they both refused to say it and for more reason than because when he turned them out he would feel conscience-bound to return the rent money; more than this on his part anyway, who was thinking *They had only twenty dollars. And that was three days ago. And there is something wrong with her,* the doctor now speaking louder than the provincial protestant, the Baptist born. And something (perhaps the doctor here too) talking louder than the provincial Baptist in her too because this morning she waked the doctor, calling him from the window where she stood shapeless in the cotton nightgown shaped like a shroud and with her gray hair screwed into papers, to show him the man coming up the beach at sunrise with his belted faggot of driftwood. And when he (the doctor) came home at noon she had the gumbo made, an enormous quantity of it, enough for a dozen people, made with that grim Samaritan husbandry of good women, as if she took a grim and vindictive and masochistic pleasure in the fact that the Samaritan deed would be performed at the price of its remainder which would sit invincible and inexhaustible on the stove while days accumulated and passed, to be warmed and rewarmed and then rewarmed until consumed by two people who did not even like it. . . .

[2] Sidney Alexander, "The Nobel Prize Comes to Mississippi," *Commentary*, XII, 2 (August, 1951), p. 177.

And when the doctor gives the gumbo to the young couple he does it as an "uncompromising Christian deed performed not with sincerity or pity but through duty."

Sometimes Faulkner is aware of the churches as a part of the landscape, and therefore as a part of the character of the people. Thus, in *Intruder in the Dust*: "he remembered the tall slender spires which had said Peace and the squatter utilitarian belfries which said Repent and he remembered one which even said Beware but this one said simply: Burn." In a number of stories Faulkner is undoubtedly saying that the principles Protestantism has added to the mores often make it hard to experience "Peace," and that deep within it, out of the old Calvinist heritage, is a terrifying willingness to say "simply: Burn."

In the genealogy of the Compsons, 1699-1945, which Faulkner did especially for *The Portable Faulkner*, edited by Malcolm Cowley, he thus characterized Quentin Compson:

> Who loved not the idea of the incest which he would not commit, but some presbyterian concept of its eternal punishment: he, not God, could by that means cast himself and his sister both into hell, where he could guard her forever and keep her forevermore intact amid the eternal fires.

It would require a very considerable distortion to find any aspect of the spirit of Protestantism at the center of *The Sound and the Fury*, in which Quentin figures so prominently. But in *Absalom, Absalom!*, which is narrated by Quentin, one aspect of Protestantism seems very close indeed to being the exact center of the novel.

In *Absalom, Absalom!* the spirit of Southern Protestantism is opposed to Latin Catholicism, the former exhibiting a stern, inflexible morality and unbending principles, the latter a more relaxed morality and a willingness to satisfy human desires at the expense of principle. At one place in the novel, there is a long passage in which the Protestant Mississippi background of Henry Sutpen is contrasted with what he sees in Catholic New Orleans:

> I can imagine him, with his puritan heritage — that heritage peculiarly Anglo-Saxon — of fierce proud mysticism and that ability to be ashamed of ignorance and inexperience, in that city foreign and paradoxical, with its atmosphere at once

fatal and languorous, at once feminine and steel-hard —
this grim and humorless yokel out of a granite heritage where
even the houses, let alone clothing and conduct, are built
in the image of a jealous and sadistic Jehovah, put suddenly
down in a place whose denizens had created their All-
Powerful and his supporting hierarchy-chorus of beautiful
saints and handsome angels in the image of their houses and
personal ornaments and voluptuous lives. Yes, I can imagine how Bon led up to it, to the shock: the skill, the calculation, preparing Henry's puritan mind as he would have
prepared a cramped and rocky field and planted it and raised
the crop which he wanted. It would be the fact of the ceremony, regardless of what kind, that Henry would balk at:
Bon knew this.

The two societies are juxtaposed to show that Henry Sutpen lives
by the letter of the law, inside rigid mores. Charles Bon has a child
by an octoroon mistress. Though in effect his mistress and not his
wife, Charles Bon has gone through a marriage ceremony with her.
He does not look on the marriage as really binding. But Henry, who
has no problem accepting the custom of Negro mistresses, balks at
the formality of marriage. Marriage involves the letter of the law,
the fixed principle. And though horrified at first at the idea of
marriage to a Negress, he none the less sees it as binding, and is
equally horrified that Charles Bon, a Catholic of sorts, is capable
of ignoring it and wanting to enter into a new marriage, a new formality, with a white woman, Henry's sister.

We cannot go into all the details of the plot here, but we may
say that the entire story can be read with this incident as a clue to its
meaning. As a part of the social context of Negro and white relations is this inflexibility of principle. Charles Bon, it develops, is not
only Henry Sutpen's half brother, but also has some Negro blood.
Thomas Sutpen had married the daughter of a plantation owner on a
Caribbean island, not knowing there was any Negro blood in the
family. Upon discovering it, he had left her and their son, Charles.
The action of the story turns upon the son, who is the adult Charles
Bon, trying to move, if only temporarily, inside the circle of his
father's white world, the world in which Thomas Sutpen accepts
formalities and legalities. (Charles Bon is using the engagement
to his half sister as a threat or weapon in case he is not accepted by

his father.)   One of the legalities, one of the principles, is that the
Negro belongs to a lesser order of human beings and therefore is
not to be recognized as a son.   Charles Bon's human need, outside his
father's fixed principles or formalized fiction, is to be recognized, if
only by a gesture, as Thomas Sutpen's son.   But Thomas Sutpen, like
Henry, his white son, is unable to relax the principle.   He refuses
to make the gesture, thereby precipitating a string of disastrous events.
In other words, it is possible to study the thematic line of *Absalom,
Absalom!* as having its origin and center in Faulkner's belief that the
Protestant or puritan spirit is one of the most significant factors, even
the key factor, in the tragedy of Negro and white relationships.   This
theme had been even more explicitly worked out and elaborated in
the earlier (and probably greater) novel, *Light in August.*

II

If one does not perceive that the Calvinist spirit is the central
issue of *Light in August,* the novel of necessity will seem confused
in theme.   It is episodic in structure, but the meaning is clear.*   The
Civil War and the black shadow of slavery do, as some critics insist,
suffuse the book.   It is proper enough to observe the position of
Hightower in the story, to relive with him the imagined scenes of
galloping horses, burning buildings, the wounded and dead of the
Civil War — these do live on into the 1920's, even in the minds of
those less crippled by such memories than the defrocked old minister.
But the greater force, in which the War and the black shadow are
caught up, is Calvinism, and, larger than it, rigidity of principle and
harshness of spirit; and it is this force that menaces Joe Christmas,
the putative Negro, and that persecutes Hightower.   Byron Bunch
and Lena Grove are more than comic relief; they are proof that one
need not succumb to such a force.

The irony of the name Joe Christmas is noted by every reader
of *Light in August.*   (And it is obvious that certain other names in
the novel have their appropriateness also — Gail Hightower, Calvin

---

* Malcolm Cowley and others say that the novel is two separate stories, the Lena
Grove-Byron Bunch story and the Joe Christmas-Joanna Burden-Hightower-Jefferson
story. This, I think, is not so. There are three strands to the novel (1) Lena Grove-
Byron Bunch, (2) Hightower and (3) Joe Christmas, all of which relate to the theme of
rigidity of spirit as opposed to the need for acceptance of human fallibility and the
need for pity and sympathy.

Burden, Bobbie [Barbara] Allen, and so on.)   Certainly the major significance in the name is the irony of his being pursued and harassed throughout his life by voices of Christian righteousness, Old Doc Hines, his mad grandfather, McEachern, his stern foster parent, and Joanna Burden, his guilt haunted lover, and finally the society itself insofar as its religion, as Hightower claims, drives the community to *"crucifixion of themselves and one another."**

Euphues Hines is certain he is doing God's will in killing the man who had seduced his daughter, in refusing to allow a doctor to assist his daughter in the birth (after which she dies) of her illegitimate son, in getting a job at the orphanage where he has secretly put the boy, then taking up a position as a threatening presence at the edge of the boy's consciousness, in allowing the boy to be adopted by Simon McEachern, and, twenty-five years later when Joe Christmas, now a murderer, is captured in Mottstown, in screaming that he should be lynched.   Through it all runs the assurance that he is God's instrument.   One of his mad speeches is a bitter parody of the doctrine of predestination:

"It was the Lord.   *He* was there.   Old Doc Hines give God His chance too.   The Lord told old Doc Hines what to do and old Doc Hines done it.   Then the Lord said to old Doc Hines, 'You watch now.   Watch My will a-workin.' And old Doc Hines watched and heard the mouths of little children, of God's own fatherless and motherless, putting His words and knowledge into their mouths even when they couldn't know it since they were without sin yet, even the girl ones without sin and bitchery yet: Nigger! Nigger! in the innocent mouths of little children.   'What did I tell you?' God said to Old Doc Hines.   'And now I've set My will to working and now I'm gone.   There aint enough sin here to keep Me busy because what do I care for the fornications of a slut, since that is a part of My purpose too,' and old Doc Hines said, 'How is the fornications of a slut a part of Your

---

* Joe Christmas is also the victim of another kind of excess, the bypassing of deserved punishment.   When as a five year old he steals and eats toothpaste, he expects to be punished, but the dietician, who believes he has witnessed the intercourse between her and a young intern, tries to buy him off.   Later Mrs. McEachern attempts to scheme with him to outwit the restrictions and rigidity of her husband, but young Christmas is more at ease with the excesses of McEachern than he is with the softness and weakness, as he sees it, of Mrs. McEachern.   In other words, he wants to live inside a system of rules and sanctions.   He associates softness and blind devotion with women and is contemptuous of them.   His tragedy, caused by the severity which he has suffered, causes him to reject love, and he gives back violence for violence.   One cannot afford, however, to sentimentalize Joe Christmas.   He is a victim and he is sacrificed, but he is also a sadist, a pervert, and a murderer.

purpose too?' and God said, 'You wait and see. Do you think it is just chanceso that I sent that young doctor to be the one that found My abomination laying wrapped in that blanket on that doorstep that Christmas night? Do you think it was just chanceso that the Madam should have been away that night and give them young sluts the chance and call to name him Christmas in sacrilege of My Son? So I am gone now, because I have set My will a-working and I can leave you to watch it.'

Twenty years after the event Joe Christmas knew that the most lasting mark from his boyhood had been made the Sunday McEachern whipped him for failing to learn his Presbyterian catechism. The punishment had been given in all righteousness. McEachern's "voice was not unkind. It was not human, personal, at all. It was just cold, implacable, like written or printed words." Several times, always after the passage of a full hour, the boy was whipped again. McEachern sat stiffly watching the boy, "one hand on his knee and the silver watch in the other palm, his clean, bearded face as firm as carved stone, his eyes ruthless, cold, but not unkind." Later the man knelt with the boy to ask "that Almighty be as magnanimous as himself" in forgiving the boy's disobedience. That day Christmas learned silent resistance. And that evening, in refusing food brought by Mrs. McEachern — dumping the dishes on the floor — he learned how to refuse sympathy, to harden himself against the feminine world. He felt she was trying to make him cry. "Then she thinks they would have had me." Joe Christmas was almost eighteen before he learned how to outwit McEachern in his niggardly denials of the flesh. A waitress, Bobbie Allen, also a semi-professional whore, is the first person from whom he accepts any sympathy, and he does this at first because of sexual desire for her. But McEachern destroys this relationship by following them to a country dance where, like the "representative of a wrathful and retributive Throne," he calls her "harlot" and "Jezebel." Joe strikes him down with a chair and after stealing a small amount of money from Mrs. McEachern runs away. But Bobbie Allen is offended at the treatment she has ha (Faulkner makes high comedy of her indignation at being calle "harlot"), screams at him that he is a nigger, and allows her friend to beat him up.

The climactic parts of Joe Christmas' life are lived in Jefferson where he becomes the lover of Joanna Burden, the spinster descendant of an abolitionist family from New Hampshire. The family had been Unitarians (Faulkner probably made a mistake in designating it as Unitarian) with the "agonized conscience" described by George Santayana in a well known passage. They believed

> that sin exists, that sin is punished, and that it is beautiful that sin should exist to be punished. The heart of Calvinism is therefore divided between tragic concern at its own miserable condition, and tragic exultation about the universe at large. . . . Human nature, it feels, is totally depraved: to have the instincts and motives that we necessarily have is a great scandal, and we must suffer for it; but that scandal is requisite, since otherwise the serious importance of being as we ought to be would not have been vindicated.

Her grandfather and brother had been killed in Jefferson by Colonel Sartoris for "stirring up the Negroes." And she had heard such insistently held opinions as this of her grandfather's: "He got off on Lincoln and slavery and dared any man there to deny that Lincoln and the Negro and Moses and the children of Israel were the same, and that the Red Sea was just the blood that had to be spilled in order that the black race might cross into the Promised Land."

In conversations with Joe Christmas she rehearses the actions and long held opinions in her family that establish their being outside the Latin desire to be at ease with the world. (In fact, there are passages in her story of the family history curiously similar to those in *Absalom, Absalom!* in which the two worlds, Protestant Mississippi and Catholic New Orleans, are contrasted.) Joe Christmas knows that her helping the Negro is a duty undertaken, but that it is abstract and impersonal. She acts not out of sympathy for other human beings but out of an obligation to carry out God's design in a depraved world. It is a helpless world, and the Negro's plight finally is irremediable. Her father tells her: "You must struggle, rise. But in order to rise, you must raise the shadow with you. . . . You can never lift it to your level." The suffering of the Negro *and* the guilt over slavery are the outward signs of a terribly guilt-ridden world — and both are permanent. Joe Christmas believes that the demonic quality of her sexual perversions are the excesses inevitable to one who believes in the New England biblical hell and who feeds her emotion-starved body in spite of it. Christmas' own life, "for all its anonymous promiscuity, had been conventional enough, as a life of healthy and normal sin usually is." Faulkner describes her corruption as it appears to Joe Christmas:

> At first it shocked him: the abject fury of the New England glacier exposed suddenly to the fire of the New England biblical hell. Perhaps he was aware of the abnegation in it: the imperious and fierce urgency that concealed an actual despair at frustrate and irrevocable years, which she appeared to attempt to compensate each night as if she believed that it would be the last night on earth by damning herself forever to the hell of her forefathers, by living not alone in sin but in filth. She had an avidity for the forbidden wordsymbols; an insatiable appetite for the sound of them on his tongue and on her own. She revealed the terrible and impersonal curosity of a child about forbidden subjects and objects; that rapt and tireless and detached interest of a surgeon in the physical body and its possibilities. And by day he would see the calm, coldfaced, almost manlike, almost middleaged woman who had lived for twenty years alone, without any feminine fears at all, in a lonely house in a neighborhood populated, when at all, by Negroes, who spent a certain portion of each day sitting tranquilly at a desk and writing tranquilly for the eyes of both youth and age the practical advice of a combined priest and banker and trained nurse.

Driven mad by a sense of lost youth and her fear of damnation, she none the less holds unquestioningly to her own beliefs. Like Euphues Hines she sees herself as God's instrument — that it is God, not she, insisting that Joe Christmas pray:

> They looked at one another. "Joe," she said, "for the last time. I don't ask it. Remember that. Kneel with me."
> "No," he said. Then he saw her arms unfold and her right hand come forth from beneath the shawl. It held an old style, single action, cap-and-mall revolver almost as long and heavier than a small rifle. But the shadow of it and of her arm and hand on the wall did not waver at all, the shadow of both monstrous, the cocked hammer monstrous, back-hooked and viciously poised like the arched head of a

snake; it did not waver at all. And her eyes did not waver at all. They were as still as the round black ring of the pistol muzzle. But there was no heat in them, no fury. They were calm and still as all pity and all despair and all conviction. But he was not watching them. He was watching the shadowed pistol on the wall; he was watching when the cocked shadow of the hammer flicked away.

The pistol misfired. Then he killed her, almost severing the head from her body.

Following the murder, Christmas is hunted and finally caught. During the days he is a fugitive he is involved in a number of violent acts, one of which is especially appropriate to the theme the novel is dramatizing. It is the scene, reported by a member of the Negro congregation, in which Christmas breaks up a revival meeting:

> He [the member of the congregation] had come direct from a Negro church twenty miles away, where a revival meeting was in nightly progress. On the evening before, in the middle of a hymn, there had come a tremendous noise from the rear of the church, and turning the congregation saw a man standing in the door. The door had not been locked or even shut yet the man had apparently grasped it by the knob and hurled it back into the wall so that the sound crashed into the blended voices like a pistol shot....a woman began to shriek...."It's the devil! It's Satan himself." Then she ran, quite blind. She ran straight toward him and he knocked her down without stopping and stepped over her and went on, with the faces gaped for screaming falling away before him, straight to the pulpit and put his hand on the minister...."We could see Brother Bedenberry talking with him, trying to pacify him quiet, and him jerking at Brother Bedenberry and slapping his face with his hand ....And he begun to curse, hollering it out, at the folks, and he cursed God louder than the women screeching . . ."

It is as though Christmas knows, and perhaps we are to infer that he does know, that the church, far from making his life easier, is one of the agents of his destruction.

The tragedy of Hightower is presented less directly than that of Christmas, mostly as remembered experiences.* Hightower's speculations upon his own history and the character of Jefferson furnish most of the explicit commentary on the significance of the action. We learn that he was born to middleaged parents, an invalid mother and a fifty-year-old father, a minister and doctor, who though strongly opposed to slavery served four years in the Confederate army. A point is made about the father's character by stating that he would neither eat the food nor sleep in a bed prepared by a Negro.

Hence during the war and while he was absent from home, his wife had no garden save what she could make herself or with the infrequent aid of neighbors. And this aid the husband would not allow her to accept for the reason that it could not be repaid in kind. "God will provide," he said.

"Provide what? Dandelions and ditch weeds?"

"Then He will give us the bowels to digest them."

Hightower was born after the war, inheriting organs which "required the unflagging care of a Swiss watch." As a child he was fascinated, bewitched by the war and lived with "those phantoms who loomed heroic and tremendous against a background of thunder and smoke and torn flags." Thinking of it caused him to "experience a kind of hushed and triumphant terror which left him a little sick." Hightower's grandfather, a gruff man who smelled of whiskey and cigars, had greeted his son's bride with this observation: " 'I reckon you'll do,' he said. His eyes were bluff and bold, but kind. 'All the sanctimonious cuss wants anyway is somebody that can sing alto out of a Presbyterian hymnbook, where even the good Lord himself could not squeeze any music.' " The boy and his invalid mother looked upon the father as foreign to them, almost an intruder. One of the grandfather's amusements was to turn church revivals held in a grove into "a week of amateur horse racing while to a dwindling congregation gaunt, fanaticfaced country preachers thundered anathema from the rustic pulpit at his oblivious and unregenerate head." The grandfather had been killed in "Van Dorn's cavalry raid to destroy Grant's stores in Jefferson." This too was one of young Hightower's torturing phantoms, causing him shudderings of delight. His own father, although alive, was also a kind of phantom to the boy. Hightower

---

* Hightower's relationship with Christmas is never made quite explicit, but there is surely a strong hint of homosexual relations. In the Modern Library edition (1950), see pages 61, 68, 77-78, 87 (chap. 4), 340-343 (chap. 16), and 406 (chap. 19).

lived in a twilight vision of a cavalry troop galloping into Jefferson.

In the seminary, to which he was drawn by its promise of peace, he told himself repeatedly — "God must call me to Jefferson because my life died there, was shot from the saddle of a galloping horse in a Jefferson street one night twenty years before it was ever born." That the seminary had not proved to be the sanctuary for the "garment-worried spirit" he had hoped for did not trouble Hightower greatly because it was merely a preparation for his getting to Jefferson. In the seminary he met his wife. She was the daughter of one of the ministers who was a member of the faculty. Hightower did not live in the everyday world and did not know that she could have lived there all her life and not be beautiful, nor did he know that for "three years her eyes had watched him with almost desperate calculation, like those of a harassed gambler." Once she spoke suddenly of marriage and escape.

> "Escape?" he said. "Escape from what?"
> "This!" she said. He saw her face for the first time as a living face, as a mask before desire and hatred; wrung blind, headlong with passion. Not stupid: just blind, reckless, desperate. "All of it! All! All!"

Hightower's congregation in Jefferson had thought him a little mad when from the pulpit in his rapt, eager voice he preached of God, salvation, his grandfather and galloping horses. Looking back at his life Hightower said he had failed his congregation because he had not preached to them of mercy, pity and the forgiveness of human frailty. He knew too that he had failed his wife. Eventually she had scandalized Jefferson by not attending church, going away suspiciously for weekends, once screaming at her husband during his sermon, and finally jumping from a hotel room in Memphis where she had been registered under a fictitious name as someone else's wife. Higtower had refused to resign and for a time, before the parishioners locked him out, he had preached and prayed in an empty church. The congregation wanted him to leave Jefferson and gave him a sum of money, but he refused to leave and settled on a little side street. He remained even after he had been taken out of town by the K.K.K., tied to a tree and beaten unconscious. The last trial Hightower is subjected to is a request from Byron Bunch (who is scheming for his own purposes) and Christmas' grandmother, Mrs.

Hines, for him to swear that Christmas could not have killed Miss Burden because he had spent the night of the murder and many other nights with Hightower. The old minister refuses to suffer this last outrage, but when Percy Grimm pursues Christmas into Hightower's house he does try to prevent the murder by declaring that Christmas had spent that night with him.

Because Hightower, despite his many weaknesses, was capable of nobility of motive and action, his view of the church, stated shortly before his death, must be stressed:

> It seems to him that he has seen it all the while: that that which is destroying the Church is not the outward groping of those within it nor the inward groping of those without, but the professionals who control it and who have removed the bells from its steeples. He seems to see them, endless, without order, empty, symbolical, bleak, skypointed not with ecstasy or passion but in adjuration, threat, and doom. He seems to see the churches of the world like a rampart, like one of those barricades of the middleages planted with dead and sharpened stakes, against truth and against that peace in which to sin and be forgiven which is the life of man.

Earlier in the story Hightower had singled out one service, that on Sunday evening, as the only one during which "there is something of that peace which is the promise and end of the church." It is an hour of faith and hope. Hightower looks forward to this hour in the week when from his darkened window he will watch the people move toward the church. On Sunday nights during the summer he loves to listen to the organ tones rich and resonant. But on the Sunday before the lynching of Joe Christmas he thinks to himself:

> Yet even then the music has still a quality stern and implacable, deliberate and without passion so much as immolation, pleading, asking, for not love, not life, forbidding it to others, demanding in sonorous tones death, as though death were the boon, like all Protestant music. . . . Listening to it he seems to hear within it the apotheosis of his own history, his own land, his own environed blood: Pleasure, ecstasy they cannot seem to bear. Their escape from it is in violence, in drinking and fighting and praying; catastrophe too, the violence identical and apparently inescapable. *And so why*

*should not their religion drive them to crucifixion of them-
selves and one another?*

Of the lynching, he says:

> And they will do it gladly, gladly. . . . Since to pity him
> would be to admit self-doubt and to hope for and need pity
> themselves. They will do it gladly, gladly. That's what
> is so terrible, terrible.

Hightower was right about how it would be done. Percy Grimm,
another of the avatars of self-righteousness, is the town's instrument
in the killing of Joe Christmas. He does not act in the name of deity,
but he moves with the same aura of assured virtue. He sees himself
the agent of pure patriotism — which in the context means the protection of each detail of the mores, whatever its source. Faulkner
insists on the righteousness of Grimm: "There was nothing vengeful
about him either, no fury, no outrage" as he pursued Joe Christmas
across ditches, behind cabins, and finally into Hightower's house.
And the righteousness is further insisted upon in the description of
his voice when Hightower, lying to prevent the lynching, says Christmas
had spent the night of the murder with him: " 'Jesus Christ,' Grimm
cried, his young voice clear and outraged like that of a young priest."
Then the outrage turns into an insane kind of fury (like that of Hines
or Joanna Burden) and Grimm castrates Joe Christmas with a butcher
knife.

Lena Grove and Byron Bunch are not merely the comic sub-plot,*
relief from the terrible anguish of the lynching. They are a part of
the complexity of the community, and by what they are and the way
they act they insinuate powerfully what is wrong with the community.
Only rarely does Faulkner allow them to comment explicitly on the
other part of the action, as when Lena Grove sees in Hightower's
face "that ruthlessness which she had seen in the face of a few good
people, usually men." Neither she nor Byron Bunch is the intelligent
refractor, in Henry James' terms, of the action; it is by being what they
are that they imply a commentary.

Lena is a creature of faith, humility and endurance. Setting out
from Alabama in her eighth month of pregnancy and with only thirty-

---

* It is quite possible that Faulkner takes from Shakespeare his episodic structure
and free intermingling of characters from two different levels.

five cents, she hopefully expects to find her seducer. In her trustful-
ness and willingness to be helped, she accepts the attentions and assistance of many, including Bunch. Her manner causes the people she
meets, or most of them, to treat her in kind, generously, courteously.
But she is not without guile. She knows how to lead Byron about,
taking an almost but not quite innocent advantage of his abject
devotion. She belongs among those who are fallible but who live in
"tranquil obedience . . . to the good earth." She is a minor earth
goddess. Harshness of spirit and rigidity of principle are completely
foreign to her.

Burch (or Brown), the seducer of Lena, is characterless. He
stands outside the two groups that dominate the novel, those with the
religious beliefs that cause them to crucify their fellowman and those,
like Lena and Byron, with the kind of belief that makes existence
sufferable and even pleasant. He is a kind of Judas (and is called just
that) in his willingness to sacrifice his friend Joe Christmas, but actually he is amoral and therefore hardly human at all. Byron says Burch
"was just living on the country, like a locust." He has no pride in himself and he has no sense of responsibility. He is capable neither of
loyalty nor love.

Byron Bunch, on the other hand, has committed himself to the
moral life, to a Protestant orthodoxy. He is the friend of Hightower
(who however offers him the conventionally good man's advice to
avoid Lena), and he is a choir leader. Obviously a product of the
Protestant ethic, he is described as having "a still stubborn, ascetic
face: the face of a hermit who has lived for a long time in an empty
place where the sand blows." He believes in the sanctity of work,
that a man gets into mischief when he is not working; therefore he
works on Saturday afternoons and keeps a record of the hours he is
not working. He attempts to search out the truth and he worries
his conscience but he is never self-righteous. Except that he has
humor about himself, he belongs to the tradition of Piers Plowman
and of Bunyan's Christian, a kind of Protestant Everyman. Faulkner
identifies him as belonging to the hill people, the pine hill farmers,
and describes him as "small, non-descript, whom no man ever turned
to look at twice." He is the only significant character whose background is not explored. But Byron is free from the excesses of the
Protestant tradition. He is not in search of martyrdom, but he endures
the hardships that his sense of obligation tells him are his to accept.

WILLIAM FAULKNER 169

He can admit self-doubt, he can pity, and he is charitable. Faulkner describes him as acting kindly "as a reflex." He is fallible and, like Lena, capable of guile, but Byron Bunch believes in "that peace," as Hightower describes it, which results from sinning and being forgiven "which is the life of man."

That *Light in August* is not a sociological document is clear enough. The whole manner of its telling cries out that it is highly stylized: The complex and subtle patterns of imagery, the frequently exaggerated situations, the furiously mad or idyllically sane characters, the paralleling of details from the life of Christ until the death of Christmas seems a monstrous and grotesque irony, and so on. The variety of characters, the interplay of carefully selected episodes, as well as the furiously sustained and the sometimes facile flow of language establish the greatness of the novel as a work of art. A different sort of essay from this one might pay detailed attention to the nature of this stylization. Again it might be studied with an emphasis on the psychology of sex. But it is also necessary to examine, as we have done here, his primary subject matter, the relation of the Protestant spirit to the mores. It seems hardly necessary to observe that it is a mark of his genius that he can carry through the primary theme, the terrible irony that it is out of the religion itself that the lynching comes, without resting in it, and is able to introduce the complementary theme, that inside the religion one can also find direction, discipline and consolations.

ROBERT D. JACOBS

Faulkner's Tragedy Of Isolation

A young man named Quentin Compson tells his father that he has committed incest with his sister, trying to redeem her from putative sluttishness by alleging an act of such transcendent evil that it will isolate her—and him—"amid the pointing and the horror beyond the clean flame." Failing to preserve his pride in family he smashes his grandfather's watch, symbol of time and tradition, and isolates himself only, by suicide.

Joe Christmas, not quite so young, spends thirty years trying to escape from himself because he does not know whether he is black or white, slashing with equal fury at both races, rejecting all overtures of kindness with violence, reaching the symbolic height of his rebellion by cursing God in a Negro church whose congregation takes him for the Satan he has become in his rage at the scheme of things. Then he too evades responsibility by choosing death.

Not driven like these, Thomas Sutpen drives himself. He thinks that by simple exertion of the will, by courage, cleverness, and endurance he can impose his own scheme upon life. Divine justice or injustice does not concern him. He orders his own affairs, tears a mansion and domain out of the wilderness, chooses his consort, and proceeds to found a dynasty. But in his innocence, his ignorance of the nature of things, he thinks that he can go it alone. Those human beings who stand in the way of his scheme can be removed. He has no responsibility other than simple economic justice. He will rigorously discharge his debt to those who might consider that he has wronged them, and he will do it in cash. But within one lifetime his domain has reverted to the wilderness from which it was torn, the mansion he reared almost with his blood has burned down upon the head of his aged and dying son, a fratricide, and his sole descendant is an idiot mulatto, howling around the ruins.

These are the chief protagonists of William Faulkner's tragic drama, and in spite of their surface disparateness, they have a common ground: each tries in his own way to make himself a master of time; each in his solipsism fails in what Faulkner again and again has insisted is not the human burden but the human privilege, the capacity for "love and honor and pity and pride and compassion and sacrifice" (the Stockholm address). These are the "old universal truths." These represent the responsibility of humanity in time, and an attempt to escape time and responsibility, by smashing a watch, by suicide, by rejecting the human race, or by founding a dynasty, is foredoomed. It does not take time's embodiment, a scythe, beheading a ruthless Sutpen, to make us aware that Faulkner, perhaps the only writer of genuine tragedy today, believes in a moral universe. For Sutpen, of all Faulkner's figures, is captain of his soul. He works his own doom. As F. L. Lucas writes (*Tragedy*, 1928), "the deepest tragedy is not when men are struck down by the blow of chance or fate . . . but when their destruction is the work of those who wish them well or of their own unwitting hands."

Quentin Compson loved death, Faulkner wrote in his appendix to *The Sound and the Fury* (Modern Library edition). He did not love his sister's body but "some concept of Compson honor . . ." In his love of death and in his jealous protection of this "honor" he preferred incest (family sin) to promiscuity (public sin). He did not love "the idea of the incest which he would not commit, but some presbyterian concept of its eternal punishment: he, not God, could by that means cast himself and his sister both into hell, where he could guard her forever and keep her forevermore intact amid the eternal fires." It is hard to construe this comment as other than an assessment of pride. For all of Quentin Compson's gentleness to children, his love of the idiot Benjy, his agonizing over injustice, he is unwilling to leave God's business to God. He is the self-appointed guardian of his sister's honor, a meaningless honor because it is not based upon inner worth or dignity but only "temporarily supported by the minute fragile membrane of her maidenhead. . . ." Contrast this honor, this wrong kind of pride, with the honor of Sam Fathers, or even that of the runaway slave of "The Red Leaves," who did not need to be ashamed because he ran well, and one begins to have some idea of the piteous folly of Compson pride.

Because he is piteous, however, because his choice of usurpation involves evasion rather than challenge, Quentin Compson's story is not tragedy. He smashes the watch, futile gesture, not because Father had said "time is dead as long as it is being clicked off by little wheels" but because he wished to get out from under what Robert Penn Warren's Jack Burden (*All the King's Men*) called the "awful responsibility of Time."

To read Faulkner without some knowledge of the attitude toward individual responsibility, toward God, and toward history of the Southern Agrarian tradition is to run a risk of misreading him. To read him as totally within that tradition is to run an equal risk; but to date the best commentator on Faulkner has been former Agrarian Robert Penn Warren, himself undeniably influenced by the Mississippian's work. The misreadings, which seem even more incredible when one still finds them seriously proposed (see Henry Steele Commager's comment on Faulkner in *The American Mind*, 1952), usually center around what has been called Faulkner's "naturalism," his allegedly morbid concern with idiots, perverts, and monsters to the exclusion of more elevated social and moral interests. Yet at least since George Marion O'Donnell's fine essay in 1939, Faulkner has been recognized as a moralist. Actually, he is a moralist of such fervor that the struggle between good and evil in his novels at its worst suggests medieval allegory and at its best provides a tragic drama of titanic proportions. To read Faulkner traditionally, and it is easy to do with the Agrarian prolegomena *I'll Take My Stand* in mind, is to grasp the nature of his evil *and* the nature of his good, which is all too often overlooked. Of course one does not really need *I'll Take My Stand*, nor should one account for Faulkner strictly by formal Agrarianism. Faulkner has made his own stand not once but many times. Still critics, one of the more recent of whom is C. I. Glicksberg ("The World of William Faulkner, *Arizona Quarterly*, Spring, 1949), persist in looking around what Faulkner says, sometimes directly, sometimes indirectly, to find ambiguities that "reveal" what he must have meant to say.

Far from depicting a world of moral chaos, of blind chance, wherein the good are always subjected to the same inscrutable and cruel fate as the bad, Faulkner posits a world of moral order. There is an ultimate standard above and beyond man, in short, a providence whose workings may seem inscrutable and indeed are so to those who would remake the world nearer to their heart's desire. But to the genuinely humble and the genuinely proud—these two terms are not antithetical in Faulkner—the Byron Bunches, the Dilseys, the Ike McCaslins, and the Sam Fathers, who have the humanity to feel love and compassion and the courage to endure and to sacrifice for something or someone beyond self, providence generally provides. As Walton Litz wrote recently in a perceptive article on Faulkner,

> Man's freedom is an inner, moral one. It is his responsibility to endure and attempt to expiate the evils which he inherits from the past. Then, secure in the knowledge that this free choice will improve the lives of succeeding generations, he will be able to reconcile himself to his fate and prevail over it ("William Faulkner's Moral Vision," *Southwest Review,* Summer, 1952)

Believing that in Faulkner's view every man shares in the general responsibility for his fellows, one can begin to see the kind of tragic failure in the three central figures in Faulkner's three great novels, *The Sound and the Fury, Light in August,* and *Absalom, Absalom!* It is a failure of human responsibility in time.

For twenty years most commentators have found that tragedy is the term that springs most readily to mind when one thinks of Faulkner's legendry of the South. Tragedy, in its old sense, helps us tremendously in getting at the essential moral conflict which is the basis for his most powerful work. Like the great Greek dramas, Faulkner's novels set the individual free will against omnipotent law or Fate. His characters often refuse to recognize this law, and even more often they misconstrue the nature of the Fate, which is of human working, not divine. The jaded determinism of Quentin Compson's father, which has so far degenerated from Calvinist predestination as almost to amount to moral nihilism, leaves nothing for the boy but the equally degenerate code of honor which requires him to make a formalized defence of his sister's virginity. Lacking the physical hardihood to act according to the code, Quentin has left only a memorized concept of Presbyterian hell, which he hopes to create on earth by alleging the terrific act of incest. As Rabi points out, incest is associated with "the flight beyond the boundaries of time, and the escape from the world of suffering" (In *William Faulkner,* ed. Hoffman and Vickery, p. 131). But Rabi, too, fails to understand the nature of the guilt. To him, Faulkner shows "a massacre of the Innocents." The modern rationalist assumes that every one is innocent who has not committed a crime. In such a manner was Oedipus innocent, but as Elliott Coleman in a recent lecture at the Johns Hopkins University pointed out, incest is guilt, unwitting or not:

> It represents a desire for self-sufficiency . . . What a great temptation, how god-like, to be whole, to be alone, unified, integral, to be the more completely self sufficient, entirely independent, something reserved for a deity, by union with a part of oneself. And I would add, doomed to fail, because a totally new thing, another and new wholeness, a further reach, is not thereby arrived at in a unique creative act, but rather, a retrogression to solipsism. . . .

This was Quentin's sin; he attempted in his way to be Godlike, to isolate himself, conjoined with his sister, beyond the clean flame. But Quentin could not perform this act; he could only destroy himself, and thereby his tragedy becomes pathos. Faulkner makes it easy to understand Quentin as victim by providing his revery with Freudian symbols of infantile regression (See H. M. Campbell and R. E. Foster, *William Faulkner,* Ch. III). It is harder to understand the nature of his guilt; but in his pride he is not an innocent slaughtered but a man who placed a degenerate code higher than love or duty. Only contrast Dilsey, who assumes the burden of all the Compsons, misguided and vicious alike. Faulkner's cryptic remark about Dilsey is "They endured," but the endurance is not simply a patient primitive stoicism but is compounded of a faith in providence, and those old qualities of love, compassion, and honor which Faulkner has never ceased to write about.

Joe Christmas is the central figure in *Light in August,* in many senses the most tragic of Faulkner's studies of isolation. Perhaps a further development of the Popeye of *Sanctuary,* Joe Christmas has been warped from normality both by his childhood in an institution and his knowledge of his mixed blood. Lost between the two races, he repudiates both and isolates himself in brigandage somewhere between, in a long and narrow road of his own choosing, defending that road against the enemies of both colors.

Sentimentalists and sociologists are bound to regard Christmas solely as a victim. Perhaps they will cite Faulkner's intention to parallel him in some way with Christ. Literary psychoanalysts will point to the early determination of his neurosis by his childhood persecution. Certainly Christmas is driven, from the age of five until his death, by the self-appointed minions of morality who often dared usurp the functions of God Himself. The foster-father, McEachern, demanded that "the Almighty be as magnanimous as himself." The mad grandfather, Eupheus Hines, justified his sadism and brutality because he was an instrument of God's will. Certainly in many aspects Christmas is a victim, but as William Van O'Connor reminds us, he is also a "sadist, a pervert, and a murderer." (*Southern Renascence*, 159). In fact his deliberate and brutal repulse of every attempt to establish some kind of human fellowship with him is emphasized throughout the book, from his contemptuous refusal of Byron Bunch's proffered food to his deliberate decision to murder Miss Burden because she had begun to try to "save" him. Clearly Christmas chose his isolation, his self-immolation to the God of his own pride. Even if we interpret Christmas in Freudian terms as a victim, we must admit that the adult who never rises above the level of infantile behavior actually works his own doom. Society cannot permit the uninhibited functioning of the world-devouring ego of the child.

Christmas's most striking acts of rejection are of food, the traditional symbol of fellowship and generosity. Give me bread, says the fainting pilgrim, and the traditional Good Man opens his larder. Three times Christmas rejects food, the first as a boy when he takes the hot meal Mrs. McEachern has prepared him and deliberately hurls it to the floor, because he resents her kindness as an invasion of his hitherto inviolate citadel of pride. She is endangering his isolation, which can be maintained easily within the limits of the crime and punishment code of his foster father. The second time he smashes dishes of food is occasioned by the fact that Miss Burden, the food-giver, has locked the front door of her house against him and he has had to enter the rear. Finding the food set out in the kitchen, the quick refraction of his pride from the mirrored situation lifts the dishes and hurls them against the wall, thinking *Set out for the nigger. For the nigger*—not remembering that to this woman who had inherited the burden of the abolitionist conscience, his negro blood would have been a sight-draft on the best she had to give. The third time he rejected food was unqualified by foresight or afterthought. Byron Bunch, a traditional good man with uncomplicated generosity, offers to share his lunch with Christmas. "I aint hungry. Keep your muck—" is the sneered reply.

Reading traditionally rather than psychoanalytically, with the ancient symbol of the breaking of bread well in mind (though it is now formalized into something that has lost its meaning as "Southern hospitality") one can say that three times Christmas rejects the fellowship of the human race. One last time he is given food. In his last flight, after he has driven out the negro congregation and has cursed God in the church, Christmas comes close to some sort of spiritual resolution, at least not to run any longer. Then in the symbolical act of the breaking of bread (this Christ has no disciple except himself and always must eat alone), he begins to realize his predicament. He invades a negro cabin,

> Then there was food before him, appearing suddenly between long, limber black hands fleeing too in the act of setting down the dishes. It seemed to him that he could hear without hearing them wails of terror and distress quieter than sighs all about him, with the sound of the chewing and the swallowing. 'It was a cabin that time,' he thought. 'And they were afraid. Of their brother afraid.'

The knowledge that the course he has taken was of his own choosing, that he has wrought his own fate, brings Christmas closer to the situation of the tragic hero than Quentin Compson. As Robert Penn Warren wrote, Christmas is a "mixture of heroism and pathos" (*William Faulkner,* ed. Hoffman and Vickery, p. 97). He is heroic in his struggle to break out of what might seem his pre-charted course, but he is pathetic as a victim of soul-warping forces beyond his control. One feels, however, that too much has been made of Christmas as victim. In such a sense was Oedipus a victim of Fate, but as tragic hero Oedipus has engaged the imagination for nearly twenty-five centuries. If tragedy in the old sense is a conflict between human will and Fate, then Christmas can qualify as tragic hero, but one must have a notion of the Fate which dooms him.

William Van O'Connor (in "Protestantism in Yoknapatawpha") has made it quite clear that the Calvinist concept of inexorable punishment is one kind of doom that provides the tragic atmosphere of *Light in August.* Subjected to this doom from his cradle on through his formative years, Christmas was quite willing to accept it as the operative regimen of existence. It was simple, it was relentless, and he could define himself within its limits. But when ordinary compassionate humanity intervened between the crime and the punishment, then the code broke down and all was chaos. He could in no way clear the record but could only allow the crimes to accumulate for eventual reckoning at some awful and deferred Judgment.

The first female violation of the Calvinist code within Joe's experience occurred when he was only five. Having stolen toothpaste and eaten it like candy (perhaps an inconceivable act in the antiseptic fifties, but I can remember young school children in Faulkner's Mississippi devouring sample tubes of toothpaste which salesmen left in primary class rooms), he expected inevitable and justified punishment, but the young woman who discovered him hiding in her room, thinking that a five year old child was capable of revealing, actually intended to reveal, her own liaison with a doctor, offered to reward him for *not* telling.

> It never occurred to her that he believed that he was the one who had been taken in sin and was being tortured with punishment deferred and that he was putting himself in her way in order to get it over with, get his whipping and strike the balance and write it off.

To be offered a reward instead of being given a just punishment confused the child who had begun life within the Calvinist discipline. Twelve years later he had begun to think of the female, compassionate and corrupt, as always standing between the crime and the punishment (compare here the attitude of the old Officer in Kafka's "The Penal Colony," who thought that the ladies of the world-colony corrupted guilty prisoners by feeding them sweetmeats, making them less capable of experiencing the stern justice of the Machine). Mrs. McEachern, trying childlessly to act the role of a mother, mediates between Joe and her husband, who arrogates to himself more the Judgeship than the Fathership, meting out punishment and reward with equal impersonality. She, the eternal, compassionate woman, full of solicitude, through her "fumbling and dumb instinct,"

> would try to get herself between him and the punishment which, deserved or not, just or unjust, was impersonal, both the man and the boy accepting it as a natural and inescapable fact until she, getting in the way, must giving it an odor, an attenuation, and aftertaste.

Joe Christmas, busily hammering out his own doom, an act of pride comparable to but transcending that of Quentin Compson, simply thinks that he can choose his punishment by choosing his crime. Women, who try to save him, commit an act of violation; they seek to invade his hellish privacy. When, in his final renunciation he murders Miss Burden, it is because she has tried to save him. The temptation to let her work her will was there, but pride forced him to reject it, thinking, "No. If I give in now, I will deny all the thirty years that I have lived to make me what I chose to be." She, woman-like in her desire to save but more fanatic than woman (from her father and grandfather she has inherited the "burden" of the negro race), had asked him, " 'Do you realize . . . that you are wasting your life?' And he sat looking at her like a stone, as if he could not believe his own ears." A little later, failing as Savior, she tries to become Judge and even Executioner, failing in both as Christmas slashes her throat.

Though the immediate motivation of Christmas's act of murder seemed to be self-defence, its final cause was the code that allowed him to define himself as the arch-criminal, even perhaps as Satan: "he believed with calm paradox that he was the volitionless servant of the fatality in which he believed that he did not believe. He was saying to himself *I had to do it* already in the past tense; *I had to do it; I had to do it*." This was his thought *before* he used the razor.

If the crime and punishment code of Eupheus Hines and Mc-Eachern can be blamed for Christmas's feeling of fatality, then the symbolic nature of his role as victim becomes clear. He, like Christ, is sacrificed by the Pharisees, but there the resemblance ceases. The symbol is not carried throughout the story. Christmas was sacrificed before Percy Grimm ran into the Hightower kitchen. He was sacrificed when he was subjected to a religious code which tempted him to become, if not God, at least the great antagonist. To paraphrase Elliott Coleman's words, quoted earlier: What a temptation, how God-like, to be self-sufficient, choosing your own punishment, arrogating to yourself the judgeship, within the regimen of an inexorable fatality.

Christmas's final act of defiance, cursing God in the pulpit of a negro church, is the climax of his rebellion. Correctly assessing the role he has chosen to play, a negro woman screamed "'It's the devil! It's Satan himself!" as Christmas ran into the church. Fulfilling his own presumption of himself as the mighty antagonist, Christmas blasphemed in the pulpit, and since no lightning bolt struck him down, he was able to make only one last choice, death. He had ended where he had begun:

> Though during the last seven days he has had no paved
> street, yet he has travelled farther than in all the thirty years
> before. And yet he is still inside the circle. 'And yet I have
> been farther in these seven days than in all the thirty years,'
> he thinks. 'But I have never broken out of the ring of what
> I have already done and cannot ever undo' he thinks
> quietly. . . .

If the Calvinist code of doom tempts Chirstmas to choose his punishment, another kind of doom helps determine the nature of his choice. This is the old Southern belief that blood—black or white, blue or red—will always out, a belief that Faulkner is able to survey with critical detachment, even though it is a part of his own heritage. Mrs. Compson, Cassandra-like, is the prophetess of doom in *The Sound and the Fury* because of her belief in the bad blood of the Compsons, reinforced by her triumphant conviction that "people cannot flout God's laws with impunity." Ironically it is her son Jason who confirms her prophecies. Not a Compson, as she proudly asserts, but inheriting the traits of the Bascombs, Jason repudiates even the ties of blood-kin and with transcendent Snopesism, drives Caddy's daughter into viciousness. She, of all Faulkner's characters, is most clearly a victim, because an immediate personal agency seems directly responsible for her destruction; but the larger forces, the code of crime and punishment and the traditional doom of blood provides the seeming Fate of the tragedy. Seeming, because Faulkner plainly makes this Fate a matter of human contrivance, not divine.

The spokesman of *blood will out* in *Light in August* is Gavin Stevens, who is too often taken as the spokesman of Faulkner himself, but who is really speaking only for Gavin Stevens, one of the most responsible and far-seeing of Faulkner's characters but one who speaks out of the ethos of the South. Faulkner, as Robert Penn Warren has observed, creates a legend, not only of the South, but of a world in moral confusion.

Stevens explains Christmas's last flight in terms of his white and his black blood—black blood, we remember, that up until his death we have had only a presumption of his possessing. Stevens sees the nature of Christmas's flight as the operation of his mixed blood, just as Cousin McCaslin Edmonds explains to Ike McCaslin in "The Old People" that Sam Fathers, part-Negro and part-Indian, probably believed that

> it was the same warriors' and chiefs' blood in him . . . that was betrayed through the black blood which his mother gave him. Not betrayed by the black blood and not wilfully betrayed by his mother, but betrayed by her all the same, who had bequeathed him not only the blood of slaves but even a little of the very blood which had enslaved it; himself his own battleground, the scene of his own vanquishment and the mausoleum of his defeat.

Of such stuff was Christmas made, less fortunate than Sam Fathers who could define himself in nature. Not that Faulkner believes uncritically in the doom of blood, but the South believes it. It operates in the choice that Sam Fathers makes and it operates in Joe Christmas' choice of doom. In choosing at last the doom of blood, Christmas again becomes the victim, the scapegoat, bearing the guilt of the South.

> For a long moment he looked up at them with peaceful and unfathomable and unbearable eyes. Then his face, body, all, seemed to collapse, to fall in upon itself, and from out the slashed garments about his hips and loins the pent black blood seemed to rush like a released breath. It seemed to rush out of his pale body like the rush of sparks from a rising rocket; upon that black blast the man seemed to rise soaring into their memories forever and ever. They are not to lose

it, in whatever peaceful valleys, beside whatever placid and reassuring streams of old age, in the mirroring faces of whatever children they will contemplate old disasters and newer hopes. It will be there, musing, quiet, steadfast, not fading and not particularly threatful, but of itself alone serene, of itself alone triumphant.

So Christmas seems to leave this earth like an ancient martyr, with his blood suffusing the very firmament. Is he a martyr? Faulkner does not make the answer easy, as so many critics have thought he should do. To those who followed Grimm into that tiny kitchen and were revolted by his actions, Christmas's blood would remain as a triumphant symbol of his martyrdom. To us who have followed Christmas act by act through his terrible rebellion against the order of things, no such affirmation is possible. However, his story is of the nature of tragedy, and its looming fatality is compounded in equal parts of the doom of church and the doom of blood. In the words of Gavin Stevens, speaking for the South, one can make out Faulkner's conditions for survival. Christmas's white blood, "rising in him for the last and final time, sent him against all reason and reality, into the embrace of a chimera, a blind faith in something read in a printed Book." But it was the black blood that had made him struggle, that had snatched up the pistol, though the white blood would not let him fire it. Remembering Faulkner's other negroes, Dilsey, who "endured," the slave of "The Red Leaves," who ran well, we can see that Christmas's black blood was both his doom and his salvation. It made him struggle, it gave him heroic stature, and it made him a martyr. But his white blood gave him his temptation (which was pride) to isolate himself from the human race and to defy the judgment of God. One must conclude that Faulkner prefers the man who ran well.

Of the other characters in *Light and August* who, juxtaposed to the hero, Christmas, assumed their human burden or denied it, Gail Hightower (whose name indicates his role) is the most significant. Lena Grove and Byron Bunch both have simple faith and humanity. Byron, within the limits of the religious code, at first flees the appearance of evil and with egocentric self-righteousness isolates himself from life. But with the advent of Lena Grove he assumes responsibility for another and thereby saves himself. Hightower, at first making a doctrinaire denial of any virtue in Bunch's act, finally comes to an act of charity himself. Delivering Lena's child, he thinks:

> That will be her life, her destiny. The good stock peopling
> in tranquil obedience to it the good earth; from these hearty
> loins without hurry or haste descending mother and daughter.
> But by Byron engendered next.

Having performed an act of human responsibility, having breached the walls of his own prison, Hightower manages a kind of redemption. He had thought to make a bargain, a compact with Time. He had bought and paid for his dream of the past, the past that became his prison. In his final recognition, however, he becomes aware of his solipsism, of how he had sacrificed his wife to his own desire, to his pride of blood: "You took her as a means toward your own selfishness. As an instrument to be called to Jefferson; not for My ends but for your own." He had resigned his pulpit with the appearance of

> a martyr's reasons, . . . bearing in the town's sight and hearing, without shame, with that patient and voluptuous ego of the martyr, the air, the behavior, the *How long, O Lord* until, inside his house again and the door locked, he lifted the mask with voluptuous and triumphant glee: Ah. That's done now. That's past now. That's bought and paid for now.

He had bought his ghost.

Ironically Hightower's most complete vision of the past comes to him in a mystic experience only after he has assumed the burden of his humanity, after he has learned in his soul that it was his ego that had been the instrument of his wife's despair and shame. Thinking this in agony, against his will, the wheel of his thought turned on "with the slow implacability of a medieval torture instrument, beneath the wrenched and broken sockets of his spirit, his life." He learns at last that for fifty years he "had not even been clay," but had been "a single instant of darkness in which a horse galloped and a gun crashed." Coming to this recognition, this tragic *anagnorisis,* the torture wheel of his thought ran more easily. The imperial ego has been dethroned, and Hightower can endure his redemption. Dying, he thinks he should pray, but he does not try. Now he can think of someone besides himself.

With all air, all heaven, filled with the lost and unheeded
crying of all the living who ever lived, wailing still like lost
children among the cold and terrible stars . . . I wanted so
little. I asked so little. It would seem. . . .

The wheel turned faster now. The little he had wanted from the Almighty had been too much, because it had amounted to absolvement
from time and responsibility. It had amounted to isolation within a
heroic moment lived and done with.

Dying, having seen the self-centeredness of his whole existence,
Hightower fully experiences the heroic vision he had sought for fifty
years:

It is as though they had merely waited until he could find
something to pant with, to be reaffirmed in triumph and
desire with, with this last left of honor and pride and life.
He hears above his heart the thunder increase, myriad and
drumming. Like a long sighing of wind in trees it begins,
then they sweep into sight, borne now upon a cloud of
phantom dust. They rush past, forwardleaning in the
saddles, with brandished arms, beneath whipping ribbons
from slanted and eager lances; with tumult and soundless
yelling they sweep past like a tide whose crest is jagged with
the wild heads of horses and the brandished arms of men
like the crater of the world in explosion. They rush past,
are gone; the dust swirls skyward sucking, fades away into
the night which has fully come. Yet leaning forward in the
window, his bandaged head huge and without depth upon
the twin blobs of his hands upon the ledge, it seems to him
that he still hears them: the wild bugles and the clashing
sabres and the dying thunder of hooves.

Is not Faulkner saying that this complete vision of the men who
had "the gift of living once or dying once instead of being diffused
and scattered creatures drawn blindly from a grab bag and as-
sembled" (*Absalom, Absalom!*) is possessed only by those who have
proved themselves worthy? This is like the vision glimpsed by the
watcher at the wall in Tate's "Ode to the Confederate Dead," the vision
of a sacrifice beyond self, a total participation, a total involvement,
not a dying by pieces nor a living by parts. Allen Tate once wrote

that his *Ode* was a poem about modern solipsism; and, in large measure, that is the theme of *Light in August*.

More than a decade ago George Marion O'Donnell found in all of Faulkner's work a "striving toward the condition of tragedy." *Absalom, Absalom!,* which he calls an "action of heroic proportions," most nearly reaches that condition. Part of this striving is distinctly explicit, purposive, with the tragic parallel being proposed by one of the characters. Mr. Compson, Quentin's father, whom we remember from *The Sound and the Fury* as the purveyor of a spiritless and jaded determinism, projects the house of Sutpen against the dark background of the house of Atreus. Sutpen names his illegitimate daughter Clytemnestra, but Mr. Compson says, "I have always liked to believe that he intended to name Clytie, Cassandra, prompted by some dramatic economy not only to beget but to designate the presiding augur of his own disaster. . . ." Mr. Compson sees Sutpen as an actor, "still playing the scene to the audience, behind him Fate, destiny, retribution, irony—the stage manager, call him what you will . . . already striking the set and dragging on the synthetic and spurious shadows and shapes of the next one."

Undoubtedly Greek tragedy, with its paramount situation of the guilty but mighty family, with its symbolic actions of incest and the slaying of kin, and with its terrifying manifestation of the guilty mind in the pursuing Erinyes, furnishes a shadowy background of precedent for the plot of *Absalom, Absalom!* The theme, however, is peculiarly Faulknerian, as is the mode of narration.

Sutpen, unlike the heroes of the two novels previously discussed, has none of the qualifications of victim. He arouses no pity and has the large dimensions of the Renaissance tragic hero. We are really with Tamburlaine rather than Agamemnon, although Mr. Compson is rather insistent upon the Greek parallel (Shreve, drawing upon Mr. Compson's story, actually calls Sutpen "a widowed Agamemnon"). Knowing at last that Mr. Compson as well as Miss Rosa is wrong, that it is a false view of history that he has passed on to Quentin, we must consider his analogy is imperfect also. The fatality that engulfs the house of Sutpen is a doom of Sutpen's own contrivance, but projected through Mr. Compson's consciousness, it becomes darker, more ominous, an outmoded Fate seemingly springing from the causeless whim of the Omnipotent Jester.

As has been suggested more than once, Faulkner's narrators, among whom was Mr. Compson, act severally in the roles of chorus, witness, or messenger, through whose partial vision, through whose misinterpretation and true reporting alike, the dramatic irony becomes sharpened. Such a function is served by Rosa Coldfield also. It is partly her "demonizing" that provides Sutpen with his larger than life dimension (although Mr. Compson's Agamemnon parallel certainly does not dwarf him). Through Miss Rosa's voice Sutpen materializes into Quentin Compson's mind:

> Out of quiet thunderclap he would abrupt (man-horse-demon) upon a scene peaceful and decorous as a schoolprize water color, faint sulphur-reek still in hair clothes and beard, with grouped behind him his band of wild niggers like beasts half tamed to walk upright like men. . . .

That Miss Coldfield is an untrustworthy witness is soon apparent. Through the tortured rhetoric of her story, surely more heightened, more Marlovian than that of any other Faulkner character, Quentin gets, not the truth but a kind of irresponsible personal history which deprives him of the will to endure because of inescapable guilt handed down from a tremendous and accursed past. Miss Rosa, seizing upon the Sutpen story as *her* history of the South, gives Quentin a full measure of the doom of blood, preordained and established by the doom of Heaven.

> Yes, fatality and curse on the South and on our family as though because some ancestor of ours had elected to establish his descent in a land primed for fatality and already cursed with it, even if it had not rather been our family, our father's progenitors, who had incurred the curse long years before and had been coerced by Heaven into establishing itself in the land and the time already cursed.

Surely it is this sense of doom, this feeling of fatality, that destroyed the Sartorises, the Compsons, and would have destroyed the McCaslins had not some of them possessed a capacity to expiate the sin. If guilt could be handed down, so could the right to expiation; so Isaac McCaslin (his given name suggests his role) repudiated his pride in blood and possessions with his barony, thereby foregoing a son. His wife, holding on to family and pride, admits him to her bed once to persuade him to keep the land. But he would free his heir of ancestral guilt, putting aside his inheritance. The son is never conceived and his wife leaves him (See "The Bear," in *Go Down Moses*). Charles Mallison (*Intruder in the Dust*) bearing McCaslin blood though not the name, balanced the scale by saving his distant negro relative, Lucas Beauchamp, from an undeserved execution. This is a complete reversal of the Sutpen behavior. It is no accident that Charles Mallison is of the McCaslin line, and it is no accident that Andrew Nelson Lytle, one of the original Agrarians, reading no more in Faulkner than what is there, pointed out the true significance of the boy's act: "He will face dangers both physical and meta physical comprised in an undertaking beyond his capacity to perform but in his decision he assumes the moral responsibility for his human ity" (*Sewanee Review*, Winter, 1949). Charles is superior to the doom of blood because he feels moral responsibility, something Quentin Compson never achieved, lost as he was in the Sutpen Compson legend of the past interpreted for him by doom-ridden minds. Quentin felt only the responsibility to a nominal honor, an honor meaningless in Time.

But *Absalom, Absalom!* is not really Quentin's book, even though it may represent for him the meaning of history (William Poirier "Strange Gods in Jefferson," *Sewanee Review*, Summer, 1945). The story is about Sutpen, and as Cleanth Brooks has made clear, it is largely about Sutpen's innocence (*Sewanee Review*, Autumn, 1951) Sutpen is the character in Faulkner who most nearly possesses *hubris* he is the character who will take the scheme of things and remold it to his heart's desire. He is unable to conceive of ethical respon sibility, only of justice in the purely rational, almost the purely economic sense. With this blindness, this innocence, which one fears is the innocence of modern man, he makes the most heroic effort of all Faulkner's characters to conquer time, not by suicide, nor by choosing his punishment, but by establishing a dynasty, the traditional way of the monarch. In allowing Sutpen this grander, more heroic mode of action, Faulkner deprives the character of the role of victim It is the Renaissance ethos rather than the Greek, and Sutpen is Modern Man.

How Sutpen works his own doom gradually becomes clear, looming up out of the partial disclosures of Miss Rosa and Quentin's
father as the shape of a mansion gradually becomes clear through
wind-rifted fog.

Coming from a primitive background (the mountains) where
what a man can *do* is the measure of his worth (reading Faulkner
at large here, Sutpen is the American archetype), Sutpen encounters
an established tidewater society wherein the assessment of value is
different. It is something complex, related not only to what one has
but also to the history one represents; in other words, he finds a
traditional society. Sutpen assumes that because he has courage,
strength and the will-to-succeed, he can establish himself within that
society. All he has to do is get the land and the negroes and the fine
house. Then he would have defined himself as a man. It was that
simple, he thought.

Through an incredible display of courage he obtained himself
a wife and fortune in the West Indies. A child was born, an heir-
presumptive to the Sutpen barony; but then he discovered that his
wife—and child—had Negro blood, so they could not be "adjunctive"
to his design. His first act of simple injustice consisted of putting
away his wife and child, relinquishing to her his estate, in what he
considered fair payment for any wrong he might be considered (he
did not consider it a wrong, himself) to have done.

In the proper mode of Renaissance tragedy, it seems that Sutpen
is going to succeed. By sheer will and courage and by a liberal employment of the ruthless behavior that he did not consider injustice,
Sutpen acquired his hundred square miles of land and his mansion.
Then he chose his wife, not out of the compulsion of any human
emotion but because in her impeccable respectability she would be
"adjunctive" to the design.

Very soon Sutpen's behavior indicated his isolation within self.
As in *Light in August,* shunning the fellowship of the table becomes
significant. Sutpen repudiates his Coldfield kin. When they come to
dinner, he is always absent, as Miss Rosa says,

> because since papa had given him respectability through a
> wife there was nothing else he could want from Papa and
> so not even sheer gratitude, let alone appearance, could force

him to forego his own pleasure to the extent of taking a family meal with his wife's people.

The repudiation of kinship is outrageous in the South. Family dinners are a social institution, but here there is a deeper implication. Sutpen had no friends. People came to his hunts, it is true, loafers, hangers-on, sycophants to the monarch, but only Quentin's grandfather (General Compson) stood in any definable human relationship to the man who would shape his own destiny. Sutpen had in effect repudiated mankind.

When his doom came, it was clearly of his own making. Charles Bon, the son of his first, his deserted wife, came, by the maneuvering of her lawyer to Jefferson. But what happened was beyond the capacity of the maneuverer to foresee or plan. Recognizing his father, asking only a like recognition of his sonship, a word, or even only a clasp of the hand, Charles Bon is put aside even as was his mother before him. This denial of kinship implemented the final catastrophe. Sutpen was not safe in his self-wrought isolation. Judith, his daughter, loves her half-brother, Charles Bon. Henry, his son, loving Charles himself, would permit the incest, but finding out that Charles had negro blood, would not permit the miscegenation. Thus the man-created doom of blood became Fate in *Absalom, Absalom!* Henry, after four years' reluctance, becomes a fratricide and a fugitive, abroad like Orestes, pursued by the Erinyes of his own conscience.

But just as Macbeth continues his course of evil even after the apparition of Banquo, so does Sutpen ignore the manifest warning that his house is doomed. In an Anglo-Saxon tradition far older than Faulkner's South, the slaughter of kinsmen dooms the dynasty. "Kinship true can never be marred in a noble mind!" sang the *Beowulf* poet. But the rational man can never be warned. Sutpen, now old and home from the wars, scarcely draws two breaths before he sets about reclaiming his kingdom and begetting a new heir. He knows he has little time left, but he plans to use it efficiently. He will rectify, not his wrong, but his "mistake."

Operating under his simple businessman's code of justice, he proposes to bed with Rosa Coldfield. If the issue is male, he will make good his end of the contract with marriage. If a girl, the contract is rendered null and void because she would have failed to be "adjunctive" to the design. Before this transcendent outrage Rosa retires to her demon-harrying for the rest of her life, bequeathing her demon to Quentin Compson.

Even this bargaining failure does not dismay Sutpen. He turns to the only available female, the fifteen-year-old granddaughter of his retainer, Wash Jones, and buys her body with candy, beads and a new dress. True to form Sutpen pays cash on the barrelhead, but the girl fails him, too. The child is a female, a "mare," and Milly, not having lived up to the unspoken contract outlined in Sutpen's mind, was denied "a decent stall in the stable," to which the real mare, having foaled a horse, was thereby entitled. Wash Jones, the grandfather, not enraged by the seduction but by this final denial of humanity, of responsibility to flesh and blood, beheads Sutpen with a scythe, symbol of the eternal justice of Time. But at least it was a decapitation, the death of a monarch.

Like the doom of the house of Atreus the fatality of the Sutpens outlived the death of the progenitor. Charles Etienne St. Velery Bon, the only son of Charles Bon and an unnamed octoroon of New Orleans, was brought by Judith Sutpen and Clytemnestra to live at Sutpen's Hundred, but the doom of blood was his fatality. Unlike Joe Christmas he had no Calvinist code of crime and punishment to set for him the terms of definition. Unable to choose his ultimate punishment, he could only determine the nature of his isolation. He could at least make his banishment from the white race absolute, not partial. He sought a negro for a mate, whose physical and intellectual characteristics had made her an outcast even among her own, and begot on her an idiot son, who was called Jim Bond. This boy the faithful Clytie cared for in a cabin at Sutpen's Hundred.

But the doom was not yet complete. Henry Sutpen was still alive, still the heir-presumptive. In the closing pages of *Absalom, Absalom!* we learn that someone, or something, is out at Sutpen's Hundred. Miss Rosa, still demonizing, goes out to find the secret dweller. It is Henry, old and sick. The ambulance that Rosa sends to get Henry is mistaken by Clytie for a patrol wagon. Rather than submit him to the white man's law, she burns down the house upon him, and as it burns they think that they can see her, "the tragic gnome's face beneath the clean headrag, against a red background of fire," and they can hear Jim Bond, "the scion, the last of his race," howling about the ruins.

This is the terrifying finality of the most formally realized of Faulkner's tragedies, with its theme of a titanic ego pitted against time itself. Sutpen's Hundred, like Tadmor and Persepolis, is left to the raven and the wolf, with the barely human survivor lurking in the ashes.

But does even this terrible conclusion justify a statement, like that of Sartre, that Faulkner denies the possibility of a future ("Time in Faulkner; *The Sound and the Fury*") ? Not unless we accept the viewpoint of Mr. Compson. *Absalom, Absalom!* is a tale that affirms the existence of a moral order above and beyond man by the very completeness of the destruction. Tragedy does not make its affirmation of this moral order by statement but by its formal description of a man working his own doom. We know that Sutpen is doomed, though he never knows it himself. It is tragic irony that he never seems to know it, although one wonders if *anagnorisis* in the sense that it appears in *Light in August,* might not make understanding easier for us. Yet remembering that Faulkner as moralist is not writing of Sutpen alone nor of the South alone but of something in the nature of modern civilization, then Sutpen's failure to understand the nature of his guilt becomes necessary, because it is a failure of rational man to understand the moral universe.

In one of the rare omniscient passages in the story Faulkner comments that the cold room at Harvard in which Quentin and Shreve sat talking of Sutpen was "dedicated to that best of ratiocination which after all was a good deal like Sutpen's morality and Miss Coldfield's demonizing." Thus the farther reach of Sutpen's doom encompasses modern man who relies upon reason to solve the ancient problem of evil. Sutpen is simply the materialist who sets his rational will above the traditional code of values (the old universals of love and honor and pity and pride and sacrifice).

But there is another meaning, one restricted to the saga of Yoknapatawpha. As William Poirier indicated, Sutpen is the meaning of history to Quentin Compson, more specifically, the meaning of family history. After all Sutpen differs from Compson only in the dimension of time. The first Compson in Mississippi, Jason Lycurgus, came riding into Yoknapatawpha with only a fine mare and a brace of pistols, trading the mare to Ikkemotubbe for a square mile of the hitherto inviolate wilderness. Thus, with the beginning of the

Compson dynasty in Mississippi begins the exploitation of the land, begins the rape of nature and the doom of blood, for the doom of blood is nothing more than the formalizing of family pride (encompassing racial pride) into Fate. If Sutpen made his fortune at least in part by gambling, so did the first Jason Compson (and the last one tried to), betting shrewdly on the given characteristics of his mare, parlaying her four-furlong endurance into a barony. What Quentin should have learned from Sutpen's story was the hollowness of the Compsons' pride. Only Time decreed that the Compsons were more worthy than the Sutpens, and, in the enormous sweep of eternity, Benjy, the last Compson, like Jim Bond, the last Sutpen, is left howling about the ruins. Jason, the survivor in *The Sound and the Fury,* is not really a Compson but a Snopes. The parallel between Sutpen and Compson is clear. Equally clear is Faulkner's premise that economic exploitation is the sin of the Southern great families as well as of the industrial North, and that the pride in family and race and the consequent doom of blood is often based less upon inherent moral worth than upon the economic brigandage of the past. Such pride can isolate the individual within the island of his own desire, depriving him of an ethically responsible will. When the pride of blood suffers the final degeneration into pride of possession, Compson is turned into Snopes, the degenerate economic man.

The alternative is equally clear: accept the responsibility of time, expiate the guilt. Until man abides by the "old verities and truths of the heart . . . he labors under a curse. He writes not of love but of lust, of defeats in which nobody loses anything of value, of victories without hope, and, worst of all, without pity and compassion. His griefs grieve on no universal bones, leaving no scars. He writes not of the heart but of the glands" (The Stockholm address).

Faulkner's tragic theme is solipsism, the isolation of the individual behind the walls of Self, but he shows clearly the way to breach those walls. It is the old way.

IRENE C. EDMONDS

Faulkner and the Black Shadow

"Tell me about the South. What's it like there. What do they do there. Why do they live there. Why do they live at all . . ." demands Shreve McCannon of his Harvard roommate Quentin Compson. The tortured answer which Quentin attempts in *Absalom, Absalom!* is as much Faulkner's as Quentin's. To both it represents a tenacious search for a philosophical interpretation of the South's history and society in terms of present day relationships between expediency and principle. For Quentin there was no answer except the futility of suicide; for Faulkner there is still the search, still the involutions and convolutions of miasmic thought—and still no answer. For Faulkner realizes, more than any of his interpreters, that sooner or later the collapse of Southern morality and tradition must be explained in terms of a society which embraces the concepts of Christian doctrine while denying its practice instead of as a death struggle between decadent Sartorises and materialistic Snopeses. Thus we come to the cause for this dichotomy, the burden and obsession of white Southern conscience—the Negro, the black shadow.

> I had seen and known Negroes since I could remember, I just looked at them as I did at rain, or furniture, or food or sleep. But after that I seemed to see them for the first time not as people, but as a thing, a shadow in which I lived, we lived, all white people, all other people. I thought of all the children coming forever and ever into the world, white, with the black shadow already falling upon them before they drew breath. And I seemed to see the black shadow in the form of a cross . . . 'The curse of the black race is God's curse. But the curse of the white race is the black man who will be forever God's chosen own because He once cursed Him' (*Light in August*, p. 221)

Miss Burden's voice trailed away into the night stillness, and Joe Christmas, part Negro, lay still, sullen and brooding. Here we have one of the pervasive themes of practically all of Faulkner's work—a theme he formulates with such painful circumambiency in a 1600 word sentence in *The Bear* (Part IV): the belief that the South, cursed and doomed by slavery, must find its own expiation. But contraposed to this, over and above the resultant compendium of violence, horror, seduction, illegitimate children, rape, incest, and perversion in Faulkner's novels, is a second theme: the theme of Negro blood as a source of defilement. This he mirrors as an abomination in the collective psyche of the South. There are even times when one senses overtones, conscious or unconscious, of the same phobia in Faulkner himself. The shadow then assumes two forms, the curse of slavery and the horror of miscegenation.

Because Faulkner's drive for honesty is so intense and direct in his effort to refine the presentness of the past into something which might explain evil and violence and a vitiated morality, one hestitates to confine him entirely to the "school of doom" Southern writers. To one who has observed the southern scene without rancor or sentimentality, the tears of this group over a lost tradition seem as maudlin and sentimental as the overworked theme of the purity of white southern womanhood, or the magnolia blossom-mintjulep philosophy of the "southern colonel." The same honesty impels one to make an objective attempt to appraise the shadow as it obsesses William Faulkner and then to draw some conclusions. Perhaps the best way to study the impact of Faulkner's brooding sensitivity on the objective correlative of the South's guilt—the black shadow—is to observe the progression in his thinking as shown in this treatment of his more memorable Negro character creations from Dilsey (*The Sound and The Fury*, 1929) to Nancy Mannigoe (*Requiem for a Nun*, 1950).

There are few novelists who know the South as well as Faulkner or who can recall its past so vividly. Surely in the characterization of Dilsey, the Compsons' maid, cook, nurse and housekeeper, one feels Faulkner's nostalgia for a period lost, an institution disappearing; for Dilsey has basically the elements of the old Negro mammy, a stereotype which is very common in southern literature. Faulkner says of her "They endured." Her character, though not fully realized, is convincing. Thus Dilsey emerges not so much as a living, breathing, individual human being, but more as an institution, a tradition, a force which held the crumbling Compsons together until their final disintegration. How else, then, could Faulkner refer to her kind except as "They"?

Yet there is one question which insists upon an answer. Why in *The Sound and The Fury* was Dilsey's story told in the third person and not in the stream-of-consciousness technique of the Benjy and Quentin sections, or the first person of the Jason section? Faulkner is such a master of his own form and structure, his own techniques, that the method of telling Dilsey's story must represent a preconceived and conscious artistic choice. Why, then, the third person? There is a dual answer.

First, Dilsey was not a person to Faulkner, the narrator of Dilsey's story. To him she was a force, a symbol of endurance, a nostalgic reconstruction of remembered past.

Secondly, he did not truly understand her as a personality nor did he feel he needed to. She acted, but he did not get inside her being to ascertain "the why"; she was a tower of strength for others, but he did not divine her personal thoughts and feelings. What he saw were "the coruscations of immolation and abnegation and time" on her fallen cheeks. And so he reports, not tells, her story—in short simple sentences as a child might. He does this not only because the basic simplicity of his characterization demands such treatment, but also because he saw through the glass darkly of her mind. There is one thought he allows to break through, and this significantly has implications for her charges, the Compsons, and not for her as a human entity—"I've seed de first and de last." Dilsey could have been Aunt Mollie Beauchamp. There were no real personality differences between them. Both were matriarchal servants who attempted to hold their white families together, and hence they were interchangeable. Such, traditionally, were their function and their significance as related to the Southern scene.

What Faulkner does is to add stature to the stereotype, thus giving Dilsey's personality dimensions above and beyond the plantation tradition. Her concern with the fundamental questions of human dignity and justice elevate her to this level. The quality of endurance, inherent in Dilsey, is presented by Faulkner as a human quality that the South, black and white, must possess if it is to survive. And so the mammy becomes something more than a holder-together of a white family, or a fountain head of love and protection for it, though the subserviency and unquestioned acceptance of status are still there.

Joe Christmas, (*Light in August,* 1932) knowingly embracing evil, sardonic and sinister misogynist, forever at war with himself and the world, forever brooding over the "taint" of his Negro blood, presents another picture. As Faulkner described him:

> He looked like a tramp, yet not like a tramp either . . . He did not look like a professional hobo in his professional rags, but there was something definitely rootless about him, as though no town nor city was his, no street, no walls, no square of earth his home. And that he carried his knowledge with him always as though it were a banner, with a quality ruthless, lonely, and almost proud.

All of Christmas' behavior stemmed from the belief that his Negro blood was a genetic curse. Though he looked white and thought white, he symbolized the supposedly "tragic" consequences of miscegenation, the crime of crimes in the South. In his desire for "purification" and release from his inner torment he went north where he sought vainly to identify himself as a Negro.

> He lived with Negroes, shunning white people. He ate with them, slept with them, belligerent, unpredictable, uncommunicative. He now lived as man and wife with a woman who resembled an ebony carving. At night he would lie in bed beside her, sleepless, beginning to breathe deep and hard. He would do it deliberately, feeling, even watching, his white chest arch deeper and deeper within his ribcage, trying to breathe into himself the dark odor, the dark and inscrutable thinking and being of Negroes, and with each suspiration trying to expel from himself the white blood and the white thinking and being. And all the while his nostrils at the odor which he was trying to make his own would whiten and tauten, his whole being writhe and strain with physical outrage and spiritual denial.

Thus Christmas committed every act forbidden to white men by Southern mores, but it is significant that this excruciating effort occured only as a violent reaction to the suddenly acquired knowledge "that there were white women who would take a man with a black skin." Joe Christmas could not escape the white South.

It is very interesting to conjecture about Faulkner's original intentions in writing *Light in August*. Aside from the story of Lena Grove and Byron Bunch, or of Gail Hightower, one feels that the initial conception of the Joe Christmas story became more comprehensive in breadth, scope, and idea than Faulkner was spiritually capable of handling. One feels that he had a very definite connection in his mind between Christmas and Christ. The vagueness with which he establishes the connection suggests that the magnitude of his theme was too great for the limits of his imaginative powers to assimilate. Regardless of the symbolic washing of Joe's feet by Mrs. McEachern; that he was betrayed for a thousand pieces of money; that Hines, his grandfather, imagined himself to be God; that the middle years of his life lay in obscurity; that he was crucified by Percy Grimm at 33 years of age—all of which bring to mind the life of Christ—one feels that Faulkner, a Southerner, when confronted by the enormity of his attempt to liken a man with Negro blood in his veins to Christ, could not find the moral courage to make the analogy inescapably clear. And so it remained a suggestion, trailing away into the obfuscation of It-Could-or-Could-Not-Have-Been.

I cannot leave Faulkner's characterization of Joe Christmas before pointing out two other things. First, that Faulkner, like Paul Green and other southern writers, thinks in terms of an actual war between the white and the black blood in the veins of a person of mixed blood as if there were a struggle between two disparate and infusible elements. In other words, we have here another Negro stereotype, the "tragic mulatto." In reality this assumed conflict represents but another facet of the belief that miscegenation is a mortal sin, and hence there must be some prima-facie evidence to prove its eternal verity. In reality the conflict is between the individual in toto and his environment.

In this same vein Faulkner has Gavin Stevens say of Joe Christmas as he (Christmas) willingly runs to meet death—

> It was not alone all those thirty years which she did
> not know but all those thirty years before which had put
> that stain either on his white or his black blood. whichever
> you will, and which killed him. But he must have run with

believing for a while; anyway with hope. But his blood would not be quiet, let him save it. It would not be either one or the other and let his body save itself . . . He did not kill the minister. He merely struck him with the pistol and ran on and crouched behind that table and defied the black blood for the last time, as he had been defying it for thirty years. He crouched behind the overturned table and let them shoot him to death, with that loaded and unfired pistol in his hand.

This "tragic mulatto" theme appears again and again in Faulkner's characters—in Charles Bon, in Lucas Beauchamp, in Velery Bon. But Joe Christmas is tragic from another angle. In the stereotype, the character is acted on from without, a victim of fate against which it seems useless to struggle. Joe Christmas chooses evil himself—he is the victim of his own doom because he consciously chooses it. He figuratively and literally runs to meet his emasculation, his crucifixion.

The second thing I want to call attention to is Faulkner's pointing up of the delusion of the repressed South's conception of the Negro male as maniacal of his sex urge—ever a potential rapist. We have the pathological mental explorations of the women who comfort the spurious rape victim in *Dry September,* and of the crowd in *Light in August* after they find the murdered body of Miss Burden. Of Joe Christmas, lover and murderer of Miss Burden, they speculate:

Among them the casual Yankee and the poor whites and even the southerners who had lived for a while in the north who believed aloud that it was an anonymous negro crime committed not by a negro but by Negro who knew, believed, and hoped that she had been ravished too: at least once before her throat was cut and at least once afterward.

Next in the progression of Faulkner's Negro characters is Charles Bon (*Absalom, Absalom!* 1936). He did not choose evil as did Joe Christmas; that he left for his son Velery Bon. In fact, his drop of Negro blood disturbed him little, if any. But he, like Christmas and Velery, sought recognition as a human entity as justification for his existence. Although prepared by his mother as the potential avenger of her repudiation by his father; Colonel Sutpen (because Sutpen discovered after she had become his wife that she had a trace of Negro blood), what he desired most was to be recognized by his father "out of the shadow of whose absence my spirit's posthumeity has never escaped."

Bon is even willing to sacrifice the love of Henry, whom he senses is his brother; because he sees in Henry's face the image of "the man who shaped us both out of that blind chancy darkness which we call future." He is willing, too, to renounce the love of Judith, Henry's sister, if only Sutpen would acknowledge him as son but for a moment.

> . . . I will renounce love and all: that will be cheap, cheap, even though he say to me "never look upon my face again; take my love and my acknewledgment in secret, and go" I will do that; I will not even demand to know of him what it was my mother did that justified his action toward her and me.

But Sutpen, the father, refuses to give the slightest sign to Charles Bon, the son.

There is but one alternative left for Bon to take in order to finally attain his sonship—either to commit incest with Judith or to accept death at the hands of his brother. Either choice would establish a form of father-son acknowledgment. And here lies the significance of Bon's story for this paper. Henry, acting from a moral-social code that transcends his love for Bon, kills the man he knows is his illegitimate brother in order to prevent Bon's marriage to their sister. Henry does this, not because of any inherent objection to incest, but because of the insuperable barrier of miscegenation. Quentin, reconstructing the last scene between Bon and Henry, has Bon say—"So it's the miscegenation not the incest, which you can't bear. Henry doesn't answer." (*Absalom, Absalom!* p. 356) By death, then, Bon finds his ultimate recognition, and Henry performs his moral obligation to the traditional mores of the region.

And now we come to Sam Fathers ("The Bear"—*Go Down Moses,* 1942), half Indian and half Negro, possessor of two qualities in man which Faulkner seems to respect—primitive endurance and physical contact with nature. Faulkner evidences a profound admiration for the Dilseys and the Sam Fathers; the first, whose prototype existed in actuality (Caroline Barr, "who was born in slavery and who gave to my family a fidelity without stint or calculation of re-compense and to my childhood an immeasurable devotion and love") and the second, who was the creation of Faulkner's atavistic primitiv-ism. But Sam Fathers remains, as do the others, an abstraction or symbol of a quality, a way of human behavior.

What Sam Fathers also represents is a breaking away from any hint of a Negro stereotype—a complete creation of Faulkner's own making. He is neither a variation of the "tragic mulatto" nor a variety of Uncle Tom. He is a primeval force suggesting a way of life for modern society.

Lucas Beauchamp (*Intruder in the Dust,* 1948) unyielding, re-calcitrant, chewing his gold toothpick, fingering his gold watch chain, stoic, stolid, "refusing to mean mister to white folks even when he says it," emerges as an implacable reminder of past guilt and present sins unexpiated.

Intruder in the Dust raises many controversial questions, depend-ing on one's point of view. Again a very strong Negro character ap-pears in the story. But what is Faulkner trying to say other than tell a corking good detective story?

Fundamentally the novel is about a young white boy, Charles Mallison, Jr., nurtured in the tradition "of that time when it's still not yet two o'clock on that July afternoon in 1863" and Pickett is "looking up the hill waiting for Longstreet to give the word." Charles, who at the beginning of the story wished with such rage and im-potence that Lucas "would be a nigger first, just for one second, one little infinitesimal second," is beset by the problems of "the reaffirma-tion of his masculinity and his white blood." His efforts to erase the shame his manhood and "whiteness" have suffered at the hands of Lucas, who denied his racial superiority by keeping him (Charles) under obligation to him (Lucas), forms the background for the action. The novel, then, concerns itself with the education of Charles Malli-son, Jr., whose enlightenment began when he found out that "you didn't have to *not* be a nigger in order to grieve."

Although Faulkner often becomes involved in grandiloquent rhetorical sprees, the first attempt to preach occurs in this novel. He very obviously steps outside the character of Gavin Stevens, uncle and mentor of Charles, to espouse the thesis that the South should be al-lowed to work out its salvation alone and without advice or compul-

sive laws from "outlanders." In three different and very long speeches
Gavin declares that—

> . . . We must resist the North: not to preserve ourselves
> but to keep intact the postulate that Sambo is a human be-
> ing living in a free country and hence must be free. That's
> what we are really defending: the privilege of setting him
> free ourselves . . . We—he and us—should confederate: swap
> him the rest of the economic and political and cultural
> privileges which are his right, for the reversion of his capacity
> to wait and endure and survive.

and again—

> . . . I'm defending Lucas Beauchamp. I'm defending Sambo
> from the North and East and West—the outlanders who will
> fling him decades back not merely into injustice but into
> grief and agony and violence too by forcing on us laws
> based on the idea that man's injustice to man can be abolish-
> ed overnight by police.

But Gavin Stevens unwittingly negates his professed humanitarianism and social emancipation. He refers to the aggregate Negro
as Sambo, and thus unconsciously reflects a mode of thinking which
still relegates Negro to the comically pathetic status of Sambo, the
caricature and the stereotype. Such a condition could *not* insure that
someday, as he hoped,

> Lucas Beauchamp can shoot a white man in the back
> with the same impunity to lynch-rope or gasoline as a white
> man; in time he will vote anywhen and anywhere a white
> man can and send his children to the same school anywhere
> the white man's children go and travel anywhere the white
> man travels as the white man does it.

With almost the same breath that he voiced the above lofty sentiments Stevens suggested to Lucas:

> . . . "Has it ever occurred to you that if you said mister (the
> symbol of superiority of white over black in the South) to

white people and said it like you meant it, you might not be
sitting here now?"

"So I'm to commence now," Lucas said. "I can start off
by saying mister to the folks that drags me off here and
builds a fire under me."

Faulkner has Gavin Stevens, adhering to type, make no attempt to re-
concile the word with the thought.

In Lucas Beauchamp, of *Intruder in the Dust,* Faulkner completely
breaks from the "tragic mulatto" stereotype. It is not the duality of
his blood which is the basis of Lucas' action; it is something above
and beyond this. What Faulkner does is to make him, "once the slave
of any white man within range of whose notice he happened to come,
now tyrant over the whole country's white conscience," not only the
symbolical conscience of Jefferson City, but of all the guilty "nation"
called the South. Lucas here is more the embodiment of the "black
shadow" as defined by Faulkner than any of his other Negro characterizations.

Like a number of Faulknerian characters, Lucas Beauchamp has
appeared before this. In "The Fire and the Hearth" from *Go Down
Moses,* Faulkner very definitely makes an effort to get inside Lucas'
mind—an experiment he seldom attempted with his Negro characters
except in brief flashes. Usually Faulkner's Negro characters are seen
through the eyes of the white people with whom they are involved.
But this earlier Lucas is revealed by the techniques of both mood
study and objective narration. Through the stream-of-consciousness
approach, Faulkner plumbs the bitter agony which must be Lucas'
when he suspects that his wife Molly has become (by command) not
only the "mammy" for his white landlord's child but also his mistress.
And so Lucas cries out—"How to God can a black man ask a white
man to please not lay down with his black wife?" When Lucas does
demand her return, we get a foreshadowing of the moral stature he
exhibits later in *Intruder in the Dust.*

The whimsical humor of the middle section of "The Fire and the
Hearth" is a little puzzling, and, upon reflection, a trifle disconcerting.
Is it pure fun, or reminiscent of the humor-tinged indulgent condescen-
sion of traditional southern paternalism in Negro-white relationships
—the "you-know-they-are-just-like-children" attitude? Whatever one's

answer to this query may be, Lucas, in this story, is a real person even though he is done in bas-relief instead of the round.

Though Lucas loses most of this personal, intimate quality in *Intruder in the Dust,* he stalks forth here with the commanding dignity of a free spirit, his strength evolving from his ability to contain suffering, and from the certain knowledge of his spiritual independence. One senses that Faulkner has come to realize that the Negro is not so easily understood by the white man as he may have formerly readily believed or taken for granted. In this unspoken recognition of the subtle intricacies of the personalities of his Negro characters, he pays silent tribute to their basic human reserve and dignity. Thus in the Lucas of the novel Faulkner may have lost some of the intimacy and the immediacy of the short story, but the moral proportions of his later Lucas, even though he has resorted to a portrait from the outside, do represent an enlargement of view.

At last we come to Nancy Mannigoe. She appeared briefly in *The Sound and The Fury* and was the subject of a short story *That Evening Sun* (*These Thirteen,* 1931) where she is to all appearances killed by a jealous husband. However, Faulkner resurrects her in *Requiem for a Nun* (1951) since he needed her as a backdrop for Temple Drake Stevens' drama.

Of all Faulkner's Negro characterizations Nancy Mannigoe is most puzzling. Even the title of the novel contains a double entendre. Who is the nun? Temple or Nancy? Here is "an ex-dope fiend whore," who in *That Evening Sun* presents one of the most admirably drawn studies of fear, desperation, and final resignation, suddenly performing an act, the murder of Temple's baby son, which she knew would demand the supreme penalty—her life. And she does all this for the sake of saving the soul of a woman more a sister of iniquity than a sister from love. What could possibly impel her, a southern Negro, to commit the premeditated murder of a white person, and a white child at that? What compulsion was strong enough to make her act contrary to everything she had been taught and accepted? How could she still remain Nancy Mannigoe and also become the force whereby a questionable regeneration of Temple might take place? Where did Nancy find the requisite spiritual strength for such an ex-aggerated sacrifice when such strength of character had never been foreshadowed in any previous acts?

I can answer none of these questions; for I believe that even in distortion there should be some form, some order, some relation of principle to expediency. It is this lack of motivation for Nancy's act that makes *Requiem for a Nun* fall to pieces.

Faulkner has Stevens say to Temple:

> You came here to affirm the very thing which Nancy is going to die tomorrow morning to postulate: that little children as long as they are little children, shall be intact, unanguished, untorn, unterrified.

A little later this dialogue takes place:

NANCY

I don't know. But you got to trust Him. Maybe that's your pay for the suffering.

STEVENS

Whose suffering, and whose pay? Just each one's for his own?

NANCY

Everybody's. All suffering. All poor sinning man's.

STEVENS

The salvation of the world is in man's suffering. Is that it?

NANCY

Yes, sir.

STEVENS

How?

NANCY

I don't know. Maybe when folks are suffering, they will be too busy to get into devilment, won't have time to worry and meddle one another.

Here we have Faulkner, then, providing a rational basis for Nancy's act—but the basis rests in Faulkner's mind, the characterization does not supply it.

What Faulkner has done is to give us a modern variation of the Dilsey character—a variation clothed in the garments of an ex-dope fiend woman of the streets. The disguise may obscure the prototype. But Temple says of Nancy, in the current idiom, what Mrs. Compson may have said of Dilsey:

> . . . Then the son and heir came; and now we have Nancy:
> nurse: guide: mentor, catalyst, glue whatever you want to
> call it, holding the whole lot of them together—not just a
> magnetic center for the heir apparent and the other little
> princes or princesses in their orderly succession, to circle
> around, but for the two bigger hunks too of mass or matter or
> dirt or whatever it is shaped in the image of God, in a
> semblance at least of order and respectability and peace; not
> ole cradle-rocking black mammy at all, because the Gowan
> Stevenses are young and modern . . .

Both Dilsey and Nancy acted as Greek chorus in a drama of the fall
of a family.

Though Faulkner must have had Temple choose Nancy as nurse
for her child in order to point up Temple's complete acceptance of
evil, still it is he who makes Nancy a variation of the Dilsey character.
This time he has the "Dilsey-Nancy" sacrifice herself for all suffering
humanity, not just for one family.

It is also interesting to note that Gavin Stevens has lost the
overtones of insincerity in his moralizing, and that he makes no reference to "Sambo." He has grown as a character, and one senses
that at last he has affirmed the truth of his protested beliefs. In
speaking of Nancy's impending execution he says:

> . . . We're not concerned with death. That's nothing: any
> handful of petty facts and sworn documents can cope with
> that. That's all finished now; we can forget it. What we are
> trying to deal with now is injustice. Only truth can cope
> with that. Or love.

It is most significant that this is the first time that Faulkner has suggested the expedient of brotherly love in human relations, black and
white.

The study, then, of Faulkner's gallery of Negro characters reveals
that he has taken the "mammy"-type (Dilsey, Aunt Mollie Beauchamp) and the "tragic mulatto"-type (Joe Christmas, Charles Bon)
stereotypes and made them into symbols of qualities quite different
from those for which they formerly stood. They are neither plantation
tradition menials nor happy-go-lucky comics. The characters, in fact,
have outgrown the stereotypes to such an extent that in his later charac-

terizations (Sam Fathers, Lucas Beauchamp, Nancy Mannigoe) the stereotypes are no longer recognizable. Faulkner did this, not out of any desire to purge southern literature of types long objectionable to Negroes, but because he wanted to dramatize human qualities he respected and admired. For him the Dilseys and Nancy Mannigoes and the mythical Sam Fathers signified a stoic endurance to survive; the Lucas Beauchamps, the black shadow, connoted the projection of the South's guilty conscience.

And now—what significance the sound and the fury? What are the conclusions, and what do they signify? Faulkner brings such an intensity of feeling and emotion to his art that if he is obsessed with the "black shadow," as he most certainly is, some reason must be found in his artifacts.

One of the first things we observe is that Faulkner does not presume to preach; he makes no attempt at propagandizing some sociological determinism. He does not attempt to justify a way of life. He is fiercely intent upon the truth, and the truth he sees is tragic. He knows the South in all its guises of good and evil and still loves it.

We must also conclude that Faulkner does not understand fully Negroes as persons—as he says, "what white man does?" He continually refers to their "inscrutability." Perhaps that is the reason that he usually approached his Negro characterizations from the outside and seldom worked from the inside outwards. Thus he writes more about them than through them. There are even times, as with Nancy Mannigoe, that his artifacts are not consistent with his characterizations. Plausibility, as related to the subtle complications of behavior in his Negro characters, seems to elude him. However, there are startling flashes of insight when he does get into his Negro characters. At such times he reveals with uncanny penetration their acute awareness and sullen understanding of the bitter life they are doomed to live in a degenerate hate-ridden South.

Anyone who uses as many Negro characters as does Faulkner is usually expected to have some philosophy, arrive at some conclusions about Negro-white relationships. Surely a serious study of his work as a whole does not lead one to the conclusion that he hates the Negro as Maxwell Geismar suggests. On the other hand, neither can one agree with those who claim that he loves the Negro, unless they are referring to the Dilsey-type Negro servant. A more tenable inference is that his thinking about the problem is unsettled and inconclusive. That there has been an expanding development in his liberalism is evident in more ways than one; but until he himself can conquer the psychological dualism of his feeling toward the total Negro, no coherent statement about Negroes can be expected in his novels.

What Faulkner has done is to present situations and reserve any personal judgement. He does not write social protest. He describes the condition of the Negro as he sees it in all its bitter sordidness—the poverty, the never-ending subordination, the "nigger-baiting, nigger-hating" atmosphere, the injustice of the whites. On the white side of the ledger he pictures the pathological fear of "black blood"; the lusting after Negro women, the morbid preoccupation with the imagined details of real or spurious rape committed by Negroes; the exaltation of southern womanhood; the perverse love and hate for the Negro.

If any conclusion can be attributed to Faulkner it is that slavery was the doom of the South, and hence it is forced into an ambivalent need to justify and atone for the crime perpetrated on its victims. It follows then that so long as the burden of guilt exists, so long as the sin remains unexpiated, just so long will the "black shadow" hover over the land as an eternal reminder of that doom. Yet, withal Faulkner's picturization of the degeneracy of the South, if one were to ask him why he hates the South, he would answer, as did Quentin Compson, "I don't. I don't! I don't hate it! I don't hate it!"

CHARLES R. ANDERSON

Violence And Order In The Novels Of Robert Penn Warren

The works of major authors often have a unity that tempts the critic to look for a central theme, even a controlling symbol, that focuses their vision of life. I find all the novels of Robert Penn Warren to be variations on a single theme, symbolized in the polarities of violence and order. He could not have chosen two concepts more arresting to the modern reader or more deeply embedded in the history of his country and his region.

American history began with a tremendous uprooting from settled European cultures because of uncompromising religious dissent and economic restlessness. The first century and a half was a continuous chronicle of international rivalries, Indian wars, and struggles for survival against a hostile environment—threatened famine, extremes of climate, wild beasts and savages. Then came the violence of revolt from the mother country, with the doctrine of continuous revolution announced as an inalienable right, followed in less than a century by a bloody Civil War. And all along, just beyond the settlements, there was always the frontier with the original conditions of violence repeated in wave after wave across the continent until the end of the nineteenth century. The smooth surface of contemporary life in this country does not conceal from the poet the same patterns reappearing today in the ruthless drive of big business and power politics, as well as in the more obvious orgies of speed, prohibition, race riots, and gangsters.

Robert Penn Warren has uncovered the historical sources of American violence and made them available for literary purposes, all four novels taking off from violent episodes in history that are used to illuminate modern meanings. But in writing tragedy, though the downward plunge into action takes up the most space and provides the greatest interest, violence alone is not enough. The tragic note cannot be struck without a positive world view. There can be no fall unless there is something to fall from; disorder is meaningless without order, at least a concept of order, as a point to measure from. Hemingway's fiction is an instructive example. He writes of violence in a world of violence, even the milieu being carefully placed outside the ordered daily life of man. Though each of his heroes has a sort of code to live by—that of the soldier, the sportsman, even the criminal —it is not a discipline applicable to the normal world. This is perhaps best illustrated by bull-fighting, where the violence of the bull is contrived and the code for fighting him is entirely artificial. It is aesthetically pure, like a problem in geometry, and hence devoid of moral meaning. It is not tragedy. In Warren's fictions, though violence predominates at least on the surface, a concept of order is always there as a touchstone; and since the source of both is to be found in his Southern heritage, this may explain why Warren (and Faulkner) alone of modern American novelists can write tragedies.

Collective myth has fixed on the South as the embodiment of violence in America. The witch-burning of New England, the bandit of the Wild West, the underworld of Chicago, all of them fade before the succession of Southern images of violence that fascinate the popular mind: the lash of the slave-driver, the Bowie knife of the old Southwest, the duelling pistol of the hot-headed gentleman, the rebel yell of the fire-eater, the gasoline torch of the lyncher, the fiery cross of the Klansman. One can indeed point to certain historical factors that made for greater potential violence in the South. By reason of its geographical shape as a fringe of seaboard states, this region was more continuously exposed to the frontier than other more compact areas of settlement. With a third of its population only a few generations out of African savagery, there was always the fact of primitive behavior as well as the threat of slave insurrection. The plantation system made the enforcement of discipline and the democratization of culture harder than in the more populous townships of the North, so that the poor-whites tended to sink into lawlessness instead of being educated into good citizenship. When the power of the ruling class was smashed, the incidence of violence in the post-bellum South rose above that of the rest of the nation, as the recent statistics of a criminologist have proved.

However interesting all this may be to the historian and sociologist, it merely provides a subject matter—not a theme—for the novelist like Warren who is concerned with something quite different from the game of cops and robbers. He is concerned with moral order and moral violence, which sometimes coincide with physical order and violence in the world of men yet sometimes seem strangely to clash with them. So for the fictional artist, who must embody his theme in society, there are opened up rich possibilities of ambiguity and irony. For Warren murder, rape, and arson are simply the most effective dramatic means of developing one half his theme: that *violence is life without principle.* Nor, to illustrate the other half, does he use orderliness for its own sake (there are no police chiefs or private detectives among his heroes); to him *order is living by principles,* even when the particular effort to do so falls far short of perfection. Yet sometimes the man of principles also may be forced into violent action to defend or reassert a concept of order, when corrupt or misguided men have risen to power and society has lost its moorings. Again, external order on the political and economic levels may all too frequently be achieved, at least temporarily, by the kind of compromise which is a "deal" based on the abdication of principles. By such conflicts of appearances and realities Warren renders in his fictions the ambiguities of the actual world, as opposed to the blacks and whites of an imaginary one.

A further irony is woven into his stories by discriminating the man of principles from the idealist, with whom he is popularly confused. Without attempting to fix the final meaning of that vexed word, *principles,* one may begin with the dictionary definition: "the general or accepted laws governing conduct" that have come down through history. Quite opposite are those flights of the spirit enjoining us that we should love our neighbors as ourselves, that all men are created equal; these are aspirations, not principles. So with the humanitarianism of the abolitionist, the absolutism of the Puritan dogma of man's depravity, as well as the transcendental insistence on his divinity. Such are the so-called "principles" that frequently lead to extreme and even violent action, to the over-throw of the existing order in a search for Utopia; they are, instead, abstract ideals born of man's pride in his reason or of spiritual naiveté. At certain crises in the world's history, when stagnant traditionalism has retarded overdue reform, anarchic idealists play a legitimate role. Only after they have announced their extremist doctrines is it possible to take the middle of the road. Then the man of principles, accepting the mixture of good and evil in his nature, can take account of the new ideas as well as the traditional codes of morality drawn from human experience and re-establish an ordered society.

This is, at least, what Poe meant by principles and what Twelve Southerners took their stand on in 1930: man must accept his middle place in "nature" between the animals and the angels, neither sinking into naturalism nor aspiring to perfection, but creating the best possible order out of his recognized limitations and preserving it. It is chiefly, I suspect, what gives continuity to the literary tradition in the South (as distinctive as that in New England), from the pragmatic humanism of William Byrd to Faulkner's concern with "the old universal truths" that lie at the heart of his fictions, as summed up in his Nobel Prize speech. At any rate, the sociologists who have been appalled by Southern violence in the physical world have overlooked an equally high incidence of Southern concern with the principles of order, in the literary theory of Poe and Lanier as well as in the social and political theory of Jefferson and Calhoun, a tradition that has flowered anew in the agrarian poets and critics of the twentieth century. (It is precisely those elements of idealism based on abstract reason in Jefferson's philosophy that have been rejected in the South.)

The civilization of the South was founded on the concept of an ordered society. The basis for this is probably agrarianism, predicated on the European philosophy of a settled order, as opposed to industrialism, predicated on a belief in progress—with the necessary corollary of a changing way of life, however orderly the process. The South has always distrusted progressivism and all the other isms that seem disruptive of a traditional society, a clearly defined order of human existence. That is, until the twentieth century, when cracks in this conservative civilization begin to show as the South, more and more industrialized, tends to lose its identity and become gradually transformed into the money economy of standardized urban America. It is a sense of this breaking-up as tragic that has focused the vision of the new Southern writers, who call back images of an older order— that they find better because more human—to measure the collapse into the political and moral chaos of the modern world. Warren's values are not founded on any theory of politics, economics, or religion, however, though most of his illustrative action takes place in these areas. He is a psychologist and a moralist, concerned with a particular conception of human nature (as Irene Hendry has pointed out, *Sewanee Review*, January 1945): Man cannot live in the world without a center of self-knowledge; hence the archetypal hero is the man with a full and immediate awareness of the fundamental principles according to which one acts in any given situation. Warren's concepts of violence and order are defined in Southern terms. Being a true artist, he does not argue these concepts nor use the terms explicitly in his novels; rather, he implies them in his symbolism, he renders them in the speech and behavior of his characters. Principles are embattled equally by corrupt materialism and by abstract idealism.

His first novel, *Night Rider* (1939), is set in the Kentucky Tobacco War of 1904. The association of farmers, organized for protection against the buyers' monopoly, at first seems based on principles. Some of the founders are high-minded, and there is much righteous indignation about unfair prices, much talk of justice and order. But unable to get justice fast enough by orderly methods, they set up the "night riders" to coerce reluctant farmers to join the association by scraping their plant beds, and even by burning barns and horse-whipping their owners. For a while the leaders managed to keep a sort of military discipline; but they have substituted force for principles—armed men operating in masks—and violence soon takes over. Recalcitrant members are shot down in cold blood by their fellow "klansmen"; mobs a thousand strong march on the towns and engage in mass arson, dynamiting the warehouses of the tobacco trust. A virtual war is precipitated, of such violence that the state militia has difficulty in restoring order. The background handling of this historical episode is almost documentary, but the center of interest in the novel lies elsewhere.

The author merely uses the tobacco war to illustrate the fall of Percy Munn from a sense of order to a fascination with violence for its own sake. His dæmonic flaw is clarified by comparison with several other characters. The nearest to an idealist in this story is the combination of theory and practice represented by Professor Ball and his son-in-law Dr. MacDonald, who organize the night riders. They are determined men who produce effective action; they have noble convictions about justice but their abstract ideals of human behavior bear little relation to human experience, so that their goals can be achieved only by the ruthless application of force. They are not bad in the sense of being corrupt, but because their fanaticism does not recognize human limitations—a different kind of evil from that of pure material-ism (which is represented, ironically, by a family named Christian). Further along in self-knowledge is the peasant Willie Proudfit, whose adventures in the far West and the religious conversion that brings him back to primitive agrarianism in Kentucky are told in an em-bedded story. Although these experiences do not furnish him with any articulate "ideals" about life, his rebirth gives him a sort of center from which to live—a not altogether successful embodiment of the regionalist theme of the small farmer who has returned "home."

The ambiguity of appearances is best brought out in two con-trasting leaders of the association whose example led Munn to join. Only Captain Todd, whose character sets the moral tone of the early meetings, always acts on principles. But when he withdraws in pro-test at the formation of the night riders, Munn is too deeply involved in the excitement to follow him, rationalizing that he is just a Con-federate veteran too old-fashioned to be effective in public affairs any longer. Instead, his eye is caught by the shining figure of Senator Tolliver, whose suave manners and eloquence in behalf of the op-pressed farmers strike him as the qualities of a true leader who knows his direction. The reader from the beginning doubts his sincerity and gradually suspects him of being a confused and fragmentary man who must fulfill himself in other people, whose craving for applause and prestige may well lead to opportunism. But the hero does not recognize him as the hollow man he is until he sells out to the trust, a man of price rather than principle. (It is apparent now that Tolliver joined the association in the first place for political advantage, just as he resigned and secretly went over to the enemy for a greater advantage.) By this time Munn, from a promising young lawyer aspiring to an ordered life, has sunk to an anonymous group-murderer and a fugitive from justice. The completeness of his disintegration is revealed by his final resolve to murder the Senator, whom he at last sees as a moral negation ("You were always nothing," he tells him); but he lacks the will to carry out even this, and in the night he is riddled with bullets by the posse sent to capture him. Such is the tragedy of Percy Munn, who lacked the ability to formulate a set of principles adequate to conduct, or even to recognize them in the noble example of Captain Todd whom he admired and who, at least for the reader, is a point from which to measure the hero's fall into violent and suicidal action.

Warren's second novel, *At Heaven's Gate* (1943), is based on the actual career of Luke Lea, who built up a precarious financial kingdom in Tennessee through ruthless business methods and political corruption and was criminally prosecuted for his part in a multi-million-dollar failure in the crash of 1929. But the financier Bogan Murdock could never have been a protagonist to Warren, as the titan Cowperwood was to Dreiser. For, wholly given over to a blind drive for economic power—modern "civilized" violence—he has no principles from which to fall. He cannot be a center of interest but only a point of reference, and a device for irony. Murdock is the sham man-of-principles, heightened and extended from the Senator of the first novel. Outwardly he is an accomplished man of the world, a perfect host, unfailingly courteous, impeccable in speech and behavior. His apparent mastery of life is symbolized in his mastery of a horse, his flashing equestrianism seeming the final flourish of the eighteenth-century gentleman. It is only gradually that the reader realizes the moral vacuum beneath this polished surface. It is his economic adviser Blake who first sees that he is empty inside ("When Bogan looks in the mirror he don't see a thing," says the cynical Ph.D.). Order, we learn, is not the same thing as decorum, though this may be the form in which it clothes itself. Order is living by principles, and Murdock has given them up in his abstract passion for financial power; he is as ruthless in this as men of an earlier day had been in action. This not only brings us nearer to the contemporary world, but it proves that moral violence is more destructive than physical violence, because it results from the corruption of principles and produces a continuing state of chaos rather than a temporary one.

Most of the evil in this novel operates under cover of big business or respectable society, and the center of interest radiates out to the circle of characters surrounding Murdock. The first inkling of disorder is the discovery that he has no control over his own family. His senile father, whose past murder of a political rival Bogan is covering up, is threatening at all points to blurt out the secret; his neglected wife is an alcoholic; his daughter is a nymphomaniac. Sue and Murdock's protégé Jerry, the Phi Beta Kappa football hero, unconsciously feel the emptiness of their lives attached to this man of no principles;

they indulge in violent and joyless copulation in an unhappy effort
to find their identity in each other, then break off their engagement
and lose all direction as they throw their weight around generally.
Physical violence, which has been kept off-stage in flashbacks and
embedded stories, is saved for the denouement where it is piled on
too thick to be disentangled here. Among the minor figures there are
plenty of grubby materialists hanging on Murdock's coat-tails ready
to use physical force if necessary to cash in on the potentialities for
corruption in his interlocking system, but as the epitome of modern
moral violence the boss is careful to maintain appearances. As a result, most of the external violence is deflected from him to his daughter
and her fiancé. Sue, in her desperate flight from her father's emptiness and Jerry's confusion, has gone to live with a drunken chaotic
group of Bohemians. She has an abortion performed because one of
them, a Marxian bruiser, refuses to marry her; she is strangled by another, a homosexual, in impotent rage; the family's negro butler is
nearly lynched for her murder; and Jerry lands in jail as the scapegoat
for Murdock's financial collapse.

In this complex novel the emphasis is so distributed among a
large gallery of characters, most of whom suffer in various stages
from the modern disease of "division," that any attempt to summarize
their meanings must be tentative. There are several partial manifestations of the idealist. Blake, who gives Jerry worldly advice on how
to achieve financial eminence, is an inverted one, as proved by his
cynicism and his sentimental discovery in the end that some things
really matter. The most fully developed idealist is Sweetwater, a
preacher's son who ran away from home to become a strike-promoter
for the unions, and who has managed to define himself through
identification with the abstract cause of the working man. But he
is not a man of principles. He can only find direction from the outside, from the Marxist's code, a partial one invented by man's reason
to right an economic wrong; and he carries over this code to his love
affair with Sue, rejecting the human relation of marriage because it
would interfere with his dedication. (The inner discipline of the
man of principles aims at a whole view, self imposed by reference to
the orders of religion and traditional society against which imperfect
man can be measured.) If Sweetwater fails in wholeness because he
is dominated by reason, the opposite is true of Wyndham, the fanatic
of the interpolated story, though his primitive religion at least pro-

vides him with an adequate understanding of evil; but both men lack balance and are led into violence by their idealism. The most vivid symbol of the divided man is the sexual ambivalence of Slim Sarrett, the intellectual who oscillates between pugilism and poetry, between a tendency to homosexuality and a desire to have Sue as his mistress. It is dramatically fitting that she should come to a violent end at his hands, for she is as incapable of finding a center from which to live as he (or as Percy Munn). The bewildered Jerry Calhoun, like all the others, is a divided modern man, but he alone finds a measure of redemption. In his bumbling, persistent way he finally recognizes Murdock as an a-moral monster in time to save himself from contamination and makes a symbolic return to his humble home and father (the favorite pattern of all Warren's "Billy Pottses"). But neither he nor old man Calhoun, the simple, clumsy dirt-farmer, is strong enough to serve convincingly as the exemplary man of principles. At best, this almost naturalistic novel is a study in the disintegration of modern society, the confusion of man lost in the disorder of his blindly competitive urban economy and trying to find some truth by which to live. But it falls short of tragedy; there is no cruel defeat through excess of virtue. And since the hero who acts on principles does not appear except in shreds and patches, there is no standard from which a fall can be measured.

All the King's Men (1946), first drafted as a play, is his fullest achievement of tragedy. Though it follows in some detail the outward career of Huey Long, dictator of Louisiana from 1928 until his assassination in 1935, it was not Warren's purpose to write a fictional biography of the King Fish. By the device of the narrator he frames one story within another, so that the rise and fall of Willie Stark become merely illustrative matter. Though this master of violence is the one who comes to a tragic end, the reader's interest centers in Jack Burden the rootless and alienated modern man, a symbol of the "terrible division of his age" that makes a Stark possible. He alternately withdraws as a spectator to formulate a theory of life and swings back into action to reform the world (at least by proxy); but he continues his search for self-knowledge which, in the end, saves him from physical catastrophe.

In his first novel Warren had effectively used "night" as a symbol of the darkness in which men move. In his ironically titled *At*

Heaven's Gate, the representative image seems to be "pus," the evil being now clearly in the blood-stream, a part of man's essential nature and not an external thing that can be eliminated automatically by reform and progress. So in *All the King's Men* essential evil is internal, chiefly expressed in terms of political corruption. And the outward manifestations of order are again ironical symbols.* The network of paved highways Stark builds over the state, with Route 58 forming a sort of structural spine for the novel, is to be the pattern of his new order of prosperity. But they are never shown to be paths of direction: nobody knows where he is going in this book, so the roads lead everywhere and nowhere. Instead of economic aids to the common man, they chiefly produce speed and meaningless action, or bring the wool-hat boys pouring into the capital to chant like primitives, "We want Willie!" It is from an accident on one of these shining concrete strips that Tom Stark, rebelling against the domination of his action-mad father, receives his basic injury. The second instrument of the new order Stark had promised the people was education, but his emphasis is on football, with its artificial discipline mimicked in the parades of bands and organized cheering. It is his forcing Tom into a game when not in condition—anything to win!—that results in the final injury. This leads to Willie's third panacea, free medical care. But the only use we hear of the hospital being put to—besides an operation to restore a schizophrenic to singleness—is Dr. Stanton's effort to save Tom. Science, alas, cannot make him whole again, and action for its own sake ends in paralysis. Order, we learn through tragic irony, cannot be imposed mechanically from the outside.

Stark's new order can only lead to destructive violence because

---

* Norman Girault, the only critic who has noted the contrasted symbolism of violence and order in this novel, has already pointed out two examples (see *Accent,* Summer 1947). The stagnant water covered with algae that surrounds the little island of civilization in Louisiana Warren describes as "the bayou, which coiled under the moss . . . heavy with the hint and odor of swamp, jungle, and darkness, along the edge of the expanse of clipped lawn"—a juxtaposition of uncontrollable brute nature and man's rationally controlled efforts to stake out a claim. Closely connected with this is a second symbol, Highway 58, and the novel opens significantly with the dare-devil driving of Sugar boy down this new road cut through the swamp. Even nature seems to resent this, as it does Stark's blind drive for power, "the ectoplasmic fingers of the mist" reaching out to snag the roaring Cadillac; but the dictator's body-guard shows his pride in the mastery of machinery, and his hatred of nature, by deliberately swerving to run down a snake. Warren seems to be saying that modern man's attempt to control the external world through the orderly will, unguided by an understanding of irrational violence, is not the way to the good life.

he plunges headlong into action with no clearly defined principles.   In
his drive for power he becomes an opportunist who makes deals, and
is soon entangled in a mesh of bribery and graft demanding coercive
measures to hold his empire of outlaws in check.   The air is charged
with potential violence as the police state takes shape: the bullet-
proof limousine, the body-guard Sugar Boy practising fast draws with
his .38, the natty élite State Patrol, the threat of illiterate mobs.
But during three-fourths of the book it occurs only in the embedded
story of Cass Mastern, whose history Jack was trying to make into a
doctoral dissertation but was stopped because unable to read the
meaning of violence and order in his ancestor's life.   This lesson is
learned in a bath of blood as the novel roars to its end.   Judge Irwin
resigns from his post as Attorney General because he can no longer
stomach the dictator's methods, then commits suicide when confronted
by Stark with the dirt from his past previously dug up by Jack; and
Jack learns too late, from his mother's confession, that he has unwittingly killed his father.   Anne Stanton, whose world of ordered
values is shattered by discovering that her father had been implicated
in the Judge's guilt, breaks her engagement with Jack and throws herself into the arms of Stark, the one man in all this chaos who seems
to have strength and direction.   This brings on the climax.   For her
idealist brother, Dr. Adam Stanton, who learns of her dishonor through
the jealousy of Stark's rejected mistress Sadie Burke and the welching
of Tiny Duffy, assassinates the dictator under the dome of the capitol.
Sugar Boy pumps him full of lead from his automatic, the squealer
Tiny narrowly misses a like fate, and Sadie collapses in a mental
hospital.   So the bodies pile up in the tradition of Elizabethan tragedy,
and only Jack and Anne are left to find their way back to a meaningful
life.

The ambiguities of real life are reproduced so faithfully in this
fiction that all Warren's characters become people instead of types,
but it may help clarify his meanings to look for the main springs of
his creative thinking.   The foreground is crowded with corrupt
materialists—almost all the king's men.   There is his machine organization of political henchmen, most fully delineated in the predatory
Duffy; and there is a whole implied ring of unscrupulous capitalists
who finance his reforms for a cut or a monopoly.   The brute materialism of some of those closest to him is slightly humanized by being
based on blind love and devotion to the dictator instead of selfish

greed, as with the moronic Sugar Boy and the carnal Sadie. The wool-hat boys whose suffrage supports him are only materialists in the sense of having never been sure of a square meal; hence their fanatic loyalty to Willie, because of their naive trust in his promises. It is not implied that they are corrupt, but they are capable of mass violence if it is needed to keep him in the saddle. Stark himself is not a pure materialist, for he is far less concerned with any tangible "take" for himself than with a mania for abstract power. This of course is largely motivated by selfish passions: ambition, the drive to compensate for being born a "have-not," and revenge against the politicos who duped him at the beginning of his career. But it is also curiously mixed with an initial idealism, to redeem government and give it back to the people, threads of which keep reappearing. He is constantly trying to persuade himself that his purpose is to bring good out of evil, and he makes at least one striking attempt to put his power at the service of a humanitarian ideal by excluding the politicians from influence in the medical center where Dr. Stanton is at the helm. None of this, however, must be confused with principles. A man of principles is above all one who can understand and control himself, and this is precisely what Willie cannot do, though he can face and manage everything and everybody else. His genius is for action, without waiting to formulate principles; in the material world this leads to opportunism, pyramiding violence, and final destruction.

Warren is just as critical of the idealist as he is of the materialist, and there are several of them here to complicate the issues. Jack Burden's supposed father is a pious fool who deserts his wife and withdraws from the world into an impossible religion, trying to live out quite literally in the slums the gospel of Christ. (Warren may find the Christian scheme of things close to the facts of experience, as one critic suggests, but he is too much of an empiricist to trust the adequacy of an idealized Christianity to cope with the chaos of contemporary life.) His fiancée, Anne Stanton, is likewise a sheltered idealist who has never outgrown the innocence of childhood and is equally helpless in finding direction for herself or poor confused Jack. Her brother Adam is another case of withdrawal, too purely a man of ideas, who spurns the world of men for the truth of science (the emphasis on the abstraction of scientism is even stronger in the stage version, with its continuous chorus of surgeons chanting doggerel). His one venture into action is almost ritualistic, though by it he rid the state of a dictator. Yet one feels that all of this group—remnants of a traditional society—had drifted into their various idealisms because the codified principles of their civilization had become too formal and functionless, and because these characters were not secure enough in self-knowledge to dare acquire that knowledge of the modern world necessary to bring them into effective action. In a happier day they could have served, even though passively, as supporters of a way of life based on principles.

Even Jack Burden has this same tendency towards idealism, or its reverse, a wise-cracking cynicism, which keeps him wavering throughout most of the story from one half-truth to another. But he has a strong sense of social obligation and is too courageous a seeker to be content with so negative a life, and in the end his tragic experience of life makes possible his rebirth. From all he has learned, he defines his perfect exemplar as the man who has a body of principles which both initiate and control his actions, a balance resulting from knowledge of the world and moral certainty of self. Warren is too much of a realist to set up such a paragon in any single character, but from all the people at Burden's Landing one can be pieced together. Judge Irwin, the hero's real father, though a gentleman of the old school, was still capable of functioning effectively in public affairs; and he always acted on principles except for one slip in early life, but his failure to face the consequences of this resulted in his suicide. Cass Mastern, his great uncle from the previous century, died a hero (at least in the religious sense) because he acknowledged his evil for what it was and lived with it, never violating principles thereafter. From these imperfect examples Jack can construct his model. He can now accept the responsibility of being human, face the evil in the world and his part in it. He can find the faith and courage to give up his role of narrator and go back "into the convulsion of the world" —the contemporary world, which includes cities and science, political machines as well as industrial ones.

Warren's latest novel, *World Enough and Time* (1950), is an epitome of all that has gone before, but the author gives himself new dimensions by completely breaking with realistic fiction. He adopts melodrama as his subject matter and allegory as his vehicle, but shoulders them both off onto the "diary" kept by his hero. The foundation of his story is the famous "Kentucky Tragedy," a murder that took place in Frankfort in 1826 and has come down in elaborate documentary records. Though Jeremiah Beaumont of the novel goes through many of the acts of the original murderer, the theme is again the tragic search for order in a world of violence. As the hero says (though the documents are silent): "The idea by which a man would live gets lost in the jostle and pudder of things."

The vivid background of violence in early Kentucky, when civilization was just raising its head in the wilderness, is epitomized near the beginning in the description of a frontier revivalist:

> He belonged to that old race of Devil-breakers who were a terror and a blessing across the land, men who had been born to be the stomp-and-gouge bully of a tavern, the Indian fighter with warm scalps at his belt, the ice-eyed tubercular duelist of a county courthouse, the half-horse, half-alligator abomination of a keelboat, or a raper of women by the cow pen, but who got their hot prides and cold lusts short-circuited into obsessed hosannas and a ferocious striving for God's sake.

This summary is profusely illustrated throughout the novel, culminating in a carnival of violence in the embedded story of "la Grand' Bosse". He is a humpbacked pirate who rules over his kingdom of outlaws on an island in the swamp, where they wallow in filth and obscenity, liquor and lechery, ignorance and brawling, renegades of mixed blood and creeds. From this retreat they conduct raids on the Mississippi River traffic, murdering, burning, and bringing back the plunder of civilization to their primitive village built on stilts over the mud flats. This we are told, with an irony that undercuts the ideal of the primitivists, is "the innocence of nature." Man, it is clear, should not live according to Nature, but according to the principles of human nature.

The most significant violence, of course, is that in which the hero is involved as a major participant. With a romantic gesture Jerry breaks off his legal apprenticeship to Cassius Fort, whom he had looked up to as the ideal statesman, and seeks out in marriage a society belle whom Fort has seduced. For a while he tries to live with her in retirement from the world. But feeling a compulsion that her honor must be avenged he issues a challenge. When Fort, though admitting his guilt, refuses to duel his "adopted son," Jerry murders him in cold blood. At his trial he is very nearly acquitted through a web of shrewd lies, but is finally convicted by an even more intricate one. Condemned to be hanged, he is joined in the cell by his previously estranged wife. In a parody of rediscovered love they indulge in an orgy of sexual intercourse; failing to find escape in life they seek one in death, but the suicide pact fails to come off—the laudanum contained an emetic. That same night, just before the hour of their execution, they are rescued in a hairbreadth jail-delivery and taken to the island of la Grand' Bosse as a hideout. Here Jerry gradually sinks into that life of violence, while his wife loses her mind and kills herself with a hunting knife. A final prick of conscience sends him back to civilization to give himself up to the hangman and find expiation in facing his own guilt at last. But he is overtaken on the way by a hired assassin, decapitated, and only his head is brought back to justice. So much for the melodrama in which the violence is manifested.

This sensational sequence of events on the frontier reproduces convincingly the violent growth from which modern America has come, but in summary it reduces the novel unjustly to a tale of blood and thunder. Further, though the surface action may seem obvious, the meanings Warren draws from it are not. For example, to assume that America has progressed to better times by policing all this physical violence into law and order is to be brought up short with the implications of the end of la Grand' Bosse's career. It is the advance of "civilization" itself, we are told, that put the river pirate out of business, by inventing methods of making profits too subtle and complicated for him to understand or cope with: "He was simply the victim of technological unemployment." And we are not spared the ironical conjecture that some of his bastard descendants, masquerading in the world as respectable leaders and business men, "still carry under their pink scrubbed hides and double-breasted sack suits . . . the mire-thick blood of his veins and the old coiling darkness of his heart"—thus linking this pioneer incarnation of evil with the Bogan Murdocks and Tiny Duffys of his modern fictions. Warren always makes it clear that he is concerned with the unchanging nature of man rather than with the changing social fabric in which this nature manifests itself. He chooses a particular time and place merely because of its illustrative value; and the profuse display of physical violence in early Kentucky makes vividly dramatic Jerry Beaumont's struggle towards a concept of order.

The author's meanings are made most explicit by the allegorical cast of the hero's mind, as he spells out the events and characters of his story in a diary. But one cannot always be certain of them because of his excessive ambition to corner the ultimate truth; for the defect of this novel lies in too many unresolved ambiguities, the failure to clarify some of its immensely complex significances. In a sense all the characters in *World Enough and Time* are projections of various aspects of the narrator (in the opening chapter the whole story is spoken of as "the drama Jeremiah Beaumont devised"); and his interpretations of them, recorded in a deliberately unrealistic style, tend to the abstractions of allegory. Two of them, his best friend and his wife, are clearly *alter egos* who give new definitions to the polarities of violence and order. Wilkie Barron is the purest Man of Action in all Warren's fiction, too engrossed in the act of living to be concerned with its meanings; if he ever attempts to express an idea it becomes rhetoric, and he laughs at his own mock eloquence. He is the instigator of every action the hero takes part in—his marriage, his political brawling with the reformers, his mud-slinging campaign for the legislature, his murder of Colonel Fort. In the end Jerry recognizes him as at once his adversary and his shadow, calling him specifically "the mask of all the world." Rachel Jordan, the injured heroine "immured in an autumn world" of poetry, is the symbol of his dreaming; and he tries to escape with her into the inner secret world of love and honor, in a house from which the public is quite literally locked out. At the peak of their romance they are described as "high allegorical figures acting out their ritual." Standing midway between them is Skrogg, the newspaper editor who lashes the Relief Party into violent action to secure justice for the downtrodden. He is a fearless idealist, we are told, "because the world outside himself was not real, . . . was nothing but chaos which could become real only in so far as it was formed by his idea." Lest there be any doubt about the author's attitude towards this purest Man of Idea, his career after the reform movement failed is sketched in brief: by a fantastic reversal he entered the world he had scorned, became a professional duelist who killed half-a-dozen men, and was finally shot down by a man he had defamed.

As Jerry is drawn alternately to order (which in his idealism he defines as "the idea of the world") and violence ("the world itself"), he finds both inadequate and cries out for singleness, for some truth

by which a man can live. In his search for principles he has many
partial teachers. The first is Dr. Burnham of the classical academy,
scholar, physician, and loving preacher, who holds up to him the example of the noble Romans; his second is Colonel Fort, the intelligent man of action, who tries to do what good he can in public affairs
within his limitations, and takes Jerry on as a protégé. They are not
perfect men, not even great men save that "they took their world
greatly . . . and knew that in study, field, and forum they bore the
destiny of men." But the youthful hero, in his obsession with perfection and certainty, drifts away from one and turns his dagger against
the other. (In his effort to provoke Fort to a duel he tries to unite
his inner and outer worlds, seeking in that code the formalized public
act that embodies the idea of honor, but he is refused this ritualistic
evasion. Condemned to death he tries to blame his botched life on
Burnham for setting him impossible ideals, but his old teacher's last
heroic act of goodness closes that escape from responsibility.) In
the end Jerry's idealism, which had rejected the limitations of humanity
and spurned the demands of society, humbles him enough to admire
once more man's struggle to live by principles. The two lawyer-
statesmen who volunteer to defend him at the murder trial provide
him with a composite example: Hawgood, who lived selflessly for a
high concept of truth, and Madison, a more experienced man, who
felt honor bound to help all those suffering from injustice. For that
one moment "the seasoned campaigner and the Platonic student" stood
together, "worldly decency conspired with unworldly truth."

Jerry's life has partaken in some degree of all these, chiefly
fluctuating between the extremes of idealism and materialism, in his
search for a center. As he sifts for the meaning of his tumultous and
tragic experiences, he records his three great errors. The first was his
withdrawal into "cold exile from mankind" believing that "the idea
was all." The second was, "when we find that the idea has not redeemed the world, the world must redeem the idea"—which led to
the confusion of means with end. The third error was "to deny the
idea and its loneliness and embrace the world as all," to try to live
in the innocence of nature. These had been the ways of his tragic
life. His conclusion must be quoted in full:

> There must be a way I have missed. There must be a way
> whereby the word becomes flesh. There must be a way

whereby the flesh becomes word. Whereby loneliness becomes communion without contamination. Whereby contamination becomes purity without exile. There must be a
way, but I may not have it now. All I can have now is
knowledge.

His diary ends with a question, the age-old human question, "Was
all for naught?" But Warren's four novels, if we probe beneath the
living tissue of the text, help to define Jerry's conclusion: Man must
live *in* the world of violence, *by* whatever principles of order he can
formulate and believe in. The man who makes up personal rules as
expediency dictates or abstract ideals based on imperfect knowledge
of the world falls into violence, moral or physical, almost as surely
as the materialist who denies the validity of morals in a naturalistic
universe. They all act against, not with, the ethical currents of their
society. A didactic novelist unconcerned with tragedy might well
have opposed to them the formalist, who rigidly adheres to the accepted civil and religious codes; but he can only function as a preserver
of law and order in an established society. Instead, the heroic figure
in these fictions is the man of principles whose beliefs are founded
upon a full knowledge of the ethos of his civilization, including its
unwritten laws and modes of behavior, so that his actions have a
frame of reference more ample and human than any rationale of conduct arbitrarily devised. Never fully embodied in any one character,
this hero is implied throughout as the exemplary Southern gentleman
of tradition. But Warren is not guilty in this of any nostalgic retreat
into a romantic conception of the Old South; he is searching for
modern meanings in its civilization, especially in its frontier strivings
and its efforts to avert collapse today. As he says elsewhere (in an
essay on Faulkner):

> The old order [in the South] . . . allowed the traditional man
> to define himself as human by setting up codes, concepts of
> virtue, obligations, and by accepting the risks of his humanity.
> Within the traditional order was a notion of truth, even if
> man in the flow of things did not succeed in realizing that
> truth.

With full recognition of all his imperfections, such a man could still
be heroic. What counted was the human effort.

HARRY MODEAN CAMPBELL

Warren as Philosopher
in *World Enough and Time*

Since Robert Penn Warren is a competent poet (in addition to being an important critic, novelist, and writer of short stories), it is not surprising that one of the most striking characteristics of his style in his fiction is the frequent use of functional imagery—usually functional even when, as often happens, the extended metaphor folds within itself a series of subordinate comparisons. Even when one finds this imagery tiresome, as in Jack Burden's perpetual wisecracking under happy and tragic circumstances alike, one usually has to admit that it is still dramatically appropriate to the character from whose point of view it is presented. (Jack Burden is an intelligent, sensitive, sometimes sentimental, more often cynical, young man for whom a flow of jesting imagery helps to wash away some of the dreariness of existence.) This kind of attention to realism in imagery is especially well illustrated by Warren's consistently careful distinction in *World Enough and Time* between his own imagery and that of the characters—for example, the old-fashioned rhetorical flourishes of Jeremiah Beaumont, which always appear as quotations from Jeremiah's journal.

Indeed realism in the sense of making character, scene, and action dramatically convincing (but realism elevated by a poetic imagination) has always been characteristic of Warren's fiction. *World Enough and Time,* for example, contains many such devices as historically accurate dates and geographical details, professions of uncertainty about material not recorded in historical documents, and speculations about what a character might have been thinking in a certain situation, all of which permit the author to vary creatively from fact (of which there is much in this historical novel) without sacrificing the illusion that he is a scrupulously accurate historian of real events. In one respect, however, *World Enough and Time* marks an important departure from the type of realism in point of view to which Warren has adhered rather carefully in his previous fiction. Nearly all of *Night Rider* is presented from the point of view of Mr. Munn. In *At Heaven's Gate* there are various points of view, with quick (impressionistic) shifting from one to the other to get the effect of a dramatic, contrapuntal presentation of modern degeneracy—with very little author intrusion. In *All the King's Men,* with all the careful consistency of Henry James, Warren uses only one narrator, Jack Burden, whose every word and thought fit his character perfectly: even the subordinate story of Cass Mastern purports to be a manuscript that has come into Jack's hands, and it is vitally related to the main plot in that Cass's repentance for his sins acts as a reproach, though an unheeded reproach, to Jack's conscience; and certainly there was no basis for the charge made by several critics that Jack was really speaking for Warren, any more than for their identifying the moral casuistry of Willie Stark with the views of Warren.

In *World Enough and Time,* however, Warren has chosen to project himself again and again onto the stage with the intimacy of a Thackeray, though with more penetrating comments than Thackeray's. In trying to discover why Warren has chosen to comment thus, we cannot suppose that he considered such explanation necessary for a tale of the past, because the complex situation in *Night Rider* is made perfectly clear with very little author intrusion. The answer, I think, must lie partly in the fact that the characters in *World Enough and Time,* like their models in real life, were romantic, accustomed to high sounding speeches, sentimental poetry, etc. No matter how realistically they were portrayed, Warren no doubt felt that he as author would be censured for their melodramatic qualities, unless he made it clear (by his own comments) that he considered parts of the drama farcical from the modern point of view, but that it had to be presented in this way or it would not have been the drama of Jeremiah Beaumont. The "Confessions of Jereboam O. Beauchamp" (the true narrative which gave Warren the idea for his novel) and other authentic documents indicate that he has presented the personalities of his characters (as well as the complex political struggle of that time) very much as they actually were. Of course he could have changed the personalities of the characters, but then he would have needed a completely new plot, since it all revolves around the tragedy that results from acting on an idea that combines genuine idealism and foolish sentimentalism in almost equal proportions. Here was a challenging theme with irony piled on irony, but Warren was probably afraid that, unless he carefully pointed out the ironies, many readers might think him unable to distinguish between nobility and foolishness himself. And, he no doubt decided, the supreme artistic irony would be to go even further and point out all the philosophical ironies that might appear in an attempt to analyze the total meaning of this fable. Certainly such a philosophical level added to the story would, for one thing, distinguish it from the work of the Costains and Shellabargers, as *Hamlet* is distinguished from *The Spanish Tragedy*.

Indeed such a distinction has been observed by the more intelligent reviewers, notably by Mr. Robert B. Heilman (*Sewanee Review,* Winter 1951). Mr. Heilman says that *World Enough and Time* compared to any other of Warren's novels is like *Hamlet* compared to *Othello: World Enough and Time* is not so neatly constructed as the others, but it is richer in philosophical meaning. The trouble with Mr. Heilman's comparison is that in *World Enough and Time* we have two Hamlets—Warren and Jeremiah—and that seems too many for any drama. And then the tone of Warren's reflections—ironical, detached, and witty, with an undertone of melancholy—seems more like that of Anatole France than like that of Hamlet. There is also another objection to what seems to be one of Warren's purposes in philosophizing here: conflicting reflections (intended no doubt to be paradoxical) can be pursued to such lengths by the clever thinker that he is no longer pulling our leg but his own. Mr. Heilman praises Warren's comments for "the alternate embrace and rejection of theory which are the co-ordinates of moral and philosophic growth." I don't deny Warren's moral and philosophic growth—he no doubt felt that in these comments, along with a certain amount of leg pulling, he was fulfilling the "arduous obligation of the intellect in the face of conflicting dogmas"—a quality for which (in *Kenyon Review,* Winter 1942) he praises the fiction of Katherine Anne Porter, to whom he dedicated his volume of short stories. But since Warren does not have the dialectical dexterity or profundity which he attributes (a little too enthusiastically) to Katherine Anne Porter, real confusion sometimes appears beneath the thin robe of his ambiguity.

Let us inspect some of Warren's philosophizing in relation to the story and attempt to distinguish at strategic points the "embrace" from the "rejection" of theory, or theories. He introduces the story with a skillful reference to its source in

> the diaries, the documents, and the letters . . . bound in neat bundles with tape so stiffened and tired that it parts almost unresisting at your touch . . . . We have what is left, the lies and half-lies and the truths and half-truths. We do not know that we have the Truth. But we must have it.

Of course all this could be part of the artistic illusion of the conscientious historian, but it later becomes evident that Warren's purpose is more complicated than this, for he begins on the very next page, and continues at intervals throughout the story, to speculate (far more than the historian illusion would require) about the nature and the significance of the life drama in which Jeremiah Beaumont was the main actor. "It was," Warren tells us,

> a drama he [Jeremiah] had prepared, an ambiguous drama which seemed both to affirm and to deny life. But it may have been the drama Jeremiah Beaumont had to prepare in order to live at all, or in order, living, to be human. And it may be that a man cannot live unless he prepares a drama, at least cannot live as a human being against the ruck of the world.

Here Warren seems certain that Jeremiah prepared his own drama, but he thinks that perhaps Jeremiah had to prepare this particular drama if he was to be "human." In other words, in order to keep from living at the sub-human sensual level, Jeremiah may have had to carry out his foolish determination to kill Judge Fort, who had lived for a short while in adultery with Rachel Jordan before Jeremiah married her, indeed before he knew her at all.

But two pages further on, Warren is not even certain that Jeremiah prepared his own drama at all. "Perhaps," says Warren, "the land and the history of the land devised Jeremiah Beaumont and the drama in which he played, and the scene is the action and speaks through the mouth of Jeremiah Beaumont as through a mask." Again, on page 125, Warren's statement that "Jeremiah Beaumont had to create his world or be the victim of a world he did not create" indicates either that Warren is still uncertain about the responsibility for Jeremiah's tragedy, or that he is certain that Jeremiah had the choice of being the author of his own drama or acting in one he did not create. If Warren's ambiguous sentence means that Jeremiah had a choice, it seems to have been an idle one: the drama would have necessarily been the same in any event, for Warren now says positively that

> the obligation [to kill Fort] sprang from the depth of his nature . . . . Out of his emptiness, which he could not satisfy with any fullness of the world, he *had* [italics mine] to bring forth *whatever fullness might be his* [italics mine]. And in the end must not every man, even the most committed and adjusted worldling, do the same? If he is to live past the first gilded promise of youth and the first flush of appetite?

The author means here—there can be no doubt of it—that the nature of Jeremiah's "fullness" could have been no different from what it turned out to be. No longer does he say that this "may have been the drama Jeremiah Beaumont had to prepare" if he was to be "human"; now Warren states positively that Jeremiah "had to bring forth" this disastrous kind of "fullness," or (the only real alternative) burn himself out in the youthful realm of "appetite."

At the time of the trial, furthermore, Warren applies to Jeremiah's situation a metaphor which foretells (perhaps not too subtly) the tragic ending of the story, and which must indicate that Jeremiah, even before the trial, was doomed to disaster: "Jeremiah Beaumont was a chip on the tide of things, a tide shot through by sudden rips and twisted currents." It does not seem likely that a free agent before the trial would suddenly become no more than "a chip on the tide of things." In the next paragraph Warren elaborates the metaphor in the same vein:

> But if Jeremiah Beaumont was a chip on the tide, he was a thinking and suffering chip, and his dearest thought was that he was not a chip at all but a mariner who had made calculations of tides and a decision for his course.

This passage only superficially resembles Pascal's famous metaphor which says, "Man is but a reed, the most feeble thing in nature; but he is a thinking reed"; for the effect of Pascal's comparison is to exalt the dignity and responsibility of man, but the effect of Warren's is to emphasize only the pathos of Jeremiah's hopeless situation. The "chip" can "think and suffer" and even vainly imagine that it is "not a chip at all," or that there is no all-determining tide on which it (and Everyman?) floats from birth. Warren concludes his reflections here by a variant, reinforcing the deterministic implications, of the same metaphor: ". . . . events followed their own blind, massive drift, with Jeremiah Beaumont caught up in them."

And, to return to the central metaphor in Warren's comments, what of Rachel Jordan's role in the drama? At times he seems to grant her voluntary action. "She could," he says,

> ascend the high and secret stage, join Jeremiah Beaumont there, and take her stance and make the gestures and speak the words that would transform the commonness of things.

Again, in a sequence that becomes almost a pattern in his exposition, Warren elaborates the meaning of his first eloquent metaphor with a second even more eloquent:

> She could gather the waste and wreckage of her life, its vain furniture of old hopes and threadbare desires, its frustrations and guilts, and fling them all disdainfully into the flame to make it leap higher and higher and gild with light ruddy as gold and blood the dark landscape that in that combustion would leap to life.

This second metaphor—with its emphasis on words like "waste and wreckage," "vain furniture of old hopes," "frustrations," and "gold and blood"—indicates that the apparent freedom suggested by the first was really not important, and it prepares the way for the author's complete negation of the brief (Cabell-like) dream which he allowed his characters. On their "high and secret stage"—a reference to the sentimental poems which Jeremiah and Rachel wrote to each other during the trial—Jeremiah called her " 'Soul sister . . . . Bright taper of the heart's desire . . . . Fair Sphinx, whose smile is truth and pain.' But what was she?" says Warren.

She was an unfortunate young woman on whom life had played every trick. It had given her a clod for a father and a fool for a mother. It had given her a first lover but to snatch him away in betrayal. It had given her dead children. It had marked her for slander and shame. It had given her a strong young husband who came in nobility, but came too late. It had given her a high heart, clear aspiration, grace, and beauty, and had marked her for place and happiness, but all had come to nothing.

It is perhaps beginning to appear that Warren's conflicting speculations after all may be drifting toward a kind of generalization in determinism. From this point of view, perhaps he means that "the most serious speeches and grand effects"—the parts of this "confused and comic and pretentious and sad" drama at which "we" in the modern world laugh—are only ironically amusing to us because "pretentious" little Jeremiah thought he was creating the effects but in reality was only "the mask through which the scene speaks." There are of course still some positive statements (in terms of the extended metaphor about the drama) that seem to contradict this trend toward determinism. For one thing, Warren tells us, there are times when "the big speeches are fluffed or the gestures forgotten, when the actor improvises like a lout." But if the scene is speaking through Jeremiah as through a mask, how can he improvise? Surely he must be doing at least some creating of his own. And at one time—to the great amusement of the spectators, the contemporaries of Jeremiah and Rachel, not "we"—these two main actors "trip on their ceremonial robes, even at the threshold of greatness, and come tumbling down in a smashing pratt-fall"—an ironical reference to their unsuccessful attempt at suicide. Surely the metaphor here contradicts the deterministic view: the actors can make mistakes. But Warren may be implying that even the mistakes are part of the big show created and directed by some kind of fatality—which would explain why "we," more understanding than the boorish spectators, feel the pathos at such times as this. Of course there is still another possibility, which contradicts the idea of the planned drama but not the determinism. Warren says positively elsewhere, as we have seen, that Jeremiah was "a chip on the tide of things" and that "events followed their own blind, massive drift, with Jeremiah caught up in them." Blind chance, in a deterministic theory, can determine human lives quite as completely as any other force or forces—which might explain why Warren says that "confusion" is one of the main characteristics of this whole "drama."

But since Warren has brought "us" in the modern world into his speculations, let us further test his general theory by seeing what he thinks of us. We pity Jeremiah, he says, "for with us pity for others is the price we are anxious to pay for the privilege of our self-pity." Are we, then, degenerate, and responsible for our degeneracy? It seems so at times, for Warren says some rather harsh things of us. "Perhaps we have lost our faith in beauty," he says,

> not only on canvas, and know that even in the flesh it [the beauty of women] is only line and color, after all, and that if there are breath and fire they promise only a hot contact and a poor moment of coupling and only a supple thigh and not truth would be ungirdled, after all.

The story of Jeremiah Beaumont seems strange to us, because, unlike him, "our every effort is to live in the world, to accept its explanations, to do nothing gratuitously." This clearly indicates that we are inferior to Jeremiah, as does the epigraph (for the whole novel) quoting three stanzas from Spenser's "Faerie Queene" about "present dayes, which are corrupted sore" as contrasted with "the antique world . . . . When good was onely for it selfe desyred." But just two pages beyond his condemnation of our "effort to live in the world," Warren seems to find Jeremiah's gratuitous act exceedingly foolish. Jeremiah at first wanted to fight a duel with Fort. If this had happened, says Warren, what would have been "the real content of the act?" One man would probably kill another because

> one of the two men, the older, had done something perfectly natural. He had been in a lonely house with a handsome, young, neurotic, desperate woman, had brought her sympathy, and had, finally, tupped her in a dark parlor. At the time the young woman was not even known to the younger man. Hecuba had been nothing to him and he nothing to Hecuba.

We can agree with a newspaper of the day in calling such duellists "dunces." "But, on second thought, we may be like the dunces. We do not stand up at dawn, but we lie in a scooped-out hole in a tropical jungle and rot in the rain and wait for the steel pellet whipping through the fronds," and do other foolhardy things in foolhardy wars. All of this surely indicates that we, too, are foolish and to be condemned for it. But not so; the next paragraph contains Warren's clever and yet bitter attack, not on us apparently, but on our fate:

> For who is Hecuba, who is she, that all the swains adore her? She is whatever we must adore. Or if we adore nothing, she is what we must act as if we adored. And if we adore her, we must do so, not because we know her, but because we do not know her . . . . Or to regard the matter in a different light, we can never leave Hecuba. She is what we must carry in the breast, though we can never know her. She is our folly and our glory and despair. And if we do not adore her, we can adore nothing or only Silly Sal, who was found tasty in Bowling Green by the hot boys of the town.

It turns out, then, that we have the same area of choice as did Jeremiah Beaumont—no more, no less: we must follow out a foolish (though in part glorious) idea with disastrous consequences or submerge ourselves in sensuality.

The villain for Warren, if there is one, in all this "confused and comic and pretentious and sad" story is the land—"the brutal, vibrant, tumescent land, which drowsed and throbbed and brooded with its own secret but cared nothing for her [Rachel] or her secret"; the "violent and lonely" land; the "wild" land which "possessed" its inhabitants so that their characters became compounded of "the fiddle and whiskey, sweat and prayer, pride and depravity"; the land which may have "devised Jeremiah Beaumont and the drama in which he played . . . ."

The drift of Warren's philosophical speculations, then, though at times they are contradictory, is toward a determinism not unlike that of Theodore Dreiser, although Warren is much more sophisticated and intellectual in considering all the angles than Dreiser. Our final conclusion must be that, from the artistic standpoint, Warren would have done better to omit all these speculations, since he was unable to give them the daemonic intensity which successfully dramatizes the philosophy in the fiction of Dostoevsky and, to a lesser degree, Faulkner and D. H. Lawrence. In his essay on Hemingway, Warren said, ". . . . what good fiction gives us is the stimulation of a powerful image of human nature trying to fulfill itself and not instruction in an abstract sense." In spite of his embodying them in some concrete and interesting imagery, Warren's comments (but not Jeremiah's agonized reflections on his own destiny) in relation to the story of *World Enough and Time* must be classified as "instruction in an abstract sense"—abstract, that is, in the sense of being drawn from the story in vaguely moralizing digressions.

From the moral point of view, Warren is also condemned by his own earlier critical theory, whether we consider that he leaves the responsibility for the tragedy unresolved, or whether we consider that he indicates enough of a drift toward determinism to make that his "view." If the former, then he has violated the requirement that he made for good literature in his essay (*Kenyon Review*, Spring 1944) on Eudora Welty: ". . . . a piece of literature should intensify our awareness of the world (and of ourselves in relation to the world) in terms of an idea, a 'view.'" And the statement made in the preface to *Understanding Fiction*:

> They [Warren and Brooks speaking in third person of their own views] would not endorse an irony which precluded resolution but they would endorse an irony which forced the resolution to take stock of as full a context as possible. The reader wants the resolution, but he does not want it too easy or too soon.

If determinism is his view, then all his earlier emphasis—again, for example, in his essay on Hemingway—on the necessity for good literature to "embody moral effort" and to serve as a "document of the human will to achieve ideal values" becomes meaningless. Mr. Heilman defends the question "Was it all for naught?" (which Warren asks at the end of this story) by saying, in part, that "it raises the issue of whether such a tragic fable can be meaningful now." This is a curious defense, for without determinism it is obvious that a portrayal of human character in a crisis can always be meaningful, and Mr. Heilman does not recognize determinism as an issue here, except in moderns, who will find the moral hard to accept because we don't want to go along with Warren in emphasizing the "crime of self." What Mr. Heilman does not notice is that it is Jeremiah, and not Warren, who speaks of the "crime of self." When Warren says, "The crime was himself, and the crime was worse than the crime of Wilkie Barron," he is merely paraphrasing, still from Jeremiah's point of view, a condensed quotation in the preceding sentence from Jeremiah's journal. In his own comments on the self, Warren never goes beyond the assertion, made when he is considering the sad expression on the face of Fort, that it is impossible to clear up "the blankness of the last secret," oneself.

Warren's trouble—a typically modern one—is due to his trying to be too evasive, too subtle, too profound, too "difficult." Mr. Heilman says that "the excellence of *World Enough and Time* is precisely its difficulty." I should say that this is precisely its weakness, its only important weakness. The roundabout speculations of Warren, like those of Carlyle, prove to be after all rather commonplace when they are digested, and hardly worth the effort, either aesthetically or morally. Their only difficulty, after they have been analyzed, lies in the fact that they are sometimes contradictory. *Contradictory*, not *paradoxical*, is the word, for Warren is not a theologian, and only theologians can successfully claim the dignity of paradox for the contradictions in their speculations.

World Enough and Time remains a good novel in spite of Warren's philosophizing—it is a profoundly moving story both in the narrative and descriptive (and historical) sections and in the moral and philosophical comments of Jeremiah, wrung from him by his agonized efforts to "justify" himself and to understand why he has suffered as he has. Let us hope that in the future Warren will let his characters do all (or almost all) the philosophizing, as he did in his earlier novels. Their contradictions at least can, and no doubt will, be dramatized in the story. Warren will be protected, and so will we.

JOHN EDWARD HARDY

Ellen Glasgow

A good many people may still buy or borrow her novels, although I doubt that even her popular following is as large as it used to be. But it is certain at least that Ellen Glasgow no longer has much of a critical audience.

Her work becomes more and more the property of the literary historian. Even the best of the few primarily critical studies in late years (see, for example, N. Elizabeth Monroe's excellent essay in *Fifty Years of the American Novel*) never get far away from historical considerations. One reason for this is that Miss Glasgow thought of her fiction itself as social history, or history of manners—a fact which would in the nature of things endear her to historical scholars, while it would operate as a decided disadvantage for her with our present generation of critics, who are habitually formalist.

Since even historians must be somewhat sensitive to the pressure of contemporary critical tendencies, it becomes increasingly difficult to account for the importance she is supposed to have. The feeling that Miss Glasgow must somehow be taken into any thorough account of the development, not only of the modern Southern, but the modern American novel, does seem to be more of a feeling than a conviction. But I suppose it is thought simply that she wrote a great deal, and yet not enough, considering the long time she was at it, to make her a hack, so that the bulk of the work is in itself impressive— or, again, that she had too much concern for style, and not enough sensationalism, to be dismissed just as a moderately successful popular novelist. And if she should seem, then, not a great novelist, nor even one whom very many people could reasonably be persuaded to read, but only, by some way of default, a *significant* one, even this need not be discouraging to the scrupulous literary historian.

For it appears further, still without too strenuous an examination of the fiction, that she took some kind of antithetical view of the conventions of the older romantic novel of the South, and yet that she became increasingly estranged from the new realism of the twenties and later. This observation makes it expedient to assume that the significance is of the *transitional* sort—and there is nothing, of course, ever more dear to the chronicler than that. It is an uncomfortable position, a singularly undignified one for a fine Richmond lady, but she is usually left, and probably will be for some time, rather gingerly straddling the near half century that was the period of her active career.

For my part, I do not advocate a Glasgow critical revival. The fact that her work does not lend itself to formalist criticism makes any such thing highly unlikely just now; and it is probably just as well. But a brief critical study might put a little light on the historical problem at least, of a kind that literary history always needs. Further, her work, and some of the effort at criticism of it in the past, should provide a good test of the meaning of certain critical terms, so that I might try to justify an essay on Miss Glasgow simply with the hope that it will help to furnish a clearer vocabulary for criticism of other novelists who are more exciting in their own right.

For example, we might get a little closer to what *realism* does, could, or should mean. In the thirties, or even earlier, Miss Glasgow's critical champions were already pretty clearly conscious that they were talking through something that had started to look rather old hat. She had early been praised, and even condemned, as a realist, the first or nearly the first to bring any measure of realism to the Southern novel. But with the kind of tough, professional competition she had by the end of the twenties, even among Southerners, that line became clearly untenable (at least without serious qualification) as a commentary on the significance of her later work. (Her novels, in fact, became more and more realistic, but the progress of the literary age made it less and less telling to point out the fact).

And yet when the qualifications were made, they inevitably sounded only rather defensive. Miss Glasgow was still realistic—although she recognized the reality of beauty and heroic myth as well as the reality of ugliness and the present commonplace. Or, Miss Glasgow was a realistic critic of man and his society, but this was and always had been secondary to her purpose as a prose stylist—with the nicer beauties of whose writing the semi-illiterate sensationalism of the younger writers could not be compared in any terms. Or, Miss Glasgow's apparent lack of contact with modernism was simply a matter of her having an ironic detachment *so* severe that she saw the follies of the Southern, post-World War society and its literature as clearly as she had in her youth seen the last follies of the post-Civil War South. She was, in short, just a bit too much of a realist for the naive younger generation to understand what she was about. Or, on a specific question, Miss Glasgow recognized the importance of the sex motive, and gave it due emphasis in her novels, but she was, again, too keenly realistic to *over*emphasize it.

There was a tendency also to retreat to a more or less elaborate statement of the "paradoxes" of Miss Glasgow's literary character and from there to defy any impudent detractor to try even so much as defining a single position for her in which he could bring her under attack. The drift of this argument, recurrent over a period of at least ten years, is latterly summed up in a statement, sufficiently objective and yet clearly sympathetic, of Kazin's (*On Native Grounds*, Chapter 10, p. 258): ". . . critics who need to brand writers like steers must always find Ellen Glasgow disturbing. She began as the most girlish of Southern romantics and later proved the most biting critic of Southern romanticism; she was at once the most traditional in loyalty to Virginia and its most powerful satirist; the most sympathetic historian of the Southern mind in modern times and a consistent satirist of that mind. She wrote like a dowager and frequently suggested the mind of a nihilist; she was at once the most old-fashioned of contemporary American novelists and frequently the wittiest."

One remark of James Southall Wilson's pointed a way off the perilous ground of the problem of realism altogether: ". . . but that was an anachronistic idealism rather than a critical realism which made her view the effects of slavery and aristocracy in the old South in a spirit more akin to that of an abolitionist than of a philosophical historian." For Wilson, the observation only qualifies a rather conventional statement on her irony, which he seems still to consider generally realistic; he shows no inclination to follow up the possible implications for her attitude toward problems other than that specifically of slavery and aristocracy. But the implications are there.

It seems to me that there is no problem simply of qualification. Ellen Glasgow, in most of her work, is in *no way* essentially a realist.

She is, in many ways, essentially a sentimentalist. No one of her novels is entirely sentimental, and she is less sentimental in her later work than in her earlier. But there is none of the novels that is entirely without sentimentality. In her early novels, much of what seemed at the time to many critics a radical reversal of older attitudes in the Southern novel—and it was radical, but not quite in the way it was usually defined—was simply a sentimentalizing of themes that the earlier post-war novelists had romanticized.

I mean, for example, the attitude taken toward a character like General Battle, in *The Voice of the People*. A certain disillusionment, to be sure, was required to produce a figure so absurd in the old, legendary type of the returned Confederate officer. General Battle, who was commissioned a colonel by official action and upon his return a general by popular acclaim, who has eaten and sat himself into a shape twice too big for his old uniforms, who congratulates himself upon an act of noblesse oblige and of kindness to his daughter when he sits for a half hour on the sagging front porch of his house to talk about crops with the youthful, poor farmer's son Nick Burr, unknowing that Nick has already had at least one kiss from the daughter, is absurd; and unquestionably Miss Glasgow intended, or hoped, that he should be laughable. (The same comic type, on radio programs and in newspaper cartoons, still does, in fact, get laughs). We are to understand that he is ridiculous and ineffectual, that his age is hopelessly past, and so on. But he is *pathetically* ridiculous; the laugh has to get around what Miss Glasgow also undoubtedly hoped would be a large lump in the throat. According to a pattern that became standard in the social usage of the immediate post-Victorian South, she has made him absurd so that she can, through Eugenia the daughter, be tender and motherly with him.

Miss Glasgow had too her own, gratuitous sentimentalities, that had nothing to do with any patterned attitude toward the themes of the older, literary romanticism. She was not president of the Richmond S. P. C. A. for nothing. Through all the novels, from first to last, supernumerary dog characters wander at will. In Eugenia's tender reminiscences beside her father's death bed, it becomes difficult during the extremity of her sorrow, if not indeed at any other time, to distinguish the character of the general himself from that of a faithful old dog named Jim. In the incident of *Vein of Iron* that is oddly reminiscent of the famous scene of the idiot and the cow in

Faulkner's *The Hamlet*, Miss Glasgow is plainly *determined* not to permit any sentimentality on the idiot's account. But the expected sympathy for Ada is necessarily sentimental. Ada is not, of course, a cow, nor even a cow-like girl, and clearly does not have to depend upon the idiot for admiration—which would be the only circumstances under which the reader could be expected to feel genuine pity, or horror, or any other legitimate emotion on her account.

In a sense, an emotional response to the experience of almost any of her characters must be sentimental. Miss Glasgow was fond of saying that "the pathos of life is worse than the tragedy." The saying was, of course, an effort to justify the fact that her novels seldom attain to anything approaching tragedy. A good many of her sympathetic critics have chosen to ignore the remark altogether, and gone on talking about her tragic sense. But Miss Glasgow's own insight into her work was best in this instance. She apparently never at all understood the principle of ethos on which tragedy, or the tragic character, must be constructed. Her characters do not act, but suffer. They suffer delight just as they suffer sorrow. Things are always "happening" to them; the novels frequently have the atmosphere of soap opera.

One of the strongest influences on Miss Glasgow's art, to whatever extent consciously, was unquestionably that of Thomas Hardy; I suppose she took much of her philosophical conviction on the problem of will from Hardy. But Hardy's characters have usually at least a strong illusion of will, and act mightily upon it. And I am inclined to think that at least such an effective illusion is absolutely essential to anything approaching tragedy. Miss Glasgow's characters have not even the illusion. They are moved only by desire, or the failure of desire, and at times the desire itself is not clearly motivated in the individual character. It is, for example, impossible to understand, if we look at them as the individuals they nearly become and not as pathetic counters in a play of social forces, why Nick Burr and Eugenia, in *The Voice of the People*, do not after all marry (the misunderstanding over the ruined girl and the cowardly brother is the purest romantic hokum as a justification); or why Roy, of *In This Our Life*, does not do something to prevent or to avenge the theft of her husband, except that she, and through her her father, must be made to suffer every possible indignity again as passive victims of social irony. Or, where at least the immediate motivation is clear enough,

as that Milly of *They Stooped to Folly* wants to get away from her
mother, it is never clear just *what,* beyond going away, her desire is,
what, precisely, the "happiness" is or might be that she monotonously,
passionately, almost hysterically, and very effectively at least in keeping
Virginius Littlepage in a torment of conscience, protests her "right"
to throughout the novel. Pathos does not, perhaps, always involve
sentimentality. But when it is the result of a conflict or frustration of
desires so obscurely motivated or vaguely defined as in these instances,
any effectiveness which it may have is purely sentimental. And if it
should be argued that Miss Glasgow, in a case like Milly's, is only
writing about "things (people) as they are," that the Millies of the
post war American world simply *were* vague in their motivations—
certainly she risks the worst effects of the imitative fallacy in doing so.

But we may put the matter in more positive terms. Miss Glasgow
was not only not a realist, she was an idealist. Because she was not a
romantic idealist, in the manner of the older Southern novelists, the
error was common among a certain class of her early critics to call her
a realist. And most of those who have not preserved that error are
equally wrong in calling her a comedian of manners. The truth is that
where she is not purely and simply a sentimentalist, or an apologist
for one thing or another, women or dogs or land reform or the plain
man in politics, she is usually a satirist. And satire, though it may
employ many of the techniques of realism in the treatment of details
of action or character or setting, is always based on a philosophical
idealism.

Realism is hardly to be thought of as contentment with the world
as one finds it, but if it does not imply an attitude of objective acceptance of fact, then the term has no meaning that I can define. Miss
Glasgow, on the other hand, is not only discontented but, albeit very
courteously, indignant. Further, she has habitually a very strong notion
of what society ought to be, and if she has no real hope of persuading
it to become that perfect thing, she is in any event determined to give
it little peace in its follies. *The Romantic Comedians* and *They
Stooped to Folly* are *light* satire, if you like; the criticism of society
never penetrates much below the level of manners, into psychological
or economic or religious or other causes (or manifestations either, for
that matter); these novels fret and annoy much more often than they
disturb; but they are satire. They are not comedy. Miss Glasgow
is neither sufficiently genial nor sufficiently detached for that. What

might appear as a genial detachment is only a weary joke, a decorously contrived wit, a jaded gentility, an exquisitely tired courtesy that is too smooth to be very effective as satire but that, at the same time, fails to look deeper not because of an overplus of sympathy but only because it is not, again, good manners to do so.

In other words, she takes manners with what is for her ultimate seriousness; her moral sense is identical with her sense for manners. Corruption of manners is inevitably accompanied by trouble for somebody, as real trouble as Miss Glasgow knows how to portray. And it matters little that it is not always trouble for those whose manners are most corrupt, but often trouble for those whom they know. That is only because, as I have suggested before, Miss Glasgow's morality is not a morality of individual will and conscience. Her very habit of working ironic reversals, whether in action or in epigram, upon the expectations or the formulas of those who do hold with will and the conscience, is only a part of her technique for defining and enforcing her own very rigorous code of social morality.

To return to the central point, then, Miss Glasgow is, in my mind, most the idealist precisely in those novels on which her reputation as a realist has, I believe, usually depended, the novels of manners. She achieves, as I see it, a considerable measure of realism only in two novels that I choose to call pastorals—one, *Barren Ground,* which she herself thought her best novel, for which she would have been most pleased to reserve "the double-edged blessing of immortality," and the other, *The Miller of Old Church,* a novel that has been neglected by almost all her critics.

Generally speaking, it should not be too surprising that her pastorals make at least a special effort to be realistic. Despite the fact that pastoral conventions usually work themselves out into extreme artificiality (which happens for one thing, I suppose, because the point of view, necessarily sophisticated, gets mixed up with the thing viewed), the original impulse to pastoral is perhaps always a quest for realism—for a material of more basic and/or stable passions, for "the real language of men," and so on. Simply as generalization, this and everything else about pastoral ought to be obvious enough after Empson. But it is worth re-stating here as a background defense for a position which, I have tried to indicate, has apparently not been so obvious to most of Miss Glasgow's critics. The criticism of *Barren Ground* that does take note of its realism does not associate the realism necessarily with the pastoralism of the novel; and I do not remember that it has occurred to many commentators to talk about *The Miller of Old Church* at all when they approach the problem of realism in Miss Glasgow's work.

It seems to me that the essential realism of *Barren Ground* is inseparable from the pastoralism. The novel has a good deal of the realism of exact, descriptive detail, and even a few successful touches of the calculated irrelevance kind of thing. But that is not what I mean by its essential realism. There is no more of this in *Barren Ground* than in any of Miss Glasgow's mature novels. And this realism, of technique, is not consistent enough in this novel, or in any of the others, to deserve much attention as a distinctive characteristic. It is, in fact, one of the strangest, and most disconcerting, features of Miss Glasgow's sensibility that she can be as hard and meticulous almost as James Joyce in *The Dead* on one page and then on the very next give us something as gauzy and palpitating and patently false in the way of a flight of feminine emotions as anything that, say, a Francis Parkinson Keyes might rig up on a wire to pull across her stage—and that with obviously equal enthusiasm for both, without the slightest tone of irony to relieve, or anything of dramatic consistency to justify, the shock of the transition.

The special realism of *Barren Ground* has something to do with the *identity* of Dorinda, with her being a real, single person. I do not find that most of Ellen Glasgow's characters ever achieve any sense of personal identity. This sense is, I acknowledge, obviously supposed to be the hard core of reality in the main characters of *Vein of Iron,* for example—that which finally justifies their existence, and their struggle to continue existing, under circumstances of the defeat or loss of all their most cherished desires and ambitions, of disillusionment in their finest faiths, of material and moral dispossession in a society that is utterly indifferent to their system of values. But it seems to me that I know it is supposed to be only because Miss Glasgow has the characters rather flatly say that it is so. The sense of identity does not, as a sense, communicate itself. I am inclined to think there are only two ways in which the reality of a fictive personality can be communicated. Either it emerges in a pattern of effective action through involvement with other personalities, or it emerges in a pattern of private, but symbolic, perception. And the two principal characters of *Vein of Iron* neither effectively act nor, with the possible exception of the passage of the novel describing the death-return of the philosopher, ever privately experience anything in such a manner that their perceptions become symbolic—that is, take on a significance that relates them to the probable perceptions of other people or to processes, human or non-human or both, which can be supposed to involve principles not limited in their operation to the one, present set of circumstances. I suppose what I am saying is that an identity in a novel can never be very 'personal,' that there is no such thing even as an entirely private illumination for the fictive person. But I think that is true. Whenever it is otherwise, what we have is not a character real in anything of his own right, but either the author or the reader talking to himself.

Dorinda, however, does have an identity. And her sense of having it is communicated. Miss Glasgow does not succeed much better with Dorinda than with any of her other characters in getting her involved with other people, as an acting as well as re-acting personality. It is, for example (cf. my remarks on Roy of *In This our Life*), impossible to tell just why Dorinda permits Jason to 'ruin her life'—except, it seems, that she must, or even perhaps that Miss Glasgow means Youth must, be betrayed. (This initial improbability makes the irony of Jason's helpless return to Dorinda in the last phase of the story somewhat less effective). The soap opera technique shows up again when Miss Glasgow can think of no better way to get Dorinda into the doctor's house in New York than to have her knocked down in the street by his car. It is rather the point of Dorinda's marriage to the storekeeper, of course, that she should never know him, or become emotionally involved with him, as a person in his own right. But the point in this instance would have had a greater, more special significance if it were not true that Dorinda, like most of Miss Glasgow's characters, has never known anyone as a person in his own right. And so on. But what is true of her relationship with other people is not true for Dorinda and the land of her father's farm.

The land is, literally, the ground of her own action. In her novels with urban settings, where in short even the non-human, physical surroundings are the product of human art, Miss Glasgow's characters have a tendency to become merely *representative* of some aspect of their time and place. But in the rural settings, a relationship at once freer and more intimate, less abstract, develops. The person and her actions are definitely associated with, can to some extent even be accounted for by, the circumstances of the time and the place. But the environment is here not an imponderable and accomplished fact, arising from an inscrutable interplay of social forces, in relationship to which the individual must be either ineffectually typical or quite as ineffectually anti-typical. It is an environment whose control is more passive, therefore more calculable, and ultimately less intractable, absolute, once a course of will in the individual has been determined.

Indeed it is an environment that makes the determination of a course of will more likely in the first place. The results of human effort, or at any rate of individual human effort, whether in success or failure, are simply more tangible and evident upon the land. Dorinda can see, in the specific, tangible evidence, the condition of the soil and the crops, the condition of her father's own body and mind, precisely what is wrong with his relationship to the land; she can make to herself certain specific proposals as to what might be done to change that relationship when she assumes control of the farm. Her own way of dealing with the land is not altogether satisfactory, of course. The outcome of her life is meant to be tragic. And the tragedy, if that is what we are to call it, has to do with the fertility of the land itself being secured at the expense of human sterility. Dorinda is sterile—the ground remains barren for her. But the point is that we can here, as not often in Miss Glasgow's other novels, regard the problem as a real problem, with real and definite causes. This is not true of the ostensible problems with which Miss Glasgow is concerned in most of her novels, or of the characters who are involved in them. Usually, the problem of the individual in her stories is a pale allegory of some abstractly conceived social disorder or condition, or some 'universal' state of human existence, of Youth, or Age, or Motherhood, or whatever. Or else, if it does not appear as directly related to a social pattern, although it may or may not in such cases be supposed to have a social origin, it is a phantasmal manifestation of individual neurosis —again, unreal. Not, I should hasten to say, that I have any objections to novels about neurotics, provided that the author knows that is what his characters are. I should not recommend the history of Dorinda Oakley, if what I am saying seems to be a recommendation at all, because Dorinda is a more wholesome, normal sort of American girl than, say, either Stanley or Roy Timberlake. But Miss Glasgow has a habit of dealing with a good many of her neurotics (and Roy *is* just as much a neurotic as Stanley) in a way that is distressingly like the neurotic's characteristic way of looking at himself—either in ignorance of the fact that he is afflicted, or, if he is technically aware of his malady for what it is, with a sentimental affection for it and an obstinate conviction of its real and supreme importance.

The Miller of Old Church is more obviously pastoral than *Barren Ground*. One becomes aware only rather slowly that the author in *Barren Ground* is looking at the country scene in conventional pastoral perspective, at the 'simple' world from the viewpoint of a more sophisticated society, and with an appeal to the judgment of the latter. To be sure, the point that Miss Glasgow wants the picture put in that perspective ought to be clear when Dorinda goes to New York, as it were to purge herself for the struggle of her return. But in that novel it is still largely a matter of author attitude, while in *The Miller of Old Church* there is a sophisticate, Jonathon Gay, who is one of the principal characters, acting in relatively uncomplicated opposition to the simple man, the miller; this opposition provides the central pattern of the plot. In short, the problem of perspective *is* the novel. And this makes it easier for the author to stay out of the novel. It is not necessary for her to try so hard, and so obviously, to identify with any of the characters, as she does with Dorinda, at one point, and then at another to contrive some stylistic device (e. g., the disconcerting shifts of tone in *Barren Ground* to a kind of professional metaphor which no one could possibly imagine to be available to the relatively uncultivated country girl's mind—we are carefully assured that Dorinda has read a great deal, but that is about as convincing as Ellen Dean's similar explanation to Mr. Lockwood in *Wuthering Heights*) to remind the reader that the identification is not intended to be complete. The fact that such identification is never established in *The Miller of Old Church*, that the style need therefore never be strained to break it, gives the characters in this novel an independence of existence, and an integrity, that is nearly unique among Miss Glasgow's creations. The perspective is established at the outset, and kept constant. The reader sees the people and the action at a distance, somewhat reduced and formalized, almost quaint perhaps, but relatively stable at any rate, and therefore probable. Once he has measured the distance, and set his eyes to it, he need not be constantly re-checking his calculations.

An effect of the independence of existence allowed the characters here is the working of a kind of irony that is also unusual in Miss

Glasgow's novels. The Glasgow irony, as I have said before, is usually a matter either of verbal paradox, epigrammatic wit, or of soap opera fortune. Here the irony is actually dramatic irony, the structure of "wit" is synonymous with the plot structure, the paradox is worked out in the pattern of action, not simply in verbal patterns—and that not by a series of accidents of circumstance, but on a clear principle of moral probability.

To get back to the stuff of the novel, it turns out that Jonathon Gay, not the miller, is the simpler, the more innocent, of the two. The fault of his attitude toward his rights of ownership in the land, and therefore toward his relationship with the Revercombs, is a fault of simplicity. The folly, that is, of his attempt to return to his estate as a lord—beating the miller's brother for poaching on his land, acting the conventional roué with the pretty milkmaid that he sees in Blossom—is merely the folly of being old-fashioned. Gay is simple, innocent, in that he tries to restore an age of simpler (if in some respects more formal) manners, and simpler economics; or, he is even more simple in failing to realize that the age has passed, that it would have to be restored.

Jonathon's relationship with his tyranically fragile mother, who keeps him a child—a statement of a theme that elsewhere becomes one of Miss Glasgow's most unfortunate 'modern psychological' kicks —serves here, and quite effectively, merely to reinforce the theme of innocence as it is defined in his other relationships. It provides the occasion, or the excuse, for his secret marriage to Blossom, and is therefore essential; but the affair with Blossom is finally significant only as a part of his total relationship with the Revercombs and the community as a whole—and it would be easy to over-emphasize the son-and-lover situation in trying to account for all of Gay's troubles.

But, what is significant for making the novel unusual among Miss Glasgow's stories, the fall here is worked out as a matter of misjudgement of character—principally Jonathon Gay's misjudgement of his own character. In brief, it is a part of his simplicity that he should see himself, in relation to the country folk, as complex—a disillusioned sophisticate. And this error leads directly to his ruin—his secret marriage to Blossom, his belated realization of his admiration for folly, and his death at the hands of Blossom's father. The sequence has, as I have said, a moral probability which is rare in Miss Glasgow's work and which gives the novel its peculiar substance.

By moral probability I do not mean moral justice. I am not at all sure that Gay's death is just, or that its consequences for the happiness of Revercomb and Molly are just—although I suspect that Miss Glasgow thought so. What I do mean by moral probability in this novel is simply that in Jonathon Gay—or, for that matter, in Abel Revercomb or Molly Merryweather—Miss Glasgow has created a person, who acts, and discovers the consequences of his action, in the particular circumstances in which he finds himself, and toward his particular ends as an individual. Which is the way people do act. Something like what happens in this novel *could* happen. It is not, as in most of the novels, a matter of something that *has to* happen to demonstrate a theory of social criticism.

Beyond the probability of Gay's career, however, and the end of it, Miss Glasgow does manage to make a rather sorry mess of this novel too. The ending, with the marriage of Molly and Revercomb in prospect, is really intolerable. The author obviously wants to invest the marriage with some ritual significance—the all-enduring strength of the land finally asserting itself in the emotions of the native son and daughter, and so on. But Miss Glasgow is working at cross purposes with herself. In the first place, one cannot use the main characters for such a purpose. And although she has not entirely succeeded—Jonathon Gay has, willy-nilly, become the hero of the novel— Miss Glasgow is plainly trying at the last ditch (as a concession I suppose to some ignoble conception of her reader's taste) still to make out of the story a romantic comedy with Revercomb as its hero. Further, the figure of Revercomb has been stuffed too full of progressive sentiment by now to cut much of a figure in a Diggory Venn style, bottle-green coat. Ellen Glasgow read Thomas Hardy, but, as I have suggested before, I feel she did not read him very carefully. Of course, it may be that all American rustics, from the very start, have been stuffed too full of progressivism to participate in a ritual of any kind; the fault is not Miss Glasgow's alone. But then, if one is to persist in trying to make a pastoral out of the situation, he must be ironically conscious that the tradition he is working with *is* deficient in this respect.

I feel that Ellen Glasgow never fully realized her best potentialities as an artist. I am not thinking so much of the aesthetic sense which she always lacked. She had no sense of form, actually. She had a sense of style, but something about as close as she ever got to making it a formal principle is the rather mechanical adjustment of prose rhythms to the voices of the several characters in *Vein of Iron*— and this sort of thing is more a matter of *decorum* than of formality in any organic sense. Symbolism almost never becomes structural in her novels—the one exception I think of is the open, limitless, featureless land itself of the farm in *Barren Ground,* references to which always function symbolically and recur in a pattern relevant to the emotional and intellectual development of Dorinda. Most of her symbols are isolated, wooden, obviously contrived—Revercomb's old mill, the harp-shaped pine in *Barren Ground.* Her intellectualism *was* basically hostile to legend. Even the legend of the haunt's walk in *The Miller of Old Church,* which is her best effort, is finally window dressing; the death of the older Gay has nothing essentially to do with the younger's. And the lack of a sense of form is bad. I am not saying simply that Miss Glasgow is old-fashioned. It is bad for any novelist, at any time; it is only a little *worse* for one who has to establish her reputation in a period in which criticism, and critical reader sympathy, has come consciously to expect a novel to be (what good novels have always been) as formally perfect as a poem. The lack of a feeling for legend, particularly, is bad for a Southern novelist. The Southerner's best bid for universalism has always been to make himself a good regionalist; and legend is an essential part of regionalism. But in all this I have no sense of an opportunity lost. What I do feel Ellen Glasgow could have been, and never quite became, is simply a good story teller.

She never, unfortunately, quite got over her youthful intellectual enthusiasms. Her fondness for "ideas" was always too superficial to become really involved with her feeling for character; it was just strong enough to falsify the feeling, and constantly to make her impatient with the materials of what was "merely" a good story, about people. There is nothing really very mysterious about Mr. Kazin's 'dowager [who] frequently suggest[s] the mind of a nihilist." We should have to go as far afield, perhaps, as Dostoyevsky's *The Possessed* to find it adequately satirized, but the social if not the artist type is familiar enough even in America. In fact, we have an educational tradition perfectly designed for producing that kind of mind always as its extreme intellectual type. It is the tradition, of university and college co-education, which Ellen Glasgow herself exactly anticipated, at least for the South, when she first alarmed but, and this is the point, never dismayed the complacent defenders of the principle of male supremacy with the success of her private studies at the University of Virginia—a tradition of liberalism born out of the decadent excess of gentility, and beautifully equipped to digest with a minimum of discomfort any ideas that might be absorbed into it.

EDD WINFIELD PARKS

James Branch Cabell

James Branch Cabell has artfully employed many tinselled words to obscure the fact that he is in part a humanist. True, on the rare occasions when it has been visible there could be plainly seen on his humanistic shield a bar sinister; and Cabell as a genealogist may have felt that his literary ancestry was not of the highest and finest. For his line of descent is not from such mighty works as Dante's *Divine Comedy;* it is rather from Dante's admirer and biographer, Giovanni Boccaccio. In so far as it is in the humanistic tradition, the Biography of Manuel stems from the *Decameron* and the *Genealogy of the Gentile Gods.*

Like Boccaccio, Cabell is frequently lewd, and sometimes blasphemous. The Italian writer devoted many pages to demonstrating, in a period of rigid Christian orthodoxy, that the mythological gods of Greece and Rome were entitled to a place in the minds of men; and considerable scholastic arguments to prove that "not only is poetry theology, but also that theology is poetry." Symbolism, allegory, and fiction are their common properties, and their common device for showing without direct statement the existence of mystic correspondences. For a poet, religious or pagan, intuitively understood that which could not be comprehended through logic or reason; but neither could it be expressed directly, for it "proceeds from the bosom of God."

Mr. Cabell has avoided this old-fashioned phraseology, but the difference is mainly in the wording. He is enough of today to believe that man is an animal; he talks in terms of aspiration rather than inspiration; not only is he aware of the imperfections of this world but he is frankly sceptical about the perfection of any possible world to come. What he has is an abiding faith in man's spirit, however much he may doubt the existence of any God. He puts his faith in the artist, especially in the literary artist, rather than in the priest: it is the function of the artist, the duty of the poet, to give

> Those things of which I most poignantly and most constantly feel the lack in my own life . . . man alone of animals plays the ape to his dreams. Romance it is undoubtedly who whispers to every man that life is not a blind and aimless business, not all a hopeless waste and confusion; and that his existence is a pageant (appreciatively observed by divine spectators) and that he is strong and excellent and wise . . . The things of which romance assures him are very far from true: yet it is solely by believing himself a creature but little lower than the cherubim that man has by interminable small degrees become, upon the whole, distinctly superior to the chimpanzee . . . I prefer to take it that we are components of an unfinished world, and that we are but as seething atoms which ferment toward its making, if merely because man as he now exists can hardly be the finished product of any Creator whom one could very heartily approve. We are being made into something quite unpredictable, I imagine: and through the purging and the smelting we are sustained by an instinctive knowledge that we are being made into something better. For this we know, quite uncommunicably, and yet as surely as we know that we will to have it thus.

> And it is this will that stirs in us to have the creatures of earth and the affairs of earth, not as they are, but "as they ought to be," which we call romance. But when we note how visibly it sways all life we perceive that we are talking about God. [Conclusion of *Beyond Life*.]

This ennobling quality is of the mind and in the imagination. It does not square with the realities of life; indeed, it transcends them. Yet it too is a reality, "for the sufficient reason that man has nothing to do with certainties. He cannot ever get in direct touch with reality. Such is the immutable law, the true cream of the jest." These are the words of Felix Kennaston in *The Cream of the Jest,* but the fictional novelist has in every way except physically an amazing resemblance to his creator. For Kennaston too sees life as given meaning through man's dream, and it is ironically through his appreciation

f art that he becomes, as Mr. Cabell has been, a decorous and firmly
believing member of the Episcopal Church. The words of the pseudo-
biographer of Kennaston are Cabell's own words: "it is only by preserving faith in human dreams that we may, after all, perhaps some
day make them come true."

The qualifications are ever-present, but so is the belief. Everything that Cabell has written he has surrounded as though to defend
a fortress with thorny, even barbed-wire complications. In *The Cream
of the Jest* a fictional narrator, Richard Fentnor Harrowby, is attempting to get at the truth about a fictional novelist, Felix Bulmer Kennaston; and both men are, and yet are not, a novelist named James
Branch Cabell. But both men voice his sentiments. Near the end of the
book, Harrowby is tempted to prove to Kennaston that his magic sigil
and his dreams can be explained prosaically as the top of a peculiar
cold-cream jar and as self-hypnotism; but as he looks at the unroman-
tic, un-godlike Kennaston, the narrator realizes that the history of the
race is epitomized in "an inadequate kickworthy creature": whatever
man's delusion of his ultimate truth might prove to be,

> it is in this inadequate flesh that each of us must serve his
> dream; and so, must fail in the dream's service, and must
> parody that which he holds dearest. To this we seem con-
> demned, being what we are. Thus, one and all, we play
> false to the dream, and it evades us, and we dwindle into
> responsible citizens. And yet always thereafter—because of
> many abiding memories,—we know, assuredly, that the way
> of all flesh is not, not merely, a futile scurrying through din-
> ing-rooms and offices and shops and parlors, and thronged
> streets and restaurants, 'and so to bed' . . .

This is the humanist Cabell, concerned with the ethical conflict
in the individual; concerned with doubt and belief; concerned always
with what man is and what he may—or might—be; concerned, in
short, with philosophical and religious problems that have troubled
man from the beginning, and one hopes will trouble him to his
eventual end. Cabell is writing of man's impossible yet somehow not
improbable journey toward perfection, toward self-realization, toward
a possible afterpiece in the form of salvation. Yet a phrase in the
quoted paragraph hints at the fundamental weakness in Cabell's
philosophy: men dwindle and subside into being "responsible citizens."

This to Cabell is the supreme and yet inevitable crime of the artist. It reveals the essential dichotomy of his mind. If the first refrain running through his non-fictional books is that man alone of animals plays the ape to his dreams, the second and almost equally important one is that the artist should create force-producing illusions by writing perfectly of beautiful happenings. The artist is always in conflict with every-day life. When he accepts and conforms, as so many of Cabell's protagonists eventually do, he may become reasonably contented but he ceases to be an artist. In *Quiet Please* (1952), Cabell has rephrased but not changed the attitude voiced in earlier books:

> In brief, I esteem it the hall mark of a literary genius not ever to sympathize with our human living here, and not ever to arrange with it a satisfying compromise, whether in his personal over-transitory flesh or in print. Rather it is his vocation, his exalted calling—or it may be, his mania—to invent an expurgated and a re-colored and a generally improved version of life's botcheries . . .

This is the purpose of art and the justification of romance, that it gives us a glimpse of the supremely beautiful and that it whispers to us of the unattainable. The ordinary doings of mankind are not the concern of the artist: "veracity is the one unpardonable sin, not merely against art, but against human welfare." This is a denial of the importance of facts, not a denial of truth in the ultimate sense "for in life no fact is received as truth until the percipient has conformed and colored it to suit his preferences: and in this also literature should be true to life." All enduring art must be an allegory it must deal with contemporary life by means of symbols; it must be faithful to what man has dreamed of becoming rather than a portrait of what he is.

II

"There is but one fable which holds true everywhere. The man goes upon a journey: that is all." That is the one universal story, the subject-matter of folk-lore and the clear allegory of every human life says Cabell, and "I, too, have re-told the old fable, over and yet over again." There may be many reasons for these journeys, but ordinarily a quest is involved; and with Cabell that quest is nearly always a search for the unattainable.

This quest leads his protagonists into dark and unfamiliar places strangely compounded of geography and of imagination; it involves magic symbols such as bright mirrors and oddly-worded spells and antique sorceries; it may be a journey of the mind instead of the body. But the goal is never fully attained, since those things most ardently desired lose value when they have been achieved and retain their value only when they have not been wholly possessed. So the journeys end with a man giving up his quest for the unattainable to return to his familiar commonplace ways and commonplace chattering wife, or finding that on the journey he has somehow missed that which his heart desired. Yet the quest alone may bring sufficient reward, as it did to Alfgar in *The Way of Ecben*:

> I am content. For I have served that dream which I elected to be serving. It may be that no man is royal, and that no god is divine, and that our mothers and our wives have not any part in holiness. Oh, yes, it very well may be that I have lost honor and applause, and that I take destruction, through following after a dream which has in it no truth. Yet my dream was noble; and its nobility contents me . . . and in the heart of every person that is royal this dream may be fulfilled, even in the while that his body fails and perishes.

Alfgar is destroyed, but Manuel and Jurgen and Felix Kennaston make an uneasy peace with life. Yet on them all an obligation is laid by an inexorable world, and it can "not be lifted either by toils or by miracles. It is the geas [obligation] which is laid on every person, and the life of every man is as my life, with no moment free from some bond or another." These are the words of Manuel, but they are the wryly humanistic thoughts of James Branch Cabell as he portrays man questing for the unattainable, falling short of his goal, yet somehow, almost inexplicably, being the better for having followed after his dream.

In the Prefaces to the Storisende edition of the Biography of Manuel and in other writings, Cabell has insisted that the work should be considered as one book in eighteen volumes. It is an elaborate and ambitious work, meant to challenge attention; yet the basic structure is simple, and the themes often repeated. In a non-fictional prologue, *Beyond Life,* he has defined his attitude toward life and literature; in an epilogue, *Straws and Prayer-books,* he has set forth his literary creed. The eighteen fictional parts in between

> deal with the life of Manuel as that life has been perpetuated
> through some twenty-three generations. For that life always
> is my protagonist. Time, as I have said, has altered this pro-
> tagonist unceasingly and subtly, but only as time alters any
> other life. Fundamentally my protagonist does not change
> . . . Meanwhile the Biography has become a completed and
> individual book. Its major theme I take to be the theme and
> the truly democratic doctrine of our own world's Author,
> that the average of one human life should not, or at least
> does not, differ appreciably from the average of any other
> human life . . . It follows that in every incarnation the living
> of Manuel can but work out, through not dissimilar situa-
> tions and through very much the same emotions, to very
> much the same comedic ending upon, at happiest, a resigna-
> tory question mark.

Louis Untermeyer has suggested that "the Cabellian 'biography' assumes the solidarity and shapeliness of a fugue, a composition in which all the voices speak with equal precision and recurring clarity;" Warren McNeill in *Cabellian Harmonics* (1928) relates it to the sonata form with its three themes. Mr. Cabell has made it plain that the three recurring attitudes toward life are the chivalrous, the gallant, and the poetic. These, respectively, have "viewed life as a testing; as a toy; and as raw material"; and these attitudes provide both the contrast and the unity. Manuel in *Figures of Earth* best symbolizes the chivalrous attitude; Jurgen, the gallant. Manuel also represents the man of action, Jurgen the man of thought; and the two books of which they are the protagonists are so far the best in the series that it is easy to lose sight of the poetic attitude as reflected by Madoc in *The Music from Behind the Moon* or by Gerald Musgrave in *Something About Eve.* Indeed, it becomes dominant only in the *Cream of the Jest,* for Felix Kennaston is more convincing than the chivalrous Colonel Musgrave in *The Rivet in Grandfather's Neck* or the gallant R. E. Townsend in *The Cords of Vanity.*

This recurring symbolism is emphasized by Cabell's use of musical devices. There is the suggestive resemblance to the sonata form in the handling of the three themes; there is also the steady employment of the leit-motif and of what Cabell terms contrapuntal prose. Manuel is "tall, squinting Manuel," with other adjectives, especially gray, to vary the phrase by which he is identified to so many of the persons who know him, and incidentally to readers. Possibly the most striking use of this musical repetition is in *Something About Eve*, with the recurrent description of women described as surpassingly lovely:

> Her face was the proper shape, it was appropriately colored everywhere, and it was surmounted with an adequate quantity of hair. Nor was it possible to find any defect in her features. The colors of this beautiful young girl's two eyes were nicely matched, and her nose stood just equidistant between them. Beneath this was her mouth, and she had also a pair of ears. In fine, the girl was young, she exhibited no deformity anywhere, and the enamored glance of the young man could perceive in her no fault. She reminded him, though, of someone that he had known . . .

This refrain is employed to describe many women, and in its final usage it is broken up into conversation, to further emphasize that the woman's beauty is created in the mind of man, existing far more in the concept or dream than in the physical persons. It is effective for this purpose, and possibly Cabell's finest use of the device; but the leit-motif in his hands is never merely an identifying tag: it has always a psychological and frequently a metaphysical end in view.

That which he denominates contrapuntal prose has a less close correspondence with the musical form. This is a passage "shaped in a pre-meditated and self-complete pattern of which the parts are correspondent, that shall harmonize with the whole and at the same time be intrinsically melodious." As one reads this precisely patterned inset, one keeps on with the prose story, yet hears a poem— quite possibly a non-existent poem. The two melodies, ideally, blend and contrast in the reader's ear. It is a verbal and rhythmical pattern, so marked that Warren McNeill in *Cabellian Harmonics* has convincingly demonstrated that many of the passages can be recast into regular verse. In gnomic form these lyric interludes sum up an attitude, an action, or a character: each has an integrated place in the structure of the while book. But only in a vague way do they suggest counterpoint. Another device, even more frequently employed, comes at least as near: when two people are in conversation, one man will be over-ridden after he speaks a word or two, and the first speaker continues serenely on his way; but the attitude of the interrupting person has been made clear enough that we seem to hear his objections under the written words. Two ideas, one voiced and one suggested, are present in unison.

Although he claims that he has written in several well-differentiated styles, Cabell's prose seems basically of a piece. He has mastered an elaborate, finicky, and fluid style; the changes that he works on it do not change the essential features any more than a new hair-do changes the essential face underneath. Certain devices are sure hallmarks of Cabellian prose: the trick of beginning almost every sentence with a connective, so that the sentences seem to flow together; the repetition with little or no variation of key words, sentences, and even paragraphs; beginning one chapter with a sentence lifted from the concluding part of the preceding chapter; embedding what are essentially poems in prose in his narrative.

Each novel too is rounded in structure, with a circular effect secured by linking the ending with the beginning. When Manuel is introduced, he is making the figure of a man, with results not quite to his thinking or his desire; when we leave him, he is working at the same task, with the same unsatisfactory result. *The Music from Behind the Moon* opens with a severely patterned, musical chapter; it closes with one that plays variations upon the words and ideas introduced at the beginning. This looping back to connect the last with the first is true also of the entire Biography, for Felix Kennaston of Lichfield, Virginia, returns to Poictesme in his imagination, and the last descendant of Manuel is circuitously linked, in *The Cream of the Jest,* with his ancestor and his ancestral home.

III

Cabell has taken a seemingly perverse delight in erecting obstacles for readers who attempt to follow the descendants of Manuel in their journeying. From the historical romancers he borrowed the somewhat childish paraphernalia of lengthy protests as to the authenticity of the tale. In Cabell's hands these non-existent old documents and bogus authorities have been developed into a pedantically mock-pedantic system that might in small doses be amusing, but when treated with such a generously heavy hand become tiresome. This long and intricate wind-up has caused many readers to lose interest in whether he delivers a fast ball or a curve; these protestations of authenticity, with their learned remarks about *Les Gestes de Manuel* and *La Haulte Histoire de Jurgen,* seem infinitely more artificial than the romances themselves.

Even in the novels Cabell maintains a deliberately artificial tone that partakes of the nature of an elaborate cross-word puzzle. He likes to employ a phrase like "The tale tells" as an introductory; and he sprinkles in enough easy anagrams (Turoine for routine, Caer Omn for romance, Sesphra for phrases) to leave the reader uncertain about the presence of more abtruse ones. The tone is frequently one of mockery, satiric rather than sustainedly ironic.

More important is the fact that this satire operates against an undefined background. Cabell has frequently represented the writer as a deity omnipotent in the universe he has created, and when writing of the Biography he has talked about the imaginary kingdom of Poictesme and its people and its laws as though these followed a comprehensible pattern. He has even with genealogical fervor traced out the lineage of his Poictesme-Lichfield descendants of Manuel. But he has not defined the bases of his allegory, either in the novels or in his numerous writings about them. His works are heavily sprinkled with magic talismans and magic formulae, but many of these are presented in a satiric, mock-pedantic, spoofing tone.

When the symbol leads to self-hypnosis, and the journey into another realm is patently of the mind, this does not matter. A Felix Kennaston may be led on his imaginary travels and marvelous communings with Ettare by the broken top of a cold cream jar as by any more potent and believable symbol; part of the cream of this particular jest lies in Kennaston's desire to escape from every-day life. But the journeyings of Jurgen are another matter, for they appear to happen consecutively and to be founded on some undefined and inexplicable magic; yet at the end neither Jurgen nor his creator is quite sure whether these were a dream or a reality. The same indecision, though never voiced, seems to afflict the account of Manuel and his fellows of the silver stallion: the rather feeble satire on the United States as Philistia is all too readily grasped, its incidents and many of its persons too easily identifiable; but in other parts the author seems aiming at cosmic truths; and in yet others only to be dallying with fantasy for its own sake. It is this mixture of purposes that ultimately makes Cabell's work suspect, because he allows the allegory to get out of hand.

The age-old conflict of the imagined versus the factual (of things as they appear within the mind versus things as they are) makes a worthy subject for allegory. The fact that Cabell has encompassed so much of it so convincingly lifts his work effectively above that of the historical romancers. But the fact that the pattern of allegory works so capriciously prevents it from having the constant and universal applicability that Dante's *Commedia* has.

Cabell has claimed often that he wrote mainly for his own diversion. Apparently it diverted him to trace out with precision the genealogy of the characters but to let the fundamental pattern of his work veer and turn according to his whimsy. If he had imposed upon his allegorical structure the same iron control that he imposed upon his experiments in rhythmical prose, the Biography would be at once more comprehensible and more convincing.

For all his insistence that the Biography is one symmetrically architectural book, it is not likely to be read as a unit, and there is no real need for it to be so read. The recurrences of major attitudes and of situations, and above all the failure to integrate and define the touchstones of allegory, make it inevitable that a few books can convey nearly all that can be got from the whole. Cabell's essentially humanistic aesthetic was best stated in *Beyond Life;* his later writings on literature have become so egocentric (permeated with irritations at people who ask how to pronounce his surname or ladies who offer him more than he desires) that he frequently seems to have lost sight of his work in his self-concern with the artist. Even in *Beyond Life* there are notes of pettishness, but these are subdued except in his over-treatment of the ephemeral in literature; and the book in its entirety presents a somewhat precious but yet a valid and defensible literary aesthetic.

Today, *Figures of Earth* towers above the other novels. Although uneven, the fantasy is usually controlled and the meaning recognizable. Manuel as man of action, as symbol of chivalry here on earth, and finally as a legendary redeemer, has in truth as much to do with contemporary life as with Poictesme. The man who takes literally the injunction to make a fine figure in the world embodies within himself so many of the enigmas which make up every man that he epitomizes life—epitomizes it strangely and sometimes bewilderingly, yet with so much of implicit reality that his book stands out as Cabell's best. It seems strangely disregarded nowadays, but it appears to have the stamp of enduring value in that it also epitomizes the romantic irony of our time (a none-too-popular attitude, in comparison with naturalism and realism) at its best.

The gallant attitude of *Jurgen* wears less well. The book has fewer complexities than *Figures of Earth;* for all its subtly-phrased accounts of how Jurgen dealt fairly with many women after his fashion, it is a glorification of man's mind, a tribute to the powers of an imagination which has created for itself heaven and hell out of life on earth. It is a story of man's dream that brings him in reach of the unattainable, and of his fears that force him back into compromise with actuality. Here too are Cabell's favorite symbols of the girl not as she is but as she has been created in one man's mind and re-created in memory, contrasted with the talkative, shrewish, comfortable wife—the recurring symbols of the ideal and the actual throughout the Biography. *Jurgen* presents one phase of Cabell's thought, *Figures of Earth* another; and these two novels best adumbrate the aesthetic embodied in *Beyond Life.*

The difference is one of degree rather than of kind. The parts of the Biography are of a piece, and there are likely to be for many years devotees of Cabell who will pick other and less familiar work as his best. But the devotee is attracted mainly by the novelist's manner. To most readers it will seem that Cabell has concentrated on an exotic and whimsically-flavored sauce that conceals the flavor of the meat—and at times is served up without the meat. *Jurgen* and *Figures of Earth* have plenty of meat under the characteristic sauce.

It may be that he has tried too hard to write perfectly of beautiful happenings. For that part of his work which seems likely to endure will do so in spite of his manner, and because of the strong though perverse humanistic philosophy that guides and controls his best work.

DONALD DAVIDSON

Theme and Method In *So Red the Rose*

During the nineteen-twenties, when H. L. Mencken, Sinclair Lewis, and Theodore Dreiser were still the flourishing idols of the new American literature, realism was consistently recommended as a sovereign cure for the sentimentalism with which the South was said to be afflicted. Sentimentalism, it was argued, had produced the so-called magnolias-and-moonlight type of Southern literature. But realism in heavy doses would purge the South of the infection, much in the way that the medical doctors were conquering hookworm and pellagra. T. S. Stribling, Laurence Stallings, Howard Odum, Gerald Johnson, Paul Green, and even DuBose Heyward and Julia Peterkin (at that time the darlings of the liberal *avant-garde*) were held to be administering the cure with much success in what seemed to be regarded as a series of clinical demonstrations.

Preposterous though this school of thought may now seem, its influence has lingered on. A good deal of its sustained momentum has come, doubtless, from the great prestige of Vernon L. Parrington and such professors of American literature as have followed his social type of diagnosis. And this lingering tendency, I suppose, would explain why a critic, as late as the mid-nineteen-thirties, could say that Stark Young's *So Red the Rose* was "heavy with the scent of camellias." He did not know that camellias have no scent; but since magnolias do not flower prominently in Young's novel, while camellias do occasionally appear, he wished to damn the book by connecting it with what he considered a deplorable non-realistic tendency.

The material contained in this essay is presented in enlarged form in the author's introduction to the Modern Standard Authors edition of *So Red The Rose* (Charles Scribner's Sons, 1953) and is used by permission of Charles Scribner's Sons.

The times have changed, and critics who think that camellias have an exotic odor are fewer—and more careful. They can no longer afford the luxury of an ignorance that would make a Florida tourist laugh. Under the new critical regime William Faulkner and other once neglected authors have received extended consideration, but the writings of Stark Young, particularly his prose fiction, have been given no such attention. They have remained an unexplored realm, to which hardly even a reportorial Marco Polo has journeyed.

This neglect seems the more remarkable when one recalls Stark Young's astonishing versatility and productivity. Since the beginning of his literary career, early in the nineteen-twenties, he has been, first of all, one of the few really distinguished dramatic critics writing in English. His dramatic criticism, furthermore, has been translated into foreign languages as distant as the Chinese and Japanese. His fine articles and essays on non-dramatic subjects have had wide circulation, and some have been gathered up, selectively, with his stories, in such books as *The Street of the Islands* (1930) and *Feliciana* (1935). Then, most important of all for the present discussion, there are his four novels: *Heaven Trees* (1926), *The Torches Flare* (1928), *River House* (1929), and *So Red the Rose* (1934). The six books named are closely related. Taken all together, they form a definite organic unity—a kind of "war and peace" of the American scene, with the focus chiefly but not exclusively on the South; and they apply in the medium of prose fiction the artistic principles and moral philosophy that animate the dramatic criticism and that Stark Young has more recently expressed in his book of reminiscences, *The Pavilion* (1951).

Although all these books have claims upon a critic's sober attention—and *Heaven Trees,* among them, has a peculiar and charming perfection of its own—*So Red the Rose* is clearly the greatest. In this instance the judgment of readers has run ahead of the judgment of critics. From the time of its first publication, *So Red the Rose* has commanded a large audience of devoted readers. For twenty years it has remained in print without benefit of criticism new or old. Since it is a complex and difficult novel—not at all the simple romance that a camellia-minded critic might guess it to be—the phenomenon of its popularity is not easy to explain. Some would explain it, I suppose, by calling the book a "Civil War novel."

But though it deals with events of the eighteen-sixties, *So Red the Rose* is no more to be catalogued as a mere "Civil War novel" than the *Antigone* of Sophocles is to be catalogued as a drama of the Theban civil war. The dramatic conflict of *So Red the Rose* is not some special sort of conflict that pertains only to the people of the South or of a limited region of Mississippi. It is a conflict of the same order and nature as we find in the works of Dostoevsky, Hardy, Yeats, Eliot, or Faulkner. The novel draws into focus the battle between tradition and anti-tradition that has been waged with increasing vehemence since the Renaissance. In it Stark Young deals with what is, for the serious artist, the great inescapable subject, and he dramatizes that subject in its own terms, without imposing special views upon it. By his method he "realizes" that subject in a full-bodied fiction that implies in every part the whole of which it is a symbolic rather than a merely pictorial or argued representation. There is no other "Civil War novel" that can compare with it because no other such novel has so convincingly brought the special historical subject matter into the realm of the high art that alone can give a local fiction general application and lasting relevance.

So Red the Rose is a large-scale narrative in which events of national importance exert catastrophic force upon the life of the Bedfords, the McGehees, and their kin, friends, visitors, slaves—the whole complex of plantation life and, by implication, of Southern life in general. Beginning with the birthday party for Hugh McGehee, in November, 1860, the narrative covers the period of the election of Lincoln, Southern secession, formation of the Confederacy, and the Civil War. It ends in November, 1865. More than fifty characters appear in the novel, and at least a score of these are of major importance.

Yet despite its large scope, numerousness of characters, and wealth of detail, *So Red the Rose* is singularly compact and at every point sharply dramatic in its method of rendering characters and events. This dramatic quality and compactness are the more remarkable if one recalls, by comparison, the diffuse or laborious treatment generally found in novels dealing with the same period. It would seem that a writer who chooses the Civil War period can hardly achieve dramatic concentration unless, like Stephen Crane in *The Red Badge of Courage*, he takes the safe course of centering his narrative on a single person to whose point of view everything is related. This limitation of course assists the dramatic concentration, but at the cost of impoverishing the context of great events and great persons in which the chosen mentality must perform. On the other hand writers who, wishing to offset this limitation, attempt to supply richness of context by romantic, panoramic, or documentary devices inevitably lose dramatic concentration and produce mere "historical" novels.

In *So Red the Rose* there is no single character on whom the narrative is focused throughout; nor is there any narrator or disinterested participant whose angle of vision affords a consistent point of reference. A single point of view may be maintained for a while during a single episode. We may enter the brooding mind of Lucy McGehee when, after the battle of Shiloh, she has her vision of dead Charles Taliaferro riding through the gate, putting his hand to his side, and saying, "That night at Shiloh, lying in my blood, I remembered how you sang." But after such moments the focus soon shifts or, rather, merges into the impersonal current of the general narrative.

Evidently Stark Young wished to retain the breadth of perspective and richness of context afforded by the "omniscient point of view" —that is, the method of classical narrative. But he also wished each scene or narrative bit to carry the sharp particularity, the firm dramatic immediacy, afforded by the modern method of dramatization in prose narrative. This method bars intruded explanation. It noncommittally subjects the reader to the flow of inferences and sensations and ideas that the performing characters encounter at any given moment.

It is this combination of methods, applied with consummate skill, that gives *So Red the Rose* its wonderful compactness and dramatic force, together with its richness of narrative meaning. But though the classical method allows the author to shift the focus continually and also, by way of "exposition," to orient the reader as to the course of events in general—the war, for example—the dramatic method requires that the author never "intrude" the meaning of the dramatization itself; it must be implicit in the action. Therefore, in combining the two methods, Stark Young had to take the risk, first, of some confusion or uncertainty of orientation, especially during the opening chapters of the novel; and, second, the far greater risk that the total and true meaning of his narrative would be missed or only dimly apprehended. For the conscientious Southern writer in our time, the latter risk is peculiarly painful. Anything that looks like a declaration on his part will be viewed as partisanship. Yet if his real meaning does not somehow emerge, it will not be grasped at all or else will be confused with some conventional interpretation of Southern life.

It might be argued that confusion of orientation is, in a way, a part of the dramatic effect. Stark Young has said, in *The Pavilion*: "It does not matter at all if some reader of these pages should find he cannot keep straight various characters or stories that appear in them. . . . The point is the quality represented here and there in one name or one story and another and the memory that remains of them." This would apply to *So Red the Rose*, to some extent.

When we encounter Malcolm Bedford, in Chapter I, writing his humorous obituaries of relatives and friends—a remarkable scene— we may suppose, accustomed as we are to the limited point of view, that we will continue with Malcolm's point of view for at least one complete episode. But no, presently we are in the carriage with the Bedfords and Mary Cherry, proceeding to Hugh McGehee's birthday party, without knowing very precisely who the Bedfords and McGehees are. Momentarily, as we look back at Portobello from the avenue, we slip into Mrs. Bedford's mind. But on the next page we reach Montrose and are in the midst of a very large group of interesting people who know one another but do not stop to lecture us on their identities and backgrounds. The author is not going to lecture us either. And we may proceed for fifty pages, even a hundred, before the identity of the characters and their relation to historic events begins to form a narrative pattern that can be completely and definitely grasped. This confusion, as Stark Young says, "does not matter"—meaning that perfect clarity, if striven for by rigid outlining and explanation, would destroy the sense of vitality and spontaneity that are needed at the outset.

Still, in *So Red the Rose*, it is not a question of a few names and relationships but of a convergence of many names and multiple relationships. And the narrative is complicated by the fact that the author presents two complete households, where most novelists might have been content with one. At Portebello, the Bedford plantation, there are Malcolm Bedford; Sallie, his wife (née Tate); Duncan, their son; Valette Somerville, their adopted daughter. At Montrose, the seat of the McGehees, there are Hugh McGehee; his wife Agnes (sister of Malcolm Bedford); their son Edward; and their daughter Lucy. Adding to these two groups Mary Cherry and General Sherman, we have ten major characters to deal with, as persons of critical importance. There are also forty or more "minor" characters—none of whom, however, can be dismissed as unimportant. It would seem that we cannot really "know" the characters of the novel and establish them in the pattern of the narrative until the two families are understood, as families. It is clear that the minor characters of the book either belong to the Bedford or McGehee households by blood or principle; or else are pathetically unattached; or represent, like Sherman, a hostile principle. And the two families, united by ties of marriage and blood, are in a sense one family as the South in a still larger sense is one family. The Bedfords and McGehees, in their histories, dwellings, and personal peculiarities, represent different and complementary aspects of Southern life.

The Bedfords seem to represent a strain more definitely English, in certain ways, than the McGehees. This is the strain deriving from Virginia antecedents that became dominant in Tennessee and Kentucky and blended with other strains in settling the western parts of the Deep South. The name Bedford is English. The Bedfords' house repeats the name of an ancestral house in Virginia, Portobello, which, like its contemporary, Mount Vernon, echoed the English affiliations of the pre-Revolutionary Washingtons and their friends. At the outbreak of the war Duncan Bedford, son of Malcolm, is attending the University of Virginia. His war service is with the Army of Northern Virginia, under Lee and Stuart.

These small particulars, perhaps only mildly symbolic, belong to the frame of reference by which the Bedfords are to be differentiated from the McGehees. The Bedfords are rather extrovert, practical, and realistic; inarticulate in the expression of strong feeling; reliant on good sense rather than intuition—while the McGehees tend the other way. The Bedford household has grown by generosity as well as by biological increase, for it includes their adopted daughter Valette, the child of friends who perished in a yellow fever epidemic, and little Middleton, the child of Malcolm's dead sister, as well as Rosa Tate ("Aunt Piggie"), Mrs. Bedford's sister, and Rosa's senile brother Henry, in addition to the Bedford children themselves. The good-humored tolerance of the Bedfords is further suggested by the near presence of that curious savage, Uncle Billy McChidrick, and his famous parrot which can make noises like a seasick person. Dock, the Choctaw Indian, retained in an anomalous relationship as hunter and hanger-on, links the family and the plantation with frontier days that are, after all, in the very recent past.

Since realism and good sense are not in the end a sufficient defense against all the irregularities of life, Malcolm is likely to confront serious issues with his sense of humor rather than with a system of philosophy. That humor, especially when aided by large potations, turns prankishly toward thoughts of the grave. Like John Donne, Malcolm makes quips about the shroud when he is faced with a conflict between idea and reality. The humorous obituaries are products of this mood. And in general Malcolm (like Dr. Clay in *Heaven Trees*) is an inveterate practical joker and tease, not far distant from the Sut Lovingood tradition. Off at the war, he writes his wife to send him some shirts with his name marked on the tails, together with his copies of Sterne and Lucretius. But for all his addiction to the classics, his talk is homely. "I could stand my children being taught transcendentalism, witch-burning, even abolition," he says, "but I'm damned if I'll have them taught that all things work together to make life sugar-coated." Sallie, his wife, is cut from the same cloth. "She was a woman who naturally, in whatever ways a man seemed to her to be like a man, let him alone."

If the Bedfords seem somewhat more definitely to stand out as a family established in Mississippi but otherwise not shown to be widely connected, the McGehees are a clan of which the McGehees of Montrose are only the part that appears in the foreground for the purposes of this particular novel. They are Celtic rebels, descendants of the outlawed McGregors of seventeenth century Scotland. Hugh McGehee's choice of "Montrose" as the name of his home suggests this rebellious past. The McGehees incline to be mystical and intuitive. In the old Scottish sense they are "fey." Montrose, like the house of Airlie, is doomed to be burned by a foeman as cruel as "the great Argyle," though more self-assured logically. Edward is doomed to die in battle. His mother Agnes (though a Bedford by blood) "knows" beyond all reasonable persuasion to the contrary, when news comes of a battle at Shiloh, that her son is dead. Like the mother of some ballad, she must straightway go to seek him among the slain and to fetch his body home. In this same moment of tragic tension Lucy McGehee has her ballad-like vision of the boy for whom she has cherished an unavowed love. While the Bedfords send their son far away to the University of Virginia, the McGehees, more locally attached and "clannish," send their Edward to Louisiana Military Academy, where in 1860 W. T. Sherman is commandant.

But though the McGehees, in comparison with the Bedfords, are more clearly exemplars of the frontier wanderings that peopled the western South, this frontier restlessness, as the historians like to call it, has nevertheless seated a part of the McGehees firmly in Mississippi. Hugh McGehee, elegant, philosophical, and well-provided, has put the frontier behind him and thinks in terms of an established society.

In Hugh McGehee, the wild Celtic strain has been tempered. The combination of fierce passion and cool reason that gave the South such a political leader as Calhoun and such a military leader as Stonewall Jackson is, in Hugh McGehee, a fusion of tenderness and wisdom. Completely articulate, he is able to detach his mind from the melee of raw events and to judge them under the laws of reason, but never with a logic that is merely logical. No doubt we are to assume—although Stark Young as author does not say so—that in Hugh McGehee Southern society has produced an example of the unified personality, in tune with its environment while also commanding it; and that Southern society at the outbreak of the war was tending toward such an ideal. When war comes, the Celtic intuition seems in Hugh McGehee to become prophetic insight, so that, while intensely loyal to the Southern cause, he can also stand apart from it in his thought about events and judge what the fruits of war will be both in North and in South.

To follow the code of the Bedfords and McGehees requires an establishment like theirs in principle but not necessarily of the same scale. It means ownership of land, respect for God and nature, devotion to agriculture and its allied pursuits, and, with these, a healthy mistrust of what towns and trade, or in the later phrase, "industrialism," may seductively offer. In So Red the Rose this is everywhere the underlying implication. In his contribution to I'll Take My Stand, four years prior to the publication of the novel, Stark Young is explicit. It was, he says, the landed class that gave Southern society "its peculiar stamp." He is willing to concede that other classes "reflected certain traits from the planter class," but in his opinion "the manners and customs of the South do not wholly arise from the bottom mass; they have come from the top downward." At the same time he speaks sharply against those who would defer to the mass in order to exploit it and warns against false notions of "aristocracy," which, if it means anything at all, is nothing boastfully pretentious, but rather "a settled connection with the land . . . the fact that your family had maintained a certain quality of manners throughout a certain period of time, and had a certain relation to the society of the country."

With such cues to interpretation, it is possible to understand the role of Mary Cherry and of certain minor figures who appear in the narrative. Mary Cherry has neither husband nor lover. Worse still, she has no kin. She owns no property except the famous trunk and few meagre personal belongings, and she will never inherit or acquire any. She has no occupation. She spends her time in long visits at household after household. Under the inviolable code of hospitality, it would be a breach of manners not to receive her and allow her the privileges of a lady and, as it were, of a member of the family, even though, away from her presence, the family groan under her loud assertiveness and domineering exactions.

In *Heaven Trees* Mary Cherry is treated at greater length, and it is in that novel that she avows her personal credo: "The world owes me a living." This she interprets as meaning that she can walk into a merchant's establishment and demand shoes or a coat, with no questions raised either as to cash or credit. In *So Red the Rose,* although she remains "an Amazonian in buckram," her rougher traits are toned down somewhat, except as, during the fearful abstraction of war, they can be turned to account against the enemy. Nevertheless, if we take the Mary Cherry of *Heaven Trees* and of *So Red the Rose* as one and the same person, it is clear that she is, in contrast to the Bedfords and McGehees, the perfect semblance of the individual who, having neither kin nor property, has no place whatever in society. In the modern term, she is dissociated. The orphan Valette might have grown up into a Mary Cherry if she had not been adopted by the Bedfords. Mary Cherry, less fortunate, must remain unattached. The society of the Bedfords and McGehees, acknowledging the tragedy, takes the private responsibility of accepting her as a charge. This is charity which, however, must never be publicly advertised as charity. The Bedfords and McGehees prefer the private obligation, however onerous, to any plausible schemes that might be devised for shifting Mary Cherry onto the shoulders of the general public.

In her behavior Mary Cherry necessarily represents a kind of a parody of the culture by which she benefits and in which she heartily believes—though without understanding. Her exaggerated independence, her loud voice, her dictatorial sending away, at table, of dishes that do not please her, her solitary singing of hymns, her fire-eating pronouncements—all such mannerisms, which are her crude exercise of what she conceives to be the prerogatives of a lady, naturally are grotesque and even when amusing are empty of real meaning because there is no substance back of them to give them meaning.

As long as the Bedfords, McGehees, and their ilk flourish, Mary Cherry can do little real harm. Her gaucheries are ignored because she is an isolated case; and a similar tolerance is extended to the northern governess, the seamstress from Iowa, and to the invalids from the North who are visiting Montrose for the climate; all of these are in something of a Mary Cherry condition. Later on when the society of the Bedfords and McGehees is weakened and partly destroyed by the war and its aftermath, the Mary Cherrys will multiply enormously and become a menace. In one form they will become that familiar nuisance, the "professional Southerner"; in other forms, the homeless, rootless, isolated individuals of the modern world, whether of the industrial proletariat or intellectual elite.

Opposed to the Bedfords and McGehees are, of course, the armies, political leaders, and people of the North. In a very general sense all these together may be thought of as the Antagonist, which, in the trite and empty modern phrase, could be called a Social Force. The term is invalid, however, with reference to *So Red the Rose,* which is nearer to Aeschylus and Sophocles than to Zola or Dreiser. Since to depict the Northern counterparts of the Bedfords and McGehees with any great circumstantiality would merely increase the size of the novel at the risk of blurring its focus and diluting its dramatic power, Stark Young uses General William Tecumseh Sherman to represent what is most hostile, in principle and in deed, to the Bedford-McGehee tradition. Sherman is the Enemy in military fact as well as in fully rationalized intent. In trying out his policy of "total war" in the Natchez-Vicksburg area—long before it was applied in Georgia and elsewhere—Sherman represents the logical and realistic side of the humanitarianism to which Lincoln at this time was giving a very persuasive but misleading rhetorical expression.

But while the historical facts of Sherman's military career bring his path directly and jarringly athwart the Bedford-McGehee orbit, and therefore make him highly eligible for the role of chief antagonist, it is even more important to note that, in person, he typifies the opposite of what the Bedfords and McGehees stand for. If they represent the culture of the whole personality, Sherman is a grand apotheosis and cataclysmic realization of the cult of the divided personality. Between Sherman the man and Sherman in his efficient function as general there is no connection. The man may be courteous, gentlemanly, artistic, kind, and "good," but the code that determines his behavior as man does not carry over into the behavior of the general, the political thinker. In Sherman, then, "thought" and "feeling" act in separate compartments. A code is allowable for matters of "feeling," but it must not go beyond ordinary drawing-room behavior—manners in the superficial sense. In practical matters, to which logic must be applied, "thought" rules absolute, and therefore no code operates. So, while the code of the Bedfords and McGehees, not thus split, but having a certain all-inclusiveness, can distinguish between soldier and civilian and confine destruction to the field of war proper, the rational philosophy of Sherman denies the validity of any such code, refuses to distinguish between soldier and civilian, and thus infinitely extends the sphere of destruction.

For Sherman the man we should also note that it creates the peculiarly modern kind of tragedy. For Sherman in his grief over the death of his son Willie, there is no consolation. The logical half of the man, divided from the hurt emotional half, has no comfort to offer. Sherman is incapable of grasping the assumption of Hugh and Agnes McGehee that his grief for Willie will naturally lead him to pity and regret for the slaughter that has brought low their Edward —symbolic of the Southern dead. Sherman's view of that is strictly rational: "If the Southern people don't like what they are getting, all they have to do is to declare their loyalty and come back into the Union." He is convinced of the expediency of his war plan, but nevertheless on the one hand he writhes under the ill impression the

Southern people have of him, and on the other hand he uses that ill impression as an instrument to further his ends. Agnes McGehee, intuitively, sees Sherman as "tormented and wilful." "This conflict of policy had become a conflict in his own nature, and . . . the story that was building up of him as a ruthless monster did at the same time both serve him and his purposes as a picture of war, and antagonize, grieve, and enrage him as a picture of himself."

Once the leading characters and groups of characters are thus differentiated, the profusion of persons, scenes, and particulars that marks *So Red the Rose* is no longer bewildering, and the dramatic structure can be apprehended, not as elaborate and pretentious, but as simple to the point of austerity. The action of the narrative divides naturally into successive stages, of growing intensity, from the time when war is a mere probability to the time when it becomes an actuality and yet is still distant as a physical fact; and then on to the stage when war, at last physically present, is known for what it truly is. What it truly is, in terms of this particular conflict, is not wholly apparent until Sherman enters the scene—until, in fact, after making his courtesy call on the McGehees, as the parents of one of his former cadets, Sherman has his private conversation at the gate with Hugh McGehee and tells him the planter class must be "replaced" after the victory of the North.

Thus the focus of the general narrative, very wide at first, is steadily narrowed until the point of greatest significance is reached. That point comes, it would seem, when Hugh McGehee says, after his conversation with Sherman, "Yes. He's good. I can't understand it." At once, like a commentary on Hugh's generous restraint, comes Lucy's violent emotional reaction. She is outraged that Sherman has been received into the house. "How could you all, how could you, when they killed—?" Almost immediately, confirming Lucy's bitter personal judgment, comes the burning of Montrose by negro soldiers under the command of a white officer:

> She [Agnes] could hear them tramping in the parlors
> and the rattle of their sabres and spurs. She rushed in to
> her daughter. There they were. Lucy was in the bedroom
> and the negroes were tramping through the sitting-room,
> threatening, cursing.

"Get out, Agnes ordered. "Get out of my house. Get out of my sight!"

A big black who seemed to be in command gave a guffaw, and the other negroes, watching him evidently, followed. One of them came up to her and with his open hand boxed her on the cheek. At once another negro put a pistol against her breast; she could smell his sweat. Then the big negro who had struck her said, "Don't shoot her, Mose, slap her. Slap the old slut." He broke into a stream of abuse.

The powerful scene in which the sack and burning of Montrose are depicted is rendered in straightforward prose, unornamented, matter-of-fact, without any officious coloring or pointing-up to connect its dramatic meaning explicitly with the episodes immediately preceding. It is as "objective" as, say, Hemingway's account, in *A Farewell to Arms,* of the Italian retreat from the Caporetto, but is far richer in its complex of meanings, since Stark Young's total narrative scheme ranges further and wider than does Hemingway's, and his use of a shifting focus allows a depth of perspective which Hemingway, committed to the limited perceptions of Lieutenant Frederick Henry, cannot possibly attain.

For the scene, brief though it is, reveals not only the gross violation which ultimately implies (as Hugh McGehee says later on) the collapse of civilized society, but also the plight of the Confederacy, symbolized in the futile skirmishing of the little Confederate detachment for which the McGehees have been cooking a hasty breakfast, as well as, in the details of the ravaging, the nature of the defeat that the McGehees and the South are experiencing and must continue to face. Nor is the narrative so ordered as to deprive the individual invaders of all humanity or the McGehees of all their natural charity. The negro soldiers, raw recruits under a white man's orders, are both brutal and sacred. In parody of their wantonness and fear we are shown, with almost a kind of tenderness, a brief picture of the little black boy who steals a handkerchief and starts to run. Bessie, one of the house-servants, catches him as he runs.

"What you got in yo' han'", boy? Show me what you got in yo' hand," the girl was saying, as she jerked his elbow and shook him. She snatched his arm from behind him and pried open the little black fingers, which were clutching a red silk handkerchief. Hugh McGehee, who liked anything that was alive, stood watching the little negro's eyes, from which the tears ran down to make a worse smudge of his sooty face. It eased Hugh to see the destruction and pillage reduced to this level, when a piece of red cloth gave the feeling of excitement and booty. He looked down at his daughter with her drawn features and shut eyes, and at the green grass around her pallet. "Let him have it, Bessie," he said.

Considered in narrative terms, the burning of Montrose is a dramatic continuation of the talk at the gate during which Sherman reveals to Hugh McGehee the pitilessly logical half of his schizoid personality. Such, too, is the nocturnal episode in which Sallie Bedford witnesses the hanging of Federal marauders by a small group of Confederate cavalry who are taking Sherman's abandonment of ethical principle to a vengeful extreme—correspondingly "logical" on their side.

These and other such scenes in the closing phase of the novel are "historically" true in that they could be documented from the *Official Records of the War of the Rebellion* or the reminiscences, diaries, and letters of numerous participants on both sides of the conflict. In 1864, after the initiation of Sherman's famous policy, the war in all parts of the western theatre of operations took on precisely the character indicated in Stark Young's narrative. Much of his material comes from papers of his own family or from oral reminiscence. The source of his information about the burning of "Montrose," for example, was a manuscript of his Aunt Mary's—an account which she composed and finally published in a Mississippi newspaper. Bowling Green, the plantation at Woodville which belonged to Edward McGehee, Sr., was sacked and burned by the Third United States Colored Cavalry, commanded by Colonel J. B. Cook. A similar "documentation" could be supplied for other historical details and episodes. Portobello, for example, is drawn from Rosedown, a house still standing two miles from St. Francisville, Louisiana. The real Billy McChidrick belonged to Stark Young's own Uncle Hugh McGehee of Panola, Mississippi. The selection from the diary of Agnes McGehee —at the end of Chapter LIII—originates in a note by Mrs. Edward

McGehee—and so on. Furthermore, the details of manners, dress, and speech have been worked out with minute and subtle scrupulousness. And while a large chapter could be written on the prose style in general, it may here be said, with regard to speech in particular, that *So Red the Rose* stands without a rival in its skillful representation of the nuances of tone, pronunciation, and idiom of Southern speech. The Southerners of this book talk like real Southerners; not like stage Southerners.

But *So Red the Rose* is literature, not documentation. The question of the "authenticity" of historical material of course arises in a work of fiction dealing with the Civil War. Any novelist who deals with the past knows that his fiction in some sense is competition with documented history as Homer's fiction was not. But such authenticity however necessary, is a subordinate, not a major element in a work of art. *So Red the Rose* is literature, not because of mere documentary authenticity but because it strives to evoke reality at the highest plane of which the art of prose fiction is capable, and because it succeeds in this evocation. It is literature in the full sense, not with the partial meaning we use when we apply such terms as realistic, romantic propagandist, or the like.

The tragic scenes of *So Red the Rose* rise above any specific feelings of resentment or horror such as might be aroused by a more partisan account in a reader whose particular sympathies might naturally be engaged on the Southern or the Northern side of the actual historical conflict. Sherman, the historical general, can be investigated and argued about in matter-of-fact terms; and the Bedfords and McGehees, or their numerous parallels, can be studied in the various aspects of the social and economic situation. But Sherman the fictional character and his fictional opponents and victims appear here not for argument but for the kind of contemplation we would give to *Richard III* or *Macbeth* or *Antigone*. The characters of *So Red the Rose* move upward toward the large conceptions of "myth," in the high sense not downward toward the always arguable and provocative issues of "realism." They submit to the Aristotelean principle and can be viewed as universals. What we see, if we look closely enough, is not only the specific personal tragedy of the Bedfords and McGehees confronted by a clearly identifiable and historic soldier-leader, but the two parties of a great conflict recurrent in one form or another throughout human history, though brought to an intense pitch in modern times. One party integrates, in terms of a harmonious life that blends substance and spirit, subject to God's inscrutable will and the contingencies of nature; the other disintegrates and, using disintegration itself as a tool of power, presumes to mount beyond good and evil and to make human intelligence a quasi-God. Since the Bedfords and McGehees of the South are by no means the only possible representatives of such integration, past or present, or Sherman the only possible representative of disintegration, the modern reader of *So Red the Rose* should be able to say, "There, but for the grace of God, go I," and find in this remarkable novel a mirror reflecting a state and a prospect to which we are more than ever disastrously and tragically liable.

RAY B. WEST, JR.

Katherine Anne Porter And 'Historic Memory'

In describing Miranda, the little girl in the short story entitled "The Grave," Katherine Anne Porter wrote: "Miranda, with her powerful social sense, which was like a fine set of antennae radiating from every pore of her skin." Miranda appears as a character in "Old Mortality," "Pale Horse, Pale Rider," and in the short stories which open Miss Porter's last volume, *The Leaning Tower*. In general, Miranda is the mask for the author when the short story is fashioned from autobiographical material and told from the author's point of view. Insofar as the short stories are concerned—as short stories— this fact is of no importance. Insofar, however, as we are concerned with Katherine Anne Porter as a Southern author, the fact is necessary information. Miss Porter's talent consists of just such a sensibility as she attributes to Miranda. She herself has said that her method of composition is to write from memory. When a remembered incident strikes her as having meaning, she makes a note; then as details accumulate, she adds other notes. At some point in the process, all of the individual details seem suddenly to merge into a pattern. With her notes about her, she sits down and writes the short story. Many of her notes begin simply: "Remember."

How such moments occur we can deduce from another passage concerning Miranda in "The Grave," where Miss Porter says: "One day she was picking her path among the puddles and crushed refuse of a market street in a strange city of a strange country, when without warning, plain and clear in its true colors as if she looked through a frame upon a scene that had not stirred nor changed since the moment it happened, the episode of that far-off day leaped from its burial place before her mind's eye." What "leaped," of course, was not

278

merely the episode, but the full composition of the picture—the events with their pattern of meaning. "The Grave" is the story of how Miranda and her brother Paul discovered a gold ring and a small silver dove, which had once served as a screw head for a coffin, in the emptied grave where her grandfather had lain before his final transfer from a home burial plot to the big new public cemetery; it is also about how Paul killed a rabbit which was just about to give birth to young, and how the knowledge of the young unborn bodies lying within the womb of the dead animal was first a secret between them, then finally forgotten, until it was suddenly remembered years later "in a strange city of a strange country": "It was a very hot day and the smell in the market, with its piles of raw flesh and wilting flowers, was like the mingled sweetness and corruption she had smelled that other day in the empty cemetery at home: the day she had re-membered always until now vaguely as the time she and her brother had found treasure in the opened graves."

This "memory" as it became a short story in "The Grave" is much more than the remembered incident. It is a story about birth and death, about the beginning of life and the corruption of life. The words "innocent" and "evil" do not appear in the story, except sym-bolically and by implication, but the story is one of the initiation of the innocent by knowledge. The gold ring which Miranda received from her brother in exchange for the small silver dove symbolizes knowledge and suggests qualities which that knowledge possesses. It is about the time "she and her brother found treasure in the opened graves," and by the end of the story, when this passage occurs, we recognize the double intention of the words: the innocent "treasure" of childhood and the sweet, mysterious, guilty "treasure" of maturity.

How did the incident come to take on this burden of meaning? No complete answer can be given, of course. We must begin vaguely by saying that Katherine Anne Porter's creative sensitivity, like Miranda's, is a "powerful social sense," which detects special and subtle meanings in experience and translates them into fiction. By this, we mean that her senses, "like a fine set of antennae," detect meanings in experience which are then transformed into aesthetic experiences, where the meanings are made available through their embodiment in recognizable images, characters, and events. What we are to be most concerned with in this account is the nature of the experience upon which that sensibility operates.

Katherine Anne Porter was born in Texas in 1894, of a family which traced its ancestry to Daniel Boone, the Kentucky pioneer. If we take the account of Miranda's background in the stories from *The Leaning Tower* as being roughly autobiographical, we can say that the family had moved, within the lifetime of Miss Porter's grandmother, from Kentucky into Louisiana, and from there to Texas. As with most Southern families, it had retained a strong sense of family unity as well as an awareness of its place in the framework of Southern history and Southern society. The grandfather, although he had died before the family left Kentucky and even though the move itself was mainly necessitated by his imprudence, moved with the family each time they were uprooted, for his grave "had been twice disturbed in his long repose by the constancy and possessiveness of his widow. She removed his bones first to Louisiana and then to Texas as if she had set out to find her own burial place, knowing well she would never return to the places she had left."

Miss Porter's experience, then, is not only of the fixed, almost absolute, values of Southern society, but also of our relationship to them in the face of a history of movement and of change. In addition, the family was Scotch and Catholic, inheriting a rugged stubbornness as its national inheritance, a determined set of moral values from its religion. When the grandmother talked about "all the important appearances of life, and especially about the rearing of the young," she "relied with perfect acquiescence on the dogma that children were conceived in sin and brought forth in iniquity. Childhood was a long state of instruction and probation for adult life, which was in turn a long, severe, undeviating devotion to duty, the largest part of which consisted in bringing up children."

I realize the dangers of talking about events from a literary work as though they were autobiographical facts. I think the danger in the case of Katherine Anne Porter is lessened, however, by the fact that so much of her subject matter lies within the areas of her own experience: her Southern background, her travels in Mexico and Europe, her Roman Catholic upbringing, and her interest in liberal social causes. Also, in describing once how she had come to write the short story "Old Mortality," her tongue slipped, so that instead of saying, "Miranda's father said. . .," she made the remark, "*My father* said. . ." In talking with her recently about her stories, I asked her about the character Laura in "Flowering Judas." I had been puzzled by this character, because so many of the background facts concerning Laura were similar to those in Katherine Anne Porter's own experience, the strict Catholic upbringing, the interest in modern social causes, and the fact that Miss Porter had taught in Mexico, and that when she returned she had brought with her an exhibition of paintings by Mexican school children. Why, then, wasn't this character called Miranda? Was Laura also an autobiographical figure? I asked. No. Laura was modeled upon a friend with whom Miss Porter had taught school in Mexico—but of course she was not merely a portrait of that girl; she was, Miss Porter supposed, a combination of a good many people, just as was the character, Braggioni, in the same story. At the same time, the events of "Pale Horse, Pale Rider"—which is a Miranda story—were many of them actual events which happened when Miss Porter was working as a reporter on the *Rocky Mountain News* in Denver during the first war.

The danger arises, of course, when a character possesses traits similar to those belonging to Miranda. But the important thing to notice is that in all cases, Katherine Anne Porter's characters possess qualities which have some point of similarity with her own experience. If they are Irish or Mexican, they are also Roman Catholic—or they are political liberals. They are usually Southerners. I don't mean to suggest this as a serious limitation, but it may help to account for the relatively small amount which Miss Porter has written. At the same time, it may also account for the consistently high level which her work represents, a level probably unsurpassed by any writer of her time. When necessary, she exhibits a range of perception of ordinary manners and mannerisms which is almost uncanny, but usually such qualities, as in the character of Mr. Thompson in "Noon Wine," are attached to a person well within the limits of her own experience. The whole atmosphere of the Thompson place, which is a Western Texas farm in the years between 1896-1905, seems to suggest that such an event must actually have occurred, even if not precisely as it is related in the story, and that the author knew very well the kind of people Mr. and Mrs. Thompson were, even if she did not know exactly these same persons. Mr. Helton, in the same story, who is a Swede and who came from North Dakota, is an interesting and successful character, but he does not occupy so prominent a position in the story and so does not bear so heavy a burden of probability. The events of "Noon Wine" center upon Mr. Thompson's guilt—

the psychological effects of an unpremeditated killing, and we can imagine that the story began from a memory either of the event or of the character of Mr. Thompson, or both, in the mind of the author who was probably about seven or eight years of age at the time of the murder and suicide. It could have begun from the events alone, and the character could have been supplied from other memories; but however it happened, the character at the center of the story was of a type which Miss Porter must have known well, while the less familiar Mr. Helton got into the story because he was necessary to the events.

The important point is that such memory as we are talking about in discussing Miss Porter's talent is not "mere memory," not only memory of something which occured, but something which occured within the long history of personal, family, and regional events— finally, within the history of mankind. In referring to the friendship between Sophia Jane, Miranda's grandmother, and her Negro maid in "The Old Order," Miss Porter writes: "The friendship between the two old women had begun in early childhood, and was based on what seemed even to them almost mythical events." Miss Porter treats her memories also as "mythical events."

Myth is, of course, a form of tribal memory, preserving events of the past as a means of justifying and explaining its views of the present. Every society adapts "myth" to its own purposes, either myths which it has transported from elsewhere and uses as a means of organizing its memories, or myths which it has created from events of its own past. Colonial America, as Constance Rourke has pointed out, created its concept of the typical Yankee, which is as true of the frontier peddler as it is of the modern G.I. in Europe or Korea—and as untrue. The society of the South was particularly inclined toward the creation of myths, partly I suppose because of the amount of Latin influence in its history, partly because of the amount of Anglo-Catholicism, partly because of its Negroes, but mainly because of its closeness to nature and because of the rural nature of its plantation society. The Latin background gave it a regard for manners and romance, the Anglican a respect for ceremony, while the Negroes fused the two with primitive magic. In addition, the aristocratic and paternalistic structure of the plantation represented a means not only of creating regional and family myth, but also of preserving it in a more or less unbroken chain from earliest times down to at least the period of the Civil War.

There have been bitter quarrels with the nature of the Southern myth, but few deny its reality or its importance to the society which it reflected. We may say that the South spent the first years creating its myths, a few important years defending them (even in battle), and its most recent years utilizing them as the subject matter for literature. Perhaps their most complete use is represented in the novels and short stories of William Faulkner, where the timeless world of eternal values of the Southern past is posted against the fluid and pragmatic present. In one way or another, these contrasts have got into most Southern writing, whether the poetry of Allen Tate, John Crowe Ransom, John Peale Bishop, Robert Penn Warren, and Donald Davidson, or into the prose fiction of Ellen Glasgow, Caroline Gordon, Stark Young, Eudora Welty, Peter Taylor, Carson McCullers, Tate, Warren, and Katherine Anne Porter. With a special emphasis, it is to be found in the writings of Truman Capote, Elizabeth Hardwick, William Goyen, Tennessee Williams, and Leroy Leatherman. With an inverted emphasis, it is utilized by Erskine Caldwell, Lilian Hellman, and most of the Negro writers of our time.

Yet each author poses a separate problem—not the least of them Katherine Anne Porter. She is less the self-conscious "professional" Southerner than either Donald Davidson or Truman Capote; she shares somewhat in the tendency toward inversion—the liberalism— of Erskine Caldwell. The question of how much an author owes to his region has been discussed endlessly and is now seen as a futile preoccupation, at least insofar as an evaluation of his work is concerned. Even as it concerns the author himself, it has only a limited and often questionable value. But it is tantalizingly present as a puzzle in personality. Just what kind of writer might Katherine Anne Porter have been had she been born and raised in a fundamentalist, Protestant New England family in, say, Rutland, Vermont? The question is hypothetical and nonsensical, but it does emphasize the importance of Miss Porter's Southern, Roman Catholic background. How much her sensibility was affected either by her place or her religion must remain a puzzle, but her sensibility is her *self*—including her memory, which she would have had in any case, and she, herself, *did* grow up in the South of a family with a long history of living in the South, she *was* Roman Catholic, and she did, as the result of an unusually perceptive mind, recognize the importance of that background, not only as subject matter for her works, but also as representing a point of view toward all experience.

Herman Melville has spoken of "historic memory," implying that it is at least one quality of the artist's general "prescience." I can think of no better phrase to describe Miss Porter's special sensibility than to call it "historic memory." Such memory, though it does, as Melville stated, go "far backward through long defiles of doom," begins with the specific present: the young girl finding a carved dove in an abandoned grave and trading it for a gold ring, another remembering the image of a dead aunt preserved in a family photograph and the family memory and contrasting them with the living present, the memory of illness and death during the influenza epidemic at the time of the first World War, the memories of Mexican revolutionaries, of moving picture companies on location, of Mexican women and West Texas farmers stirred to violence by passion. Partly these memories are controlled by a Catholic sensibility, which seeks out the ceremony and order in the events, partly by a Southern habit of thought which metamorphoses reality into "romance"—not the romance of inferior Southern authors, who see the events as picturesque and quaint manifestations of a peculiar social order, but something nearer the "romance" which Hawthorne sought in his *The House of the Seven Gables,* a romance which links man of the present with the long, legendary concepts of man in a continued and continuing past.

The creation and utilization of myth is, then, in Katherine Anne Porter's work, both subject matter and method. Neither as a Southerner nor as a Catholic is she orthodox; that is, she does not mistake the myth for the reality; for her it is merely another kind of reality. Hawthorne called it "the truths of the human heart." Today, I suppose we should prefer such a term as "psychological truth." The important thing in a short story like "Flowering Judas" is not that Laura fails to escape the conflict between a conservative upbringing and the desire to assist in liberal political causes, but that such a conflict is at the bottom of the whole idea of man's Christian redemption; that there is something Christ-like about such a dilemma. The important thing in "Pale Horse, Pale Rider" is not that a young Southern girl found the war horrible or that she suffered from influenza and lost her lover to it, but that the sequence of events mirrored the relationship of man to good and evil. The important thing about "The Jilting of Granny Weatherall" is not merely that a proud and stubborn old lady dies, unable to forget the jilting of a long-lost lover, but that the story reflects a particular, but common, attitude toward death.

Perhaps the most complete instance of a short story which utilizes a specifically Southern background and memory for the creation of this larger, more generalized "truth" is "Old Mortality," where Miss Porter's subject matter is Southern attitudes as expressed through family history, and where the theme is concerned with the nature of reality—particularly with self-definition. The story is told from the point of view of Miranda between the ages of eight and eighteen, and its details agree with all of the other Miranda stories insofar as they detail events in a family which had moved from Kentucky to Louisiana and from there to Texas. At the center of the story are the memories of a girl, Amy, about whose long courtship and brief marriage to "Uncle Gabriel" the aura of "romance" has accumulated. We meet her first in a photograph in the family parlor, "a spirited-looking young woman, with dark curly hair cropped and parted on the side, a short oval face with straight eyebrows, and a large curved mouth." The family legend represents her as a vivacious, daring, and extremely beautiful young girl, against whom the beauty and grace of later members of the family are forever being judged. It tells of her using her cruel beauty to tantalize Uncle Gabriel until he despaired of ever winning her, of her precipitating events at a ball which caused a family scandal and disgrace. It tells of her sad suffering from an incurable illness, of her sudden and romantic marriage to Gabriel, and of her early death.

But the legend, which is more than just a romantic memory of Aunt Amy, is also a reflection of the family's attitude toward all events of the past—memories which Miranda cannot share and an attitude which she cannot adopt because of discrepancies which she senses between such stories, as related by the family, and the actual facts which she perceives in the people and events which surround her in the everyday life of the present. In the photograph of Amy, for instance, "The clothes were not even romantic looking, but merely most terribly out of fashion"; in the talk about the slimness of the women in the family, Miranda is reminded of their great-aunt Eliza, "who quite squeezed herself through doors," and of her great-aunt Keziah, in Kentucky, whose husband, great-uncle John Jacob, "had refused to allow her to ride his good horses after she had achieved two hundred and twenty pounds"; in watching her grandmother crying over her accumulation of ornaments of the past, Miranda saw only "dowly little wreaths and necklaces, some of them made of pearly shells; such moth-eaten bunches of pink ostrich feathers for the hair; such clumsy big breast pins and bracelets of gold and colored enamel; such silly-looking combs, standing up on tall teeth capped with seed pearls and French paste." Yet despite these disappointing incongruities, the child Miranda struggled to believe that there was "a life beyond a life in this world, as well as in the next"; such episodes as members of her family remembered confirmed "the nobility of human feeling, the divinity of man's vision of the unseen, the importance of life and death, the depths of the human heart, the romantic value of tragedy."

Another view is suggested in the second section of the story, when Miranda and her sister have become schoolgirls in a New Orleans convent. During vacation on their grandmother's farm, they had read books detailing accounts of how "beautiful but unlucky maidens, who for mysterious reasons had been trapped by nuns and priests in dire collusion, 'were placed' in convents, where they were forced to take the veil—an appalling rite during which the victims shrieked dreadfully—and condemned forever after to most uncomfortable and disorderly existences. They seemed to divide their time between lying chained in dark cells and assisting other nuns to bury throttled infants under stones in moldering rat-infested dungeons." In Miranda's actual experience at the convent, no one even hinted that she should become a nun. "On the contrary Miranda felt the discouraging attitude of Sister Claude and Sister Austin and Sister Ursula towards her expressed ambition to be a nun barely veiled a deeply critical knowledge of her spiritual deficiencies."

The most disheartening disillusion came, however, during this period, when Miranda came actually to meet the legendary Uncle Gabriel for the first time. His race horse was running in New Orleans and her father had taken her to bet a dollar on it, despite the fact that odds against it were a hundred to one. "Can that be our Uncle Gabriel?" Miranda asked herself. "Is that Aunt Amy's handsome romantic beau? Is that the man who wrote the poem about our Aunt Amy?" Uncle Gabriel, as she met him, "was a shabby fat man with bloodshot blue eyes, sad beaten eyes, and a big melancholy laugh like a groan. His language was coarse, and he was a drunkard. Even though his horse won the race and brought Miranda a hundred unexpected dollars—an event which had the making of a legend in itself, Miranda saw that victory had been purchased, not as a result of beauty, but at the price of agony; for the mare when seen close up "was bleeding at the nose" and "Her eyes were wild and her knees were trembling."

In legend, the past was beautiful or tragic. In art, it might be horrible and dangerous. In the present of Miranda's experience it was ugly or merely commonplace. In the first two sections of "Old Mortality," we get first the view of the past as seen through the eyes of the elders with their memories of the past, not as it actually was, but as they wanted it to be. In section two, we get the view of it through the eyes of Miranda herself, who judges it merely as it is reflected in her present. By section three, Miranda is eighteen. She has eloped and married, but she is still struggling to understand her own relationship to the past. To her, her elopement seemed in the romantic tradition of Aunt Amy and Uncle Gabriel, although we soon learn that it is, in actual fact, a failure. We meet her on the train returning home for the funeral of Uncle Gabriel. His body has been returned to lie beside Amy's, as though in a final attempt to justify the dream, even though he has married again, and (it is hinted) there are better and more real reasons for him to be buried beside his second wife, who had shared the bulk of his wandering, homeless, and meaningless existence. On the train, Miranda runs into Cousin Eva, also returning for the funeral, whose own life had been burdened by a constant comparison with the legend of Amy. While Amy was beautiful, thoughtless, impulsive, and daring, Cousin Eva had been homely, studious, and dedicated to high purposes. Amy had died and had been preserved in the romantic legend; Eva had lived to develop a character and a reputation as a fighter for women's rights. In a sense, Cousin Eva's good works, too, were part of her legend of homeliness and dedication. At bottom, Miranda finds her a bitter, prematurely aged woman; but it is Cousin Eva who provides her with a third view of the legend of Aunt Amy. She hints that it was nothing but sublimated sex that caused the young girls of Amy's day to behave as they did: " 'Those parties and dances were their market, a girl couldn't afford to miss out, there were always rivals waiting to cut the ground from under her. . .   It was just sex,' she said in despair; 'their minds dwelt on nothing else. They didn't call it that, it was all smothered under pretty names, but that's all it was, sex.' "

The old, then, had two ways of looking at the past, the romantic way of Miranda's father and of other members of the family, and the "enlightened" way of Cousin Eva. Each way was different, and each was wrong. But the old did have something in common; they had their memories. Thus, when the train arrived at the station, it was Cousin Eva and Miranda's father who sat together in the back seat of the automobile and talked about old times; it is Miranda who was excluded from these memories and who sat beside the driver in the front. Yet Miranda feels that she has a memory now and the beginning of her own legend—the legend of her elopement. Strangely enough, neither Cousin Eva nor her father will accept it. When reminded by Miranda of it, Cousin Eva says: "Shameful, shameful. . . If you have been my child I should have brought you home and spanked you." Her father resented it. When he met her at the train, he showed it in his coldness: "He had not forgiven her, she knew that. When would he? She could not guess, but she felt it would come of itself, without words and without acknowledgment on either side, for by the time it arrived neither of them would need to remember what had caused their division, nor why it had seemed so important. Surely old people cannot hold their grudges forever because the young want to live, too, she thought in her arrogance, her pride. I will make my own mistakes, not yours; I cannot depend upon you beyond a certain point, why depend at all? There was something more beyond, but this was a first step to take, and she took it, walking in silence beside her elders who were no longer Cousin Eva and Father, since they had forgotten her presence, but had become Eva and Harry, who knew each other well, who were comfortable with each other, being contemporaries on equal terms, who occupied by right their place in this world, at the time of life to which they had arrived by paths familiar to them both. They need not play their roles of daughter, of son, to aged persons who did not understand them; nor of father and elderly female cousin to young persons whom they did not understand. They were precisely themselves; their eyes cleared, their voices relaxed into perfect naturalness, they need not weigh their words or calculate the effect of their manner. 'It is I who have no place,' thought Miranda. 'Where are my people and my own time?' "

Miranda is not merely a Southern child, in Southern history, reflected through the sensibility of a Southern author—even though she is, partly at least, all of these things. She is any child, anywhere,

seeking to come to terms with her past and her present—seeking
definition. Katherine Anne Porter's Southern history, whether legendary or actual, provided the concrete experience through which her
"historic memory" could function. Thus when she wrote the concluding sentence of "Old Mortality," she was expressing not the
dilemma of Miranda alone, but the dilemma of all of us who seek
understanding: " 'At least I can know the truth about what happens
to me,' " Miranda thinks, "making a promise to herself, in her hopefulness, her ignorance."

It is out of hopefulness and ignorance combined that myths are
constructed and self-definition achieved, from a sense of social need
and a vision of a society which expresses both the hopefulness and
the need. Southern society represented the proper conditions for the
perceptive talent of an artist such as Katherine Anne Porter, who responded both critically and with a warmth of admiration to her
memories, thus transforming them, finally, into something more than
mere memory.

LOUIS D. RUBIN, JR.

Thomas Wolfe In Time And Place

Thomas Wolfe was born in Asheville, North Carolina. He lived in Asheville until his twentieth year. His first and best novel, *Look Homeward, Angel,* is mainly about people in Asheville. All his subsequent books contain many chapters each about Asheville. When he died, he was at work on a novel about his mother's people in Asheville and the North Carolina mountains.

These things being so, it may seem odd to have to justify a look at Wolfe as a Southerner, as one of a number of Southern writers who in the decades after the first world war wrote books about the South. Yet the justification is often necessary. One frequently encounters, both from those who enjoy Wolfe's work and those who don't, the attitude toward him typified in Maxwell Geismar's absurd remark that Wolfe "was born in the South, but he shared with it little except the accident of birth."

The fact is that it is as a Southern writer that Thomas Wolfe is best understood: one in whose work may be found, especially if one looks below the surface, most of the characteristic virtues and vices ordinarily ascribed to other Southern writers of his time and place. There is one striking dissimilarity, too; but I think that a little reflection on the implications of that dissimilarity will show that it is equally a product of Wolfe's Southern background. I refer to Wolfe's taste for subjectivity, and I shall try later in this essay to demonstrate that it is no more foreign to his origins than, say, James Joyce's anti-clericalism is unrelated to his Irish background.

To be sure, one seldom thinks to link Wolfe with the group of poets, novelists, and critics whose work affords an explicit statement of those principles and aims we usually ascribe to the Southern writers. It was these Nashville Agrarians of *I'll Take My Stand* who in large measure formulated the credos and the critical foundation basic to most modern Southern literature. Participating membership in the Nashville group, however, is hardly a requirement for the Southern author. Certainly the political, social, and aesthetic principles of Ransom, Tate, Warren and Davidson have been abundantly put into effect by William Faulkner, and he was never a Nashville Agrarian. On the other hand, though, Faulkner has never actively attacked the Agrarians, while Wolfe did just that.

In this connection, we might remember some recent remarks of Faulkner's, made in an interview at the University of Mississippi several years ago, and reported in the *Western Review* for Summer, 1951. "If you don't think it too personal," a student asked Faulkner, "how do you rank yourself with contemporary writers?" Faulkner's reply was as follows:

> 1. Thomas Wolfe: he had much courage and wrote as if he didn't have long to live; 2. William Faulkner; 3. Dos Passos; 4. Ernest Hemingway: he has no courage, has never crawled out on a limb. He has never been known to use a word that might cause the reader to check in a dictionary to see if it is properly used; 5. John Steinbeck: at one time I had great hopes for him—now I don't know.

Faulkner's evaluation of Hemingway we can discount much as we discount Lee's remark that McClellan was the best general he had ever faced, and Grant's choice of Sidney Johnston as *his* most dangerous opponent; even so, in a day when Faulkner is king and Yoknapatawpha the specimen ground for Southern studies, it is interesting to learn that the only man Faulkner was willing to admit as his peer was Thomas Wolfe.

I want to show that Wolfe exhibits most of the characteristics we like to call "Southern" in novels. These characteristics, to be sure, are not *confined* to Southern writers; but the unusual emphasis placed upon them by most Southern writers causes them to be considered indigenous to the Southerners.

The most immediately obvious characteristic, one found in almost all Southern writing worthy of the name, is the element of rhetoric. "The Southern writer has been raised in a world that inherits a love of rhetoric," William Van O'Connor has declared in his study of

Warren in the anthology entitled *A Southern Vanguard* (ed. Allen Tate, New York, 1947). "Traditionally, Southern statesmen have been orators. A society emphasizing social rituals and manners requires a kind of reverence for words to adequately express sentiment and feeling. . . . The Southerner generally does not shy away—to the extent the Northerner does—from the use of a language that is something more than bare statement. The Northerner, with his conditioned respect for practicality and getting-to-the-point is more likely to possess a far greater reading than speaking vocabulary and to associate anything more than simple expression with ostentation. The Southern writer inclines toward rhetoric at his own artistic level."

Thomas Wolfe's "own artistic level" involved a stupendous rhetoric, appearing everywhere, often leading its author into wild flights of oratorical fancy that obscure and lead far astray any statement which might happen to be involved, until Wolfe is found mouthing all manner of irrelevancies and preposterous oddities, and the reader is left baffled and exhausted by the sheer flow of words. In Wolfe, Southern rhetoric is undisciplined and unbridled to an extent that makes even so flourishingly rhetorical a writer as Faulkner seem positively laconic by comparison. Yet its abundant presence is one kind of surface kinship to his Southern contemporaries, even though the absence of control is hardly typical.

Of far more importance is a second Southern characteristic found all through Wolfe's work: a sense and awareness of time, of past and future as well as immediate present. There is a deep and omnipresent feeling for the historical and tribal memory, for tradition and continuity: a belief and conviction, that is, that human beings exist and have existed in a condition of *becoming* as well as *being*. "After the [first world] war," Allen Tate has written about Southern writers, "the South again knew the world, but it had a memory of another war; with us, entering the world once more meant not only the obliteration of the past but a heightened consciousness of it; so that we had, at any rate in Nashville, a double focus, a looking two ways, which gave a special dimension to the writing of our school—not necessarily a superior quality—which American writing as a whole seemed to lack" ("The Fugitive: 1922-1925," *Princeton University Library Chronicle*, April, 1945). We find Wolfe, discussing the state of mind of young Southerners in the early 1920s, making practically the same point in *The Web and the Rock*:

> There was an image in George Webber's mind that came to him in childhood and that resumed for him the whole dark picture of those decades of defeat and darkness. He saw an old house, set far back from the traveled highway, and many passed along that road, and the troops went by, the dust rose, and the war was over. And no one passed that road again. He saw an old man go along the path, away from the road, into the house; and the path was overgrown with grass and weeds, with thorny tangle, and with underbrush until the path was lost. And no one ever used that path again. And the man who went into that house never came out of it again. And the house stayed on. It shone faintly through that tangled growth like its own ruined spectre, its doors and windows black as eyeless sockets. That was the South. That was the South for thirty years or more.
>
> That was the South, not of George Webber's life, nor of the lives of his contemporaries—that was the South they did not know but that all of them somehow remembered . . . . They did not see it, the people of George's age and time, but they remembered it.
>
> They had come out—another image now—into a kind of sunlight of another century. They had come out upon the road again. The road was being paved. More people came now. They cut a pathway to the door again. Some of the weeds were clear. Another house was built. They heard wheels coming and the world was *in*, yet they were not yet wholly of that world. (pp. 245-246)

Faulkner's *Requiem For A Nun* is full of this awareness of the omnipresence of the past. "The past is never dead," Gavin Stevens keeps telling Temple Drake, "It's not even past." And there is the rolling, Wolfe-like passage at the close of the sequence entitled "The Jail" (pp. 261-262):

> not that it matters, since you know again now that there is no time: no space: no distance: a fragile and workless scratching almost depthless in a sheet of old barely transparent glass, and (all you had to do was look at it a while;

all you have to do now is remember it) there is the clear un-
distanced voice as though out of the delicate antenna-skeins
of radio, further than empress's throne, than splendid insatia-
tion, even than matriarch's peaceful rocking chair, across the
vast instantaneous intervention, from the long long time ago.
'Listen, stranger: this was myself: this was I.'

"Why has it never occurred to anybody," asks Herbert Marshall
McLuhan in an essay contained in *A Southern Vanguard,* "to consider
the reason why every Southern novelist is a teller of tales? . . . The
tale is the form most natural to a people with a passionate historical
sense of life." Assuredly Wolfe was a teller of tales, just as his mother
was. All the stories of the Pentlands and the Joyners and their mystic
doings in the mountains are adaptations of the stories Wolfe's mother
told him about his Westall antecedents. Wolfe believed strongly in
the pervasiveness of the impact of past upon present. "The seed of
our destruction," he wrote in *Look Homeward, Angel,* "will blossom
in the desert, the alexin of our cure grows by a mountain rock, and
our lives are haunted by a Georgia slattern because a London cut-
purse went unhung" (p. 193). Again, in *The Story of a Novel,* he
speaks of a kind of past time in which characters were envisioned "as
acting and as being acted upon by all the accumulated impact of
man's experience so that each moment of their lives was conditioned
not only by what they experienced in that moment, but by all that they
had experienced up to that moment" (pp. 51-52). Wolfe wrote often
of the past; not only his own past but his mother's family's past,
which was to have been the subject of *The Hills Beyond,* the novel on
which he was working at the time of his death.

Time was no mere dimension for Wolfe; it became a preoccupation. There was, of course, a surface infatuation with it; he loved
to brood over the way time was passing him by, and how all his
yesterdays were lost and gone forever. Below the obvious level, however, there existed a profound and sincere contemplation of past and
present, and of the timelessness of the earth as contrasted with the
briefness of life. The extent to which Wolfe approached Proust's
attainment with the Time Experience is not generally realized. Some
of its facets were elucidated by Margaret Church in her essay, "Thomas
Wolfe: Dark Time" (*PMLA,* September, 1949). Suffice it to say
here that Wolfe's concept of essence and existence, and of the at-

tainment of lost time through memory, is subtle and complex, going far beyond any mere peripheral dabbling. The implications of what Wolfe set forth in the fourth part of his short story, "The Lost Boy," contained in the volume *The Hills Beyond,* and in the final twenty pages or so of *The Web and the Rock* would undoubtedly be a source of astonishment to many who, like Clifton Fadiman, dismiss Wolfe airily with the remark that he "simply had no intelligence." No one without a great deal of intelligence could have comprehended the Time Experience articulated in Wolfe's work.

Imbedded in this awareness of time is the consciousness of race and family. John Peale Bishop has pointed out that the sense of familial ties is one of the factors giving order and form to modern Southern literature. The blood relationship is a symbol in its own right, with all its connotations of history, tradition, family, name. McLuhan quotes James Branch Cabell: "one trait at least the children of Lichfield share in common. We are loyal. We give but once; and when we give, we give all that we have." Familial ties, with all their overtones of continuity, ritual, even mysticism, are immensely strong in Wolfe. Bishop emphasizes this in his essay, "The Sorrows of Thomas Wolfe," perhaps the best single thing ever written on Wolfe even though it approaches him from a viewpoint not calculated to appreciate much that is admirable in him. The single enduring relationship possible for Wolfe, Bishop says, is that of the child to his family, and this relationship is inescapable: "His father is still his father, though dying; and his brother Ben, though dead, remains his brother. He loves and he hates and he knows why no more than the poet he quotes" (*Collected Essays of John Peale Bishop,* ed. Edmund Wilson, New York, 1948).

George Webber, in *The Web and the Rock,* sees visions of the Joyner clan toiling up a mountain slope for hundreds of years. Eugene Gant, in *Look Homeward, Angel,* suffers anguish because he has developed the mark of the Pentlands, the itchy patch on the nape of his neck. The sense of inescapable continuity of past into present, of generation to generation, of childhood to young manhood to the moment of death, helped to cause Wolfe to evolve a Proustian metaphysic of timeless time in order to explain the apparent contradictions.

A third characteristic of so much modern Southern writing is a devotion to texture, to what Ransom calls "things as they are in their rich and contingent materiality." This is accompanied by a corresponding distrust of theory, of the abstraction of ideal structural principles from the full body and texture of existence. This lack of sympathy for the theorist is found throughout the Agrarian writings. Donald Davidson, for example, has little or no use for the social sciences. Attacking economic theorists, he wrote that

> We came at last to economics, and so found ourselves at odds with the prevailing schools of economic thought. These held that economics determines life and set up an abstract economic existence as the governor of man's effort. We believed that life determines economics, or ought to do so, and that economics is no more than an instrument, around the use of which should gather many more motives than economic ones. ("*I'll Take My Stand:* A History," *American Review,* Summer, 1935)

The Agrarians believed that the full experience of life must always enjoy priority over abstract theories about any part of life. The South, Richard M. Weaver has noted in discussing the writings of the Agrarians, "despite its great contributions to the founding of the American republic, has never done much thinking of the purely speculative kind. . . . Though the modern South has become prolific in a literary way . . . there is still hardly a trickle of analytical writing, apart from stuffy treatises of social science which emerge from university presses. . . . Southern departments of philosophy have remained pitifully small. The bane of Southern writing has been an infatuation with surfaces" ("Agrarianism in Exile," *Sewanee Review,* Autumn, 1950).

In this respect Thomas Wolfe was surely a Southerner; more than any of his contemporaries, he was never able to let reason displace the knowledge of senses and instincts. Imposing though his achievement with the Time Experience might be, it was made possible through his experience, in order to account for his experience; unlike Proust, he had no Bergson. He was unable in his writings to work from a preconceived plan, to build his art upon theory. Time and again he would start out with the idea of writing this or that kind of novel, according to this or that plan of action, but each time the plan succumbed to the material. He could not write naturalistic fiction, though sometimes there are naturalistic passages in his work, because this would entail a view of man as a fixed creature trapped by the hostile forces of environment, doomed to a vain struggle to extricate himself from these forces. Wolfe could not view man from any dialectical perspective. He could not write a Marxist, or a transcendental, or even an Agrarian novel; to do so would mean for him that he must extract a portion of experience from the whole, and write only in terms of the portion.

Wolfe could not ignore or slight any of the various aspects in which life presented itself to him. We find this illustrated in his handling of the problem of evil. Marshall McLuhan says of modern Southern writers that "in none of them is there any discernible effort to evade the very unpleasant limits and conditions of human life— never any burking the fact of evil." Awareness and acceptance of evil implies an acceptance of life as it is, and a correspondingly deep grounding in its full body and texture. The writer who overlooks any of the vital aspects of life is less an artist than a propagandist; he is trying to extract from existence only those elements which suit his purpose, and the texture of his art will inevitably suffer so that the structure may persuade. The result is going to be bare bones without the redeeming flesh.

For the Southern writers evil is seldom viewed in terms of a dialectic. It is not a mere economic or social phenomenon, brought about by environmental factors alone, and capable of being legislated or educated out of existence. "I think the enemy is single selfishness and compulsive greed," Wolfe has George Webber write to his editor in *You Can't Go Home Again.* "I think the enemy is blind, but has the brutal power of his blind grab. I do not think the enemy was born yesterday, or that he grew to manhood forty years ago, or that he suffered sickness and collapse in 1929, or that we began without the enemy, and that our vision faltered, that we lost the way, and suddenly were in his camp. I think the enemy is old as Time, and evil as Hell, and that he has been here with us from the beginning" (p. 742). The enemy there, it may be noticed, sounds very much like original sin. The passage seems similar to Faulkner's use of the jail in *Requiem For A Nun.* The presence of the worn timbers of the old Jefferson jail, built when the town was founded and still enduring under the brick and mortar of the often-remodeled building, serves as a reminder that evil and sin are forever present in the structure of society and the marrow of the citizenry.

If there is no escaping or ignoring evil, similarly there must be no evasion or overlooking of the unpleasant phenomenon of death. Contemplation of death is found in almost all modern Southern fiction. Faulkner mulls over the problem throughout his writing. The Reverend Hightower waits for death in *Light in August*, the Negro woman Dilsey awaits it in "That Evening Sun Go Down," the spinster Emily lives with it in "A Rose for Emily," and of course there is *As I Lay Dying*, in which death becomes the structure of the novel.

Assuredly Thomas Wolfe shows this trait. Death is always one of his major concerns. We find it in the titles he chooses for his writing: "Death the Proud Brother," "Only The Dead Know Brooklyn," *From Death to Morning*. As Faulkner says, he wrote "as if he didn't have long to live." W. M. Frohock, in his essay on Wolfe in the *Southwest Review* (Autumn, 1948), has declared that Wolfe "is the writer of our century who has written the most eloquently about death—the death of Grover, the death of Ben, of old Gant; and of the overpowering imminence of death everywhere . . . More surely than anything else the thought of death looses that remarkable flow of his language—the unearthly torrent of words which has always been the delight of some of his critics and the bane of the rest—and also the extraordinary resources of his rhetoric."

The acceptance and contemplation of death give a vigor and meaning to Wolfe's attitude toward life. He envisioned death not so much as the end of man's existence as the culmination of it. This quality, found in Wolfe, Faulkner, and the other Southern writers, often gives to their work a depth unmatched in writers who would ignore or look sideways at this universal and awesome final experience of life. As the late Pedro Salinas wrote of another writer about death, Lorca,

> An existence in which the idea of death is hidden or suppressed is like the representation of action on a movie screen, flat, inapprehensible, and lacking in something essential; it is lacking in the dimension of death, in the dimension that gives life its tone of intensity and drama. Man can only understand himself, can only be entire, by integrating death

into his life; and every attempt to expel death, to take no
account of it, in order to live, is a falsification, a fraud perpetrated by man on himself. (*Hopkins Review,* Fall, 1951)

Wolfe's attitude toward death varied between awe and terror. Never,
however, was he able to divorce it from his consciousness for very
long.

The unwillingness on the part of Southern novelists like Wolfe
and Faulkner to accept any abstraction from life, to take any view
of life that would ignore basic experiences such as death or evil, helps
to produce a prose notable for its complexity and its completeness.
Such a prose has one striking characteristic: a rich and varied texture
of language and imagery. It is an art that appeals to the senses as
well as to the intellect. "The quality of my memory," Wolfe wrote
in *The Story of a Novel,* "is characterized, I believe, in a more than
ordinary degree by the intensity of its sense impressions, its power to
evoke and bring back the odors, sounds, colors, shapes, and feel of
things with concrete vividness" (p. 31). Wolfe could suppress no
detail, no matter how small, John Peale Bishop has said; it was impossible for Wolfe to feel that a detail was unimportant.

At its worst, a passion for detail obscures and hampers the structure of a literary work; at its best it gives the structure body and flavor.
One need only compare a story by someone like Caroline Gordon,
say, to a story by Hemingway or Dos Passos to observe how the prose
of the Southern writer abounds in rich, variegated textural imagery,
whereas the two Midwestern writers consciously strive for prose which
is relatively poverty-stricken in sensuous material. And one can hardly
imagine Hemingway writing, or wanting to write, two sentences like
these, from Wolfe's *Look Homeward, Angel:*

Wet with honest sweat, the plowman paused at the turn and
wiped the blue shirting of his forearm across his beaded fore-
head. Meanwhile his intelligent animal, taking advantage
of the interval, lifted with slow majesty a proud flowing tail,
and added his mite to the fertility of the soil with three moist
oaty droppings. (p. 324)

It is precisely what Joyce attempts in *Ulysses:* "Local colour. Work
in all you know. Make them accomplices. . . . Composition of place.

Ignatius Loyola, make haste to help me" (p. 186). Such textural composition of place as Wolfe displays is assuredly a characteristic common to almost all modern Southern writers. In the poor ones, the odor of magolias reeks; in work by Faulkner, Wolfe, Gordon and others, the prose is made rich and sensuous thereby.

We have seen, then, that Wolfe shares with his literary compatriots (1) an addiction to rhetoric; (2) a keen sense of time and the past; and (3) a distaste for abstract ideas manifesting itself in such forms as an unwillingness to gloss over unpleasant topics like evil or death, and a taste for detail that often results in rich textural language, drawing upon the full powers of the senses as well as the intellect. There is, however, another characteristic notable in the work of most of Wolfe's contemporaries which is glaringly absent from the Wolfe novels. It is objectivity, an attitude which makes possible an external fiction.

The Southern novel, Marshall McLuhan declares, presents "a vacuum where we might expect introspection. . . . The stress falls entirely on slight human gestures, external events which are obliquely slanted to flash light or shade on character." The objective nature of Southern writing, the absence of the subjective attitude toward form and communication, presupposes that it places its entire reliance upon external communication. It is true, of course, that Faulkner is not always so objective; quite often it is Faulkner talking directly to us, telling us what is going on inside a character's head, telling us the significance of what is happening. But Faulkner can get away with it because he is still commenting upon externalities; the external still retains the main emphasis. Faulkner never violates the economy of form: the arrangement and use of subject matter to fullest artistic effect, which involves the limitation of texture in accordance with structural relevancy.

Such objectivity comes, in part at least, from a formal social tradition in which manners, custom, ritual all combine to evoke an exterior order and form. One is inclined to link it with classicism, since it takes onto itself a willingness to work in terms of limitations, of form.

Objectivity and economy of form are hardly virtues one would want to ascribe to the work of Thomas Wolfe. Where his Southern contemporaries exhibit control and an innate reticence, he is most formless and uncontrollable. Where they rely upon the external portrayal, he is appallingly subjective and addicted to injecting his own personality and presence into his already-autobiographical narratives.

Before we dismiss Wolfe's subjectivity as being alien to the Southern milieu, and atypical of his origins, however, we must consider why it is that Wolfe is so subjective. And here we are confronted with a paradox.

Wolfe is, we know, unable and unwilling to express himself by external methods. He tried it for awhile; his first literary ventures were in the form of plays, and the drama is the art medium most limited in dimension, most confined to external speech and gesture, least adaptable to direct interior communication. The dramatist cannot say "He thought that etc., etc."; he must rely upon speech and deed to show the working of the mind. Wolfe tried drama for eight years, before he turned to the novel, a form much more adequate for his purposes.

Yet—and here is the paradox—this writer, who turned from the play to the novel to achieve a more direct, immediate, total communication of ideas as well as action, whose work is most notable for authorial intrusion and direct address of author to reader, is also the *one writer most acutely conscious of the limitations of all communication.* It is Wolfe above all who is the bard of loneliness, of the human isolation. Eugene Gant melodramatically "understood that all men were forever strangers to one another, that no one ever comes really to know any one, that imprisoned in the dark womb of our mother, we come to life without having seen her face, that we are given to her arms a stranger, and that, caught in that insoluble prison of being, we escape it never, no matter what arms may clasp us, what mouth may kiss us, what heart may warm us. Never, never, never, never, never" (*Look Homeward, Angel,* pp. 37-38). Loneliness, which he considered the inescapable human condition, was one of Thomas Wolfe's most frequent subjects. He boasted of it: "My life, more than that of anyone I know, has been spent in solitude and wandering. . . . From my fifteenth year—save for a single interval—I have lived about as solitary a life as a modern man can have. I mean by this that the number of hours, days, months, and years that I have spent alone have been immense and extraordinary" ("God's Lonely Man," *The Hills Beyond,* p. 186).

Thus Wolfe is (1) convinced of the essential nature of solitude and the inescapability of loneliness, and yet (2) is also the one Southern writer least willing to rely upon the external modes of communication, most desirous of breaking through all the formal barriers. He denied that communication was possible at all; and he demanded a more nearly complete communication than art or life could possibly afford him.

What is the explanation of this apparent contradiction? McLuhan attributes it to a clash between Wolfe's instincts and his upbringing. Wolfe, he declares, partakes fully of the Southern social attitudes, with the strong emphasis upon manners, custom, ritual, formality of social intercourse: "the impersonal attitude born of formalized social symbols, which finally left each person entirely locked up in his own passionate solitude. . . ." A formal social code involves an arm's-length encounter, emphasizing civility, manners, external gestures and formalizations. Bishop has said of Southerners that "their manners gave them assurance and, because they knew the use of civilities to keep others at a distance, they preserved integrity. There is even today among the poorest Southerners a self-respect, a sense of their worth as men, regardless of what they have done or accumulated, that sets them apart from the more successful American who is lost without his bankbook and recognizes no pride but that of achievement" (*Collected Essays,* p. 11). Wolfe's last editor, Edward Aswell, in his introduction to Wolfe's unfinished novel, *The Hills Beyond,* noted that "Tom and I, being both from the South, began our close relationship on a plane of very correct formality, Mistering each other about a month before we felt we were well enough acquainted to use first names with propriety" (p. 360*n*). In early letters to Aswell, Wolfe would refer to himself in connection with his work as "he" rather than "I."

But while the social environment in which Wolfe was reared was one addicted to the "civilization of manners" and "formalized social symbols," Wolfe's own personality traits rendered him unable to accept and take part in it. McLuhan declares that Wolfe "has all the passion without any of the formal means of constraint and communication which make it tolerable." There was the instinct toward mannered, arm's-length formality of communication, and also the feeling that this was intolerable. He felt he had too much to say, too many things he thought it necessary to expiate. There were too many turbulences boiling within him. He was a child of conflicts, of divided sensibilities, whose parents were of clashing temperaments, and contradictory outlooks, whose home town was undergoing an unnatural transition from an agrarian town to a tourist and industrial metropolis. Communication of passions through externalized, formal means was increasingly impossible for Wolfe. He crashed through his society's habitual social barriers and attempted to pour out his passion directly. He was a great tale teller, a raconteur of family legends, but—usually unfortunately for his art—he was never content with the mere telling of a tale. Implied allegory was not enough. There must be an accompanying explanation of what it meant to him, in direct writer-to-reader form. He must go beyond the external process of showing, and tell in addition what he was thinking. He could withhold nothing. "He was the most open and unsecretive person in the world," Edward Aswell has said. This of a North Carolinian who believed that communication between two human beings was impossible!

To dismiss Wolfe's subjectivity as being foreign to his origins, then, is to miss the fact that the formalized social patterns of those origins served to intensify and heighten his sense of isolation and loneliness. The subjective safety valve that might have been possible to him in another place and time and society was denied him. The pent-up emotions within him required a more accessible outlet than the customary formalized means of constraint and communication permitted.

Furthermore, those very emotions he wanted to express were peculiarly related to his origins. The turbulence of his antagonistic family, with the cautious mountain mother and the violent Pennsylvania father; and the confusion of Asheville in the 1900s and 1910s, caught as it was in a two-way pull between conflicting economies and incompatible attitudes; it was from these that Wolfe's sensibilities were drawn.

Donald Davidson explains Wolfe's formlessness and subjectivity as being the product of a schism between his emotions and his intellect: "I suggest that his trouble was that he had been taught to misunderstand with his head what he understood with his heart. Thomas Wolfe had a divided sensibility which very likely resulted from his education at Mr. Howard Odum's citadel, the progressive University of North Carolina, and from his subsequent unfortunate experience at Harvard" ("Why the Modern South Has a Great Literature," *Vanderbilt Studies in the Humanities,* Nashville, 1951). Norman Foerster makes somewhat the same claim:

> *We* educated Thomas Wolfe, we educated him in Chapel Hill. I was here then, and share the responsibility. Clearly, there were elements in the university situation that helped him to become what he was, one of the finest novelists of the period between the two wars. But he was also a lost soul, beating his wings to exhaustion in an atmosphere which made breathing difficult. We did little to offset the influence on him of the sour naturalism then current. A single passage will symbolize this. You may recall that Thomas Wolfe tells of driving in the country surrounding Chapel Hill. In the fashion of the day he describes the country as simply ugly, this charming rolling Piedmont scenery which deserves *celebration* by the novelists, poets, and artists. (*North Caroline Historical Review,* April, 1946)

Quite apart from the fact that Wolfe might have been comparing the tobacco country with his own mountains, which would possibly account for his queer tastes in scenery, Foerster is oversimplifying things tremendously, and so is Davidson. Wolfe's college training, for better or for worse, undoubtedly helped make him what he was, but it is hardly sufficient to blame the deep-seated cleavages in Wolfe's sensibilities on four years at Chapel Hill and two in Cambridge. The contradictions go back far before his college days; they show up in every phase of his life, and by no means in his attitudes toward literature alone. Parents, temperament, Asheville environment, events subsequent to his college life; all these are involved. And to say, as some have said, that Asheville isn't really a "Southern" town, what with its tourists and industries, Vanderbilts and Groves, is to overlook the fact that Asheville *was* once a little town in the Southern mountains, and that it *became* what it is today while Thomas Wolfe was growing up in it. It was the cross purposes of the new and the old, personified in many ways in the antagonisms within his own family circle, that produced Thomas Wolfe. To contend that he was not one of the Southerners is to mistake the issue; it was because he *was* a Southern writer to the marrow of his bones that Wolfe wrote and thought as he did.

What have we said, then, when we say that Wolfe was a Southern writer? The mere statement in itself constitutes neither praise nor accusation. All we have done is perhaps to provide a point of departure, a framework of reference which may be used in attempting an analysis of Wolfe.

In his short story "The Return of the Prodigal," Wolfe wrote of Eugene Gant returning home for the first time in seven years. "And suddenly," he says, "Eugene was back in space and color and in time, the weather of his youth was round him, he was home again." So often the space and color and time are present when Wolfe is writing of his childhood, and absent elsewhere. If it is in space and color and time that a writer creates his art, then it is in the use of these ingredients that the ultimate criticism of Thomas Wolfe must rest.

ROBERT DANIEL

The World of Eudora Welty

The tone of Eudora Welty's stories ranges from the broad satiric comedy of "Petrified Man" to the delicate, restrained pathos of "June Recital." Less written about than other contemporaries who have published fewer books, she is sometimes spoken of as though her work were a miscellany of unrelated effects, now funny, now touching, and always a little odd. Her stories do indeed show great variety of both tone and manner, but they also develop a consistent attitude towards the world in which she lives—towards her shaped experience of that region whose present she knows directly, and whose past she has reconstructed in a legendary way from her elders' talk and from her own reading.

She was born April 13, 1909, in Jackson, Mississippi. Twenty-seven years later, when a magazine called *Manuscript* brought out her first published story, she was living in Jackson, and she lives there today. The University of Wisconsin, New York, San Francisco, Great Britain—all these she has visited for one reason or another, and they have given her material for her fiction. But by far the greater and the more distinguished part of it has found its settings in the state of Mississippi. Sometimes it treats of the middle-class world of beauty-parlors and card-parties that presumably is Jackson; sometimes of villages in the Delta, with their storekeepers and salesmen and ill-to-do farmers, white and black; sometimes of decayed mansions in Natchez and Vicksburg. And beyond all these, in her stories, lies the encompassing countryside of fields and woods and rivers, or even the primeval wilderness, when she writes of the region as it was a century and more ago. With interruptions for college, Guggenheim Fellowships, and just "trips," she has lived and worked in Mississippi, observing its people and places, all her life.

These biographical particulars take on additional interest when one considers Eudora Welty's predicament as one of those young

Southern writers who came to maturity some two decades ago. In 1929, when she was twenty, William Faulkner published *Sartoris,* the novel in which he began to construct that fictitious world that 'stands as a parable or legend of all the Deep South," as Malcolm Cowley has said. *The Sound and the Fury* followed in the same year; and by 1931, when Eudora Welty came home from Columbia University to write copy for the radio station, supply the Memphis *Commercial Appeal* with news of Jackson society and try her hand at photography, Faulkner had extended his parable with *As I Lay Dying, Sanctuary,* and *These Thirteen.* After the appearance of *Light in August* (1932) and *Dr. Martino* (1934) Faulkner's version of the modern South was complete in its main outlines. On the young Southern writer, particularly the young Mississippian, this version of the Southern experience—from which he too must draw his material —exerts an almost irresistible spell. If he wishes to write about his own region (and how can he avoid doing so?), the question before him is bound to be how to avoid rewriting Faulkner.

To say that Faulkner's books were appearing at the time Eudora Welty started writing is not, of course, to say that she read them. Her work contains indications that she did, but in nearly all her different kinds of stories the problem of influence is one that she has successfully solved. Indeed, she affords an instructive study in the proper use of an influence: Faulkner may have given her an enriching conceptual background, but the foreground of her stories—the incidents, characters, dialogue, and feelings—is largely her own. This article purposes not to dwell on her debt to Faulkner, but to describe a few aspects of the unique achievement that gives her her place in modern letters.

So far she has published five books, of which, since the novel *Delta Wedding* has been comprehensively and justly praised in a recent *Sewanee Review* ("Delta Wedding as Region and Symbol," by J. E. Hardy, Summer, 1952), and the fantasy called *The Robber Bridegroom* is only for her special admirers, we may confine ourselves to the three volumes of short stories. These differ from each other as greatly as any three novels by the same author; they are in separate veins. (She is still writing actively; her latest stories have appeared, somewhat incongruously, in *The New Yorker;* and a fourth collection, markedly unlike the others, may be expected in a year or so.) *A Curtain of Green* (1941) contains the best examples of her humor—"Petrified Man" and "Why I Live at the P. O."—as well as some of the finest stories embodying her gift of pathos, such as "Death of a Traveling Salesman." *The Wide Net,* published two years later, draws in part on the same sort of material; but the best things in it are those exquisite scenes laid in the great forest at the beginning of the 19th Century, the times of Aaron Burr, Audubon, and the highwayman Murrell. All the stories in *The Golden Apples* (1949) are concerned with characters who grow up in the hamlet of Morgana, Mississippi, a few years back. They belong to a class that appears not very often in Southern fiction and had not figured prominently in Eudora Welty's earlier books: the upper-middle class of the small town, those who can afford servants and music-lessons for their children, though not very easily. The book is more than a collection of short stories; the parts are independent and conclusive, but the same characters appear in most of them. This method draws on the mastery of the short-story form that Eudora Welty had attained, and adds to it the advantages of scope and fulness provided by the novel. At the end of the book we seem to have seen not only the life of Morgana in its entirety, but even the later lives of some of its people who leave it. Except for the delicate, pervasive melancholy in *The Golden Apples,* it might be called a Mississippi *Cranford.*

Turning from a description of Eudora Welty's separate books to a division of her stories according to their characteristic settings, we see that they fall into four groups. "First Love" and "A Still Moment" concern the Natchez Trace and the nearly untouched forest of a century and a half ago; these are the stories involving historical characters. They dramatize the era in her world that may be described as Before the Fall. In it nature is paramount, or at least man and nature are equal, reverencing one another. The incidents are narrated gravely, as befits the subject, in a controlled style marked by words chosen with great deliberation. The characters are dignified, free from the quirks that usually identify her people of more recent times. The action even when violent is gently disclosed, its point often being rendered by a symbol. In general it may be said that the farther back the era on which her imagination is working, the more symbolically she is inclined to write. Whereas her stories of the recent past report directly on what she seems to have herself observed, symbols carry the weight of the meaning when she is working on what she has read or been told about. The essential quality of the wilderness stories is found in the scene where Audubon shoots the white heron: "The gaze that looks outward must be trained without rest, to be indomitable. It must see as slowly as Murrell's ant in the grass, as exhaustively as Lorenzo's angel of God, and then, Audubon dreamed, with his mind going to his pointed brush, it must see like this, and he tightened his hand on the trigger of the gun and pulled it, and his eyes went closed. In memory the heron was all its solitude, its total beauty. All its whiteness could be seen from all sides at once, its pure feathers were as if counted and known and their array one upon the other would never be lost. But it was not from that memory that he could paint."

The stories concerned with the countryside in recent years are far more numerous. It is in this group that we find characters who can only be described as heroic, sometimes depicted with Eudora Welty's kind of pawky humor, sometimes with her characteristically restrained pathos. There are the unfortunate couple who sacrifice even the bedclothes to save the tomato-crop; Old Phoenix, with her December journey in search of medicine for her grandchild; and, in the two stories about traveling salesmen, the guitar-player and the tenant farmers who support their lot with grace and dignity. " 'Same songs ever'where,' said the man with the guitar softly. 'I come down from the hills . . . . We had us owls for chickens and fox for yard dogs but we sung true.' " Then there is a whole group of naughty characters—William Wallace Jamieson, Livvie, Ruby Fisher, Mattie Will Holifield—who are busily escaping from the trammels of marriage and asserting their untamable humanity.

A third group of stories, those set in the towns, must itself be divided. Some of them concern the dwellers in the big houses, the ruined mansions; others, the townspeople who work for a living. In writing of the former, Eudora Welty often employs a device that may reflect her earlier interest in photography. This is the arrested moment, the scene that is, as it were, caught by a click of the camera's shutter, where the very immobility of the scene is essential to its meaning. In "Asphodel," for instance, three old maids picnic near six white columns, which, with a fragment of the entablature, are all that remains of a Doric portico. Behind it the house has burned and become a habitation only for goats. " 'This is Asphodel,' they repeated, looking modestly upward to the frieze of maidens that was saturated with sunlight and seemed to fill with color, and before which the branch of a leafy tree was trembling." In other stories the well-born characters include Mr. Marblehall, who has two wives and a son by each, and Clytie, who cares for her paralyzed father, drunken brother, and half-mad sister. Clytie at last drowns herself in the rain-barrel, "with her poor ladylike black-stockinged legs up-ended and hung apart like a pair of tongs." The working class of the towns is represented by the family in "Why I Live at the P. O.," a dramatic soliloquy that has enlarged the boundaries of American humor; by several of the characters in "Lily Daw and the Three Ladies"; and by Tom Harris and R. J. Bowman, the salesmen in "The Hitch-Hikers" and "Death of a Traveling Salesman." These two stories, perhaps the finest that Eudora Welty has written, juxtapose town and country characters in a manner entirely her own. One sentence from "The Hitch-Hikers" will illustrate her sensitivity to the pathos that lies in the lonely root-lessness of modern life: "Walking over to the party, so as not to use his car, making the only sounds in the dark wet street, and only partly aware of the indeterminate shapes of houses with their soft-shining fanlights marking them off, there with the rain falling mist-like through the trees, he almost forgot what town he was in and which house he was bound for."

A fourth setting that Eudora Welty has occasionally employed is that of the metropolis: New Orleans, San Francisco, New York. Such stories as "Flowers for Marjorie" and "Music from Spain" develop further the sense of exile, of human beings on whom quite inhuman lives are imposed. Though the locale is inhospitable to her talent, and no admirer would say that these stories are among her best, they complete her view of the modern world. "Music from Spain" was first published separately, by the Levee Press, and seemed then to lack force and point. Read as part of *The Golden Apples*, it makes clear what Morgana stands for. Morgana is the kind of little town from which all but its more vegetable inhabitants must from time to time consider fleeing. Yet in the loneliness of his San Francisco exile, Eugene MacLain looks back with longing to the comparatively primitive life of his boyhood. For Morgana, with all its simplicity was an organism, to which its people could feel that they belonged. It must, however, be written of in the past tense: most of the incidents in *The Golden Apples* take place in 1910 or a little later.

Eugene MacLain's life was transformed by his moving to San Francisco. For those who remain, as his twin brother Randall does, the transformation occurs in the people and the towns themselves.

The high point of Randall's story is his seduction of a girl on an iron bedstead in a tourist cabin. The incident recalls the coarseness of the women in "Petrified Man," which had appeared in Eudora Welty's first book, but "The Whole World Knows" is told with compassion, in place of the horrified amusement that the women's absurdity had inspired. Taken together, these stories of the modern city and the modern town imply the level of existence to which humanity is drifting, across the span of years that extends from the death of the white heron to the present day. The simplicities of life in Morgana, Mississippi, caught at the moment that its organic life is dissolving, represent perhaps the mid-point of the process.

One must immediately add, however, that when Eudora Welty's stories are spoken of as a "process," when her settings are schematized and her symbols and implications made into explicit criticisms of life, they begin to be falsified. The abstracting explanation may be needed to make clear her coherent view of things and her relation to other modern writers, particularly Faulkner, but it omits both her humor and the wealth of ambiguity in her "middle" stories, stories that involve characters of the small town and the small farm, often pitted against one another. Moreover, to break an author's work into its components of setting and character is to violate its form; and this wrong ought to be redressed by an inspection of a single story in its integrity. For this purpose it is tempting to select "Death of a Traveling Salesman," and perhaps to contrast it with the play that it evidently inspired. However, this story is not only well known but is the first that Eudora Welty published. To choose the best from her latest volume would be more useful, since it will show the stage to which her talent has by now developed.

The title of *The Golden Apples* recalls Greek myths, and its first story compares its hero to Zeus; but the action is firmly grounded in the ordinary life of a Mississippi town some forty years ago. (That is not to say that its dominant episodes are ordinary occurrences.) It affords countless examples of Eudora Welty's ability to catch the absurd but authentic mannerisms of her characters, as in Mrs. Morrison's answer when her daughter asks her if she could have learned the piano: " 'Child, I could have *sung*,' and she threw her hand from her, as though all music might as well now go and jump off the bridge." Lightly told as most of the stories are, however, the theme of *The Golden Apples,* like that of "A Still Moment," is the Loss of

Innocence, the journey from childhood to maturity, or, in keeping with the Hellenic title, we should more properly say the Golden vs. the Silver Age. All of Eudora Welty's books show her sympathetic insight into the emotional lives of children; here, this interest is fused with her alienation from the workaday world of the present. But whether or not the sadness inherent in growing up is a peculiarly modern experience the reader is left to determine. The book is concerned with the experience itself, and is even able to persuade us that the children realize what is happening; at least some of them do, such as Nina Carmichael. "Again she thought of a pear—not the everyday gritty kind that hung on the tree in the backyard, but the fine kind sold on trains and at high prices, each pear with a paper cone wrapping it alone—beautiful, symmetrical, clean pears with thin skins, with snow-white flesh so juicy and tender that to eat one baptized the whole face, and so delicate that while you urgently ate the first half, the second half was already beginning to turn brown. To all fruits, and especially to those fine pears, something happened—the process was so swift, you were never in time for them."

In *The Golden Apples*, the most ambitious and the most successful story is the one called "June Recital." It is a story of points of view—based, we may imagine, on Henry James's remark about windows. One point of view belongs to the younger Morrison child, Loch, who is spending a summer afternoon in bed with malaria. His boredom explains his interest in the house next door, visible from his window; and because he has malaria he is permitted to use his father's telescope. His fever also produces a slight distortion in what he alone can see occurring in the other house, both because he has the telescope and because there is nothing to distract his attention. As the story develops, these circumstances are seen to be symbolically related to Loch's innocence of sex, love, and the pathos of a lonely old age.

In the next room, meanwhile, Loch's sister Cassie, who is less ignorant about at least the first of these, is dyeing a scarf to wear this night on a hayride. Loch cannot get her attention to the strange activities that he is watching in the other house, an almost abandoned old house, inhabited only by a nightwatchman, who sleeps in the afternoon. Loch has seen a sailor carry a girl in at the back door and make love to her on a bare mattress in a room upstairs, but that interests him less than the old woman who enters at the front door and begins to festoon the living-room with newspapers. (She has escaped from her keepers and intends to set the house on fire.) Then she goes to the piano and plays the opening bars of a piece called *Für Elise*—which brings Cassie to her window.

Cassie looks towards the other house, but in the sunlit afternoon she cannot see inside. The tune, however, takes her thoughts back to the events that led up to the present degradation of the girl and the old woman. The woman is Miss Eckhart, who once gave music-lessons in the room that she is now trying to destroy, and Virgie Rainey was her only talented pupil. *Für Elise* was Virgie's particular piece—though at the annual recital she played concertos by Liszt and even harder selections. She was the consolation of Miss Eckhart's bitter and lonely existence, yet on finishing high school she has become the piano-player at the local picture-show.

It is unnecessary to summarize the rest of "June Recital." Cassie, who fully recalls the past incidents that lead up to the present, cannot see into it; for one thing, she "was practicing on her ukelele again so she could sing to the boys." Loch, at the other window, sees the present fully, but is too inexperienced to understand it. When Miss Eckhart throws the metronome, a symbol of time, into the yard, Loch climbs down a branch outside his window and retrieves it. But he does not know what a metronome is. He imagines, half-seriously, that it is a bomb. He returns to his bed and, as the sun sets, sinks to sleep: "A cloud lighted anew, low in the deep sky, a single long wing. The mystery he had felt like a golden and aimless bird had waited until now to fly over."

When Cassie comes back from the hayride, her thoughts return to Miss Eckhart and Virgie Rainey; and as she too falls asleep she grasps at least a part of the mystery. "Both Miss Eckhart and Virgie Rainey were human beings terribly at large, roaming on the face of the earth. And there were others of them—human beings, roaming, like lost beasts."

The Golden Apples unites many of the themes and settings that distinguished Eudora Welty's earlier stories. If it lacks the broad comedy of her best humorous pieces, and makes little use of her knowledge of rustic ways, it contains some of the most striking proofs that she excels at dramatizing the inward, individual emotional life of characters caught in a historical process, which occurs in a vividly depicted region, who are at the same time human entities important in themselves. Eudora Welty's sense of the historical process she may owe to Faulkner; her ability to interest her readers in her characters' inner life results solely from her own gifts. The whole matter of her relationship to Faulkner is worth a short discussion.

It is evident that one can define Faulkner's world only by identifying the classes that collide or are overwhelmed in it. His fictitious Yoknapatawpha County, as is beginning to be well known, is populated mainly by the two classes of characters represented by the Sartoris and Snopes clans: the latter in the act of seizing power and wealth as they slip from the enfeebled grasp of the former. Characters of other names are assimilated to one of these groups: Compsons, Griersons, and Sutpens are by social position Sartorises, yet certain of their members, notably the unspeakable Jason Compson, are essentially Snopesian. Two other groups, possessing neither power nor wealth and not likely to, complete the picture: virtuous but ineffectual educated men, such as Horace Benbow, and the illiterate, long-suffering, and admirable poor—some of the most memorable being Cash Bundren, Mrs. Henry Armstid, Sam Fathers, and most if not all of the Negroes. These are the characters whose relationship to nature, though often harsh, Faulkner regards as being essentially right.

Faulkner of course possesses a masterly ability to depict character, but his readers seldom think of Faulkner's characters apart from the groups to which they belong. Attention is therefore centered on the clash of mighty opposites, rather than on the innermost feelings of individuals who come between their fell-incensèd points. Here lay Eudora Welty's opportunity, which she has magnificently seized. While her reader is made aware of the forces that change the world surrounding her characters, he is mainly intent upon the sensations that the characters as individuals are experiencing. And the foremost of these is loneliness. Faulkner's people are frequently wretched; in his crowded, seething world they are seldom lonely.

Occasional passages in Eudora Welty's stories come a little too close to Faulkner for entire comfort. Asphodel and Clytie's mouldering mansion may recall Sutpen's Hundred ·and Miss Emily's house when they ought not to. Eugene MacLain, uprooted and transported to San Francisco, has more than a little of Quentin Compson in him. His story consists largely of a nightmarish walk along the cliffs overlooking the Bay, an obscurely motivated journey reminiscent of Quentin's walk by the River Charles shortly before his death. In the story

"Moon Lake," Loch Morrison, now a Boy Scout, is forced by his mother to act as life-guard at a girls' camp. Throughout the week his only emotion is an incessant, comical rage against his situation, a sort of juvenile version of the feelings of Jason Compson or the convict in *The Wild Palms*. The style in which he is described is touched by a note of Faulkner: "He came and got his food and turned his back and ate it all alone like a dog and lived in a tent by himself, apart like a nigger, and dived alone when the lake was clear of girls. That way, he seemed able to bear it; that would be his life."

But echoes of Faulkner are exceptional in Eudora Welty's work. The more pervasive likeness is seen in the grouping of her stories— her preoccupation with settings and periods that are common to Faulkner. Her wilderness stories compare to Faulkner's "Red Leaves" or "The Old People"; and the white heron is just such a symbol as the bear. The same holds true of her stories dealing with farms, small towns, and plantation-houses, as well as her rare excursions to the metropolis. In all probability the parallels result as much from a common upbringing as from direct influence. "Mississippi has two cities," says the proverb, "—Memphis and New Orleans." It comes natural to any Mississippi writer to see life in terms of countryside and county seat, as consisting of a present impregnated with the past, and as achieving its ultimate degradation in the cities beyond the state's boundaries.

The best of Eudora Welty's fiction bears little direct resemblance to that of any other writer. In it the reader feels the form and pressure of a coherently organized view of the world in which the author lives, and perhaps she has inherited that view from Faulkner; but the deep, inward response of her characters to the conditions of existence is her unaided achievement. If we began by wondering how her gift could thrive in Faulkner's gigantic shadow, we end by deciding that it has grown and flourished all the more for being rooted in prepared ground.

ROBERT HAZEL

Notes On Erskine Caldwell

In books about our writers, whether in transition, mid-, or uneasy passage, we usually find an essay about Erskine Caldwell tacked on to the end like the little red caboose behind the train. A procession of our novelists would not be complete without that smudged and inherently funny little car, yet we seem embarrassed by its presence and the need for it.

This attitude toward the necessary but unwanted has always perplexed me. My experience with Caldwell was from the first one of almost constant delight. I am not embarrassed about, by, or with Caldwell. My reaction to him involves both exasperations and admirations, and this may explain certain excellences and defects, but not explain them away. Likewise, they may have to do with Caldwell's Southernness, or lack of it, but neither does Caldwell's Southern background explain them away.

I. Caldwell "can't write," in the sense that Dreiser couldn't write but James could; or to come nearer home, Jones can't write but Styron can. Style seems to elude certain men. It is really an easy distinction to draw. It is meant simply that Caldwell's language as language does not possess a very interesting life. Language is no particular friend of his and he has to go it alone, the hard way of a writer who has not found within him the capacity to love language. This does not mean a lack of ear, for Caldwell has heard accurately and put down the living speech of his men and women. It means, in practice, that the world of men and women which Caldwell creates lacks that final rhetorical dimension which transfigures the worlds of writers such as Wolfe and Faulkner. Scottsville does not lie for us amid peaks of language as do Altamont and Jefferson. This is not even to say that one wishes it did. Rather one is content that Caldwell, having a more immediate sociological concern than Wolfe or Faulkner, and further removed thereby from conditions which had nourished an heroic grammar, eschewed an English rhetoric of a sort which has lingered, which has even been caused to linger by the Agrarians, who had certainly no genuine concern with plain speaking. Caldwell could and did stake out his acre and work it. Any literature, and certainly Southern literature as a body, is a group effort. And without Caldwell's reportage this marvellous country of his would have been lost, another "country not heard from."

I am not saying that it is better to be given a world in whatever language than not to have been given it at all. An immediate sociological concern may have assigned to Caldwell a language true to his task. In this he diverges from a group of Southerners who remain suspicious not only of sociology as such but of a mode of operation based upon the semi-science. What occurs, at any rate, in the writer who has not addressed himself to the problem of language for its own sake, is that stresses are created which must be absorbed elsewhere and re-asserted within the particular mode. In Caldwell, the solution, reportage as mode, forces him into one of the excellences of journalism. Caldwell made a great virtue of dialogue as a carrier of action. His local speech advances his narrative cleanly. In Caldwell we have a functionalism of action rather than of diction, of mythos rather than melody. It would seem—and one says this with genuine amusement—as if the persons who buy millions of his books must have agreed with Aristotle that action is most important in a work. Such a statement, of course, requires modification. For in our understanding of language in relation to the world of action, we must insist upon the fact that the created world is a function of the language itself. Given this slightly different, but not invalidating, twist to our understanding, we can conclude that the nature of the action in Caldwell is precisely what its language makes it, and that the world is, among other things, one of plain speech, of local idiom, of vulgar rather then fine motivations and actions, of a uniform levelness, of a consistent and impressive monotony, a desiccated world where the lifting of a hand or foot seems to be arduous and significant, a world lacking in poetry. When poetry wants to steal into this world, it is not realized—as in the instance of the girls with eyes like morning-glories who work in the mill—it is impregnated with sentiment only. In the world created by the language of Caldwell, there is no valid occasion for poetry. There are only poetized attitudes about all the chimney-sweepers who come to dust. There is a difference. The most poetically resonant novelistic languages seem to be written by men who contain in themselves not enough poetry to be poets, but enough so that working assiduously they create good prose. Caldwell lacks this resonance. Stylistically, Caldwell is not a Southern writer.

II. This section might be called character as exaggeration, or caricature. The particular exaggeration is innocence, a peculiar and grotesque and malignant innocence which Caldwell alone has been able to fill his world with. (Faulkner has certain indestructably innocent characters, but on no such scale, or to such metaphysical degree as Caldwell.) Caldwell seems to make a world culpable, not its particulars, to make large forces guilty, not persons. The social (I use the word loosely) attitudes of the 20's and 30's had developed strongly enough that Caldwell could produce, as others did, the guiltless man. Ty Ty is irrascible and indestructible, but above all innocent. Perhaps it is because he has no consciously realized, turned and weighed values. He has not even the rudimentary and static love of land which is Jeeter's most nearly conscious value. He doesn't even stop to consider why he wants to strike gold on his farm. He is a mindless slave of processes, not ends. And from evidences of behavior in the body of Caldwell's work, we can infer safely that if Ty Ty had found gold he wouldn't have known what to do with it any more than a child would. Caldwell's people live that unexamined life which is not worth living, except of course to the tenacious egos themselves, if only because they subsist on animal faith, the final value in a world where all else is ruin. It seems that a character such as Ty Ty is able to sense the ruin: "There was a mean trick played on us somewhere. God put us in the bodies of animals and tried to make us act like people." But here he is out of character. Caldwell says this, not Ty Ty. Only when Caldwell lets Ty Ty return to his digging does he restore the character.

In force-feeding ideas of impersonal nature into his fiction, Caldwell has departed from the stream of Southern writing and taken to the brush, to a jungle of forces, not the intensely personal and dramatic area of guilt and expiation which has bounded a remnant and vestigial society, a society driven in upon itself and forced to look at motives, a process of intensification which has helped put Southern writing in its present position of leadership. Caldwell has laid his emphasis elsewhere. He has dealt with sub-men who are beyond good and evil as truly as are the super-men of the *Künstler-roman*. Caldwell's characters are certainly beyond tragedy. To show Caldwell's divergence more clearly, we can note an interesting instance in which Faulkner chose to make his persons innocent and a society guilty—*The Wild Palms*. He attempted a tragic action, but in choosing an antagonist named society, an impersonal, amorphous, faceless, characterless force, he failed. And he didn't try again in this vein. It has been said of another Faulkner novel, *As I Lay Dying,* that he singularly denied his persons tragedy, whereas in his other work he permits his characters tragic status. The inference was that in this novel the characters were *below* tragedy and, one might add, were too nearly like Caldwell's sub-men to achieve tragedy. At any rate, whether the persons of *As I Lay Dying* are tragic or not, we do note that in this work Faulkner came his closest to poaching on Caldwell's acre. There are other parallels and approximations, here significant in a picture of Southern literature, which Faulkner and Caldwell share. But the shared areas are largely reduced to particularity, not scheme. Both writers share the mules, the plowlines, and the red-necked men, but their unifying schema are as far apart, and as near, as tragedy and comedy, as terror and laughter. Given their different contexts and visionary designs, one cannot interchange particulars, cannot for example say *incest* and mean both writers at once.

The Snopes and Bundrens are cousins to Ty Ty. A third generation Snopes might own a textile mill where Ty Ty's son-in-law would go on strike. This Snopes probably wouldn't let Ty Ty come to his house in town to visit. Jason Compson rides an old Ford, a camphor rag about his neck. Caldwell's people ride old cars (or crack up new cars, so they become old—he insists upon a junk-filled world where men bale newspapers without a market for the bales—the agrarian South is shown in passage between the mule and the Model A, unable to afford, but purchasing for a spree, a new car, meeting the jangling industrial South emerging in mills, urban and rural elements juxtaposed and productive of the crackling ironies which are germane to Caldwell's situation humor.)

The innocence of which I speak, is related in simplest terms to an attitude found generally in the world of Caldwell's people: a man ain't to blame: "If you've got a rooster, he's going to crow." It is an attitude which is pre-psychological and expressive of a certain large and bland tolerance and negligence and not much questioning. This attitude, in contrast with the more inquisitive and energetic attitudes held by most of us in the audience, provides an important lever for Caldwell's humor. The boy ain't to blame if he wants to chuck a ball against the side of the house, or drive a car without oil. Another boy ain't to blame because his sister-in-law is so beautiful that he just has to have her. A man ain't to blame if he can't feed his niggers because he's got important things on his mind, has to dig holes in the ground looking for gold. I say pre-psychological and this necessitates one refining explanation. The reason why these persons are pre-psychological is not that they are guiltless for being what they are. Psychologists do not hold any man guilty of his desires, his impulses, or even certain rather destructive acts. But Caldwell's characters are pre-psychological insofar as they do not, need not, and will not alter the patterns of their desires or the patterns of fulfillment. In their innocence, they do not know enough to wish to change or to seek means to divest their acts of destructive power. Again the unexamined life, pre-psychological. A candidate for the office of county sheriff ain't to blame if he instructs other men where to find an albino and how to rope him, as long as they don't get too rough. Here is one of the cruel paradoxes that give a sting, a poisonous and vivid inflammation to the humor of Caldwell. He lances social sores, boils, cancers. The laughter produced is as fire. It burns the throat. In examining this matter, we are touching tender skin on us and our time. We do not feel like laughing anymore at a Negro boy who is forced to climb a tree to silence woodpeckers and who is pecked on the head in the dark, the birds mistaking his skull for the wood. We do not feel it is appropriate to laugh sadistically at the evil in ourselves, projected, or at the expense of other persons. It is one of Caldwell's particular virtues as a humorist that he confronts us with symbols which start laughter only to smother it in the pain of sympathy or revulsion. His is a humor of the preposterous, often free enough of pain, involved merely with such attributes as sloth (Pluto's lazy vote-counting) or stupidity (Ty Ty's insistence that his gold digging is carried on scientifically) but when the preposterous becomes outrageous the humor adds another dimension, becoming doubly pathetic.

If Caldwell's world is without tragedy, it contains pathos—often of an irritating sort. The irritation may perhaps be an encompassing emotion within us, which does not often come to the surface to disturb our enjoyment, a feeling that there is no excuse, finally, for the life lived in that world. This may be our feeling. It has nothing to do with Caldwell's success or failure. Caldwell's problem was to create a world, not to prejudge it. (Here one must except the kind of prejudgment inherent in the naturalistic method and its variants, and, further, the kind of judgment which inevitably precedes any creative act.)

III. A humor of situation, which is also a humor of the preposterous, is what Caldwell has given us with such overwhelming success that it bears further notation. There is little need to comment on its gusto, or the "Rabelesian" or "Chaucerian" labels which have adhered to it. Suffice it to say that these words contain quite precise meanings more than tag-words ordinarily do. Certainly the humor is gusty, uniquely gratifying, a largess, a bounty, for which one always thanks the giver. We cannot thank Caldwell too much or too often for giving us the robust and depraved and homely and vulgar tom-foolery as no one else has given in our time. His literalities, equivalents and approximations, particularly concerning the sex content in the lives of his people, come forth genuinely incorporated and derived from the traditional and popular mind-body of the rural South. Can anyone, esepcially those who know the region, ever forget or stop laughing at Ty Ty's praise for beautiful Griselda, remembering the thousand times he has heard it from a thousand obsequious adorers of a profaned virgin. The laughter is immense, but with just enough truth and sadness in it to keep it from being utterly coarse. And when sadness falls on Caldwell's humor, the gusto, which we associate with health, diminishes—as in the scene involving Will Thompson, when he declares he has to take his sister-in-law because when he first saw her he promised himself some of that and he just can't break his own promise. Gusto plays on the surface but is engulfed finally in our deeper apprehension of Will's sickness, and an entire landscape caving under the sickness which has produced him. As far as the eye sees, there stretches the ultimately humorless inferno of Caldwell. That the animal fails to attain humanity is not finally laughable. Or is it? Take either point of view, and Caldwell has provided amply for you. Or admit no yes-or-no answer, and Caldwell has provided a world complex enough. I do not know, certainly, how Caldwell himself feels about that world of his creation. It doesn't matter. We can know, from his stated preoccupations with certain social problems, how he must have felt about the actual world to which his fictional world bears some relation. The relation may be put thus: satire is the name of the relation of the real world of fiction to the actual world of fact. But satire is a too easy name, too easily pronounced and let pass. We must, in observing the relation between those actual and real worlds, account for the sums and multiplications of particular elements and their alignments in given instants, otherwise how could we honestly say that Caldwell's world is funnier than ours *and* crueller *and* sadder?

Let us examine. The world Caldwell makes is a Southern world. It is not simply a world economically determined and which could be any place. Although various determinisms, compatible with and suitable to Caldwell's scene, are at work, they no more provide full explanations of that work than of any other work of stature. (Take Dreiser, for example, who was fond of determinism as method. The fact that Clyde Griffiths' mother didn't buy the child ice cream cones when he wanted them is not an adequate explanation for Clyde's crimes. The determinisms of the writers of the 30's offer keys to their gardens, as it were, but not to their houses. If we were dealing with Zola or Hardy, when naturalism was still in a relatively pure condition, it would be quite another matter.) Caldwell's contextual obligation to the Southern land and what grows and dies on it is incontestable. Here he is a Southern writer. I quote a friend's recollection of Georgia country after a trip across the state several years ago: ". . . the retinal highway shimmering in the brain, the dustladen roosters, the laddered growth of corn southward, the claypowdered broad leaf tapering into pecan signs and turpentine pine, into the rutted swamp bridges, then the exotic verdure. The cold grease clotted grits, the thin etherized coffee. The 25c straw hat, the sullen, evasive eyes above beard stubble, the clay-red roadmapped neck. Hadacol, Mail Pouch peeling off the barns, J. C. Penney and Piggly-Wiggly, overalls —Lee and Headlight, brass studded. The sunset town: the all-nite Greek's in a sputter of neon, the leaner outside, the protuberant adam's-apple, the quid, the wen, the new baby-shit Florsheims . . ."

What my friend wrote was a description of an actual world, but it is also obviously, and without conscious intent, a description of Caldwell's real world. The description leads us to believe, for the moment at least, that the relation between the worlds is nigh identity—until we reflect on the grotesque alignment of particulars from the actual world, which distinguishes the real. From this actual description, we could not even begin to predict the variants, the singular monads reflected by their fictional universe, that one stubbled face would belong to a Pluto Swint, another to a man who was tricked into paying money to copulate with his own wife. No, the real world is as different as it is superior. It permits combinations of elements in mixtures not actually possible. Caldwell permits us to be surprised. He also inures us to surprise by building consecutive layers of surprise. When we see Ty Ty digging for gold, we are surprised. When Pluto suggests an albino to divine the lode, we are surprised. But by the time Darling Jill drives away in Pluto's car, we are prepared. And, if in *God's Little Acre*, a man should walk on the scene and offer to buy dead souls of negroes, would the reader be surprised? I think the answer is no. Such is the construction of Caldwell's world as to support such goings-on.

IV. To build a world demands an inclusion of vigorous terms, and to build an infernal world of instinctual human life, without the purity of the instinct of animals, requires Caldwell's terms, his special troupe of irrational puppets, his dusty stage hung with burlap. In his zeal to make ample provision, Caldwell runs the risk of over-stocking, of the needless multiplication of examples, of displaying the same set of objects in a too little varied action. But this is to err on the right side. Many "tests" of a novelist have been put forward. I suggest that among these tests, one which is of first importance is: How adequate, how complete is a writer's projection of a world? To apply this criterion we must disregard the nature of that world. The failure of critics as a tribe to effect this separation between the completeness of and the nature of worlds has resulted in impossible hopes for and demands upon our writers. It is customary for the critic to hold up the fictional world to *the* actual world (as though he knew what *the* world is) and to judge by the mirror theory. But no writer can project *the* world (nobody can write a description even of a mule as it actually appears, much less describe *the* world) and the illusory hope that some writer can, and that all writers should try, leads to such absurdities of thought as enabled us to speak once of the Great American Novel. We do not even re-create *the* world; we create worlds. A writer creates a world and populates it with a set of objects—forces, ideas, persons, etc., and signifies these things by an elaborate system of signs—or he fails to do so. From the drift of these notes, I hope it will be supposed that Caldwell created a world abundantly and successfully, a world sufficient unto itself, which bears significant relation to other fictional worlds (to the Southern worlds particularly) and, further, a world indispensable to the constellation we call Southern literature.

VIVIENNE KOCH

The Conservatism of Caroline Gordon

The work of Caroline Gordon as a writer of fiction appears to have suffered a curious lack of appreciation when compared to the lively admiration which has greeted the efforts of some other Southern women writers during the last two decades. It is my impression that of the group of talented Southern women, including Katherine Anne Porter, Carson McCullers, and Eudora Welty, whose work is widely acclaimed not only by an intellectual élite but by a popular reading audience, only Miss Welty possesses in terms of actual achievement anything like the merit attributed to her. Miss. Porter has by an almost alchemical word-of-mouth campaign rolled up a reputation far out of touch with the realities of her small and precise talent for the short story. Miss McCullers' is another story and her dependence on the more decadently baroque elements in what is taken to be a Faulknerian outlook has served her, as the saying goes, only too well.

But it is not my purpose to reduce others in order to raise Miss Gordon. I wish only to place her against her contemporaries· and to suggest that it is her un-modishness that is in a measure responsible for a want of wider recognition. She has not accommodated the austerities of her method to that cultivation of violence and oddity for its own sake, whether in subject-matter or style, which is one of the more distressing infantilisms of an otherwise vital and growing Southern expression in literature. And while there is nostalgia and backward glancing in her early novels of the old South, she sternly reminds herself in the title of one of them that "None shall look back." Thus she loses out, as well, at the popular romancing level of Southern fiction, for she has not gone with the wind.

Caroline Gordon, whose prose is perhaps the most unaffected and uniformly accomplished that is being written by any American woman today, should be seen as the conservator in contemporary Southern fiction of the great classical tradition of the nineteenth century novel as formulated by Stendhal, Flaubert and somewhat later, Henry James. Miss Gordon's sense of her role is inherent in the instructive critical comments on the art of fiction which she makes in her analyses of other writers' stories in her recent anthology *The House of Fiction,* co-edited with Allen Tate. While the editorial material is a joint contribution, the matter of it so faithfully reflects the principles by which Miss Gordon has won her reputation as a brilliant teacher of writing at various universities about the country that one can easily tap the author. In the Preface we are told,

> . . . James exacted of the work of fiction "a direct impres-
> sion of life"; and very nearly his whole demand is in the
> adjective. The direct impression is the opposite of the
> blurred and easy impression; it creates the immediate sense
> of life, not the removed report. Of this school, Flaubert,
> Chekhov, Crane, Joyce and James were the great masters.
> Since Flaubert, fiction has extended or changed its subjects,
> but where it transcends its social or other documentary
> origins it is still in the Impressionist tradition; or it is some-
> times called the tradition of naturalism or realism, descrip-
> tive terms with a philosophic ring, but often standing only
> for a sentiment about the values of life. Neither the senti-
> ment of naturalism or realism nor any other could have, un-
> aided, produced the art of *Madame Bovary.* A single plainly
> discernible principle of imaginative reality distinguished this
> art, by means of which it has achieved something of the self-
> contained objectivity of poetry. Once you get inside one of
> the great works of naturalism you find this principle inform-
> ing with a specific actuality whatever values the author may
> have. This actuality reaches us as the intense *dramatic activ-
> ity* of everything in the story: a snowstorm, Emma's blue
> eyes, the crest of a wave, an after-dinner speech. Nothing is
> left inert.

Miss Gordon's allegiances are clearly formulated here and in her last novel, *The Strange Children,* her fidelity to the tradition of "naturalism" as she has defined it emerges with a mature authority. It is in this finely thoughtful work that her real service to the realm of Southern letters as the conservator of the heritage of "naturalism" and thus of the mainstream of the great fiction of the western world is most powerfully demonstrated.

It would be misleading to imply that Miss Gordon has arrived at this clarity about the role of the fiction writer easily or all at once. The evidence of almost twenty-five years of writing suggests much wrestling with and re-shaping of formal intentions and means. But one can see in her first attempts at fiction, "The Long Day" and "Summer Dust," two short stories written in 1928 and now included in *The Forest Of The South,* how firm the primary sense of lively "impression" was. The choice of the short story form indicates that this sense had not yet expanded into a program confident enough for the novel. "Summer Dust" especially foreshadows the virtue of her later writing although it is episodic and somewhat uncertain of short-story limits. The theme is the insistent impingement of the world's evil upon a child's innocence. But what *dramatically* elucidates this problem is the fine tissue of circumstance which flows from the social and psychological structure of the South. Thus, the past and innocence is not merely Sally's preoccupation with the fairy tale of the little princess with whom, both by social credit and imagination, she has identified herself; on her peach-picking expedition with her playmates she thinks realistically with the cruel self-awareness of a child: "I'm not a nigger . . . I'm the only one who's not a nigger." The dramatic evocation of the past is in the forest in which Sally gets lost, in the sick old Negro woman endowed by local legend with mysterious witch-like powers, in the white tenants whose slyly just denunciation of her family suggests an opaque history of deprivation and degradation. The totality of this dramatic rendering of a limited context translates into that evil summer dust which conspires to invade the cool green herbage of Sally's innocence.

A few years later, Miss Gordon's first novel *Penhally* (1931) maps out the territory in which her naturalistic method will operate for about the first decade and a half of her work. In its first pages, the nostalgia for a lost grandeur which was the ante-bellum South is expressed obliquely through the thoughts of Nicholas Llewellyn surveying his Kentucky plantation one fine day in 1826:

> But everything was breaking up nowadays. The country was
> in the hands of the New England manufacturers—men who

> gave no thought to its true interests. The tariff of abomina-
> tions, as they called it, made it almost impossible to feed and
> clothe your negroes . . . His people had left Virginia because
> everything was breaking up there. Now everything was
> breaking up here. The women might very well keep on cry-
> ing. They would be the first to feel it if the roofs of the old
> places fell about their heads.

The drama of this "breaking up" is enlarged by Nicholas' memories of his boyhood, of his parents' tales, so that the perspective is pushed back some sixty years into the eighteenth century. Thus the structure of life at Penhally in the nineteenth century gains the melancholy richness of depth and distance, as if its tragic destiny were already lurking in the luxurious ambiguities of its past.

Nostalgia may be the initial impulse directing the novelist toward these materials. But even in 1931 Miss Gordon was too informed and objective toward her craft to rely naively on the sustaining power of impulse. In the fratricide committed by Nick's twentieth century descendent, Chance Llewellyn, who turns against his brother Nick, the legal heir to Penhally, for selling the estate to rich Northerners, Miss Gordon was clearly, perhaps too transparently pointing a parable. Chance (the name is useful) cannot stay the hand of time except by violence. And death to his brother is the final destruction of one link to the past he so loves. Nostalgia succumbs to the ironies of chaos.

By 1934 Miss Gordon was involved in the matrix of the Alec Maury stories. In the novel, *Alec Maury, Sportsman,* and in the shorter stories which were, no doubt, shavings from it not possible to integrate into its scheme, she found a way to present the past ironically through exploiting its rich secret life in the mind of the central figure. "Old Red," one of the best short stories Miss Gordon (or, for that matter, any contemporary Southerner) has written, is a useful place to look into the more mature habits of her art as it explores the humours of nostalgia. The plot is Time; and it is a plot with which Alec Maury will have no truck:

> "Time, he thought, time! They were always mouthing the
> word, and what did they know about it? Nothing in God's
> world! He saw time suddenly, a dull leaden-colored fabric

depending from the old lady's hands, from the hands of all of them, a blanket pulled about between them, now here, now there, trying to cover up their nakedness . . . But time was a banner that whipped before him always in the wind! . . . Where, for instance, had this year gone? He could swear he had not wasted a minute of it, for no man living, he thought, knew better how to make each day a pleasure to him . . ."

The unstated equation between Alec Maury and Old Red, the elusive fox of his hunting days, raises the memories of the old sportsman to a symbolic plane where his own evasion of those who would run him down as ruthlessly as any animal quarry takes on a heroic gallantry. But it is a gallantry tinged with pathos because we know it is time who is the real antagonist. In this story the past, as sensed through the mellow texture of Maury's sensibility (he is the kind of individualist only the old South or other societies resembling it could afford to produce), has a double function, as if cause and effect were inseparable, with protagonist and antagonist locked in a beautiful but deadly embrace.

Alec Maury, Sportsman is the extension of this atmosphere into the magical evocation of a whole vanished way of life with something of the same effect of a self-contained universe of reference as one feels in Turgenev's *Memoirs of a Sportsman* to which it bears no little resemblance. The made-upness of the world of sport, like the made-upness of "the self-contained forms of poetry," to which Miss Gordon compares the fiction she admires, is the perfect objective correlative for the kind of society old Alec stands for, and for the formal classical interests which, in the modes of rhetoric and poetry, complement in his inner life that ardent pursuit of the thing-in-itself which his fishing represents.

Miss Gordon's next three novels, *None Shall Look Back* (1937), *The Garden of Adonis* (1937), and *Green Centuries* (1941), continue the exploration of her imaginative centre, the South, at a number of levels which suggest some uncertainty of purpose. In *None Shall Look Back,* a Civil War novel with General Nathan Bedford Forrest as a more than life-sized First Cause who dominates the landscape, the level is carefully historical with a good deal of social exposition worked in. In this sense it is a *serious* historical novel (something which most novels in this genre are not) just as the later *Green Centuries* is a serious historical study of the late eighteenth century Kentucky settlers and their battle with the new world of the frontier and the old world of the Indians.

Oddly, *The Garden of Adonis,* set squarely in modern times—the period is the depression—where for the first time in Miss Gordon's work the poor whites are of co-evalent interest with the denuded aristocrats of the land, pursues an inner theme not too remote from those of the two historical novels I have just mentioned. This theme I can only roughly delimit by calling it the theme of alienation. It is a major, a recurrent theme in Miss Gordon's writing, but it inhabits another world in the books from about 1945 on. It is often expressed in her early novels by fraternal antagonisms. Both *Green Centuries* and *Penhally* end with brother killing brother. In each case the victim is the brother who has "sold out" to the enemy—in the first instance, to the Indians; in the second, to the North.

In *The Garden of Adonis* the alienation theme is situated more complexly in the dispossession of *all* the characters from their roots in the land. Ben Allard, a descendant of the Allards in *None Shall Look Back* (it should be mentioned that Caroline Gordon has, like Faulkner, worked out a vast genealogy of over a century and a half of families in Kentucky and upper Tennessee which builds up a huge historical dossier for her to draw upon), is a landlord who really cares about the land. He is murdered by one of his most loyal tenant farmers, Ote Mortimer, a young man of considerable integrity and force, displaced from his job in the auto factory, and trying a return to the land. He is a good worker but he has not the patient love which is needed to redeem the soil and when he finally kills (or appears to have killed) Allard at the end of the novel it is a symbolic act which rejects just such a love. The novel tells a parallel story of the aristocratic but poverty-stricken Carters who marry into the Camps, a wealthy Northern industrial family whose activities have dispossessed them and thus is an attempt to handle the alienation theme from more points of view than the simpler one of historical loss which earlier satisfied Miss Gordon. It is not really successful, however, perhaps because of its attempted complexity. The Adonis symbolism, as hinted by the epigraph from Frazer's *The Golden Bough,* seems incidental rather than central to the real conflict which is social, and not sexual as the title urges. This overt reliance on myth, as we shall see in *The Women on the Porch*, fails here as there because the myth is too fragilely developed to bear the weight of the novel's meaning and so its adventitiousness to Miss Gordon's deeper interest is shown up.

Still, *The Women on the Porch* (1944) is safe to take as the initiation of Miss Gordon's most ambitious period. In this novel her absorption in Southern materials is paradoxically counterpointed by extending the frame of reference, moving from New York to Tennessee and back again. New York, as one might expect, although treated realistically enough is shadowy in comparison with Miss Gordon's South, where every aspect of setting, terrain and speech is seen with the fine clarity with which she can trace a leaf or a bug. But the novel evokes not only a rich and vaguely sinister South to which Catherine, the expatriate heroine, returns when her marriage appears threatened by her husband's infidelity, but also it introduces a kind of allegorical sociology which seems extraneous to the story.

Miss Gordon appears to be covertly arguing, as indeed she had argued more openly in *The Garden of Adonis*, that love cannot flourish without roots and that these roots lie in the land of one's birth, preferably (if this can be managed) in an ordered and predictable local society. To this end, she shows Jim Chapman, the husband, a deracinated middle-westerner teaching in New York, to have a barren emotional life of which his present affair is only a symptom. But Jim is insufficiently developed as a character for one to judge whether deracination was a cause or an effect of his problems. Jim, left by his wife, muses: "Middle-westerners, springing out of that rich, deep loam of prairie, always on their way somewhere else . . . I never felt at home but once in my life . . ." In *Green Centuries*, a few years earlier, this obsessive faith in the value of possession by the land, through a willed act of fealty to it (much as John Crowe Ransom urges this in his lovely "Antique Harvesters") was summarized by the hero, Rion, in the beautiful closing as he gazes up at the constellation for which he is named:

> But it seemed that a man had to flee further each time and leave more behind him and when he got to the new place he looked up and saw Orion fixed upon his burning wheel, always pursuing the bull, but never making the kill. Did

Orion will any longer the westward chase? No more than himself. Like the mighty hunter he had lost himself in the turning. Before him lay the empty west, behind him the loved things of which he was made . . . Were not men raised into the westward turning stars only after they had destroyed themselves? . . .

But in *The Women on the Porch,* the heroine, who in her emotional turmoil instinctively flees to the South for comfort and security, shrinks back in alarm at the static, almost paralyzed composure of her relatives at Swan Quarter. Her eventual rejection of a life as the wife of her cousin, and as the mistress of his land, a land she loves, does suggest that the claims of the South upon its lovers are crumbling under the pressures of new and inevitable alignments outside it. But the "love" conflict then is reduced to a mere illustration of the more fundamental hostility between the two cultures symbolized by Jim, the rootless intellectual, and Catherine, the land-loving Southerner. The result is a curiously passionless love story, beautifully written and with the minor characters swiftly and memorably established, yet as a whole unsatisfying. The unstated myth which is said to inform the novel, that of Iphigenia in Aulis, another story of sacrificial flight, does not, I think, in any objective way determinable by the novel alone, enhance the meaning. But certainly with the publication of *The Strange Children* (1951) it has become plain that *The Women on the Porch* was an exploratory work, designed to accommodate Caroline Gordon's newer consciousness of naturalism as symbol (something she had evoked with exquisite precision in the death-haunted short story of that period, "The Forest of the South") as well as her increasing preoccupation with the problem of the point of view.

What emerges with dazzling effect in *The Strange Children* is something that the romantic agony of the early novels only timidly hinted: Caroline Gordon's fiction is now squarely in the realm of the novel of manners, the great tradition of Flaubert and James, and like theirs her social comedy is complicated and, in the end, dominated by the perilous likeness it bears to tragedy. In this sense she connects herself with a strain abandoned in Southern fiction with the death of Ellen Glasgow, but a strain enriched both by the fuller events of her own biography as well as her more acid consciousness of what the novel, as formal means, should be doing. *The Strange Children* elegantly points the dramatic method which Miss Gordon admires as a critic and teacher of fiction. It is a novel of ideas and in it she establishes that this is her proper domain, that at last she is allowing full play to a powerful intellectual scrutiny suppressed in the earlier novels in favor of an ambivalent mystique of localism and historicism.

The Strange Children manages the seemingly impossible device of revealing a complex hierarchy of meaning through the use of a nine-year-old child as the central intelligence. As modern fiction has shown again and again, the dangers of using an immature consciousness for this task are manifold: the most obvious is the cutting down of nuance and the elimination of intellectual themes; the less obvious but the most deadly is that of the coarsely Rousseauistic sentimentalization of childhood and adolescence which is tiresome commonplace in much contemporary writing. But the choice of Lucy Lewis, whose favorite reading is the beautifully ambiguous tale of "Undine," as central intelligence is subtly right for Miss Gordon's motive, a motive adequately laid down by her epigraph: "Rid me and deliver me from the hand of strange children whose mouth speaketh vanity . . ."

It is, of course, the ironic triumph of the novel that the strange children are the grown-ups in it and that Lucy is the wisely clairvoyant agent of judgment on them. But unlike those intolerable children of modern writing she is not all innocence and imagination; nor, as in the counter-romantic to this view of child-life, all cunning and sexuality. She is, rather, a little vessel which responds to the tremors and passions of the adult world in which she is both familiar and stranger, but always with that instinctual knowledge of good and evil which seems to be the burdensome gift of innocence.

Still, there are problems to be faced in such a choice of sensibility to reflect the complicated goings-on at Benfolly, a country house in Tennessee, where a group of neurotic and self-destructive intellectuals, both Northern and Southern, are gathered in the hectic communality of an alcoholic house party. The question of the limits of Lucy's ability to re-translate the action for us is solved by Miss Gordon's subtle modulations from the child as central intelligence to an omniscient narrator when the material becomes unmanageable for the child. This violates that strict determinism which is sometimes thought to control the point of view in the naturalistic novel, but, as even the most cursory examination of *Madame Bovary* or *Ulysses* will reveal, these small shifts of perspective are always useful when the limitations of the perceiving sensibility require them. Miss Gordon's sharp awarness of this possibility is evident in the endorsement she gives to the method of the "Roving Narrator" or the "Technique of Central Intelligence" in *The House of Fiction*:

> . . . A given technique is the result of a moral and philosophical attitude, a bias towards experience on the part of the author; and as the author begins to understand what it is in life that interests him most, he also becomes aware of the techniques which will enable him to create in language his fullest sense of that interest. Material and technique become in the end the same thing, the one discovering the other . . . this method (the Roving Narrator) combines the advantages of the three others and involves the artist in fewer of their disadvantages than any other known technique. But it requires the greatest maturity of judgment, the greatest mastery of life and the highest technical skill to control it . . . We look at the situation by and large through the eyes of the central character or intelligence, but we stand a little above and to one side, so to speak, and actually use the eyes of the artist himself. We thus enjoy his privilege of omniscience without the dubious authority of the so-called omniscient narrator for here the artist makes his surmises, summaries and explanations in terms of what the central character sees and feels, and the usually inert masses of material are dramatized and given *authority* . . . The technique of the Central Intelligence is employed in one way or another in the greatest nineteenth century novels, from *The Idiot* and *Madame Bovary,* to the *The Ambassadors.*

Miss Gordon, then, has made it amply clear where her sights are trained and we need only look, let us say, at the moving end of *The Strange Children* to see her method in operation. We have just had the great cathartic climax of the Holy Roller meeting of the poor whites and the taking up of serpents which has resulted in near-death to one of the believers. Little Lucy, through the cruelly casual thoughtlessness of her parents, has been exposed to all this and, now, to complete her turmoil, her fall from virtue in the theft of a crucifix belonging to one of the house-guests is suddenly and humiliatingly discovered. But that is not all. Having lost the succor of the beautiful little image, whose magnetism she only half understands, she learns, along with the other grown-ups, that Uncle Tubby, her father's pyrotechnically successful poet-friend and Isabel, the wife of Kevin Reardon, have eloped. But the real horror of this is in the revelation by Kevin that Isabel is mad. It is at this point that the child, as central intelligence, delicately modulates into a more encompassing one which is that of her father's and, beyond that, through language, tone and selection of detail into that of the omniscient narrator or, more properly, the author herself:

> He [Stephen Lewis] walked to the railing and looked down at the drenched lawn. He raised his eyes to the sky. There was a rustle behind him. A slight form pressed up against his. He put his arms around the child's shoulders and drew her closer while his eyes ranged the heavens. There was his own sign, Scorpio: "The House of Death—unless a man be re-born." . . . He passed his hand over his brow. His eyes went to the house below where a single lamp glowed murkily. There a man still lay at the point of death. He told himself that it would have been no great matter if that man had died tonight, for all men, it appeared to him now, for the first time, die on the same day: the day on which their appointed task is finished. If that man had made his last journey tonight he would not have gone alone, but companioned by a larger presence, as the friend standing behind him had been companioned when he, too, lay at the point of death in a strange country and in a desert. But all countries, he told himself wearily, are strange and all countries desert. He thought of another man, the friend of his yonth, who only a few minutes ago had left his house without farewell . . . He saw that those days, those years had been moving toward this moment and he wondered what moment was being prepared for him and for his wife and his child and he groaned, so loud that the woman and the child stared at him wondering, too.

It is right that this concluding integration of themes should be stated through a larger vision than that of a child's. Lucy's burdens in the strange dissolution of loves and friendships that has taken place at Benfolly are profound. But it requires a more practised judgment than hers to restore the troubled movement of all the characters' lives into the universal channels of love and hate, of death and peace and rebirth. In this passage, somehow recalling in its cadences the great final lines of Joyce's "The Dead," there is no solution, only a momentary resolution into a new possibility of being.

I have scanted in this accomplished novel those elements of wit and erudition which are a new and altogether successful area of achievement for Miss Gordon, and, as a matter of fact, a province that few women writers in this country have essayed. Into this impressively knowledgable complex of reference, the issue of religion naturally enters. Miss Gordon's conversion to Catholicism has been public knowledge for some five years but there is little overt concern about religion on the part of the protagonists of the novel written concurrently with her reception into the church. Still, in the figure of Kevin Reardon, the wealthy expatriate who has become a Catholic convert, there is provided a convenient if shadowy point of reference against which to direct a subtly inferential dialectic illuminating the motives of the others: the hard-drinking mother, Sara Lewis, ambivalent in her feelings for her child and husband; Stephen Lewis, bitter and sophisticated, a historian who ridicules in his wife the mysterious inner yearning which makes her hang on Kevin's story of his "vision" with an almost physiological intensity. Oddly though, it is the child, Lucy, who in her seemingly senseless theft of Kevin's crucifix dramatically reveals the drive which they all unknowingly harbor for a saviour. The passage of Stephen's musings from which I have quoted above hints at a more open religious motive to come in Miss Gordon's writing: ". . . he would not have gone alone . . .," thinks Lewis of the two men, the Catholic convert and the crudely believing Holy Roller lying ill in his house. Suddenly, there is a kind of incandescense and we recognize that two ways of knowing have been exhibited for us, through the dramatic mode of "naturalism," as possibilities of salvation. We have not been told; we have only, in the strict aesthetic of Miss Gordon's understanding of naturalism, been shown.

It is possible to say that *The Strange Children* which, incidentally, at one level is a fascinatingly malicious roman à clef of some pretty well-known literary figures, is the first work in which Caroline Gordon exchanges the frame of reference of a vanished hierarchy of caste and grace, represented by the old South, for the universe of order provided by the more durable scheme of Catholicism and its idea of grace. Her next work, I am willing to chance, will show this sense of possibility benefited by the full flowering of the deepened vision operative in *The Strange Children*. Alienation means no longer merely to be cast out from a social class or a local society, but a removal from God to whom we have become strange children.

IV. The Poetry Of The South

ISABEL GAMBLE

Ceremonies Of Bravery: John Crowe Ransom

The poetry of John Crowe Ransom is a small but accurate mirror of the modern sensibility. In it are reflected the miraculous virtues of contemporary verse at its best: its combination of delicacy with strength, of fervor with restraint, of elegance with earthiness. One needs only to glance at the critical writing about Ransom to see how perfectly apt, for his poetry, are the favorite words of this generation's critics. He has been celebrated, rightly, as the poet of perilous equilibrium, of dichotomies and irony, of tension and paradox; his verse portrays, Randall Jarrell once wrote, "the composed and inexhaustible ambiguity of things." In addition, Ransom's poetry illustrates with beautiful clarity the interdependence of form and matter; his style emerges from the exigencies of his subjects, which are completed and composed by its perfect fidelity.

In his own Poetics — for he is preceptor as well as practitioner — Ransom has done much to convince us of the worthiness — indeed, the necessity — of these modernist virtues, and the attitudes which lie behind them. They are the attitudes, we should like to think, of a civilized man: courtesy, manners, regard for the individual as an in-dividual, refusal to simplify the complex, insistence on balanced judgment, proper respect for the facts of life and a determination to triumph over them whenever possible. Ransom's imaginary kingdom, like that of another civilized man, E. M. Forster, is Love, the Beloved Republic,

> Where the men or beasts or birds
> Exchange few words and pleasant words.

341

Somewhere is such a kingdom, though not here, not now. Forster and Ransom are, indeed, a congruent pair, sharing a good many points of view; Forster's essay, "What I Believe," might stand as a manifesto for both. "My law-givers are Erasmus and Montaigne, not Moses and St. Paul," he writes; and we remember that St. Paul fares but poorly under Ransom's scrutiny as well (see "Our Two Worthies"). The saint was a devotee of the Pure Idea, a Platonic notion to which the sceptical empiricist cannot subscribe.

> Plato, before Plotinus gentled him,
> Spoke the soul's part, and though its vice is known
> We're in his shadow still.

Ransom and Forster foregather instead under the banner of Aristotle, "pulling steady on the bottle"; if, indeed, they will accept a banner at all — for, they keep reminding us, they do not believe in Belief. They believe in personal relationships and the whatness of things.

These attitudes produce the special style we have chosen to call modern, although actually it is a recurrent style, reappearing as the cycles of history move around. Its characteristics are adumbrated in the critical terms listed above. The refusal of Belief demands an ironic style (both Ransom and Forster are masters of it), a necessity of the double vision, which wishes to say one thing while suggesting another. Allegiance to Aristotle, the natural father of poets, requires in addition a sense of the complexity of things. For the Aristotelian, Beauty is not the Pure Idea, but (as one of them has said), "in the flesh it is immortal." Spirit is incarnate in flesh and our mortal condition is ambiguous, amphibious. Rejecting the Platonic universal, distrusting the grandeur of generality, the modernist chooses instead to render the unique, the precious object. This choice enforces an oblique style, since the vocabulary of directness, smoothed by too many tongues, fits the body of the object loosely and shrouds its particularity. Ransom has declared positively that "the direct approach is perilous to the artist, and may be fatal." Circumlocution may take the form either of a dramatic-symbolic style, where images enact ideas; or of linguistic dislocation, the formation of a dialect at once thickened and subtilized until it can present the object in a fresh and therefore (so our theorists assert), a truer light. The style of Gerard Manley Hopkins is a greater exemplar of this second manner (his term "inscape" is an earlier name for the precious object); Ransom's is a diminished but scarcely less effective instance.

Devotion to the individual, the particular, imposes special burdens on the poet, which affect not only his idiom but his subject-matter. Ransom's highly personal style and his consistency of tone have driven critics almost irresistibly toward an attempt to describe his "major subject." It is usually stated in terms of "dichotomies," such as science *versus* poetry, reason *versus* imagination — in short, "the divided sensibility." There are, indeed, divisions in almost all of Ransom's poems. But if we are to use so clumsy a concept as "major subject" at all, we must use it to signify some special preoccupation that is always present in the poet's consciousness, the chasm that yawns beneath all slighter ditches. The predicaments of the divided sensibility, though serious, are less fundamental than the division persistently recorded by Ransom. It can be stated quite bluntly; best, perhaps, by another poet, who had also weighed Plato against "solider Aristotle" and, in some moods at least, found him wanting.

> Man is in love and loves what vanishes,
> What more is there to say?

This realization lies behind almost all of Ransom's poetry; his subject is the war of death with life.

Death has a special menace for the anti-Platonist, who has denied the Pure Idea and the great complacent universals that can resist time. He has lost the consolation of the unchanging and placed his values in the precarious purlieus of mortality. As Yeats wrote in another place: "Everything that man esteems Endures a moment or a day." No longer permitted to love universal Beauty, the sorrowful modernist must learn to love each new incarnation of it. "Perilous and beautiful" becomes an inevitable formula, recording the frailty of Beauty's earthly vessels. Thus Hopkins laments the felling of an ash tree: "seeing it maimed there came at that moment a great pang, and I wished to die and not to see the inscapes of the world destroyed any more." His poetic memorial to this incident is in "Binsey Poplars":

> After-comers cannot guess the beauty been.
> Ten or twelve, only ten or twelve

Strokes of havoc unselve
The sweet especial scene.

Just as the dozen strokes havoc the poplars, so Ransom's "lady of beauty and high degree" is unselved "after six little spaces of chill, and six of burning." It is a commonplace that one mark of the modern consciousness is an awareness of time's pressure; but this comes to the surface in every age when men are forced for one reason or another to love what vanishes. Elizabethan poetry is a long lament for the brightness that falls from the air; the seventeenth-century prose writers — Ralegh, Browne, Jeremy Taylor — give sonorous instruction in the rules of dying. As Hopkins sadly observed,

It is the blight man was born for,
It is Margaret you mourn for.

It is this dilemma, sharpened to acuteness in our age that has nothing to cling to except the personal, which gives Ransom's poetry its persistent elegiac tone and dictates its intention. Following Hopkins, he writes "Of Margaret":

Virgin, whose image bent to the small grass
I keep against this tide of wayfaring,
O hear the maiden pageant ever sing
Of that far away time of gentleness.

The poems are a series of images preserved against the tide of wayfaring, the dark sweep of time. They are little histories of mortals who are to be overcome by encroaching night; Ransom's books are populated with gallant but dying gentlemen and a bevy of blue girls akin to Wallace Stevens' Susanna. Reading him, we confront "a dream of ladies sweeping by" — and cry out to save it.

Let them alone, dear Aunt, just for one minute
Till I go fishing in the dark of my mind.

Wordsworth, the first "modern" poet in so many respects, also saw his poetry as a preserving medium for the talismanic "spots of time" which together make up a life. Ransom has written that "the tense of poetry" is past. "We ask what the specific poems, the ones that we cherish as perfect creations are doing. I should say that they are dramatizing the past."

Mortal is one of Ransom's favorite, or at any rate most necessary words. "The cold hearts in us mortally return"; "we are mortals teasing for immortal spoils" and "instructed of much mortality." To number his poems on the subject of mortality is almost to make a complete index of Ransom's work. There is the little cousin, "dead, by foul subtraction," and his counterpart, John Whiteside's daughter; Miss Euphemia who "sits with us only Till next Pentecost"; the lady young in beauty besieged by the gentleman in a dustcoat; Emily Hardcastle: "Right across her threshold has the Grizzled Baron come"; and Conrad in Twilight, Captain Carpenter, Grimes "subsiding slowly To the defunctive posture of the stained dead," the Old Mansion ruining quietly, Janet's hen descended to "the forgetful kingdom of death," Margaret mourning for the dead leaves and Miriam Tazewell for "her lawn deflowered" by a "villain" world, the aging lovers in "Fall of Leaf," the aging South in "Antique Harvesters," and a lady who is celebrating her birthday:

> Sure eyes, you have observed on what hard terms
> Beauty has respite from voracious worms;
> Her moment comes; thereafter fast or slow
> Her daily funerals go.

The celebration of daily funerals gives Ransom's poetry its depth of sadness. He is constrained to be a perpetual mourner because he is a perpetual lover.

> Assuredly I have a grief,
> And I am shaken; but not as a leaf.

Ransom's elegies are not only for the death of the body, but also for the thousand little deaths of the soul whose daily funerals escape eyes less surely instructed in mortality. There is the death of parting — "A cry of Absence, Absence, in the heart." There is the death of love, frail as the hollow tree in "Vaunting Oak," slain by "silences and words" in "Two in August," riding away "up the hill forever" on the messenger's bicycle in "Parting, without a Sequel." Absence of love, or denial of love, is indeed death in Ransom's world, for life can flourish only in the Beloved Republic.

> Heartless lovers are as dead
> That walk the earth unburied.

One of his saddest little poems is a dirge for a marriage, "In Process of a Noble Alliance."

> For now in funeral white they lead her
> And crown her queen of the House of No Love:
> A dirge, then, for her beauty, musicians!
> Ye harping the springe that catches the dove.

"Spectral Lovers" and "The Equilibrists" memorize the doom of those whose lives were never fully realized, "whose songs shall never be heard" because their love remained unfulfilled.

What is there to set against all this grief? Only the acceptance of brutal fact: that the perilous closeness of death is a sign of life, that "life is not good but in danger and joy" — in a word, courage. The frail mortals celebrated by Ransom are, in Marianne Moore's phrase, forms "steeled straight up" with defiance; they "accede to mortality," but with honor. The poet exhorts the birthday lady, in the face of funerals: "Dear love, rise up and proudly sing," reminding her of soldiers —

> They fling sweet oaths on high, not honouring
> The dismal nearing Thing.

Ransom makes elegies for the hopeful, courageous blue-eyed people.

> Devising for those gibbeted and brave
> Came I descanting.

Gibbeted and brave are Captain Carpenter with his "sweet blue eyes," and the dying Grimes, the "fortress," in "Puncture":

> Blue blazed the eyes of Grimes in the old manner.

Blue is a word invoked by Ransom to counter his other key word, *mortal.* It is the color of life, of hope, of bravery. Jane Sneed, one of the speakers in an Eclogue on death, dreams wistfully of faithful lovers united against Night, "the dark and fathomless." "The flame of each to the other's flame cries Courage!"

> So unafraid they keep the whole night through,
> Till the sun of a sudden glowing through the bushes
> They wake and laugh, their eyes again are blue.

Here all of Ransom's plus-terms — life, love, courage, blue eyes — converge. Miss Euphemia, who is about to die, nevertheless ventures out to count her tulips,

> Out of the frore escaping
> To the blue upper arch.

The dead lady in "Blue Girls" now has "blear eyes fallen from blue," but once "was lovelier than any of you." In another poem, Ransom praises a lady's "eyes of an extravagant hue: *Viz.*, china blue." They blaze out defiantly against the turning seasons.

> Where does she keep them from this glare
> Of the monstrous sun and the wind's flare
> Without any wear?

The lovely miller's daughter has eyes "which are a blue stillwater." And ducks, courageously building their nests "dangerous at the earth-heart,"

> will rise and go
> Where Capricornus dips his hooves
> In the blue chasm of no wharves.

In "Painted Head," body's love is invoked to "colorify" "the big blue birds" of the head. The cows who come alive joyously in "Little Boy Blue" have "hooves and horns of blue." One of Ransom's characters wakes in the morning with a feeling of joy and a desire "to be singing not talking." "Blue air" is swimming "all round his bed" — the same blue air that "rinses the pure pale head" so unwillingly loved by the Man without Sense of Direction. In "Prelude to an Evening," one of his best poems, Ransom juxtaposes his contrary themes in a single stanza — the blue of life and love, the undertone of danger and death — as the foreboding wife listens:

> Freshening the water in the blue bowls
> For the buckberries with not all your love,
> You shall be listening for the low wind,
> The warning sibilance of pines.

A final example of blue comes more ambiguously in an earlier poem, "Hilda," which mourns still another of Ransom's dead girls.

> O Hilda, proudest of the ladies gone,
> Wreathing my roses with blue bitter dust,
> Think not I would reject you, for I must
> Weep for your nakedness and no retinue
> And leap up as of old to follow you, —
> But flesh hath monstrous gravity, as of stone.

A fume of life rising upon the bitter air is the only thing left when all the nymphs have departed. But it is significant that Ransom should still insist on recognizing the "monstrous gravity" of flesh. In that two-pronged phrase he compasses the sadness of earth, and its earthiness as well — its mass and inertia, weighing heavily on the human spirit, but part, too, of its very life. It is a measure of Ransom's own courage that he has never refused to record the brutality and evanescence of life. For the poet in love with what vanishes, the temptation is strong to give his keepsakes the unreality of tombstone art. Shall he lay them up in lavender? Shall he make of them golden birds to set upon a golden bough? For a single stanza, he almost succumbs.

> Bring proper gifts to Beauty then:
> Bring topaz, emeralds, gold, and minerals rare,
> Musk that will ever be sweet on mortal air,
> Bright stiff brocades outlasting the short ken
> Of usual mortal men.

But this is the stiffness of death, not life. And so the poet who seeks to preserve his precious objects from time's tide is forced into a paradox. Change *is* life, so they must be allowed to change, lest they find in art a death more final than any other. Their deaths must be renewed a thousand times, in homage to their vitality. As Virginia Woolf wrote, "Beauty must be broken daily to remain beautiful." "The artifice of eternity" will not serve. Ransom, in a phrase that might be a retort to Yeats, has only dispraise for "the extravagant device of art," castigating it

> For having vinegarly traduced the flesh
> Till, the hurt flesh recusing, the hard egg
> Is shrunken to its own deathlike surface.

The enduring is what has never been alive, the deathlike surface of abstraction. So the poet of inscapes is left with his daily funerals, his perpetual recognition of the peril, the swiftness, the vulnerability and gravity of flesh.

The surfaces of Ransom's poetry are far from deathlike; they are as shifty, as startling and shiny, as the living things reflected in them. The poet's devotion to beauty immortal in the flesh produces, as we have suggested, his special manner, with its combination of brutality and bravery, its diction compounded of bluntness and elegance. He celebrates "ceremonies of bravery," and like an earlier poet of "brutall terminations," Sir Thomas Browne, devises a style which drawn on the resonances of our double language to reproduce their solemnity and transience. Just as "foul subtraction" might have been written by Browne, so Ransom might have composed "brutall terminations," or, "Diuturnity is a dream and folly of expectation." Both of them exploit the precision and formality of Latin, which has the stiff beauty of the golden bird, to fix their diuturnities against a background of austere eternity. Both combine with this background a foreground of love and sadness, embodied in the common English words that have a hold on our emotions. Thus the timeless and the temporal, the abstract and the concrete, spirit and flesh, intelligence and feeling, are joined to compose our mixed unity. Ransom's "Vaunting Oak" is a fine example of this technique; the poem, as usual, is about transience, and the dilemma emerges through its very language. So, on one side there are words like concumbent, eruptive, susceptive, eminent, profuse, testified, traversed, instructed, dolorous, reverberance; and on the other, shapes of earth, fashioned in an earthly tongue: "a flat where birdsong flew," "daisies and yellow kinds," "the singing of bees; or the coward birds that fly," and a flock of simple words — frail, mad, young, bitter, tall, green, steep, brag, knobs, boomed, sped. A few sentences from *Urn Burial* will show how Browne, who called man the great amphibium, records his predicament in the same ambidexterous medium.

> Sense endureth no extremities, and sorrows destroy us or themselves. To weep into stones are fables. Afflictions induce callosities, miseries are slippery, or fall like snow upon us, which notwithstanding is no unhappy stupidity. To be ignorant of evils to come, and forgetfull of evils past, is a mercifull provision in nature, whereby we digest the mixture of our few and evil dayes, and our delivered senses not relapsed into cutting remembrances, our sorrows are not kept raw by the edge of repetitions.

Ransom and Browne are alike, too, in the stateliness of their styles; both are believers in ceremony. And we remember, again, Yeats, with his "ceremony of innocence."

> How but in custom and in ceremony
> Are innocence and beauty born?

One might add, how else are they to be kept alive? Ransom's tone, uniformly severe and ironic, is a product of his belief in the necessity of ritual for civilized life. His essay, "Forms and Citizens," in *The World's Body,* is the prose *locus* for this belief; his verse is the enactment of it. It is his own form of defiance, matching the courage of his personae. Ritual masters transience by imposing an order upon it. And ritualism in poetry is, also, a mastery of emotion. It is one type of oblique style, fending off the assaults of sentiment inherent in the direct approach. "Our sorrows are not kept raw"; they are made less piercing, and at the same time are lent dignity and depth, by acquiring a pattern. Ritual, or ceremony, exposes the paradox of feeling, which gathers strength the more firmly it is controlled. The paradox was phrased by Yeats when he wrote,

> I might have had no friend that could not mix
> Courtesy and passion into one.

Ransom could have been such a friend. His style, like that of Yeats, is high talk, combining the courtesy of a courtly tongue with the heart's passionate outcry. And, like Yeats, Ransom draws strength for his rituals from an awareness of tradition, his sense of being "rooted in one dear perpetual place," even though the perpetuity may be only relative.

It is true that Ransom cannot cry out as loudly as Yeats; that the elder poet is the greater because he is capable, when the necessity arises, of abandoning obliqueness and ceremony for a terrible naked directness. True, too, that Ransom often seems too elegiac, too much concerned with dramatizing the past, and incapable of the fierceness, the positive joy and gusto that could make Yeats' Self triumphantly outshout his Soul, turning toward the future to cry,

> I am content to live it all again
> And yet again . . .

and to end, with Blakean ecstasy, "Everything we look upon is blest." Nevertheless, though we may conclude that Ransom errs on the side of too much courtesy, and may grow weary at times of his restraint and good manners, we have more need today of courtesy than of passion, of control than of abandon. Forster, in the essay quoted earlier, has reminded us of the dangers that attend Great Men. So, though we may agree that Yeats and D. H. Lawrence are greater than Ransom and Forster, we must also admit that they commit dreadful errors of judgment and taste, that they were extravagant as human beings, politically naive and inclined to take themselves too seriously. They are necessary for our health; but two are enough for one generation, and it is equally imperative that we produce the minor excellence that is the best fruit of civilization — an aristocracy, as Forster has said, "of the sensitive, the considerate, and the plucky." To this aristocracy, famous for its foolhardy allegiance to humanity in the face of darkness, Ransom belongs.

LOUIS D. RUBIN, JR.

The Serpent In The Mulberry Bush

"That poem is 'about' solipsism, a philosophical doctrine which says that we create the world in the act of perceiving it; or about Narcissism, or any other *ism* that denotes the failure of the human personality to function objectively in nature and society."

That poem, as Tate goes on to say about the "Ode to the Confederate Dead," is also about "a man stopping at the gate of a Confederate graveyard on a late autumn afternoon." Thus the man at the cemetery and the graves in the cemetery become the symbol of the solipsism and the Narcissism:

> Autumn is desolation in the plot
> Of a thousand acres where these memories grow
> From the inexhaustible bodies that are not
> Dead, but feed the grass row after rich row.
> Think of the autumns that have come and gone!

A symbol is something that stands for something else. What I want to do is to point out some of the relationships between the "something" and the "something else."

Richard Weaver has written of the Nashville Agrarians that they "underwent a different kind of apprenticeship for their future labors. They served the muse of poetry." In a certain sense that is true, but the word "apprenticeship" is misleading in Tate's instance. Allen Tate did not become a poet merely in order to learn how to be an Agrarian. He was a poet while he was an Agrarian, he continued to be a poet after his specific interest in Agrarianism diminished, and now he has beome an active communicant of the Roman Catholic Church and he is still a poet. One must insist that for Allen Tate poetry has never been the apprenticeship for anything except poetry.

"Figure to yourself a man stopping at the gate of a Confederate cemetery . . .," Tate writes in his essay "Narcissus as Narcissus." He continues: ". . . he pauses for a baroque meditation on the ravages of time, concluding with the figure of the 'blind crab.' This creature has mobility but no direction, energy but from the human point of view, no purposeful world to use it in. . . . The crab is the first intimation of the nature of the moral conflict upon which the drama of the poem develops: the cut-off-ness of the modern 'intellectual man' from the world."

> The brute curiosity of an angel's stare
> Turns you, like them, to stone,
> Transforms the heaving air
> Till plunged into a heavier world below
> You shift your sea-space blindly
> Heaving, turning like the blind crab.

If the Confederate Ode is based upon a moral conflict involving "the cut-off-ness of the modern 'intellectual man' from the world," why did Tate choose as his symbol the Confederate graveyard? The answer lies in the history of the region in which Allen Tate and his fellow Fugitives and Agrarians grew up. Tate was born and reared in the Upper South, and he attended college in Nashville, Tennessee, and there was a symbolism in the South of his day ready for the asking. It was the contrast, and conflict, between what the South was and traditionally had been, and what it was tending toward. "With the war of 1914-1918 the South re-entered the world," Tate has written, "—but gave a backward glance as it stepped over the border: that backward glance gave us the Southern renasence, a literature conscious of the past in the present."

What kind of country was the South upon which Tate and his contemporaries of the early 1920s looked back at as well as observed around them? It was first of all a country with considerable historical consciousness, with rather more feeling for tradition and manners than existed elsewhere in the nation. There had been a civil war just a little over a half-century before, and the South had been badly beaten. Afterwards Southern leaders decided to emulate the ways of the conqueror, and called for a New South of cities and factories. Such Southern intellectuals as there were went along with the scheme.

Men of letters like Walter Hines Page and John Spencer Bassett preached that once the provincialism of the Southern author was thrown off, and the Southern man of letters was willing to forget Appomattox Court House and Chickamauga, then Southern literature would come into its own.

When it came to forecasting a literary renascence in the South, Bassett and his friends were absolutely right, but they could not have been more mistaken about the form that it would take. What brought about the renascence— what there was in the time and place that made possible an Allen Tate and a William Faulkner and a Donald Davidson and a John Ransom and a Robert Penn Warren and an Andrew Lytle and three dozen other Southern writers— was not the eager willingness to ape the ways of the Industrial East, but rather the revulsion against the necessity of having to do so in order to live among their fellow Southerners. By 1920 and thereafter the South was changing, so that Tate's modern Southerner standing at the gate of a Confederate military cemetery was forced to compare what John Spencer Bassett had once termed "the worn out ideas of a forgotten system" with what had replaced that system.

And what had taken its place was what Tate and his fellow Agrarians have been crying out against ever since: the industrial, commercially-minded modern civilization, in which religion and ritual and tradition and order were rapidly being superseded by the worship of getting and spending.

Thus the Confederate graveyard as the occasion for solipsism, and the failure of the human personality to function objectively in nature and society, because for Tate there could be no question about where the young Southern writer should stand in the matter. The agrarian community that had been the Southern way of life was with all its faults vastly preferable to what was taking place now. As he wrote in 1936, "the Southern man of letters cannot permit himself to look upon the old system from a purely social point of view, or from the economic view; to him it must seem better than the system that destroyed it, better, too, than any system with which the modern planners, Marxian or any color, wish to replace the present order." Surveying the heroic past and the empty present, the young Southerner could only feel himself in isolation from what were now his region's ways. In the words of the Confederate Ode,

What shall we say who count our days and bow
Our heads with a commemorial woe
In the ribboned coats of grim felicity,
What shall we say to the bones, unclean,
Whose verdurous anonymity will grow?
The ragged arms, the ragged heads and eyes
Lost in these acres of the insane green?
The gray lean spiders come, they come and go;
In a tangle of willows without light
The singular screech-owl's tight
Invisible lyric seeds the mind
With the furious murmur of their chivalry.

    We shall say only the leaves
    Flying, plunge and expire

We shall say only the leaves whispering
In the improbable mist of nightfall
That flies on multiple wing. . . .

We are, that is, inadequate, cut off, isolated; we cannot even imagine
how it was. All we can see is the leaves blowing about the grave-
stones. So Mr. Tate's modern Southerner felt.

The "Ode to the Confederate Dead" dates from about 1926, and
that was the year, Tate recalls, that he and John Crowe Ransom began
toying with the idea of "doing something" about the Southern situation, a project which soon led to plans for the book entitled *I'll Take
My Stand,* in which Tate, Ransom, and ten other Southerners set
forth Agrarian counsels for what they felt was an increasingly industrialized, increasingly misled South. The central argument was
stated in the first paragraph of the introduction, which Ransom composed and to which all the participants gave assent: "All the articles
bear in the same sense upon the book's title-subject: all tend to support a Southern way of life as against what may be called the American
or prevailing way; and all as much as agree that the best terms in
which to represent the distinction are contained in the phrase, Agrarian
versus Industrial."

The problem that the twelve Agrarians felt confronted the
modern South was the same problem, then, as that which Mr. Tate's
modern man at the graveyard gate faced. And in a very definite sense,
I'll Take My Stand represented their recommendations for a solution,

in a particular time and place, of the central moral problem of the "Ode to the Confederate Dead."

The Agrarians declared in their symposium that industrialism was predatory, in that it was based on a concept of nature as something to be used. In so doing, industrialism threw man out of his proper relationship to nature, and to God whose creation it was. The Agrarian quarrel, they declared, was with applied science, which in the form of industrial capitalism had as its object the enslavement of human energies. Since all activity was measured by the yardstick of financial gain, the industrial spirit neglected the aesthetic life. It had the effect of brutalizing labor, removing from it any possibility of enjoyment.

It must be remembered that most of the Agrarians were speaking not as economists or sociologists or regional planners or even as professional philosophers; they were speaking as men of letters. They believed that an Agrarian civilization was the way of life which permitted the arts to be an integral and valuable social activity, and not, as Ransom put it, "intercalary and non-participating experiences." Donald Davidson wrote of the Agrarians that "they sought to force, not so much a theory of economics as a philosophy of life, in which both economics and art would find their natural places and not be disassociated into abstract means and abstract ends, as the pseudo-culture of the world-city would dissassociate them."

In an Agrarian community aesthetic activity would not be subordinate to economics. The artist would be a working member of society, not a person somehow set apart from the everyday existence of his neighbors. Nature, religion and art would be honored activities of daily life, and not something superfluous and outmoded, to be indulged when business permitted. Knowledge—letters, learning, taste, the integrated and rich fullness of emotion and intellect—would be "carried to the heart," as Tate said in the Confederate Ode, and not an unassimilated, discordant conglomerate of fragments. In the words of the poem,

> What shall we say who have knowledge
> Carried to the heart? Shall we take the act
> To the grave? Shall we, more hopeful, set up the grave
> In the house? The ravenous grave?

Shall we, he is asking, who still possess this full knowledge and who live in a world from which we are increasingly cut off by its insularity and isolation, in which we have mobility but no direction, energy but no outlet— shall we wait for death, or better still, court it?

In one sense, the program put forward in *I'll Take My Stand* constituted an answer to that question. But for all the book's effectiveness (and 23 years later it is receiving more attention from young Southerners than ever before in its history), it would be a mistake to believe that the Agrarian program was the only, or even the most important, statement of the problems of modern man as Tate and his colleagues saw them. One must always remember that Tate, Ransom, Davidson and Warren were poets primarily, not social scientists. The place to look for Allen Tate's ultimate statement of views is in his poetry.

Cleanth Brooks has pointed out the relevance of Tate's poetry to this central moral problem. Not only is this so in regard to subject matter, however; we find it implicit in the poetics as well. What is the most obvious characteristic of the poetry of Tate and his colleagues? I think we find it stated, and recognized, from the very outset, in the first reviews of the anthology, *Fugitives,* published in 1928. "Fugitive poetry makes one distinctly feel that one of the serious and fundamental defects of nineteenth century poetry was that it was too easy," one critic wrote. "Mr. Ransom, Mr. Tate and Miss [Laura] Riding are not for those who read and run," another reviewer asserted. The poet John Gould Fletcher, himself soon to join the Agrarians in the symposium, declared in a review that the Fugitive poets had become the main impulse in America in the leadership of "a school of intellectual poetry replacing the free verse experiments of the elder school."

The kind of poetry that Allen Tate was writing, then, represented a disciplined, intellectual, difficult poetry, requiring of the reader, in Tate's own words, "the fullest co-operation of all his intellectual resources, all his knowledge of the world, and all the persistence and alertness that he now thinks of giving to scientific studies." It was therefore a direct challenge to the attitude that aesthetic concerns were a subordinate, harmless activity "for those who read and run." It claimed for art as important and as demanding a role in human affairs as that played by science and business. As Ransom wrote, art "is a career, precisely as science is a career. It is as serious, it has an attitude as official, it is as studied and consecutive, it is by all means as difficult, it is no less important."

Another characteristic of Tate's poetry is its concentrated use of image and metaphor, as in the concluding lines of the Confederate Ode:

> Leave now
> The shut gate and the decomposing wall:
> The gentle serpent, green in the mulberry bush,
> Riots with his tongue through the hush—
> Sentinel of the grave who counts us all!

Of those lines Tate says that "the closing image, that of the serpent, is the ancient symbol of time, and I tried to give it the credibility of the commonplace by placing it in a mulberry bush—with the faint hope that the silkworm would somehow be explicit. But time is also death. If that is so, then space, or the Becoming, is life; and I believe there is not a single spacial symbol in the poem. . . ."

Why, though, if that is all that Tate "meant," did he not write something like the following:

> Let us leave the graveyard now.
> Time runs riot there
> And time brings death to bear
> And wears it on its brow.

The answer is that those lines are simply the abstract statement of what Tate was saying—and not even that, because Tate was not simply declaring that one should not remain in a graveyard because it reminds one of time and time brings death. Such a statement represents merely the "message" of the lines. Its purpose would be to give instruction concerning the course of action to be followed at a cemetery gate. One may decide that it is "true," which is another way of saying that the idea expressed is in accord with the findings of science; or that it is "false," in which case the advice is non-scientific and not an advantageous basis for action. If the former, the poet is not saying anything startling, and certainly a clinical psychologist could present much more convincing proof of the validity of the action than the poet would be doing. And if one decides that the advice is not scientifically plausible, then what else remains? The lines contain nothing but the advice; the "meaning" represents the lines' sole reason for being.

Tate's lines, however, do not simply give "advice"; they do not base their appeal on their adaptability to counsel. They are not dependent upon any scientific 'proof' of their correctitude. Both alone and in the context of the Ode they *create their own validity*. They do not pretend to be representative of scientific knowledge and proof; they *are* their own knowledge and proof. They are about serpents and mulberry bushes and shut gates and decomposing walls, and not advice to graveyard visitors. Tate's poem isn't a mere pseudo-scientific statement, and it doesn't depend upon a paraphrase of a scientific statement, and its validity is neither confirmable nor refutable by scientists. It may or may not contain a statement of scientific truth, but that would at most be a portion, only one of a number of parts, involved in the whole creation of the poem. The poem, therefore, does not depend upon science; science plays only a relatively minor role. The relationship is obvious to the Agrarian belief in the equality of the aesthetic pursuits with the scientific.

Tate and his colleagues have insisted in their poetry and criticism that the image possesses a priority over the abstract idea. They have taken over the pioneering work done by the Imagists and gone further. They have been instrumental in reviving contemporary interest in the Metaphysical poets of the seventeenth century, constructed as that poetry is with complex imagery and metaphor. An idea, Ransom has written, "is derivative and tamed," whereas an image is in the wild state: "we think we can lay hold of image and take it captive, but the docile captive is not the real image but only the idea, which is the image with its character beaten out of it." The image, Ransom declared, is "a manifold of properties, like a field or a mine, something to be explored for the properties." The scientist can use the manifold only by singling out the one property with which he is concerned: "It is not by refutation but by abstraction that science destroys the image. It means to get its 'value' out of the image, and we may be sure that it has no use for the image in its original state of freedom."

A poetry of abstract ideas, Tate and Ransom held, is a poetry of science, and as such it neglects the manifold properties of life and nature. Just as an economist used only the special interests of economics to interpret human activity, so the poetry of ideas was concerned with only one part of the whole. This led to specialization and isolation, fragmenting the balance and completeness of man and nature into a multitude of special interests, cutting off men from the whole of life, destroying the unity of human existence.

And here we come again to Tate's main theme in the Confederate Ode, "the failure of the human personality to function objectively in nature and society," "the cut-off-ness of the modern 'intellectual man' from the world." It is a constant refrain in Tate's work. In 1928, for instance, we find these two sentences in a review by Tate of Gorham Munson's *Destinations,* in the *New Republic*:

> Evasions of intellectual responsibility take various forms; all forms seem to be general in our time; what they mean is the breakdown of culture; and there is no new order in sight which promises to replace it. The widespread cults, esoteric societies, amateur religions, all provide easy escapes from discipline, easy revolts from the traditional forms of culture.

And 25 years later he is still saying just that, as in his recent Phi Beta Kappa address at the University of Minnesota:

> the man of letters must not be committed to the illiberal specializations that the nineteenth century has proliferated into the modern world: specializations in which means are divorced from ends, action from sensibility, matter from mind, society from the individual, religion from moral agency, love from lust, poetry from thought, communion from experience, and mankind in the community from men in the crowd. There is literally no end to this list of dissociations because there is no end, yet in sight, to the fragmenting of the western mind.

Modern man of the dissociated sensibility, isolated from his fellows, caught up in a life of fragmented parts and confused impulses; thus Allen Tate's Southerner waiting at the gate of the Confederate cemetery contemplates the high glory of Stonewall Jackson and the inscrutable foot-cavalry of a day when ancestors of that Southerner knew what they fought for, and could die willingly for knowing it:

You know who have waited by the wall
The twilight certainty of an animal,
Those midnight restitutions of the blood
You know— the immitigable pines, the smoky frieze
Of the sky, the sudden call: you know the rage,
The cold pool left by the mounting flood,
Of muted Zeno and Parmenides.
You who have waited for the angry resolution
Of those desires that should be yours tomorrow,
You know the unimportant shrift of death
And praise the vision
And praise the arrogant circumstance
Of those who fall
Rank upon rank, hurried beyond decision—
Here by the sagging gate, stopped by the wall.

Times are not what they were, Tate's Southerner at the gate realizes;
it has become almost impossible even to imagine such days:

You hear the shout, the crazy hemlocks point
With troubled fingers to the silence which
Smothers you, a mummy, in time.

Even the title of the poem stems from the irony of the then and now;
"Not only are the meter and rhyme without fixed pattern," Tate wrote,
"but in another feature the poem is even further removed from Pindar
than Abraham Cowley was: a purely subjective meditation would not
even in Cowley's age have been called an ode. I suppose in so calling
it I intended an irony: the scene of the poem is not a public celebration, it is a lone man by a gate."

If in the Confederate Ode there is regret and irony over "the
failure of the human personality to function objectively in nature and
society," then in Tate's poem "Seasons of the Soul" the malady has
attained the proportions of desperation. The poem is Tate's equation of the present-day dissociation of sensibility with the medieval
Hell. It begins with a quotation in Italian from Canto XIII of the
Inferno, and the English equivalent is to this effect:

Then I reached out my hand before me
    And severed a twig from a thorn bush;
    And the trunk shrieked, 'Why do you tear me?'

The passage is that in which the poet is conducted to a wood in which the souls of lovers who died by committing suicide have become trees, and which are eternally rended by Harpies which feed on the branches. "Seasons of the Soul" is in four parts, and in the course of the poem the pestilences of modern man are set forth, each in its anguish. War—

> No head knows where its rest is
> Or may lie down with reason
> When war's usurping claws
> Shall take the heart escheat—
> Green field in burning season
> To stain the weevil's jaws.

Rootlessness, a world peopled by ghosts—

> My father in a gray shawl
> Gave me an unseeing glint
> And entered another room!
> I stood in the empty hall
> And watched them come and go
> From one room to another,
> Old men, old women— slow,
> Familiar; girls, boys;
> I saw my downcast mother
> Clad in her street-clothes,
> Her blue eyes long and small,
> Who had no look or voice
> For him whose vision froze
> Him in the empty hall.

Godlessness—

> For the drying God above,
> Hanged in his windy steeple,
> No longer bears for us
> The living wound of love.

Bestiality—

> The pacing animal
> Surveys the jungle cove

> And slicks his slithering wiles
> To turn the venereal awl
> In the livid wound of love.

In the last section of the poem, "Spring," the poet recalls his childhood:

> Back in my native prime
> I saw the orient corn
> All space but no time,
> Reaching for the sun
> Of the land where I was born:
> It was a pleasant land
> Where even death could please
> Us with an ancient pun—
> All dying for the hand
> Of the mother of silences.

As Vivienne Koch has pointed out, "the mother of silences" appears to be a figure symbolizing both the Virgin and death. In time of pestilence, the poet says, who knows what is to come, death or salvation? "In time of bloody war / Who will know the time?" he asks; "Its light is at the flood, / Mother of silences!"

With certain reservations one can say that "Seasons of the Soul" is Tate's own telling of the Waste Land. The poem is renewed evidence of the accessibility to a common tradition shared by Tate and the Southerners on the one hand, and Eliot and his followers on the other. The Southerners, Fugitives and Agrarians both, in many ways have said for their time and place what Eliot has been saying for the same time but another less particularized place. The theme of "Seasons of the Soul" could hardly be better explicated than in recent remarks by Eliot in his *Notes Toward A Definition of Culture*:

> We can assert with some confidence that our own period is one of decline; that the standards of culture are lower than they were fifty years ago; and that the evidences of this decline are visible in every department of human activity. I see no reason why the decay of culture should not proceed much further, and why we may not even anticipate a period of some duration in which it is possible to say that it will have *no* culture. Then culture will have to grow again from the

soil; and when I say it must grow again from the soil, I do not mean that it will be brought into existence by any activity of politival demagogues. . . . Culture is the one thing that we cannot deliberately aim at. It is the product of a variety of more or less harmonious activities, each pursued for its own sake.

Eliot's proposed course of action for modern man is well known: it is the deliberate and disciplined cultivation of spiritual values, through religion. That he feels that his advice will not be followed, and that disaster will result, in no way diminishes his belief that only through God can civilization survive. For the Southerners, Agrarianism was one way of saying this, too. Though *I'll Take My Stand* did not base its recommendations upon a religious revival, the role of religion in the agrarian life was insisted upon. Significantly, too, Tate's essay was on the Southern religion, calling for the spiritual values of wholeness and unity through religion.

Recently Tate has remarked, in discussing the impact of *I'll Take My Stand,* that "I never thought of Agrarianism as a *restoration* of anything in the Old South; I saw it as something to be created, as I think it will in the long run be created as the result of a profound change, not only in the South, but elsewhere, in the moral and religious outlook of western man. The South is still a region where an important phase of that change may take place; but the change will not, as I see it, be uniquely Southern; it will be greater than the South. What I had in mind twenty years ago, not too distinctly, I think I see more clearly now; that is, the possibility of the humane life presupposes, with us, a moral order, the order of a unified Christendom. . . ." (*Shenandoah*, III, 2, summer 1952.)

Again we find the philosophy mirrored in the poetics. The demand for a conscious quest for the order and unity of a spiritual existence runs throughout his poetry and his criticism of poetry. His famous definition of tension in poetry, for instance, is in direct relationship to this concept:

the meaning of poetry is its 'tension,' the full organized body of all the extension and intension that we can find in it. The remotest figurative significance that we can derive does not invalidate the extensions of the literal statement.

> Or we may begin with the literal statement and by stages
> develop the complications of the metaphor: at every stage we
> may pause to state the meaning so far apprehended, and at
> every stage the meaning will be coherent.

The definition is a demand that poetry embody and reflect a unity. Together with the belief in a poetry of rich imagery, it constitutes a pronouncement against the poetical equivalent of "easy revolts from the traditional forms of culture," "illiberal specialization," and the dissociation of sensibility. Tate insists that the poem constitute a whole, full and rich and multi-faceted, with no insular scientific abstraction from the whole for the sake of facility or "usability"; and he demands that the the whole be unified, disciplined, and coherent all along the way, rather than formless and fragmentary. It is his desire for all forms of our overly-disjointed modern life, especially the theological: "If there is a useful program that we might undertake in the South," he has recently declared, "would it not be towards the greater unity of the varieties of Southern Protestantism, with the ultimate aim the full unity of all Christians?"

Tate's newest poem has been appearing by installments in various magazines, and one awaits with eagerness its publication in full. The poem has a strong and obvious narrative level, which in the two portions thus far in print concerns the poet's childhood. The first section, "The Maimed Man," published in the *Partisan Review,* tells of a boy who is confronted with the corpse of a man with the head severed from the body. Another, entitled "The Swimmers" and published in *Hudson Review,* describes five youths out swimming in a creek:

> Bill Eaton, Charlie Watson, "Nigger" Layne
> The doctor's son, Harry Dueslér who played
> The flute; Tate, with the water on his brain.

But the narrative style is deceptively easy; and one looks with expectation for clues to something else—because that "something that stands for something else" is always present in a Tate poem, too. So that one notices in "The Swimmers" that the five youths encounter a posse searching for a lynched Negro, and that twelve men are in the posse, but only eleven men ride back:

> eleven same
> Jesus Christers unmembered and unmade,
> Whose corpse had died again in dirty shame.

And as the youths watch the sheriff, the leader of the posse, with the corpse,

> A single horseman came at a fast lope
> And pulled up at the hanged man's horny feet;
> The sheriff noosed the feet, the other end
> The stranger tied to his pommel in a neat
> Slip-knot. I saw the Negro's body bend
> And straighten, as a fish-line cast transverse
> Yields to the current that it must subtend.
> The sheriff's God-damn was a facile curse
> Not for the dead but for the blinding dust
> That boxed the cortege in a cloudy hearse
> And dragged it towards our town.

Then one remembers the story of the Crucifixion, in *John,* and of the burial of Christ's body by Joseph and Nicodemus, and it suddenly becomes clear that Tate is not just telling about five Southern boys who see a lynched Negro; the Passion is being reenacted. One recalls the lines in the first section, "The Maimed Man," which serve to preface the poem:

> Teach me to fast
> And pray, that I may know the motes that tease
> Skittering sunbeams are dead shells at last.
> Then, timeless muse, reverse my time; unfreeze
> All that I was in your congenial heat . . .

It would seem, then, that Tate is prepared in his new poem to look at his childhood again, and perhaps all his life, through the eye of his adult religious faith, and that what we shall get is a poem in which each day the Passion is reenacted for the modern man, in everything he does, all around him. One realizes, too, that the rhyme scheme of Tate's poem is that of the *Divine Comedy.* The poet seems to be reliving his past—the South, his boyhood there—against the perspective of the eternal, and equating his childhood reactions to evil, in all the innocence of boyhood, with his mature attitudes:

O fountain, bosom source undying-dead
Replenish me the spring of love and fear
And give me back the eye that looked and fled
When a thrush idling in the tulip tree
Unwound the cold dream of the copperhead.

The serpent again—the passage of time, evil, the lynching—is awakened from its sleep by an act of beauty; the child sees and flees, recognizing evil without pretense, rationalization, or callousness to it. The poet asks that now, with the strength and purposiveness given him by his belief in God, he be permitted to see things whole again, not with the untried innocence of childhood but in the experience of the adult who has been living in time.

Twenty-three years ago Allen Tate called for the South to "re-establish a private, self-contained, and essentially spiritual life." For longer than that he has been advocating a spiritual outlook which will provide a unity against chaos, a discipline of religious values against the nihilist threat of new dark ages. "As I look back upon my own verse, written over more than twenty-five years," he declared recently, "I see plainly that its main theme is man suffering from unbelief; and I cannot for a moment suppose that this man is some other than myself." During this time he has widened his scope and interests to include his nation and his civilization, without for a moment ceasing to speak to and for his native region. His poetry, his criticism, and his other writings have all mirrored his times. That he now addresses the whole of Christendom hardly makes what he has to say any less relevant for the South. For it was the South that taught him how to say these things in prose, and in his poems embody them.

ROBERT WOOSTER STALLMAN

The Poetry Of John Peale Bishop

He who would do good to another
Must do it in minute particulars
—*Minute Particulars*

I

Paul Valéry, remarking on Poe's far reaching influence (from Baudelaire to Valéry himself), contends that the surest criterion of the value of poetic genius is a long descent of prolific influence, not the production of masterpieces. As late as 1936, T. S. Eliot was rejecting Milton on the grounds that "Milton's poetry could *only* be an influence for the worse, upon any poet whatever." Reversing this stand in his recent British Academy lecture, Eliot no longer impugns Milton on grounds of influence: "The only relation in which the question of influence good and bad is significant, is the relation to the immediate future." As T. Sturge Moore first pointed out (in the *Criterion*, 1926), Valéry's notion of influence is a scientific or historical standard but not an aesthetic one. The question we should ask of any poet is: what are the masterpieces he has produced? Not influence, but achievement in terms of achieved poems should be the basis of critical assessment.

The problem of influence in terms of what the poet has borrowed from other poets is raised by Bishop's poetry more than by any other poetry of our time. Bishop's poetry is the collective catch-all of the chief fashions which his age made current. His derivations and echoes, as other critics have pointed out,[1] constitute a catalogue of contem-

---

[1] The following checklist of writings on Bishop's poetry supplements "John Peale Bishop: A Checklist," which J. Max Patrick and I compiled for *The Princeton University Library Chronicle,* 7 (Feb., 1946), 62-79. The PULC checklist provides a full bibliographical account of Bishop's books; his contributions to anthologies; poems, essays, short stories, editorial comments, and reviews appearing in periodicals. (It does not include writings on Bishop.) The starred items represent essays or reviews containing critical discussion of the poems and cataloguing some of the influences on

porary poets:—Pound, Eliot, Yeats, Tate, MacLeish, Cummings, W. C. Williams, Wallace Stevens, Paul Valéry; even perhaps Edith Sitwell and Hart Crane.[2] Pound and Eliot predominate in *Now With His*

Bishop's poetry, echoes from his contemporaries.

Christian Gauss in *Princeton Alumni Weekly*, 18 (Apr. 17, 1918), 608-609; Gilbert Seldes, *Dial*; 73 (Nov., 1922), 574-578; R. Holden, *New Republic*, 33 (Feb. 14, 1923), 329; Horace Gregory*, NYHT-*Books*, Dec. 10, 1933, p. 8; in NYTBR, Dec. 17, 1933, p. 9; R. P. Blackmur*, *American Mercury*, 31 (Feb., 1934), 244-246; Eda Lou Walton*, *Nation*, 138 (Feb. 7, 1934), 162-163; Allen Tate, *New Republic*, 78 (Feb. 21, 1934), 52-53; R. P. Warren, *Poetry*, 43 (Mar., 1934), 342-346; R. P. Warren, *American Review*, 3 (Apr., 1934), 22-28; Babette Deutsch, *Virginia Quarterly Review*, 10 (April, 1934), 298-302; Allen Tate*, *Southern Review*, 1 (Autumn, 1935), 357-364 (reprinted in *Reactionary Essays*, 1936); T. C. Wilson*, NYHT-*Books*, Mar. 15, 1936, p. 23; R. E. F. Larsson, *New Republic*, 87 (June 10, 1936), 138; John Holmes, *Virginia Quarterly Review*, 12 (April, 1936), 288-295; H. G. Leach, *Forum*, 96 (Aug., 1936), 96; F. C. Flint*, *Southern Review*, 1 (Winter, 1936), 650-672; Conrad Aiken*, *New Republic*, 102 (Apr. 22, 1940), 540-541; Louise Bogan, *New Yorker*, 17 (Mar. 1, 1941), 57; M. D. Zabel*, *Nation*, 152 (Apr. 12, 1941), 447-448; Lloyd Frankenberg, *NYHT-*Books*, Apr. 13, 1941, p. 4; Dudley Fitts, *Saturday Review of Literature*, 24 (Apr. 26, 1941), 13; Thomas Howells, *Poetry*, 58 (May, 1941), 96-99; in *Booklist*, 37 (May 1, 1941), 404; in *Bookmark*, 2 (May, 1941), 7; Conrad Aiken*, *New Republic*, 104 (June 16, 1941), 830-832; John L. Sweeney, *Yale Review*, 30 (June, 1941), 817-822; Ben Bellitt, *Virginia Quarterly Review*, 17 (Summer, 1941), 460-465; R. P. Blackmur*, *Southern Review*, 7, (Summer, 1941), 187-213; W. R. Moses, *Accent*, 1 (Summer, 1941), 250; Babette Deutsch*, *Decision*, 2 (Aug., 1941), 59-61; in *Springfield Republican*, Dec. 28, 1941, p. 7e; Peter Munro Jack, *NYTBR, Jan. 4, 1942, p. 5; Harry Brown, *Vice Versa*, 1 (Jan., 1942), 69-72; Cleanth Brooks, *Kenyon Review*, 4 (Spring, 1942), 242-247; B. Alsterlund, *Wilson Library Bulletin*, 18 (Feb., 1944), 424 (biographical sketch); Christian Gauss, *Princeton University Library Chronicle*, 5 (Feb., 1944), 41-50; R. W. Stallman, *Western Review*, 11 (Autumn, 1946), 4-19; Joseph Frank, *Sewanee Review*, 55 (Winter, 1947), 71-107; Allen Tate, *Western Review*, 12 (Winter, 1948), 67-71 (memoir, reprinted in *Collected Poems*, 1948, pp. xi-xvi); F. C. Flint, *Kenyon Review*, 11 (Winter, 1949), 165-171; Stanley Edgar Hyman*, *Accent*, 9 (Winter, 1949), 102-113.

The Collected Poems of John Peale Bishop, edited with a Preface and a Personal Memoir by Allen Tate, and *The Collected Essays*, edited by Edmund Wilson, were published in 1948 by Charles Scribner's Sons. A notable tribute to Bishop is Tate's poem *Seasons of the Soul*, in *The Winter Sea* (1945).

I wish to acknowledge the kind permission of Charles Scribner's Sons to reproduce a number of Bishop's poems in this essay. They are reprinted from *The Collected Poems of John Peale Bishop*; copyright 1917, 1922, 1948.

Portions of this essay are reprinted from "The Poetry of John Peale Bishop," which appeared in *The Western Review*, 11 (1946), and from *The Explicator* (1946), by permission of the Editors. The present essay considerably extends my earlier version and represents almost a complete revision of it.

[2] The above list of influences is not exhaustive. The points of reference between Bishop and F. Scott Fitzgerald, for instance, are considerable enough to justify a rather lengthy note, particularly between Bishop's poetry and *The Great Gatsby*.

Love (1933), Yeats and Tate more especially in *Minute Particulars* (1935). While the influence of Eliot and Pound diminishes in the later poems, that of Yeats persists beyond *Selected Poems* (1941). (For instance: *Ghoul's Wharf,* which is Yeats-like in form and seems likely to have had Yeats' *What Then?* as model.) What Oscar Wilde says of Mrs. Cheveley in *An Ideal Husband* applies to many of Bishop's poems: "A work of art, on the whole, but showing the influence of too many schools."

In tracing a poet's sources we chronicle his poetic development, but the critical question is whether the derived convention, idiom or tone, has been transformed so that what has been borrowed is now integrated anew. It is not without symbolic significance that the name he gave to his place on a stretch of salt-marsh at Cape Cod was "Sea Change." (Cf. "Full Fathom Five" in *The Tempest.*) Bishop succeeded again and again in transforming his borrowings, transforming them not necessarily into "something rich and strange," but into something that survives as his own. The paradox of his "originality" is illustrated, for one example, by *Young Men Dead*:

> Bernard Peyton is dead
> It is thirteen years:
> Son of a decayed house
> He might have made his roof
> Less contumelious
> Had there been time enough
> Before they buried his bed;
> Now it is thirteen years
> At seventeen years old.
> And Mooch of the bull-red
> Hair who had so many dears
> Enjoyed to the core
> And Newlin who hadn't one
> To answer his shy desire
> Are blanketed in the mould
> Dead in the long war.
> And I who have most reason
> Remember them only when the sun
> Is at his dullest season.
>
> (In *Now With His Love,* 1933)

"Only the best of Yeats" (to quote Tate) is better than this.

The worst that can be said of derivative writing is that it is an admission of failure in self-discovery. "My imitation of other poets," Bishop admits, "is in part a desire not to be myself." Mr. Ransom once remarked to me, though not in reference to Bishop's poetry, that a poet ought not permit himself more than two or three voices, three at most. Bishop expresses himself by over a half-dozen; and his style, even when it is not a borrowed idiom, is impersonal and neutral, as neutral as the style of Robert Bridges. His poetry lacks the signature of a personal idiom, an identifying voice or tone.

The Gregory-Zaturenska *History of American Poetry* scorches Bishop with the easy verdict that his *Selected Poems* "could be used as a textbook illustrating changes in poetic taste from 1916 to 1940— and no single poem, no matter how polished it may have seemed at first reading, has the distinction of an individually formed taste and imagination." But this criticism is rather unjust and requires some qualification. Bishop readapted current techniques, but he readapted them from their originals, employing the same attitudes (to paraphrase Warren) from which these techniques were developed. What Bishop wrote of Edna St. Vincent Millay applies equally to his own poetry: "Many of her images seem to come to her from other poets; actually she has taken them out of the public domain and by long familiarity made them her own" (*Collected Essays,* 1948, page 325).

Edmund Wilson's prejudiced notion that Bishop's poetry evidences "the finest poetic instrument that we have had in the United States since Pound and Eliot" (in *We Moderns*) can scarcely be taken literally. For a "poetic instrument" means, for one thing, an original idiom or style. The individuality that Bishop attained he attained only at rare intervals. Frost is often dull, but there is no mistaking his speech for another's. In MacLeish of the *Conquistadors* the identifying idiom is a mechanical mannerism of syntax and voice; in Cummings, a forced eccentricity of typography and prosody; the signature of Ransom is unmistakable—his witty, ironic tone. Originality, as Frost defines it, "consists in wagging the mind in one's art differently." Of course a style of unmistakable identity produces as many bad poems as it does good poems—in Cummings, for example. The critical determinant is not solely originality.

Bishop's concessions to modernity spoil no small number of hi
poems, yet there remain two groups of about a dozen poems each
(1) the poems in which these influences have been successfully trans
formed, reintegrated into structural wholes; and (2) the poem
which show no traces of influence and are entirely Bishop's own. A
third group consists of his translations; notably his renderings from
the French of two Rimbaud sonnets and his superb translations from
the Greek anthology—*To A Swallow* and *Epitaph,* which have been
rated the best translations of these poems ever written.

Bishop studied and absorbed into his poetry practically the whole
range of Western literature and art: Greek and Latin, French, Brit
ish and American. Music he knew intimately, and painting he knew
from first-hand practice. The influence of painting upon his poetry
and critical writings is seen in such poems as *Riviera* and in *Still Life
Carrots. Ballet* imitates Giorgio de Chirico, and *Fiametta* the Fiametta
of Boccaccio. *Perspectives Are Precipices* is the poem as a Dali paint
ing. His concern with painting in relationship to literature is found
in such critical pieces as "The Passion of Pablo Picasso," "The In
fanta's Ribbon," and "Poetry and Painting." This last is especially
interesting in relation to his poem *Paolo Uccello's Battle Horses.* A
for his literary echoes, they extend beyond his contemporaries to
Chaucer and Wyatt; Shakespeare and Elizabethan dramatists; Jonson
Donne, and Dryden; Blake, Shelley, Emily Dickinson, Dante Gabriel
Rossetti, Swinburne, and Ernest Dowson. Emily Dickinson is de
liberately echoed in *A Subject of Sea Change:* "Death greets us with
out civilities." Rossetti and Keats appear in *And When the Net Wa
Unwound Venus Was Found Ravelled With Mars,* a poem tha
imitates chiefly the manner of Pound: "In black silk her bosom
seemed / Taking flight for heaven in heaviest breath." Frost himseI
might have written:

> You'd think that he would cause a shock
> The scorpion with his double cock,
> Both sides erect, but not at all.
> The scorpion is a liberal.
>
> One thrusts to right, one sticks to left
> As he advances toward the cleft
> And then presents in copulation
> The New Republic of the Nation.

(This poem, untitled except by its first line, was first published in the *Collected Poems,* 1948.) Though Bishop did not care much for Frost's poetry, the influence of Frost is noticeable in Bishop's landscape poems such as *Moving Landscape With Rain. The Dream,* posthumously published in 1945, is done somewhat in the manner of Mark Van Doren. And *A Spare Quilt,* having perhaps its model in the poems of Mark Van Doren, can be read as in effect a criticism by Bishop of his New England fellow craftsman.

II

Bishop's poetic output (approximately one hundred and twenty-five poems, the same in volume as Yvor Winters's) is slight by comparison with the fecundity of Frost or Mark Van Doren. It would be absurd to label a poet "minor" on that account. A "major" poet is not a major poet by virtue of his bulky output. Frost and Van Doren are certainly bulky, but not at their best. The labels "minor" and "major" defy definition (Eliot's attempts notwithstanding), but if the perfections of poets were weighed one against another the critic would have a more accurate measurement of poetic stature than now prevails. It takes no pair of scales to decide that Bishop is a minor poet, yet his achieved poems surprise in number. Very few poets, however bulky their output, produce more than a dozen first-rate poems. There is a distinction to be made, of course, between poems that are perfectly contrived wholes and poems that are triumphs. Triumphs occur only now and then.

Bishop's elected best are *The Return* and *Perspectives are Precipices.* From *Now With His Love* (1933) I would also single out *Speaking of Poetry, Young Men Dead, Fiametta, Behavior of the Sun,* and *This Dim and Ptolemaic Man.* From *Minute Particulars* (1935) I would single out as best *Southern Pines, An Interlude, A Recollection, Your Chase Had a Beast in View, A Frieze,* and possibly *Apparition.* From *Selected Poems: The "Yankee Trader,"* perhaps also *John Donne's Statue* and *The Statue of Shadow,* but superior to all these is *Colloquy With A King-Crab.* The less said about Bishop's first volume, *Green Fruit* (1917) the better. And the same holds true for most of his uncollected and unpublished early poems reproduced in *Collected Poems* (1948). The best of his uncollected later poems seem to me *The Submarine Bed, The Parallel, The Spare Quilt,* and

The Dream; of the unpublished later poems reproduced in *Collected Poems* the only one worth singling out is *"This Critic."* A formidable list indeed; not many poets do much better!

His poetry belongs to that classification which Hopkins designated as *Parnassian,* a derivative poetry or a poetry representing one stage in the evolution of a poetic style. In Bishop it is the style of the Symbolists, almost exclusively. The Metaphysicals influenced him scarcely at all; the one exception is *The Submarine Bed,* a late poem.

It is Eliot rather than Donne that Bishop leans upon in *John Donne's Statue:*

> Proud Donne was one did not believe
> In heirs presumptive to a bone . . .

In style Bishop inclines more to Jonson or Dryden than to Donne. Dryden, whom Eliot taught us to admire, models at least one passage from this same poem:

> Proud Donne was one did not believe
> In heirs presumptive to a bone
> Or boys' pursuit of love, their leave
> To sensual oblivion.
> Come dying then! Too fine a joy
> And too intrinsic for a boy:
> Sustain that ecstasy in stone!

The Submarine Bed is metaphysical *and* symbolic. His other poems dealing with lovers or with women are, however, simply imagistic—not witty in tone, not ironical but purely sensual. The sensual characterizes Bishop's poetry almost as much as Keats' or Marlowe's: musically patterned, visually plastic, concrete and richly connotative.

A Recollection, one of Bishop's perfections, epitomizes the primary defining quality of Bishop's poetry as a whole—its tactile quality. Here is the craftsmanship of a master:

> Famously she descended, her red hair
> Unbound and bronzed by sea-reflections, caught
> Crinkled with sea-pearls. The fine slender taut
> Knees that let down her feet upon the air,

Young breasts, slim flanks and golden quarries were
Odder than when the young distraught •
Unknown Venetian, painting her portrait, thought
He'd not imagined what he painted there,

And I too commerced with that golden cloud:
Lipped her delicious hands and had my ease
Faring fantastically, perversely proud.

All loveliness demands our courtesies.
Since she was dead I praised her as I could
Silently, among the Barberini bees.

The woman is remembered as she was in life, that is, before "the young distraught / Unknown Venetian" painted her portrait. The opening stanzas of the sonnet depict her also as she is in the painting, transposed here on the fresco with the intensity and impact of life itself. Perhaps no such woman existed and the painter but "thought / He'd not imagined what he'd painted there." Where does beauty exist—in fact or in imagination? It was perhaps that very question that caused the painter to be "distraught." Has the painter reproduced the beauty he knew in the flesh or solely the beauty he imagined? Like the painter, the poet too has "commerced with that golden cloud:"—that perfection of beauty which all men seek.

His poem is a painting, but like the fresco the poem is far more than merely a faithful rendering of the original. Art, far from being no more than an imitation of reality, is an imaginative recreation possessing a life all its own. Neither the poet nor the painter has been merely copyistic. The poem implies questions about the relationship of life to art. Its fluid syntax functions to impart an ambiguity of time past and present, the one melting into the other, and simultaneously an ambiguity between fact and fiction. The ambiguity is thematic.

"Commerced" prepares for the final phrase—"the Barberini bees," by which the recollection of the poet returns him from the realms of "golden cloud" to the noisy world of fact:

Since she was dead I praised her as I could
Silently, among the Barberini bees.

"Since she was dead" transfers to the poet's vision, which is extinguished as his poem glides back to the noisy world of actuality signalized by "the Barberini bees." This vision dies away, but yet the world to which he is returned by "Barberini bees" is not without its beauty too, for the very phrase is beautiful in itself. The painter fulfilled his vision in the painting, and the poet in his poem. He is furthermore compensated by an enrichment of manner, thought, and speech—his life and ours are thus enriched. It is permissable to make one further inference: the poet, like the painter, was "distraught" during the process of composition.

In technique Bishop belongs to his own age, but in his endorsement of passionate flesh he harks back to Shakespeare's *Antony and Cleopatra,* Marlowe's *Hero and Leander,* the Elizabethan love-lyric, and Wyatt's *They Flee From Me:*

> I was the first to nakedness. Suddenly she
> Left her dress and her feet were on the floor.

This is from *And When the Net Was Unwound Venus Was Found Ravelled With Mars,* a poem about a soldier's momentary "Farewell to Arms" in time of war. (Another piece suggesting Hemingway is *In the Dordogne:* "the leaves fell / And were blown away; the young men rotted / Under the shadow of the tower.") Whereas the lovers in *The Submarine Bed* are troubled by a sense of guilt arising from their union, in *Metamorphosis* the lovers are unashamed:

> There was no shame in that
> Consuming nakedness
> For we were one; and a disparate
> Skin is love's own dress.
> But our division of air
> Was burned between ecstasies.

In *The Spare Quilt,* obversely, the lovers—frigid New Englanders—lack all passion. Poems "realistically" depicting the sex-act are rather scarce. In modern poetry among the best in this kind are Yeats' *Leda and the Swan* and W. R. Rodgers's *The Net* (in *Botteghe Oscure,* VIII); but both of these poems are symbolic as well as realistic, and Yeats' *Leda and the Swan* is also mythical. The love lyrics of E. E. Cummings, like the lewd poems of Rochester, are witty; they differ from Bishop's poems also in their lack of realistic delineation of object or act. In Bishop's *Les Balcons Qui Rêvent,* for instance:

> The lovers sleep, their dreams increased
> By shudders from the night before.
>
> His breath upon his parted lips,
> Sleeping he flows into her sleep.
> Her belly slumbers, but the tips
> of both dusk breasts are bright awake.

Here the lovers are discovered at dawn; in *Speaking of Poetry* the lovers—Desdemona and the Moor—"meet, naked, at dead of night," while "the torches deaden at the bedroom door." *October Tragedy*—another "bitter tale of love / And violations on a summer night"—vulgarly describes "The unwilling struggle and the willing fall." Bishop's realism descends to vulgarity again in *Metamorphosis of M* (Margaret, his wife), in *And When the Net Was Unwound,* and in *Venus Anadyomene.* In *To Helen,* a poem which echoes Pound, the motto used is from Tourneur's *Atheist Tragedie:* "I salute you in the spirit of copulation." That motto applies equally to almost a dozen Bishop poems. Tupping is their subject, the disrobing of the mistress, the caressed body. Bishop's love poems share with a painter the predilection for naked flesh. Their unabashed sensuality seems almost unprecedented in American poetry. Bishop, unlike Auden and Whitman, does not exploit love *as* a doctine. What he celebrates is the experience of love; not a doctrine of love, but an act of love in the sensual moment now. In his affirmation of passion one is reminded of Blake. It is from Blake that Bishop took the title of *Minute Particulars:*

> He who would do good to another
> Must do it in minute particulars.

And from Chaucer he took the title of *Now With His Love:*

> What is this world? What asketh man to have?
> Now with his love, now in his colde grave
> Allone, with-outen any companye.

The love-and-war poems of *Now With His Love,* as Joseph Frank observes, remind us irresistibly "of the early Hemingway, also obsessed with death, also seeking for a source of positive value in naked sensuous experience."

III

"The aim of all the arts," Bishop states in his essay *The Discipline of Poetry,* "is to present the conflict of man with time ... . And the famous release which the arts afford is essentially a release from time." Triumphs over time! But how shall the artist achieve them? How fix the flux of temporal experience, which is without form, into formed structures of meaning? Didacticism is not the answer. "The poem comes inevitably to its end, but the poet does not reach a logical conclusion." Almost without exception, the poems attempting to reach "a logical conclusion" fail—*viz., Hunger and Thirst, Counsel of Grief, Trinity of Crime, The Tree,* and *The Saint.* (My opinion here runs counter to that of M. D. Zabel, who listed these last three poems, in 1941, as among Bishop's best.) These poems substitute statement for symbol, and I think they fail by their didactic resolution of theme.

Bishop is at his best in the poems that *discover* their own theme, their own form, rather than in the poems that directly state their theme. He is a technician of the first order (as Louise Bogan remarked), "incapable of falling into any mawkishness or sentimentality."[3] On the other hand, he is capable of falling into banality (as in *And When the Net was Unwound*), vulgarity (as in *October Tragedy*), and downright bad taste, as in *Epithalamium.* The instance Warren singles out, where Bishop's taste fails him flagrantly, is the ending of the *Ode:*

> But he is dead,
> Christ is dead. And in a grave
> Dark as a sightless skull He lies
> And of His bones are charnels made,

Bishop's poetry of statement—the finest pure statement poem being *Young Men Dead*—is not the pure poetry of statement found

---

[3] In the *New Yorker* for March 1, 1941. Bishop is not mentioned in Miss Bogan's *Achievement in American Poetry,* 1951.

in Dryden or in certain poems of the later Yeats. The difference is that Bishop's poetry of statement incorporates also symbolism, as in *A Defense.* His poetry is mainly a poetry of obliquity, and it is in poems oblique in meaning that he scores his major successes.

Almost none of his poems, not even brief lyrics like *Green Centuries* or *Colloquy in a Garden,* delivers its meaning at once. And each poem poses a new technical problem and attempts to solve it anew—not by formula. As his critical essays testify, Bishop was preoccupied with problems of form and methods of achieving formal structures. In "Aphorisms and Notes" he writes: "A poem has unity of form when, after arousing in the reader a desire to have something happen (in the poem), it satisfies that desire in such a way that the reader is surprised but not resentful." Here Bishop is not exactly original. His definition derives from Kenneth Burke's *Counter-Statement* and reads like a paraphrase. Important is the definition appearing in "Poetry and Painting:"—"The ultimate question concerning any work of art is out of how deep a life does it come. But the question that must first be asked is whether it has a life of its own. And the life of art is in its form."

The problem of form Bishop mastered in a significant number of perfectly executed poems, and it is this primary and all-saving virtue of structural achievement that counters and largely cancels Bishop's censorable defects of eclecticism and anonymity. His poetry and criticism, as Hyman says, are substantially of a piece, each reinforcing the other.

Bishop's characteristic structure is a two-part structure of contrasted symbols: the first part being a landscape, portrait, or action by which the theme is initiated, and the second part a symbolic or mythical image contriving the resolution of theme. It is where the second part is symbolic that Bishop's poems are more likely to succeed, whether they begin in statement or in symbol. *Your Chase Had a Beast in View,* for example, pictures the hunting of leopards, whose slaughter makes the exultant hunter "A moment young." The literal situation, the hunt, described in the first part is transposed in the final stanza into symbolic significance:

> Only in singing it might be
> Supported by the sense alone,

One syllable of ecstasy
Confusing shame, confounding bone.

The slaughter of the beasts is an event of no duration *until* that
event is recreated into art-form, where alone the actual event becomes justified. Among the hunters: "The youngest sang a stranger
love." It is his singing that redeems the slaughter. The youngest
hunter is, as it were, the poet whose poetic rendering of the bestial
contest is the saving thing that makes "sense" of the senseless conquest of the hunted by the hunters. ("At times it seemed they hunted us.") The triumph of art over time is signified also in *A Frieze,*
while *Speaking of Poetry* and *Colloquy With a King-Crab* symbolize
the methods by which such triumphs are attained.

Speaking of Poetry provides the answer: Some mythos, some
ceremony or ritual of meaning must be found. This poem, which itself achieves its own prescribed dictum, uses the form-symbols of
Othello and Desdemona for the opposition of Life and Art. Set down
in ironic contrast, Life is huge and foreign and barbarous, emotionally
crude; Art is restrained and delicate, sophisticated and artistocratic.
Unions of no spiritual value may deceive the Senator (the critic) or
"outwit his disapproval; honest Iago / Can manage that: it is not
enough." Life and Art, Emotion and Intellect, how shall they be
aesthetically united?

O, it is not enough
That they should meet, naked at dead of night
In a small inn on a dark canal.

They must be wed in magnificent architectures, structures rich with
the forms of convention, rich in myth and fable. They must be clothed
in textures rich with the symbols of tradition. Their union must be
a ritual of timeless imagination, *traditional in ceremony* with antiqui-
ties of language strange—symbolic and strange "with never before
heard music." Poetry is neither naked emotion nor naked intellect
but the perfect fusion of the two. Didacticism—in Tate's canon too
that is the poet's greatest evil—will not suffice.

Procurers
Less expert than Iago can arrange as much.

The Ceremony must be found
Traditional, with all its symbols
Ancient as the metaphors in dreams;
Strange, with never before heard music; continuous
Until the torches deaden at the bedroom door.

There the music ends: in the union of Emotion and Intellect.

The best artist is the one who constructs his poems in such a way as to admit of no interpretation but the one intended, the intended meaning being determined by evidence of the poem itself. Bishop's poems are not readily exhaustible in meaning and in no instance are they incoherent at their core, ambiguous or obscure in their dominant intention. Much of the so-called Obscurity in Modern Poetry exists, I believe, chiefly in critical discussions about it. *Speaking of Poetry* leaves room for variant readings of its minute particulars, and the same may be said of Bishop's most difficult poem, *Colloquy With a King-Crab,* but the overall intention of both poems can scarcely be disputed. The Desdemona needlework of Bishop in *Speaking of Poetry,* for all "the subtlety of the stitches," is clearly enough speaking primarily about poetry. Other allegories are not authorized by this one. The present brief reading by no means exhausts the poem. The marriage ceremony in *Speaking of Poetry* symbolizes, to add Joseph Frank's reading, tradition; but only a Marxian critic would be inclined to force a reduction of the poem to a sociological tract.

IV

The difficulty of being a poet without a mythos troubles Bishop not only in *Speaking of Poetry* but again in *Behavior of the Sun. Behavior of the Sun* is Bishop's lament, as artist, for the loss of myth in our scientific civilization. In *O Let Not Virtue Seek* the sunward-soaring aviator, Icarus, represents the triumph of science over time and space, science and myth being equated and their "triumphs" obliquely compared. Identical imagery and symbolism recur throughout Bishop's poetry. The dominant imagery is of cloud, wind, sun and shadow, sand and sea. An overlapping of theme likewise links poem to poem. The theme is obversely treated in *This Dim and Ptolemaic Man:*

For forty years, for forty-one,

Sparing the profits of the sun,
This farmer piled his meagre hoard
To buy at last a rattly Ford.

Now crouched on a scared smile he feels
Motion spurt beneath his heels,
Rheumatically intent shifts gears,
Unloosing joints of rustic years.

Morning light obscures the stars,
He swerves avoiding other cars,
Wheels with the road, does not discern
He eastward goes at every turn.

Nor how his aged limbs are hurled
Through all the motions of the world,
How wild past farms, past ricks, past trees,
He perishes toward Hercules.

Modern man has misused "the profits of the sun" and sacrificed himself for the god Science, whose token is that rattly contrivance of our cheap tin age, the Ford.[4] In the motion he feels "spurt beneath his heels," the farmer—like Icarus—seems to possess power over time and space. But his power is an illusion. And science, for all its Herculean labors to conquer nature, can no more triumph over space than Hercules could do so over time. Death *was* his match. The poet's reduction of Copernican man to Ptolemaic man and again of Science to the Gates of Hercules points to his cynicism:—the one myth is no more valid than the other.

Myth provides the poet with forms of meaning amidst a world confronting him as meaningless or without absolute spiritual values. *A Divine Nativity* and *The Saints* attempt to establish, by a sensual mingling of Greek and Christian myths, an integration of values, but they fail (I think) in their rendering of the supernatural. These poems are attempts to reinstate a set of beliefs in which the poet himself does not believe. Neither Bishop nor Tate commits himself to the Christian legend. It is by Greek myth rather than by Christian myth that Bishop measures his disbelieving world. Science has stripped the modern world of the possibility for belief, of the possibility for imaginative belief in myth, and it has discredited art as but itself a

---

[4] The Ford of the 1920's, that is; not certainly the modern Ford!

form of myth. Bishop's position squares with the defense of Myths made by I. A. Richards: "Without his mythologies man is only a cruel animal without a soul . . . a congeries of possibilities without order and aim" (In *Coleridge on the Imagination*). Bishop's major theme is the loss of myth, the loss of belief, the loss of traditional values public and private.

In *Behavior of the Sun*, as in *Colloquy With a King-Crab*, the fascination of what's difficult is at its pithiest.

The artist, as if to insist upon the validity of his own aesthetic viewpoint, ironically discourses on science in terms of pictures. He embodies his theme in visual images—"the sunlight came in flashes." (We are blinded too much by the light of scrutinizing reason.) Instead of presenting a rational argument, the artist contrarily presents a poem—a piece of symbolism.

The same symbolism of sun and shadow, and with similar meaning, reappears in *Perspectives Are Precipices* and in *The Mothers*, and here again the theme is the loss of myth. And the tone is similarly one of despair: "After revolt, what triumph and what deaths?" The mothers, older myths whose heritage of religous beliefs our age of science denies, appear, distant and improbable as "vast shadows on the rocks." "And in their eyes are myths conceived." But shadows have no credible substance, no truth of existence; and "We are their sons."

> Over their eyelids, in ethereal bronze
> Deploy, Icarus! For among their rocks
> Are depths where a man might drown.

The sons of these mothers are Icarian sons, Icarus figuring as the new generation of modern science. In personifying our scientific age in the mythical personage of Icarus the poet employs irony, inasmuch as our present-day faith in science is but another myth—the modern myth. "Our course is, I think, nearer to the sun." But as our course is "nearer to the sun," so too is our destiny an Icarian one.

V

The poems in Part VIII of *Selected Poems*—including *The Saints*, *Trinity of Crime*, *Divine Nativity*, and *The Tree*—are the result of Bishop's experiment "to make more and more statements, without giving up all that we have gained from Rimbaud." None of them seems to me successful wholes. *The Saints* is quite as much a "poetry of the will" (Tate's term) as anything of Shelley, at least in this portion:

> Dilate
> Our loves beyond
> All loves that age
> Or lust consumes,
> O thirst and rage
> For the lost kingdoms!

Bishop is at his best where he is, like Keats, a painting poet. Many of his very best poems are poems *as* paintings. His perfection in this kind is *Perspectives Are Precipices:*

> Sister Anne, Sister Anne,
> Do you see anybody coming?
>
> I see a distance of black yews
> Long as the history of the Jews
>
> I see a road sunned with white sand
> Wide plains surrounding silence. And
>
> Far off, a broken colonnade
> That overthrows the sun in shade.
>
> Sister Anne, Sister Anne,
> Do you see nobody coming?
>
> A man
> Upon that road a man who goes
> Dragging a shadow by its toes.
>
> Diminishing he goes, head bare
> Of any covering even hair.
>
> A pitcher depending from one hand
> Goes mouth down. And dry is sand.
>
> Sister Anne, Sister Anne,
> What do you see?
>
> His dwindling stride. And he seems blind
> Or worse to the prone man behind.

> *Sister Anne! Sister Anne!*
>
> I see a road. Beyond nowhere
> Defined by cirrus and blue air.
>
> I saw a man but he is gone
> His shadow gone into the sun.

This is the Dali desert of Eliot's *Waste Land*. Both poems, like MacLeish's *You Andrew Marvell,* convert time into space-images. In his essay on "Poetry and Painting" Bishop cites, as an example of a poem situated in space, that passage of *The Waste Land* which begins:

> Here is no water but only rock
> Rock and no water and the sandy road

Bishop points out that "the dry rocks and the sandy road winding toward the mountain where there is still no water are but symbols of a spiritual drought, due to the disappearance of faith in the truth of Christianity, which is itself a disaster of time." These perceptions transpose into an explication of Bishop's own Dali painting. Here the symbols of that spiritual drought are the dry sand and the dry pitcher (replacing the rock in Eliot's landscape). Sister Anne's perspective of history is a perspective of broken colonnades (cultures and beliefs destroyed by the anti-religious attitude) and of a road—once the road of religious faith, now the road of scientific reason—down which man and his civilizations disappear. "Beyond nowhere" is Sister Anne's single image of hope and consolation. The road of scientific reason ends ultimately in realms of the supernatural. Yet her image defines a vacuum: The world of faith is as empty as the world of reason is desolate. Hence Sister Anne's discourse echoes with doubt (*"Do you see nobody coming?"*), of despair (*"What do you see?"*), and of fear (*"Sister Anne! Sister Anne!"*). Questioner and Answerer personify the theme of the poem, and its dialogue form is thus determined. Ironically, it is Science (or Reason) questioning; it is Religion (or Faith) answering. Bishop is using here the French fairy tale of Bluebeard (as Hyman has noted). Though the poem and the fairy tale do not bear point for point relationship, the fact of discrepancies in their literal situation does not constitute, it seems to me, necessarily a flaw in the poem. As in *Behavior of the Sun,* the poet discourses in pictures, in images rather than in statements. Tate, in his essay on Bishop (reprinted in *On the Limits of Poetry*), points out that the plastic method of the poem, its method of concretion, is violated by the Metaphysical wit of "long as the history of the Jews," but that blemish is a minor one. Except for this instance of Metaphysical wit, the poem is wholly an aesthetic discourse in terms of pictures, as distinguished from a scientific discourse in terms of statements.

Bishop's *Perspectives Are Precipices* is Eliot's Waste Land in miniature. The temporal is converted into images of space not only in these poems but also in Eliot's Sweeney *Among the Nightingales* and in MacLeish's *You, Andrew Marvell*. Keats' sonnet, *On First Looking Into Chapman's Homer,* presents two consecutive images of space to define simultaneously a single moment. The time-span symbolized by the space-images in Bishop's *Perspectives* is extended from Keats' moment to Spengler's history of man. The consecutive images of space in *Perspectives* occur successively and not, as they would in a Dali painting, simultaneously. They define a disaster of time, present-past-future: Man's present spiritual drought (the pitcher is its emblem) is the resultant disaster of his tragic past ("a distance of black yews") and images his future wasteland in the present one. *The Statue of Shadow* repeats the symbolism of *Perspectives,* expressing the same mood of fear and the same theme of history as the lengthened shadow of man.

The Return, as Bishop himself explains, is a simile with one term of the comparison omitted. The two-part structure of the poem unites fact and myth. As the form of Roman civilization was destroyed by that materialism which created it, so the form of modern civilization is threatened by the same sea of materialism. Though the poem is about the loss of form, it is (to quote Cleanth Brooks) "perfectly 'formed' itself—even the fluid grammar is functioning as 'form' in terms of the poem." The temples of the seagod become the sea itself. "Form is overwhelmed . . . The movement of the invading sea dominates the rhythm of the stanza, overwhelms the syntax."

Time as fate pitted against man, his art and his civilizations— that is Bishop's commonplace, the obsessive motif of whole poems or of their particulars. Except in *Riviera,* where the sea manifests space, the time-motif is symbolized by the sea. *Beyond Connecticut, Beyond the Sea,* in which poem Bishop catalogues his forbears, opens and closes upon the sea-symbol—the same as in *Farewell to Many Cities*. The sequence of ancestral images is thus framed in circle-form. The sea is the emblem most frequently manipulated into an expanding or a contracting spatial image (as in "Vast cities of Atlantis discovered in a skull"); it is chiefly by this device that Bishop achieves his effects of painting.

The problem of the poet centers in his choice of theme and the appropriate symbols by which to form it. This is the problem-theme of *Colloquy With A King-Crab* and *Speaking of Poetry*. In *Colloquy With a King-Crab* the poet finds his symbols in nature. Will the horseshoe crab suffice as symbol "To say what I have sought?" The answer, which constitutes one of the obliquities of the poem, is probed out of the crab-symbol phrase by phrase, line by line. There is a second obliquity in the deftly indirect comparison of the crab with the poet. Each derives from the sea of time past. But observe their differences: "This crab is no abstraction"—"His head all belly and his sword all tail, / But to the imagination is suspect. / Reject him? Why?" Well, the poet is a complex of head and heart, one part of him *abstract*, one part *concrete;* his senses reject all abstractions, and his mind suspects all sense-perceptions. As for the crab, he is "no abstraction." But he is the symbol of an abstraction. The crab thus represents these two aspects of art and philosophy: the concrete and the abstract. *That* precisely is "To say what I have sought." For the poet the major problem of his art is to establish and evoke relationships between imagery and theme, between the concrete and the abstract.

VI

"There was not one of the great Symbolist poets," writes Bishop in reviewing Mark Van Doren's poetry, "who might not have declared, as the last of them did, that his aim was to write of his race and reality." This is also Bishop's aim: not to escape from life but to report on his world, to explore, as the Symbolists did before him, the effects of a decayed civilization on modern sensibility. The province of his vision is not an imaginary Shropshire or Celtic twilightland but a reality of time past and present, the province of his vision extending across seas of historic generations from Virginia and Connecticut to Troy and Rome. The predicament of modern civilization arises from the glorification of the scientific vision at the expense of the aesthetic vision. The resultant disruption of sensibility is the problem-theme underlying much of the poetry of Bishop and the Southern poets.

Bishop is a Southern poet[5] by regional and personal ties with Ransom, Tate, and Warren, but more fundamentally by affinities in his later poems with their moral and traditional problems—the issues of our scientific civilization with its industrial economy. His closest affinity is with Tate. They are alike in their search for a historic religion, in their inquiry into the metaphysics of time and space and the nature of the *elan vital,* in their perspectives of history—time-past juxtaposed with time-present under contexts of mythological and historical symbols— and in their personal definitions of the relationship of the artist to his society and to his forbears. The influence of Tate upon Bishop's *Minute Particulars* is chiefly the influence of this philosophical bias. Again, Bishop is a Southern poet by virtue of his Southern heritage (prior to the Civil War), even as he is a New England poet by virtue of his New England residence. But though he shared Connecticut with Mark Van Doren, he has not made New England his poetic property as Van Doren has done. Nor is he "a Southern regionalist" (as one reviewer labels him). Both his Southern lyrics (only "Apparition" is specifically localized) and his New England lyrics (Part IV of the *Selected Poems*) transcend their regional material to unite with other poems on the same theme: the loss of tradition.

Another Acteon presents the personal plight of Bishop as the

---

[5] Bishop was born in Charles Town, West Virginia, on May 21, 1892; he died on April 4, 1944. At Princeton he was the editor of the Lit, the class poet, and the colleague of Scott Fitzgerald and Edmund Wilson. In 1917, during his senior year at Princeton, he published a volume of verse, *Green Fruit;* after the war, in which he served as First Lieutenant in the Infantry, he became managing editor of *Vanity Fair.* He is described in the character of Tom D'Invilliers in Scott Fitzgerald's *This Side of Paradise* (1920). With Edmund Wilson he published *The Undertaker's Garland* (1922), a collection of sketches and poems. It was not until 1930, however, that his poetry and literary criticism began to appear in the major critical journals. He published two books of Southern fiction: *Many Thousands Gone* (1931) and *Act of Darkness* (1935). From 1922 to 1933 he and his wife lived in France, and upon returning to America in 1933 he settled first at Westport, Connecticut, and then at South Harwich on Cape Cod, producing then the poems about his ancestors—as in *Beyond Connecticut, Beyond the Sea.* In the *Princeton University Library Chronicle* for February, 1944, Christian Gauss has provided a portrait of Bishop during his Princeton days.

exiled poet returning from a sterile Europe to begin his apprenticeship with domestic traditions, Southern and New England. This
poem is an apt occasion for critical judgment in terms of Eliot's criterion of the Objective Correlative. The predicaments of Acteon and
the poet do not provide an adequate solution for the emotion expressed by the poet in his plight. That solution (the meaning of his
personal plight) is located, not in *Another Acteon,* but in com-
panion-poems which answer the questions here asked and upon which
our full understanding of this poem depends. *The Ancestors* reiterates
the same mood of self-questioning fear and objectifies in a single
expanded image the reason for that fear. Again, the plight of *Another
Acteon* is restated in the less oblique *Return to Connecticut.* What
the poet seeks is sustenance in his ancestral land; but his quest ends
in disillusionment. The reason for his disillusionment is located in
Moving Landscape With Falling Rain, or again in *Conquest of the
Wind.* Time-past is severed from time-present.

Time, *The Burning Wheel,* is personified in the poem by that
name in Aeneas and Anchises. As before in flight from disastrous
Troy, Aeneas on his shoulders bore Anchises, so

> They, too, the stalwart conquerors of space
> Each on his shoulders wore a wise delirium
> Of memory and age: ghostly embrace
> Of fathers slanted toward a western tomb.

Each cycle of civilization bears on its back the death of its former
triumphs, each repeating cycle ending in oblivion. The modern
Aeneases, pioneers who conquered the West to found new Romes,
"They saw the west, a sky of falling flame". The always pioneering
course of mankind toward the West, symbolically, is toward the land
of the dead (so the West was identified by the classical poets). The
plight of Aeneas, in *The Burning Wheel,* fleeing from old worlds
lost to new worlds unconquered, is also the plight of *Another Acteon.*

In *The Yankee Trader,* the question of *Another Acteon* ("What
do I ask for?") is again answered, here by the symbol of an old
abandoned sofa. The sofa represents the Puritan tradition of New
England: faded in pattern, worn-out in form, abandoned. The sofa-
symbol speaks for those values enduring in all patterns, all forms, all
traditions. Their loss is the burden of the poem.

What has gone out of New England, since Emily Dickinson defined it in "The Missing All," is the soul sufficient to itself, whose loss Bishop sets down in his essay of that title, and again in his poem *The Spare Quilt.* Sterile even in Emily's day, Puritanism (the New England Idea, which to the post-war writers of Bishop's generation was the enemy) no longer nurtures the artist.

What history has made of the South is epitomized in the acid etching *Southern Pines.* (*Collapse of Time* develops the same theme, the loss of tradition, and echoes in images of fear the devastated landscape of *Southern Pines.*) *Southern Pines* echoes no other poet. Masefield's *Cargoes* has a similar structural ordering inasmuch as each stanza frames a portrait of an age, the progression defining by contrast a decline. In both poems the method is symbolic. Obliquities of symbol unite with theme: the loss of cultural and spiritual values. Here is the history of our spiritual degeneration:

> White pine, yellow pine
> The first man fearing the forest
> Felled trees, afraid of shadow,
> His own shade in the shadow of pinewoods.
>
> Slash pine, loblolly,
> The second man wore tarheels,
> Slashed pine, gashed pine,
> The silent land changed to a sea-charge.
>
> Short leaf, long leaf,
> The third man had aching pockets.
> Mill town, lumber mill,
> And buzzards sailed the piney barrens.
>
> Cut pine, burnt pine,
> The fourth man's eyes burned in starvation.
> Bone-back cattle, razor-back hogs
> Achieve the seedlings, end the pinewoods.

"Achieve" keynotes the irony. Stripped of spiritual values, without traditions (those pines to shadow him), man thirsts in starvation. But he no longer has a heart to ache, only "aching pockets." His spiritual death, announced by the starved hogs who alone remain to achieve for him the final devastation, is foretold by the buzzards sailing "the piney barrens." What man has destroyed is his belief in a world of values outside himself ("the first man fearing the forest") and his belief in a world of values within ("afraid of shadow, / His own shade"). What the hogs, symbolizing four generations of progress, achieve is the ultimate triumph of civilization over culture: the destruction of Southern tradition and of her hopes of spiritual growth. They "end the pinewoods." All shadow of belief is gone. Those pines, the symbol of man's source of spiritual beauty and power, once towered over man and held him in awe. That awe—his respect for a power beyond himself—is connoted in the silent "f" alliteration of lines 2-3. The silent land of "white pine" (the beauty of the forest) becomes a noisy land—"changed to a sea-charge"— by the noisy vowels in the harsher refrain of "Slashed pine, gashed pine" (the ugliness of the forest). Stripped of pines, the forest is again silent in the "l's" of "Short leaf, long leaf" and of "Mill town, lumber town." The silence, which was first broken by the "s" alliteration (lines 3-8), is replaced by the noise of "buzzards" sailing "the piney barrens," and by the "b" alliteration and repeated harsh vowels in the last stanza. Together with the refrain on "pines," these four key consonants carry the burden of the poem, define its shifts of moods, and link the four parts. Twice this refrain is broken (lines 11 and 15), the breaking of this pattern emphasizing the two intended symbols of opposition (mills and hogs) to the symbolic pines.

RICHMOND C. BEATTY

Donald Davidson as Fugitive-Agrarian

The term Fugitive-Agrarian refers to two kinds of widely divergent literary activities which have been identified with Vanderbilt University in recent years. Of the sixteen members of the group who published a little magazine called the *Fugitive* (1922-25), only four were associated with the Agrarian movement of the 1930's. The others proved indifferent or hostile to it; they became bankers, scholars, insurance executives, and the like. Those whose work tended to give to the phrase "Fugitive-Agrarian" a kind of surface but misleading identity were John Crowe Ransom, Donald Davidson, Allen Tate, and Robert Penn Warren. They were the only writers who contributed both to the *Fugitive* and to the first agrarian symposium, *I'll Take My Stand,* which appeared in 1930.

Though in common agreement about the problems which faced them—whether aesthetic or economic—these men approached the specific issues involved as individualists. Nobody actually "approved" another's poem or essay, despite the fact that an atmosphere of alert and frank "give and take" was evident throughout the period of their personal association. The reason that this atmosphere could exist at all was due, I think, to a phenomenon increasingly rare in our time, namely that they were men who belonged to an essentially common background. They understood the language of one another, and by *language* I mean the primary ways in which we think about Religion, the people with whom we live, and about the relation of the individual to the state. In other words, the atmosphere which these gifted young writers found prevalent at their university was homogeneous, not heterogeneous. They did not, for example, write in wry amazement to their parents back home when they heard a student say "Yes Ma'am" to an older lady, saw him remove his hat when any lady

entered an elevator, or bounce out of his seat and bow slightly
when he noticed any person considerably older than himself standing
up in a street car. No ice had to be broken on questions of fundamental good breeding, which is perhaps the first and simplest way
through which people come to comprehend one another.

As poets and as artists generally their inclinations and practice
differed to such an extent that the results are, on the surface, all but
untraceable to a basic origin. The poetry of Ransom, Tate, Warren,
and Davidson is so divergent in manner as to cause one to speculate
about the question of how they ever came to an agreement about anything. I offer only the tentative suggestion already indicated, but
with a demurrer that ought to be registered at every opportunity. It
is directed against such a statement as the following in the generally
rewarding *Literature of the American People* (Appleton, Century,
Crofts, 1951: Editors A. H. Quinn, Kenneth Murdock, Clarence
Gohdes, G. F. Whicher). Of Donald Davidson Professor Whicher
remarks: "He is the spokesman of the region."

A generalization of this nature is very, very bad indeed! It may
suggest the melancholy limitations of all literary histories. Spokesman? Maybe Senator Kefauver or Senator Byrd is the South's spokesman, or William Faulkner, or maybe, again—and doubtless—nobody
at all. The South is a jungle, as is every other articulate region that
has individuals willing to study themselves in terms of ther way of
thinking about life. The present essay is about certain writings of
Mr. Davidson in prose and poetry which tend to define his own attitude regarding the human predicament. Probably nobody would
grant Mr. Davidson's remarks an absolute, dogmatic acceptance. I
would reply to the critic who would cavalierly dismiss them, however,
in the words of Shakespeare's Touchstone: "Then shepherd, thou
art damned!"

The works of Mr. Davidson are of a piece and evoke a problem
in every instance—the problem of belief. A man extremely fertile in
ideas, he is rare among Southern authors in having been able to contemplate experience from a settled and definable point of view; he
has kept his sensibility undissociated in this, perhaps the most dis-
tracted of all eras since the collapse of the Roman Empire. He has
achieved this success at the cost of many repudiations, for value
after value which the society of our own time has come to esteem or

despairingly to accept he has submitted to searching examination. Always the examination has been made in the light of an attitude that is traditional to the author, who might be characterized as a highly intelligent and gifted Southerner, one who knows and cherishes his personal and cultural past, his country's history, and the intentions of the men who established its constitution.

It follows, of course, that Mr. Davidson has written about many anti-traditional tendencies in our society in unsparing terms. General attention to his criticism was first established through his "The Weekly Review: A Page About Books," which appeared in the Nashville *Tennessean,* the Knoxville *Journal,* and the Memphis *Commercial Appeal* (1927-1930). One of the twelve authors of *I'll Take My Stand,* he became also a frequent contributor to the *American Review* (1933-1937). The best statement of the views which preoccupied him at that time may be found in the *Attack on Leviathan* (1938). What he had to say in this work about such subjects as History, Sociology, Regionalism, the Northeast, Education, and Literature is fundamental to an understanding of his poetry.

Here, to begin with, is a comment in support of his conviction that "the towers of New York are built upon Southern and Western backs."

> The Southern planter or farmer (and not only the Southern one!) gullied and exhausted his lands, sold his timber, held his tenants pinned with a dollar mark, not because he was a limb of Satan but because money has to be forthcoming—and that quickly—for shoes and hats from tariff-protected factories; money for farm machinery, kerosene, gasoline, fertilizer, cooking-stoves, knives, axes, automobiles, all financed and produced under the imperial scheme; money for mortgages and loans, to placate the sucking tentacle-tip of the money octopus flung far to seize him; money for taxes to run schools on the new model furnished by the Northeast—and, yes, indirectly to swell the endowment of Teachers College of Columbia University and keeps its well-marshalled hosts employed; money for more taxes for still more public improvements—new roads, new courthouses (with steel filing cabinets) and new bureaus upon bureaus; money for interest on the national debt, covered by bonds gilt-edged, good as gold, offering Hamiltonian

conveniences to banks and security-venders; money for the new Northeastern idea of insurance, to hedge him against the liabilities and calamities forced upon him by the system and to bury him when, lifeless, moneyless, and propertyless, he delivers his soul to his Maker and his body to a mortician who is one of the highly valued members of the Chamber of Commerce. For all the while, prodigious and faithful though his labor may have been, the money for these things came to him in a niggardly trickle, if at all, but it poured Northeast in flood. The South has learned this lesson well. And now the West may learn it, too—may know that the West goes in shoddy that the Northeast may walk in silk and satin . . . The extent to which both West and South are owned, controlled, and exploited by the Northeast is set forth in detail by Walter Prescott Webb in *Divided We Stand,* which was published late in 1937 after this book went to press. The "North," Webb says—implying the Northeast plus the "border states" of the Middle West—owns or controls about $80 out of every $100 in the nation. The West and the South, in Webb's picture, are little more than the hired hands of the dominant section, which maintains control through government-protected corporations, the tariff, patent monopolies, and the credit system.

This economic dominance has been accompanied by an equally sinister cultural interpretation of the South:

The legend, thus renewed under peculiar circumstances, of the barbarism of the South, especially in its southwestern parts, and of the vulgarity and dullness of the Middle West, for a good many years has governed the approach of the metropolitan East to the phenomena of life in the so-called hinterland. Whether the approach be literary, or sociological, or merely journalistic, the assumptions have been always the same, and the ensuing generalizations have been uniformly tagged with shocked protest and pious exhortation. The South—so the tale runs—is a region full of little else but lynchings, shootings, chain-gangs, poor whites, Ku Kluxers, hookworm, pellagra, and a few decayed patricians whose chief intent is to deprive the uncontaminated, spiritual-singing Negro of his life and liberty. But what is more shocking, it is inhabited by believers in God, who pass anti-evolution laws; and more shocking still, it is in thought and deed studiously backward and anti-progressive. The Middle West—the tale says—is a land of morons, boobs, and shoulder-smacking Babbitts, in which despite a plethora of schools and modern conveniences, an artist's soul feels cramped and misunderstood; or a land of lonely farms where men and women drudge away their sterile lives; or of repressions and shams, where tender little Clyde Griffiths's who start out as bell-boys must perforce end up as murderers. Over such pictures the East stormed, or shed crocodile tears, in the clever nineteen-twenties.

On the subject of Sociology, Mr. Davidson has written most sharply in a later essay:

> For better or worse, the sociologist has become the chief expert consultant on the Negro problem, at least to that part of the American public which believes that the problem can be solved by legislative means. The reasoning of this public can be briefly stated as follows: The cause of the problem is race prejudice, which is a kind of social disease afflicting white folks, especially in the South; the sociologist is a kind of doctor, who isolates and describes the disease, and then designates remedy and treatment; apply remedy and treatment through Federal legislation, and you have the cure.
>
> The good sociologist may stand aghast at this highly simplified version of his large and serious studies. I think he ought to stand aghast, but I wish it to be understood that, in what I am about to say, I intend no disrespect to sociological study as such, but rather would offer admiration. It would be a pleasure to distinquish between good sociologists and bad ones if the occasion invited that. But here it is the abuse of sociology that raises the question, and there is also the corollary question of whether there is some defect in the method of sociological study that renders it susceptible of abuse, particularly in such a difficult matter as the Negro problem. At any rate the pressure of contemporary issues has dragged the whole question into the public forum. It is certain that hardly any proposals relating to the Negro

problem are now made that do not originate, or claim to originate in sociological interpretations. The sociologists, some quite unwillingly, others with obvious unction and high hope, have inherited the leadership formerly held by William Lloyd Garrison, Wendell Phillips, Charles Sumner, Thad Stevens and Company.

It is the indifference of sociologists to history that disturbs the author. The conditions under which Negroes were brought to this country they rarely consider, a fact which implies an anti-traditional approach to the whole complex question. All too often these men are tempted to turn reformers and to advocate special programs or panaceas with little regard for the established moves and inertia of the people they would reeducate. Theirs thus becomes a program of violence—"education to cure 'ignorance' and 'prejudice'; factories to cure poverty; and more and bigger laws, bureaus, and governments to do away with social 'injustice.'"

Such men are at heart in league with the Southern movement of Liberalism whose early post-Civil War exponents were Henry Grady and Walter Hines Page. The older Southern tradition was rotten and behind-the-times, these men argued, and ought to be replaced by the brisk and modern concepts of the victorious section. Mr. Davidson has little use for their proposals:

> It was ignorance, no doubt, that made Page assume that the modern program of universal compulsory education was identical with Jefferson's old scheme of selective education. It was something more than ignorance that made him assume that the Southern notions of life, good up to 1850, needed only to be swapped off for the opposing northern notions, if the New Jerusalem were to be entered. In retrospect, the incompleteness of Page's program makes his rashness appear the more shocking. It was bad enough to imagine that an importation of industrialism, plus a modern school system, was enough to make the South a paradise; but it was shallow foolhardiness to jeer at the three "ghosts" of the Confederacy, of Negro domination, of religious orthodoxy, without stopping to ask whether those three phenomena, that lay at the heart of all Southern problems, could wisely and safely be hooted out of existence.

About the present-day advocates of this point of view he is equally outspoken:

> The Southern liberals of the new school (Gerald John-
> son, Virginius P. Dabney, and other followers of Grady and
> Page), no doubt innocently enough, have furnished the
> screen. They entered upon Southern history at approximately
> the same moment that the Bourbons made the decision to be-
> come industrialists. The defection of the Bourbons had in
> it at least the excuse of self-preservation. Bereft of their
> lands and ruined by war, they were persuaded to think that
> industrialism offered a way out. For the first time, their eyes
> were opened to "natural resources" that meant dividends and
> bank accounts. But the liberals, with no such excuse, were at-
> tracted to the cultural by-products and social devices which
> seemed to go along with the Northern model of civilization.
> The South suddenly looked shabby to them, and the North
> glittered. So they surrendered, and their surrender was far
> more abject than that of the planter-industrialists, some of
> whom secretly hoped to revenge themselves on the Yankees
> by a financial flank attack. For the surrender of the liberals,
> made, it seems, without a quiver of concern as to the virtue
> of the institutions they were abandoning, was a surrender of
> the spirit, a recantation made by converts to a new religion.
> Perhaps they were tired of all the old talk about the war.
> Their fatigue, if it was such, had important results. At or
> about 1900, when the liberals began to break up, the real
> conquest of the South by the North got under way.

On the subject of Education, Mr. Davidson has cited the findings of the sociologists themselves when they perform in their proper role, which is descriptive. Only a complex statement, he writes, can make clear the extent of the educational deficiencies and burdens involved in this problem:

> On top of the extra expense of its bi-racial school sys-
> tem, the South has the largest proportion of children of
> school age to the total population alongside the smallest in-
> come and wealth with which to educate them. Thus the
> burden of supporting schools on a property tax in a poor
> state with a large ratio of children may be more than ten

times as heavy as for a rich state with fewer children. Some figures will make the situation plain. Mississippi, with about 47 per cent of its population of school age in 1930, had 23.5 per cent of its population in school. Its per capita net income in 1929 was $32; its total expenditures per capita for schools in 1927-28 were $9.04; of all its income it spent four per cent on schools. New York, with about 34 per cent of its population of school age, had 19 per cent of its total population in school; had $506 per capita net income; spent $23.86 per capita of its total expenditures, or 2.11 per cent of its total income.

To this melancholy contrast we might add a bit of interpretation by Rupert Vance: "For Mississippi to attain the national average in expenditures for educating her school children would require 99.3 per cent of all the present tax monies of the state."

The average annual teacher's salary in Georgia is reckoned at $546 as compared with California's $2,337.

These reminders are aside from the author's view that a fundamental misdirection took place when the traditional academic curriculum lost its struggle against the Social and Natural Sciences in American colleges and universities. Temporizing courses of study were substituted for basic courses, on the theory that the former type would equip the individual in a more immediate sense for his place in modern society. Mr. Davidson's view seems to be that a fundamental discipline in basic subjects would make one competent of function naturally in *any* society, present or future. Always, by prevailing modern standards, the gains are accompanied by corresponding losses:

Education is only one example of how the means used by industrialism to gain its ends results in perverting the ends. The high standard of living uplifted the masses at great cost to their humanity and self-respect. The mountain boy could get a college education, but the system that built him a school also took out of his mouth the traditional ballad that was his ancient heritage, and instead of a ballad gave him a 'mammy song' devised in Tin Pan Alley by the urbanized descendant of a Russian Jew. Meanwhile, the system, working through another specialized department, recorded the ballad and stowed it away on the shelf of a library to be studied and annotated, as the artifact of a lost culture, by men who would never sing it. To the country boy, newly become a mill-hand, the system gave more money than he had ever seen; but organized capital and labor told him how to spend it. The new women, advancing into pursuits denied her grandmother, gained a profession or job; but she lost her right to become a mother. The farmer got an automobile; but he lost his home.

All the tendencies which have been indicated in the above remarks may be said to represent elements in our society which are hostile to the kind of world Mr. Davidson is able spiritually to accept. He favors an interpretation of human life in biological, rather than in mechanistic terms, in terms that, while granting Economics its importance, would deny its primacy in human affairs. This is the basis of the agrarian quarrel with the philosophy of industrialism, which positively and without fail, he adds, has elevated "the economic motive to the first place in its hierarchy of human values." More specifically it defined his distrust of the Roosevelt administration. "Every important bill passed by Congress since March, 1933, has had a caption written on it in invisible ink: THIS MEANS MONEY!! And all Americans, whether friends or opponents of the administration, have been able instantly to read that invisible ink. Mr. Roosevelt in very truth has taken from the rich and given to the poor, but he has not done so for sweet charity's sake—nor in order to make rich or poor free or noble. He has done so that economic imbalance may be rectified, that depression or recession may be checked, that consumers may have money to keep producers producing and the unearned increment increasing."

And what about the Southern writer—especially the poet?

A young poet 'emerging' in the South today is in danger of following one of two courses, both of which are bad. In one case he will utterly divorce himself from all sense of locality and at once begin to write clever but trifling imitations of decadent poetasters in New York, London, and Paris. But, if he is safely illiterate, and so manages to escape the infection of our times, he may then write 'Southern' poetry containing very proper local references; and this is sure to be as empty as the other was clever. One tendency gives us modernists of every type—people who begin by grandly renouncing their birthright and by contributing to wooly Messiah magazines of the *Blues* or *Contempo* variety. The other tendency begets local laureates: cheerful infants who commit monstrosities such as state songs on the model of Katherine Lee Bates' "America the Beautiful." This happens too often not to be emphasized as a phenomenon of our times. It can be traced out in a considerable scale in such an anthology as Mr. Addison Hibbard's *The Lyric South*. It appears, though to a less horrifying degree, in the work of some of our best poets. It almost amounts to this: that a poet cannot be 'Southern' without behaving like a fool; and if he tries not to be a fool, he will not be recognizably 'Southern.'

It is this overall external compulsion which Mr. Davidson would have the Southern artist resist. He should be able to accept a tradition consonant with his social and historical background. "One ought to be able to say of it [the South] as 'A. E.' said of Ireland, that it is a good field for the arts, especially for poetry, simply because. in contrast to progressive America, it has long been defeated and poor and behind the times; or, furthermore, because it offers its people belief rather than doubt, conviction rather than skepticism, loyalty rather than distrust."

The problem here adumbrated is heavily involved, but when analyzed it may be said to reduce itself to the following question: Does the acceptance of Mr. Davidson's attitude limit the sensibility of the poet who, if he is a modern, will find himself unable to escape studying the work of his contemporaries—work which will almost inevitably affect his own performances? Moreover, what of the audience which such a deliberately delimited poet would undertake to reach, since that audience has also been corrupted through reading the "decadent poetasters of New York, London and Paris"? An examination of Mr. Davidson's own interesting poetry is perhaps the most reasonable means of approaching an answer to such questions.

An Outland Piper appeared in 1924, *The Tall Men* in 1927, and *Lee in the Mountains and Other Poems*—which might be thought of as Mr. Davidson's "Selected Poems" to this date—was published in

1938 and reissued by Scribners in 1950. *The Tall Men* is included in this book, though in revised form: some two hundred lines of the first version are omitted.

It remains, nonetheless, by long odds his most ambitious work, one which reflects the effort of a contemporary mind to integrate itself with its own personal past and with the past of the early Tennessee settlers, the tall men. In addition, it is a commentary on the present, in terms of the past, rendered by turns autobiographically, dramatically, and lyrically. The poem is also in certain passages satiric, and the validity of its structures on the artistic generation that flourished during the 1920's reads with undiminished conviction today, now that we are able to contemplate that generation in the light of a certain perspective. Broadly speaking it is epic in its intention, although the impersonal point of view usually associated with this form is interrupted from time to time by characteristic subjective intrusions:

> It was a hunter's tale that rolled like wind
> Across the mountains once, and the tall men came
> Whose words were bullets. They, by the Tennessee
> > waters,
> Talked with their rifles bluntly and sang to the hills
> With a whet of axes . . .
> Their palisades were pitched
> In the Cumberland hills. They brought their teeming
> > wives
> To rock the hickory cradles and to mold
> Bullets for words that said: 'Give way Red Man
> You have lived long enough . . .'

And the tall men actually speak in this poetry—Andrew Jackson, David Crockett, John Sevier, and whole panorama is opened for the reader to see and to believe in. "But where are they, where are Shelby and Campbell, where is Cosby" now, Sevier wants to know, just as Andrew Jackson wants to know "What makes men live but honor?" These are "the words of ghosts," the poet acknowledges. "I was not there, at Talladega, Horseshoe Bend, Kings Mountain . . . in days when men were tall . . . I have not sung old songs or danced old tunes. I have read a book."

"I have read a book." The words define the chasmic difference between the poet's present and his traditional past, the past of old men "who creep to the sun in the winter of a time that heeds them not."

> Yes, this is the Battery Lane,
> So they say. The Battle of Nashville was fought
> Somewhere around here. I suppose there's a tablet.
> We won't go back to look.

The disseverance is complete, so complete that when a child asks the Wordsworthean question

> *Where was I before I was born?*

the poet can only answer

> O questioning son of man, *I do not know*
> *Where you are now after you are born*

Out of this past do "hants" come back? They do in Mr. Davidson's poetry and speak "Right out on de porch out loud." And this brings one to the Negro problem in a passage unmistakable in meaning:

> Black man, when you and I were young together,
> We knew each other's hearts. Though I am no longer
> A child, and you perhaps unfortunately
> Are no longer a child, we still understand
> Better maybe than others. There is a wall
> Between us, anciently erected. Once
> It might have been crossed, men say. But now I cannot
> Forget that I was master, and you can hardly
> Forget that you were slave. We did not build
> The ancient wall, but there it painfully is.
> Let us not bruise our foreheads on the wall.

The section called "The Faring" is based upon the poet's experience in World War I. The grimness and misery of modern war are all there, but the humor is present also, along with the ever-present sense of racial history:

> Over the Viking road came the Viking blood

Eastward for battle, borne in the Angles' ship,
They who were Angles. They who were Vikings came
Back to Norman shores, with the Norman sinew
Strong for the oldtime faring, with Norman brow
And the Norman name, fused, molten, changed.
Saxon and Norman came to the elder land,
Jesting in casual tongue, having heard of deeds
Bruited somewhere in France or in Flanders fields . . .
                              Now they are going
Somewhere in France on roads where Roman eagles
Slanted to meet the Nervii or where
Napoleon, flushed with greetings, galloped from Elba
A hundred years before. The husky guns
Rumbled at twilight from the Western Front.
The slow column poured like moving bronze.
And something (call it civilization) struck
In the latest battle of nations, somewhere in France.

After victory speak the various voices of the living and the dead—a
Colonel and subordinate commissioned officers, a sergeant, a corporal,
a dead airman, an unknown soldier, and others. They speak in character throughout and give to this part of the poem a complex unity
and integrity. Then the protagonist, Lt. McCrory, somes home, to encounter the indifference of post-war America:

                              There were streets
Walled up with stony faces, averted eyes,
Garroting me with sneers—
                              Why, old ex-service
Nut, why what are you after now that the treaty
Ought to be signed but it's all messed up
                              and jobs . . .
She said, 'You'll have to buy an overcoat.'
I said, 'I've spent my money on railroad fare,
And Treaties of Peace and other perishable rot.
I guess I'll wear my army overcoat.'
He said, benignly posed like the annual convention
Of Y.M.C.A. Secretaries, 'Well, what are your
Qualifications?' I said, 'Qualifications?
In the army I learned the Impossibles.'

He said, 'We'll file your application.' I said,
'Thank you, sir,' and walked out buttoning tarnished
Buttons and swinging O.D. sleeves with a yellow V,
Meaning fodder for moths and spider-webs.

Faced with this ingratitude, the protagonist calls up the Devil for explanation, and the Devil as Ringmaster shows him a two-reel movie to which he provides a commentary. Reel One he terms "Disease of Modern Man." Here are the ways of life open to him:

This is Rupert of the House
Of Rupert, famed in history,
Pondering on his income tax,
Deducting genealogy.
Great-grandfather from a loophole
Potted Choctaws in the thicket;
Rupert, menaced by the Reds,
Scratches the Democratic ticket.
Rupert's mother, D.A.R.;
Rupert's father, U.C.V.;
Rupert, mounting in his car,
Zooms up to God in Rotary.
Grandma Rupert had ten children;
Rupert's father begot five.
All of Rupert's stocks and bonds
Are strained to keep one son alive.

One can mouth the dead slogans of Democracy, attend a church that advertises its services with posters, and read editorials chastizing the younger generation. But though Science is pushing back the utmost bars of space, men are shrinking up into specks. The protagonist terms these "intolerable pictures of death." He cannot bear them. "Is there no cure?" he asks. The Ringmaster reassures him, by proceeding to run the second reel, which presents various types of escapists.

First appears a Traveler, who has discovered magnificence and peace by looking to the roads:

So I have travelled,
Feasting on alien glory until I am
Myself no longer, but I have found my life.

He is followed by three expatriates. "Impossible country of bigots and warped schoolma'ams, I have left you forever," says the first. "In Paris a man may think . . . drink, talk, curse, carry a cane, wear spats, grow a moustache, and admire James Joyce without being charged with adultery." The solution of the second was equally simple:

> Until I visited Oxford I never knew
> What was wrong with me. Then I adopted
> The Oxford accent, and became a gentleman

The third discovered modern art:

> Dada is laughter, Picasso, Cezanne, Matisse
> Bring man back to his primitive clownish self,
> As I discovered in studying Negro sculpture . . .
> Black men, I am starving. Make me fertile.

These are followed by the "Satyr in a Tuxedo," who came to life in the "general scuffle / Of creed on creed"; by the "Bobbed-Hair Bacchante" who leaves the dance and drives with her lover *"jusqu'au bois"* and stays till dawn; and by the "intellectual," or academic scholar, who has repudiated his present world to lose himself among the fragmentary "Necrological beauties" of earlier times.

> "Stop the reel," shouts the protagonist:
> These negative freedoms burn
> Like rockets in my brain and then puff out
> With falling ashes. Here is no rest or peace.
> Beyond which, out of this nightmare world,
> There lie
> Green hills where moonlight falls on honest grass
> And honest men who sleep, or waking, speak
> The tongue I speak and love.

Two considerations about this unit of the poem should not be forgotten: The Ringmaster of the show was the Devil. The opportunities he revealed were rejected because the man to whom they were indicated preferred to live within the context of his own experience.

"The Breaking Mold," the section which follows, is a searching examination of the religious question, or attitude, insofar as it is accessible to a person with Mr. Davidson's presuppositions. In trying to understand his own personality, the writer once more attempts to think back into his furthest predictable racial inheritance, to the Seventh Century, and the time when, according to the Venerable Bede, King Aedwin was persuaded by Paulinus to accept Christianity. The pious Catholic was bringing a message about the primal sin of man, but with it came also the gentle Latin hymns and stories of unselfish saints. The twilight of the old Norse Gods was at hand; "The hammer of Thor was fallen forever, and Odin looked upon Asgard sadly. The Goths unbuckled the sword." Later he remembers Luther, the Reformation, Cromwell's victory over Charles I at Naseby Field, his people sailing to the New World, the Indian fights,

> And Samuel Doak, before King's Mountain, prayed
> To the ancient God of battles. Are these not blessed,
> The firm lips of mountain men who pray,
> Firm in search of God so many a year?

And then to him in person comes the Evangelist "in the blare of a cornet under a canvas tent," with borrowed piano, sweating choir, and the question "Brother, are you a Christian? Are you washed in the Blood?" He remembers what the atheling said to King Aedwin:

> 'O, King,' the atheling said, 'how the time of man
> Is like to a sparrow's flight from door to door
> Of a hall where men sit feasting, and fire is warm.
> From cold and darkness it comes. It is safe from
> Weather
> A moment only; then into the dim and outward
> Winter it flies again.

This unending cycle of nature described by the warrior is something the poet finds himself unable to forget and

> I said, this mortal plasm
> Living by process of all centuries
> Not yet has died. The seed is old as man . . .

> I who have had no beginning
> Know life only. Beyond, by either way,

Is god, whose answer has not come to men
But in the rumors of men.

For this poet is three men:

And one with pagan blood
Startles at dawn to find no sword at his side . . .

And he says in his teeth: Now who has bewildered me
A thousand years with a doctrine of strange tongues?

The second man of me is Methodist,
Who learned of a gentle mother the Ten Commandments
And read the Good Book through at the age of twelve

The third man was born to weigh the sun
And love the clean cool sureties of matter
What ever God is, this man does not guess.

Yet his is no scornful repudiation of the House of God. It is
simply a way of saying that human beings are greater than the houses
they build. "I seek the God who will not tame the manliness of men."

The Epithalamion with which *The Tall Men* proper concludes is
something rare in our day; it is a convincing love poem, done in stanzas
that echo those of Spenser on the same subject. Informing them is
the theme of paganism without sensuality which Mr. Davidson admires in his pre-Christian ancestors:

Our love
Is ours only—the old way of the world
That in itself completes itself and asks
No doctrine or memorial but its own

The frequently reprinted Epilogue, "Fire on Belmont Street," re-
emphasizes the problem of belief his writings are constantly inviting.
Some trivial bungalow, perhaps, is afire, but he discovers in it a
sweeping significance:

Why God has come alive
To damn you all, or else the smoke and soot
Have turned back to live coals again for shame

On this gray city, blinded, soiled, and kicked
By fat blind fools. The city's burning up?
Why, good! Then let her burn!

Or perhaps it would be better to arise and cry:

'Citizens, awake! Fire is upon you, fire
That will not rest, invisible fire that feeds
On your quick brains, your beds your homes,
                    your steeples,
Fire in your sons' veins and in your daughters',
Fire like a dream of Hell in all your world.
Rush out into the night, take nothing with you,
Only your naked selves, your naked hearts.
Fly from the wrath of fire to the hills
Where water is and the slow peace of time.'

Mr. Davidson's other poems in this volume are briefer but, in general, "relatively impersonal approaches" to the broad issues developed in *The Tall Men*. In "Lee in the Mountains" we have portrayed the picture of the great but defeated general, the president of an impoverished Virginia college—Lee the outlaw, no citizen of the United States, remembering how "those people came," violating his father's house. And what advice is this abused and respected man able to give the students in chapel?

Young men, the God of your fathers is a just
And merciful God Who in this blood once shed
On your green altars measures out all days,
And measures out the grace
Whereby alone we live;
And in His might He waits,
Brooding within the certitude of time,
To bring this lost forsaken valor
And the fierce faith undying
And the love quenchless
To flower among the hills to which we cleave,
To fruit upon the mountains whither we flee,
Never forsaking, never denying
His children and his children's children forever
Unto all generations of the faithful heart.

This is perhaps the most moving and eloquent passage in Mr. Davidson's poetry, and if it does not epitomize the essence of the older concept of Americanism, one is at a loss to describe it.

In "Sanctuary" and in a later poem "Hermitage," the emphasis
is still upon preserving one's ancestral tradition. "Salving our wounds,
from the moody kings we came," speaks the far-off sire of the latter
poem, who reminds his descendents, out of his knowledge of Europe,

"Lost continents ebb we have no power to save"

and concludes with a blessing and a curse

Peace be to all who keep the wilderness.
Cursed be the heir who lets the freehold pass.

And should the enemy of "Sanctuary" come—that invader whose ideas
and ways stem from the dying old world:

Go as your fathers went with woodsman's eyes
Uncursed, unflinching, studying only the path.
First, what you cannot carry, burn or hide.
Leave nothing here for him to take or eat.

The poem is a metaphorical expression of one of Mr. Davidson's
basic beliefs: the necessity of keeping free from outside contamination the culture which our forebears fled Europe in order to establish.

Mainly the other poems of this interesting book recount Civil
War stories such as the "Running of Streight," a fragment of the saga
of General Forrest, or the simple story of the "Deserter," a Christmas
Eclogue regarding the misunderstanding of the Confederate government—it could be *any* government, *any* abstract organization—in recording this word against a man who left camp overnight to see how
his people were getting along and to make some effort to protect them
against the invader. It is a poem fully understandable only by defeated peoples whose family allegiance is stronger than their devotion
to the idea of statehood. It is told in the language which Wordsworth
preferred but did not always use—the language of everyday life.
So it goes for a good many of the other selections in this part of the
volume. The alert modern, or modernized, reader will probably find

them tame, too colloquial, too unrelieved by the exciting contrasts of mood and diction which he has come to demand in contemporary poetry. In brief, it represents a kind of writing that is "provincial" in subject and character. But one should immediately add that in its overtones it is universal and that, in the judgment of the poet, every way of thinking about life is provincial, since it is limited necessarily by individual experience. (A novel tracing the tragic career of Dreiser's bellboy, with all its urban implications, is not—as Mr. Davidson has pointed out—the great American novel, for this country is in no sense completely urbanized.)

In suggesting the development Mr. Davidson's poetry has taken, it might be said that from the romantic, Blakean, and often successful qualities of the *Outland Piper* it has moved into a far more serious stage for a reason already indicated—namely that he prefers to write what in the deepest sense he believes about man's nature and place in society. Poetry is thus anything but a diversion or an escape for him. He is no experimentalist in metrics, nor is he particularly rewarding to the reader who is fond of arresting images. A certain rhetorical eloquence of speech (again like Wordsworth) is the substitute for these devices; he is most interesting when considered in terms of the total context of a given performance. Moreover, insofar as I know, he is unique in modern times in having made the effort Wordsworth undertook in his *Prelude,* which was to understand himself first, if he would later dedicate himself to a literary career. *The Tall Men* is the result of that undertaking, and its limitations are soon forgotten by anybody willing to think of the difficulties that would be involved were he to try to work them out in a similar fashion for himself.

To conclude with a brief comment on the position at which the utterances, or beliefs of this author arrive: He is certainly in the deepest sense a moralist, as Thoreau and Carlyle were moralists, and his characteristic subject matter is identical with theirs. His writings are, moreover, Christian in the fundamental sense that they recommend a drastic curtailment of emphasis upon economic values and in the further implied argument of Thoreau that men are unique and inviolable individuals whose integrity ought to be respected despite whatever institutions they have collectively evolved, either through church or state. To argue that, because of such thinking, he should be labelled a modern Jeremiah is in no sense to divorce him from the major secular prophets who have attempted to awaken Western Man to an understanding of his oldest question—What is my nature, what should I truly value, and what is my destiny?—a question which Mr. Davidson (again like Thoreau) has posed in terms of specifically contemporary issues. To add further that, so constituted, he belongs rightly in the Church is to compel the melancholy reply that the Church, being an institution, is by its nature too confined to contain him, in much the same sense that it was unable to contain Emerson.

JOHN EDWARD HARDY

The Achievement Of Cleanth Brooks

It is just to say that Cleanth Brooks has made more sense about more poems than any other American critic of our time. I think his being a Southerner, for one thing, has much to do with the kind of sense he makes; and I am coming to that later. But I want to emphasize that his peculiar virtue as a critic, as I see it, is his singular devotion to the poem, the one, unique, indivisible whole of the particular work.

And yet I would avoid implying that the achievement I am talking about is simply a large number of explications done, that the palm I am presenting here is only a kind of competitive trophy, that would have to be taken away should some still more tireless contender enter the field before the next accounting. I can testify, from the experience of my own work with him on Milton's shorter poems, our efforts to make the book a whole, that Brooks has a total perspective which has to be understood.

Mr. Brooks is original much more as reader than as theorist. He himself, perhaps a little too self-effacingly, stated in the introduction to *Modern Poetry and the Tradition* the ideological debt he owed to a number of critics. And surely the concluding chapters of *The Well-Wrought Urn* did little to change the nature of that debt, or of his awareness that it existed.

It is true also that he has consciously devoted himself to the education of a generation of readers. The education has been, even, much by formal means. Because in our age the audience for serious poetry, and so for serious criticism, at least in America, is largely a university audience, it is perhaps inevitable that any volume of strictly critical essays should have at least a tone of academic sobriety and urgency. I am not sure that Brooks's essays have this tone more noticeably than those of any non-teaching American critic. But Mr.

413

Brooks does make his living as a professor. A good half of his writing has been in text books, deliberately and directly tied to his professional concerns. The three *Understanding* anthologies have, indeed, been primarily effective, if not ultimately causative, in bringing about a pedagogical revolution.

In view especially of this, shall we say, cheerful, devotion of his to the duty of teaching—a devotion the measure of which can well be taken from the recent appearance of *Modern Rhetoric*: who else, except of course the equally astonishing Mr. Warren, would have thought of pausing in mid-career to address so many words, with such seriousness, probity, and profundity, so much laborious, kindly patience to exemplify and elaborate, to the forlorn purpose of making freshmen and sophomores articulate?—in view of this, Mr. Brooks might seem to have asked for final obscurity, for submergence in his cause. He might seem to have demanded no greater honor than recognition of his leadership in the movement to outlaw certain forms of professorial posing, hokum, and hanky-panky—a movement that has so far succeeded, in fact, that there is hardly an English professor in America now who, when he has finished telling his sophomores about Tennyson's hat or his graduate students how to translate a regnal date, will any longer dare to go into one of the classroom routines of "The man can write!" or "Gentlemen, I trust you are not blind to the beauties of this passage" that used to serve as criticism of the day's poem.

And if the textbooks, dedicated to creating a more critically responsible professoriate that it must be hoped will perpetuate itself, seem *calculated* to produce 'competition' for their authors, both in the classroom and in editors' and publishers' offices, I think the volumes of essays Mr. Brooks has published are, after all, hardly less likely to do so. To return to the point of his being primarily a reader —Mr. Brooks really has no theory of Poetry. He has a theory of the structure of poems, but that in effect is the same thing as a methodology. A systematic aesthetic theory has a certain sanctity, but a methodology is not inviolate. It invites, even demands, constant testing in practical application, and thereby risks reduction to the status of technique, available to everyone, and subject to facile, careless apprentice imitation of effects.

Monroe Spears, in his statement of policy upon assuming the editorship of the *Sewanee Review*, said that he felt we need a "consciously impure" criticism, something to relate literature to "the rest of man's concerns"—now that "the lesson [has been] learned, and we have plenty of critics able to do good formal analysis." Mr. Brooks made occasion to refer to these remarks in his reply to Douglas Bush's criticism of his essay on Marvell's Horatian Ode. (A distressing business. Poor poetry goes begging while her guardians stake their hard-earned intellectual fortunes on the turn of this criticism of criticism of criticism wheel. But perhaps Brooks is, at any rate, tempted less often than most into such improvidence). There was much truth and some legitimate hope, Brooks allowed, in what Mr. Spears had to say; but he added that he was not so sure, while Douglas Bush persists, that the lesson has been learned.

But it *is* true, as Spears says, that we have plenty of analysts. And what I have been trying to get at here is the significance of *that* fact for an assessment of Brooks's success in his educational cause.

While there is any confusion, and I think there is some, on just what the lesson is, the very increase of conversions might be looked upon as the greater cause for alarm. I would not entirely unsay what I have said, that a revolution has been accomplished, that it is well done, and that Mr. Brooks has preeminently defined its spirit and prosecuted its causes. But even at the risk of buying a clearer definition of his individuality only with an admission that his cause is not quite so well won as I might first have indicated, I think his position ought to be more carefully distinguished from some of its confused, apparent alliances. If Brooks is right in saying that he must still recognize the force of the open and intransigent opposition of such views as Mr. Bush's, and be extremely wary of submitting the dispute to the all too benevolent conciliation offices of the disinterested third power, Mr. Fiedler, I would suggest that there is at least as much to be feared from some of the latter day new critics who work in more or less apparent agreement with Brooks.

Taking the more apparent first, we do indeed have plenty of men, mostly young men in this class, who can do a competent, doctrinaire job of structural analysis on (almost) any given poem—men with a keen eye for patterns of recurrence in imagery, for balance and shifts of tone, for functional ambiguities of reference and syntax (a bit too keen here sometimes), and so on, men who are rigorously trained to avoid the fallacies, or heresies, of message-hunting, author's intention-hunting, direct emotional participation in the poem's subject experience, and the like. It is, to repeat, very often doctrinaire. A school has been formed, and so canons of taste, and so, further, a body of approved writings. Too often, the poem selected for analysis is, in fact, "given," not chosen. Only poems within fields, period or typological, previously staked out in published studies by the masters are available for consideration in any particular season. Similarly, the criticism of other modern schools, and still more, nineteenth century European criticism, against which the masters originally formulated their position, is simply neglected in the training of the followers. And the line of interpretation of the ancients is strictly defined. The philosophical basis of certain fundamental points of the doctrine—for example, the problem of distinction between form and substance—is something again with which the disciples are seldom concerned.

This is all overstated, and smacks somewhat deliberately of the irresponsibility in generalization of the Van Wyck Brooks kind of attack on the "new schoolmen." One point that ought to be made clear is that I have not used my own extended metaphor of the "school" with the idea that it reflects very accurately the real academic situation of any of the supposed "masters." In the actual schools, universities, in which these men *are* masters, I doubt that any such degenerate sectarianism has been directly fostered by their teaching. Insofar as the situation of dogmatic obscurantism I have been talking about is real, and is part of an actual academic situation, it is one created largely by the work, as faculty members, of fanatical fringe adherents of the formalist movement—a sort of part-time, night- or correspondence-course students who have taken up, from haphazard reading, the doctrines merely as shields to hide their incompetence in any other kind of scholarship. Few who have actually studied under the "masters" are among the culprits; the wrongdoers are actually, academically, embittered graduates of the old, so-called philological schools of Ph. D. scholarship in their final decadence.

But regardless of where the responsibility for its encouragement is justly to be put, the explication fad in criticism is established; and because the faddists use their textbooks and their phrases, the responsibility is charged most frequently, whether justly or not, both by many whom the fad does offend and by some whom it should but doesn't, to the willing influence of Ransom, Tate, Blackmur, Empson, Warren, Heilman, *et al,* and simply because he is the constant exegete and constant pedagogue of the group, especially to Brooks. It is not only the practising scholars and critics of other fairly well defined, opposing schools who seem unable to distinguish between the work of any one of these men (there are vast differences among the members of the "group," of course, Mr. Van Wyck Brooks's latest book still notwithstanding) and the doctrinaire imitation. There is a tendency also among those who are not in gloom but rejoice at the fact or prospect of this movement's becoming the dominant one in the universities and the literary journals, to welcome indiscriminately any kind of lip-service to the cause as an earnest of faith and good sense. And it is this tendency that seems to me cause for greatest concern. Even if the universities are always, in a sense, beyond hope, by some rule of their nature ceaselessly driven from one doctrinal slavery to another, the journals can and ought to be free. (It would be healthier, if the choice had to be made so, to fill them nine-tenths with second rate poetry, than to admit any amount of any kind of second rate criticism).

We need some means of distinguishing between the genuine contribution and the fad piece. And in the case of Mr. Brooks's work, the means are ready to hand, if seldom taken; the difference is remarkably simple, if rigorous.

It is the difference between approaching a poem as an architectural problem, or as an engineering problem. It is perfectly true, as some of his critics are fond of pointing out, that the terms of Mr. Brooks's theory which refer properly to principles of form are often used as if they referred to structural materials. But they are not so used by Brooks. He has done nothing by his own example to encourage the view that one might learn to read, or write, a poem in some sort of literary Strength of Materials course—with lessons in the tensile strength of paradox, the relative virtues of cast and wrought irony, the flexibility of reinforced concrete.

It is the difference between looking for what holds specific effects together in the whole of a particular poem, and having a facile eye only for the effects as such. The context is all for Brooks.

He has never in any sense been concerned with effects, but with all devices as manifestations of an informing and unifying principle in any poem. And for Brooks, the principle, the form itself, always emerges, as John Crowe Ransom has observed, out of the poem's "own metaphorical energy." Ransom speaks of Brooks's determining sometimes a dominant image in a poem and then "wrestling" the poem into the terms of that dominance. The figure of the wrestler is good. One might conceive of Brooks's terms—paradox, irony, and so on—as so many practiced holds that he applies in an encounter with a poem. He is wrestling a Proteus, to be sure. Brooks is insistently interested in the "common structural properties" of various poems of all periods, in "universals"—this insistence is an essential part of his quarrel with the historical scholar-critics. But if each poem is but one shape of the many that the ultimately single, wily opponent may take, still that particular form, of the individual poem, has at least an immediate, active reality that had better be respected if he *is* to be held fast, and made at last to prophesy, to tell of what is beyond the present and particular. How the holds are to be applied in each instance will effectively depend upon whether he chooses to appear a man or a serpent for the moment.

There is the difference, further, between knowing and not knowing what one is rejecting when he strips the poem to read it "as poem." I am not sure that it is well, or even that it is possible, to be a scholar first, before one is a critic. It may be that one may choose only between a responsible or an irresponsible critical attitude, that every scholarly undertaking is shaped by a previous critical judgment, good or bad, controlled or uncontrolled. But assuredly it is desirable to acquire habits of scholarly competence *along with* the practice of criticism. And Mr. Brooks is a scholar; the breadth of his scholarship, through the twenty-odd years of his work, has increased constantly with that of his critical insight, not to alter the essential purpose of the criticism, but to strengthen and confirm it in an always richer and at once more rigorous definition. When Brooks proposes to read a poem *sub specie aeternitatis,* he knows fully the cultural matrix, the biographical facts, the situation of textual doubt or certainty, from which he is releasing the poem. And he never approaches a reading without first clearing the ground, assessing the critical history of the poem. If anyone tries to practice the exegetical method simply because he is ignorant of the techniques and results of other approaches, it is not Mr. Brooks—and if the word I have of those who have labored for a Ph. D. under his direction is trustworthy, it is not his students either.

But besides those who have too narrowly adopted Mr. Brooks's method, there are others who have, from varying motives, attempted to adapt it. Now, there is little question but that a rapprochement of some kind between the method of structural analysis and other philological disciplines is desirable; I am inclined to think it is also possible. But there is a question of procedure in getting them together, so that the unique purposes of one or the other, or both, may not be lost sight of in the process.

Almost every respectable, publishing, scholar now finds it at least politic to support the 'facts' of his research on any literary work with a plausible effort now and again at structural analysis. But even when the motive is more than one of expediency, the effort is made too often without attention to the fact that structure is total structure. Mr. Brooks has not, perhaps, always succeeded in accommodating a poem to this view—and the fault may be, in one instance or another, either his or the poem's, or both—but the view is, as we have observed before, that the poem generates its own principle of form, and that the final test of validity in the reading of any aspect of a poem is the taking of the aspect as organic *part,* and submitting it to the question of what impulse it bears from and imparts to all other parts. If one takes *structure* to mean anything else, he is not speaking Mr. Brooks's language. It is well to understand that the vocabulary and the rhetorical tricks of the analytical method may be adapted without any real grasp of its principle.

I think this is what has happened in a good many instances of the grinding of old axes against the new stone. They are axes, and they are old, though usually now fitted with new handles. Biographical criticism, for example, of the sort that used to be practised especially on Milton and the Romantics, whereby poems were made out to be transcripts or allegories of the personal life experience of the poet, is pretty well discredited. But it, or something essentially very similar to it, begins to appear again in the guise of what might be called intellectual biography, an effort to plot from the development of habitual rhetorical practices and intellectual concerns in the work of a particular poet an over-all *system* of his poetic, what is spoken of most cautiously as a consistent personal myth or most rashly as a personal metaphysic, in terms of which every particular poem must be understood. The older kind of biographical study, taking literature more or less frankly as a reflection of life and largely indifferent to the internal order of the image, the text, concerned with pinpointing relationships between particular aspects of poems and particular life experiences of the poet, lacking the system, could not be easily accommodated to the view of a poem that demands an account of the functional inter-relationship of all its parts. The re-vamped approach, on the other hand, does confine itself largely to texts, the conscious utterances of the poet, for its materials. Ostensibly, at any rate, it gives to the poetic text a status at least equal to that of letters and whatever formal, critical statements the poet might have made. And having a system, so developed, a logical structure of categories into which the several aspects of all the poems can be fitted and shown to function thus and so within the frame of that logic, such an approach can much more readily read its order into any particular study with an appearance of its being an account of the total order of the poem—or the order, for purposes of relative evaluation of poems, that the poem seeks but perhaps fails to attain.

Now, there is some justification for such a procedure. Certain poets—Wordsworth, Yeats, Donne, Milton even—especially yield themselves to at least one notion that is central here (emphasis varies with the practitioner), that of the career in which all the many poems are but partial representations of the one poem, the poem that maybe never got written at all in its single, whole perfection. And perhaps my remarks on Brooks as wrestler with Proteus might be seen to imply that he is doing the same thing on a larger scale—envisioning the One Poem, not just Wordsworth's one poem or Yeats's one poem, but everybody's, of which all particular poems are shapes. Brooks would probably turn away in horror at the first sight of any such image of himself as mystic. But if there is anything at all to it, I am inclined to think that the difference of scale is all the difference. The broader the vision, the conception one has of the ultimate reality, in literary criticism as in religion and politics, the more respectful one is of particular and immediate realities. It is the very, seeming nearness of the possibility that a totality may be grasped, the mind of the individual poet, the whole form of his Thought defined, which seduces the kind of critic I have been talking about into impatience with the particular form of the single poem. And granted that there is something grand and lordly in such impatience, a fine and assured contempt in the relegation of the structural analysis to the status of example or proof—"I can *do* this, of course, but I am after something so much bigger"; granted that there is something stodgy and schoolmasterish, maddeningly patient about Brooks's procedure—"What is *this* poem saying, what is *its* dominant image, read *that* line over before you make up your mind finally about this one"; still we ought to see clearly that if the consideration of the single form *is* merely accessory, it is a *different* thing from what Brooks does, not the same thing in a larger context. And I would further suggest, as an admonition to the impatient seeker for wisdom in his essays, that Brooks is probably at his most serene when he appears at his grubbiest—a kind of monk devoutly spading the abbey garden.

But if we move beyond the uses of the poem to consider the uses of poetry, the number of purposes to which it might seem possible to adapt structural criticism multiplies astonishingly. It is, indeed, in the eyes of many who pursue these concerns, not simply a possibility but something already accomplished.

Mr. Brooks, in the reply to Mr. Bush, has voiced his own misgivings at the prospect of an alliance of literary criticism with political and religious apologetics, or with the 'higher criticism' of mythanthropsychapology. Giving assent to his warnings, I would add that if it *is* Mr. Brooks's version of criticism one has in mind, the terms of any alliance also with the purposes of semantics and other language studies, of cultural history, of social and cultural criticism, require very careful examination. It seems to me questionable whether what has been adapted so far to any of these disciplines is anything like what Mr. Brooks means by literary criticism. And even if what I would call the lines of misdirection already established are to be pursued in the future, and we must remain in doubt about where we are headed, we ought at least to be sure what blessings can and cannot reasonably be demanded for the setting forth upon such enterprise.

Since one example will have to suffice here, it might be best to make it one that is perhaps least obvious. Mr. Brooks has at times been accused of participating in a kind of critical conspiracy to dictate principles of belief and taste and craft to the poets of his generation. The kind of critical activity that does attempt this, it seems to me, is essentially a variety of what I have called cultural criticism and I think can hardly with justice be read into Brooks's own work, or even regarded as flourishing under the influence of his ideas, rightly understood. This may be, in itself, a legitimate activity; again, it is conceivable that a way might be discovered to accommodate it to Brooks's views; but as it is presently practiced, Brooks is not only not responsible for it, but the way he looks at a poem seems to me completely at variance from its purposes.

Brooks, at least in the past, as a teacher in writing courses and as an editor, has directly encouraged and criticized the work of a number of our most important younger poets, perhaps exercising some influence to shape their practice of the art. But in his published criticism, beyond the general influence that any vital critical activity inevitably has upon the creative activity of its period, the tendency has been quite away from prescribing rules for composition. In fact, Brooks has not been very much concerned even to investigate or speculate upon the nature of the poetic process.

It is true, aside from the absurdity of such dark charges as Mr. Robert Hillyer's, that concern for the development of contemporary poetic practice—for what influences are and are not available to the young poet, and to what end—has centrally informed most of T.S. Eliot's critical work, somewhat after the example of Pound. And Brooks has frequently expressed his admiration for Eliot both as poet and as critic. But in this respect at least he has not followed Eliot in his own work. Whatever he may privately think, or teach, about what poetry ought to be, or how it ought to be conceived and written, he has pretty well restricted himself in his writing to a view of poetry as constituting poems, individual works of art that are already in definable existence, and no more with the problems of the pattern of influence or the psychological process through which they came into existence or might be effective in bringing other poems into existence than he has been, say, with the question of how 'poetry' can be made a mirror for magistrates. There is little more for the deliberate instruction of the practising poet in Brooks's criticism than there is for the politician, the cleric, the school administrator. Brooks has consistently refused to put the poem to work, at least until he is sure he knows what the poem is. And he has never doubted *that* the poem is. It might conceivably be a psychological or metaphysical impossibility, this poem that is. But if it is a delusion it is none the less the one that Brooks has rigorously adhered to. At the least, one can charge him with no other.

But to leave the question of what the tendencies and alliances of his work are and are not in the whole context of modern criticism in English—it might be interesting to see what can be made of Brooks as a Southerner. He is sometimes identified with the spirit at least of the Fugitive and Agrarian groups, although he is younger, of course, than the original leaders of these vaguely allied movements. He has written a few essays, on the South and poetry, and the South and Protestantism, that show an affinity with the Agrarian philosophy. He has at various times given his voice to the defense of the doctrine. He has been directly, critically interested, in a fashion that takes account of its theoretic regionalism, in the poetry of the Fugitives. Certainly also his editorial alliances have fostered these interests. And it may be significant that the first book of his single authorship on an individual writer is the study of William Faulkner now in progress.

And yet, here as in the larger context, it is clear that his work has put the emphasis upon the poem and the story removed from consideration of its cultural origins and influence. Or, if "cultural" is too large a term here, certainly he has been consistently less interested, in his published work, than any of the other Southern critics with whom he is usually associated—Tate, Ransom, Davidson, and so on—in the *social* implications of his critical ideas.

But it is, I think, a fact essentially significant in the development of his criticism, not accidental or incidental or simply a matter of temperament and the habits of friendship, that Brooks is a Southerner. The task he set himself was different from that of any of the other Southern critics, but neither more nor less surely calculated to drive him eventually into exile than theirs, its difference in no way a matter of its being less Southern. Brooks saw no more clearly than many others, perhaps, that the greatest or possibly the only hope for the South to survive or to be redeemed, to flourish as a distinct cultural reality, lay in the practice of letters—belles lettres our lady had to be, or else, there was no other way, submit more and more willingly to the role of happy housewife, indulged in an occasional charming excess of sentimentality, to a nation accustomed to think of literature and its history as a branch of advertising. But what he either did see more clearly than most, or has kept more constantly in mind, is that critical integrity in regionalism depended upon a rigorous refusal to have the region confused with the historical and geographical and social and political province. That the regional work might be understood as work of art, and not document of provincial life or dream, it was first essential that one understand the nature of *a* work of art, the principle of form by which it always works through but transcends the particulars of its maker's time and place. And, within the boundaries of the common language, the search for the principle seemed most likely to succeed if it ranged as far and wide as possible. Perhaps, if I am right about there being a spirit if not a conscious intent of Southernism in Brooks's career, the book on Faulkner is not a new departure, but simply the first work in a new phase developing out of the former, a judgment for which the other work is a logical preparation and condition.

Further, it seems to me there is something, not universally to be sure, but peculiarly Southern, in the way itself that Brooks looks at a poem. Not every Southerner, nor even every literary Southerner, but more certainly still hardly any non-Southern American critic, could take quite so seriously this view, that not only does the poem exist, but that such things, things existing in and for themselves, have a right to exist, and that it is a proper end of man's intellectual endeavour simply to study that existence.

Brooks, then, is fairly easily convicted of Southernism. It is a Southernism, however, that takes the whole English literary world as its province, that proposes no restrictions upon either its legitimate area of study or its audience.

But the mention of audience brings up a question that is not very easily settled by reference either to Brooks's critical theory as such, or to his Southernism. These references have to do with the question of how and what he reads, and somewhat with why. But the critic is also a writer, of course. And the characteristics of Brooks's writing, his 'style,' can hardly be defined either by analogy to his conception of the organic form of poetic composition, or as deriving from anything recognizable as a Southern rhetorical tradition.

The tradition, insofar as it might impose a style, is clearly irrelevant. For Brooks's work starts from the conception of form; as a critic he has never looked at the tradition except from the point of detachment provided by that conception. On the other hand, his idea as such of poetic form does have something to do with the way he writes; but that can best be defined, I think, by distinction rather than analogy.

I think it must be the simple truth of the matter, that Brooks does regard the use of language in at least his kind of critical writing as something essentially different from the poetic use. It is unlikely that he would be much disturbed by the charges one has heard that he talks about literature, but does not *make* literature of his talk.

It may be making virtues of natural limitations, but Brooks's style seems a deliberately plain, steady, utilitarian style. The critical commentary does not emulate but only serves the poem, assists it in the performance of its "miracle of communication," like the disciples distributing the bread and fish.

One may weary a little at the limited variety of Brooks's rhetorical and logical devices—the series of leading questions, offering tentative readings of a line, a figure, picking up relevances, discarding plausible irrelevancies, toward the definitive statement; the "if not exactly . . ., still" or "it may mean . . ., but it might also" constructions; the suggesting various words that the poet might have used other than the *mot juste* he did achieve. The repetition of such maneuvers in essay after essay, designed to win acceptance of the interpretation being offered by an elaborate show of anticipation of all possible objections, even if it doesn't bore him, may finally impress the reader not as candour but as a trick, which he naturally resents, to lead him into a logical ambush. The plain, straightforward sentence structure, with few suspensions or inversions, invariably neat subordinations, and much reliance on apposition of independent clauses and the like, becomes perhaps a trifle monotonous and, like the methodical "summing up" at intervals, may seem uncomplimentary to the reader who is vain of his own intellectual subtlety. Brooks himself expressed some concern, in a concluding chapter of *The Well-Wrought Urn,* about his reader's possible annoyance at the endless repetition of certain terms—irony, paradox, and so on. And it is true that Brooks is as tenacious with his terms, when he is sure he has got hold of a good one, as he is with his famous extended metaphors.

But there is another way to look at all this. If one can avoid thinking of a critical essay as properly either a contest or an amorous exercise between the author and the reader, Brooks is perhaps simply trying very earnestly to be precise about what he is saying, and again, not saying. Further, he makes no pretensions. One perfectly good reason for putting it plainly might be that he thinks it is a plain thing he has to say. And if the terms he works with are few, they are also well-defined.

Or, possibly the best way to make the point is to repeat what I have said before, that the commentary is never allowed to get in the way of the poem. Whatever the other risks involved in the style he has chosen, Brooks avoids the greatest danger that the 'inspired' critic faces, that of having his critique become a rival or substitute poem for the one supposedly being investigated.

There is a remarkable adaptability in Brooks's style, an apparent capacity of his mind for anonymity, indicated in the fact that he has been able to collaborate with several people of vastly different interests and training and bent of thought. Yet in the books of his single authorship, he has his individuality; and, if my remarks here have so far obscured the fact, his is far from the most graceless of contemporary critical manners.

His essays sometimes give the impression that he has never read a book for pleasure. I grant that this makes me uncomfortable— probably it makes Mr. Brooks uncomfortable too. But one must after all remember that literary studies have been embattled in this generation. Both fine impetuosity and gentle refinement in the pursuit of criticism and scholarship require a leisure that our society has seen fit more and more to deny us. And that leisure, if it was ever indulged in all the freedom and beauty that some of our elders pretend to recall, is not to be purchased again simply with deploring the loss of its pleasures and graces. I cannot pretend to know just how it will be restored, if it ever is to be. But it is certain that our ideas must first be a good deal clearer than they have been before on exactly *what* it is for which we would demand license. Mr. Brooks has been both tireless and exacting in the measure that the task imposes.

HENRY W. WELLS

Poet And Psychiatrist: Merrill Moore

The thoughtful biographer of Merrill Moore will always recognize him as a Southerner; the critic concerned primarily with ideas discovers him an uncommonly poetic scientist and a poet strongly impregnated with scientific ways of thought. These are the more serious considerations. The larger public, always prone to judge from surface appearances, readily regards him as symbol for literary spontaneity, fecundity and possibly diffusion, as the astonishing man who has composed thousands of sonnets, who writes a facile style in shorthand, who hurries to print in defiance of his more scrupulous critics. Although he was at twenty much encouraged by John Crowe Ransom and others of the Fugitive group at Nashville, of which he was a younger member, his style never closely resembled that of any group of poets or even of any other poet. No sooner did he turn from magazine publication to his own books of verse, than an estrangement not only from the Fugitives but from the Southern mind generally became clear. The harshest of his critics found him at best a writer of palatable light verse, at worst, of slovenly pseudo-poetry. The more confirmed in cultism the "New Critics" have become, the less they have considered Moore in any respect. Yet he has won a perceptible audience, and a considerable praise, has remained active, and to some extent, at least, continued for more than a quarter of a century in the public eye. Also, it is probable that the cursory judgments passed upon him have often completely missed the mark. His eight books of verse have received a very fair number of reviews both in this country and abroad; one was published in New Zealand; another enjoyed a creditable translation into Spanish. He is more widely read than criticized. He remains, perhaps, all the more to be seriously examined because he stands resolutely apart from the cults of his own generation, an experimenter in new modes and an explorer of a style remarkably unlike the styles of Yeats, Eliot, Auden, Cummings, Thomas, Tate, or any of his more widely reputed contemporaries.

Whatever may be Moore's limitations, provinciality is hardly among them. He is Southern with many reservations. His position is not even sharply delimited in time, for he cannot well be described as a belated nineteenth-century naturalist in verse. There is no Southern poet with whom he has as much in common as with William Carlos Williams, who has analyzed and commended his verse with more discrimination than any other of his critics. Yet Southern in not unimportant respects Moore remains, for his style and mental attitudes were well established before he left the South in his twenty-fifth year, and the reader searching a little beneath the surface easily observes definite marks of his heritage, if not from the South in general, at least from that turbulent State, his native Tennessee. Like the majority of his fellow Fugitives, Moore revolted from Southern conservatism, though in a direction very unlike that of any of his friends.

Moore gladly admits that he learned something from Ransom. Psychological interests he shares with Warren. It is difficult to believe that his close association with Allen Tate in their most impressionable years, widely different as their temperaments are, can have been fruitless. He was one of the most frequent contributors to the unexpectedly successful periodical of verse which he and his friends sustained in common.

Then there was his father. While the Fugitive poets revolted against the conjunction of naturalism and sentimentalism long sanctioned by popular usage in the South, Merrill Moore reacted still more emphatically from the overshadowing power of a truly remarkable parent. John Trotwood Moore was one of the leading men of letters in an area at its widest describable as the South-Central part of the United States, or, at its narrowest, as Western Tennessee. The elder Moore was a successful novelist, short story writer, editor, historian, poet (possibly rhymster), essayist, propagandist not only for political measures but for the advance of amateur science and the new "scientific" farming and animal husbandry already transforming life in the more fertile areas of Tennessee and Kentucky and adjacent states. The son found contagious the father's literary ambitions, love for spontaneous expression and eloquence, and affection for the natural sciences. But while the father's innovations seemed liberal, the son's at once appeared radical. He completely renounced the peculiarly Southern social and ethical standards upheld by his father, as well as his father's literal-minded, sentimental, middle-class standards. His activity as poet may well be interpreted as focused upon his ambivalent attitudes towards his father, both in what he retained and in what he adopted as a violent revolt from the practice of a parent thoroughly representative of an important section of Southern thought. The South, like the Fugitive group, gave him a ground-work for his character as man and artist and the lively provocation to break forth unto new paths. While other members of the Nashville fraternity managed at the same time to be loyal to an older South and fugitive from it, the young Moore more poignantly contrived to be loyal to and fugitive from a beloved parent. In important respects he owed more to the South and revolted further from it than any.

The subject-matter of his first published poem well expresses this paradox. "Dendric" has as its title the pen-name which for a short while, at least, he employed. It celebrates the "primitive" art of the native African negro. Had his father really understood the piece, he would almost certainly have been shocked. Moreover, at the time when Ransom, Tate, Warren and their associates were scorning the Romantics and turning toward Dryden, Marvell, Donne, Shakespeare, Skelton and Chaucer, Moore, blandly neglecting British tradition and avoiding American chauvinism, was at least hospitable to far more remote influences. His poem owes its thought to a much more scientific or psychological anthropology than indicated by the far-fetched mythological-religious images of *The Waste Land*. With Eliot as their arch-type, the new poets, destined to evolve, by apotheosis or decline, into the "New Critics," were to become the avowed enemies of science, ascribing to it a spiritual bankruptcy in modern man. But Moore was himself to become a scientist of distinction, whose personality, for better or worse, integrates science and imagination in novel relationships, so that the scientist becomes in some respects the poet, the poet, partially the scientist.

During the six years of his literary activity in the South (1922-1928), Moore was a rebel. And during the longer and more recent period of his activity he is a willing exile in the North. As would be supposed, the South endowed him with many of his personal characteristics, but influenced his mind largely through providing incentive for counter-action. He became much that his Nashville friends profoundly distrusted: in philosophy, pragmatist and modernist; in poetry, impromptu in his inspiration and relatively open in his diction. As befitted a psychiatrist—for such was his carefully chosen profession—at times he cultivated the weighted and elusive symbol, but always rejected a metaphorical compression. He appears spontaneous where his associates appear literary; the mind employed in his poetry turns to psychology and to life, with remarkably little attention to literary tradition or current literary opinion. Well might professional critics distrust him, since he owes them so small a debt. To the most severe among them, eyeing him with condescending glances, he seems a rank amateur, but in more friendly and possibly more discerning eyes he appears a notable modern experimenter. This difference of opinion is seen in the completely conflicting views regarding him held by Ivor Winters and Dr. William Carlos Williams.

In a limited sense, then, Moore is Southern, since he achieved his style and philosophy within the first six years of his intellectually active life, which included his four years in Vanderbilt University and his two years of medical training. Although he has explored further and more deeply, the lines laid down in this early period to a pronounced degree define a literary career thus far extending to thirty years. Within a few months after he began to take poetry seriously, he embraced the sonnet form as his own and, treating this freely and with no little originality, he has sustained it as his only form ever since. His elusive symbols and perspicuous language, his colloquial idiom and expansive subject matter, appear from the very first. The fascination that psychological observation holds for him, a point of view on the whole much more commonly found today in novelist than in poet, he shows from the beginning. He explores the universal through the personal, the abiding truth through the moment of lyrical enlightenment flashing upon the contemporary scene.

This attitude he attained in various ways. A singularly independent man, he seems not to have been deeply influenced by his college training, although he enjoyed much of the reading which it encouraged, nor does he seem actually to have formed his literary character through the stimulation of the Fugitive group. His father had a fairly large library, which the boy devoured. On its shelves he found the food for the heresies that turned him away from both the Old South and the New. He was a New England pragmatist before seeing New England, a modernist before he set foot on what were, conventionally speaking, the more progressive sections of the United States and the world.

His divorce from the trodden ways of Nashville was confirmed by two trips to Europe, one while still an undergraduate, the other, at the termination of his medical internship. In Germany he came in touch with Expressionist art. He imbibed something of the Freudian climate of ideas well before he achieved his early ambition to become a psychiatrist. His trips to Europe, however, were merely summer excursions. On Southern soil Moore became substantially the man and poet that he is today. It is no accident that he married a boyhood friend who was herself a Southerner by birth, though a Northerner by temperament and education. Promptly thereafter he began his independent life as a professional practitioner and as the father of a family within the confines of Boston. Moore illustrates both how much and how little the place of birth and early training can signify for a man. His personality was molded by his youth in the South, his mind, by the reading of books written elsewhere and by the consciousness of the twentieth century, though certainly more by its social and scientific thinking than by its literary cults.

The student of Moore's art, then, discovers all its essential elements in the poems contributed to *The Fugitive,* 1922-1926. These Moore collected in two pamphlets published in 1938. One, of relatively minor value, contains all the pieces not in sonnet form; the other, obviously of much more merit and importance, is comprised exclusively of sonnets, which clearly point to his destined career. Although none of the chief features of his later work is here fully developed, all are at least present. There is already considerable freedom in rhythm and rhyme, though less than in the volumes of a decade thereafter. The early sonnets are a little less unconventional than their successors. Nevertheless, they are typical Merrill Moore poems. Rarely are the first few years of composition so definitive in a poet's life. Moore is today an admirable exponent of the general philosophy of William James and John Dewey, with many recent accretions eminently pragmatic and agreeable to the intellectual atmosphere of the North, as well as of other lands more widely removed from the South. His adjustment to New England and New York has been detailed and inclusive. Yet at least his poetical manner was completely achieved during his early years. He departed almost as far as it is possible for a Southerner born and bred to depart from his local tradition. Moreover, the physical divorce he felt virtually essential. But not until his mind was made up did he change his place of residence which, owing in part to his sanguine temperament, he found as emotionally congenial as it was intellectually repulsive. However far he may have strayed as man and artist from his original home, he has in general retained personal affection for his Southern friends, intellectual and non-intellectual, and for his home city. Especially he enjoys its negroes. It is well worth remembering that for a short while Moore taught French in Fisk University.

Part of Moore's reputation results from his peculiar publicity. Neither he nor his successive publishers have avoided a publicity making him appear more a legend of fecundity than an author of merit. In an age wherein the poetry of most repute is costively created, published in very small books, framed in short poems, and interminably revised, Moore appears in the world's eye as prodigiously spontaneous. The legend goes (partly promulgated by Mr. Untermeyer) that he writes many thousand sonnets, that he writes with almost incredible rapidity, in short hand. This is literally true, but the outlines have been rendered grotesque by exaggeration. He is not so much incapable of self criticism as impatient of it. Editorial labor he generally leaves to others. With real shyness and instinctive reliance on friendship, he has published his verses with commendatory comments by other poets and by critics, including the present writer. (There is, of course, ample precedent for this in the seventeenth century). In recent volumes humorous titles and comic-strip cartoons by the sprightly Edward St. John Gorey have pointed to the element of light verse. Especially his *M,* a volume with a thousand sonnets, drew some condescending detractions. Undeniably Moore's sonnets are of unusually unequal merit, some of the best marred by weak lines, even some of the worst containing a line or two of memorable verse. Whether or not he has revised too little, it is highly probable that he has published too much. Others may have written as much as he; many living poets have published far more lines, notably those producing verse plays. But none has followed a strategy so seriously risking the charge of diffusion. His personal optimism also encourages the view of him as wanting the severer criticism of the dedicated artist. A relatively sober critic, like Mr. Winters, is ideally constituted to fall foul of such a phenomenon as this veritable Pantagruel masked as a sonnet.

Moore's sonnets have not been especially popular with the anthologists, for they so clearly contradict many, though not all, the requirements commonly fulfilled by modern verse. Their language is not particularly "dense," their outlook, in some respects more objective than subjective. The best of them, though elusive in the major symbol, or essential meaning, are fairly transparent in diction. They show small conformity to the fashions, stylistic, emotional, or intellectual, set by *The Waste Land*.

There is even an element of wisdom behind the poet's seeming foolhardiness in publishing much. Although never written as sequences, the sonnets should be read excursively to be enjoyed most. This partly accounts for the absence of quotation in this brief article. We must accustom ourselves through some repetition to having symbols presented more in terms of the psychologist than of the linguist, for the linguists have at least temporarily won the battle of the little magazines. We need space to grow used to the real novelty of Moore's approach, to realize that he is not a bad writer following familiar ways but a new kind of writer and an experimentalist, whose merits it would be rash to appraise hurriedly.

Doctor Moore is at present the leading scientist in America writing verse of any consequence. Doctor William Carlos William is a poet at least of wider repute but not a scientist of greater repute. Only occasionally does Doctor Williams use his medical experience as subject matter for his poetry; actually, so far as we are allowed to see, Williams the physician goes one way, Williams the poet another. But Moore, creative in both fields, is much more clearly a single personality, whether working as an authority in psychiatry, in problems of alcoholism, drug mania and veneral disease, or in the writing of poetry. His "portrait sonnets," for example, are character analysis; his poetic imaginings resemble the hypotheses of science; his many scientific papers not infrequently have the breadth, the warmth, the human understanding of the artist. To Moore, poetry is not exclusively an affair of words, nor the practice of medicine wholly a transaction in exact technical knowledge. A distant heir of both Leonardo and Theophrastus, he sees imaginative literature and science as practical allies, not, as Eliot, Ransom and Tate so often describe them, antithetical. Pedantry, Moore presumes, is possible on either side; indeed, it becomes inevitable unless some harmony is attained between the two approaches to life. His poetry is designed to avoid equally the pedantry of numbers and of words.

That a scientist when writing verse should turn his back on literary tradition, is by no means strange. To the doctor, the medical books of a few generations ago are nearly useless. He must keep up with the times. So when he turns to verse, it is not impossible that he will also consult the present rather than the past. And he may experiment. Doctor Williams announces that he is in quest of a new language for poetry, a new English clear to men, using old words, no doubt, but in a new fashion. Moore is less linguistically minded than Williams but resembles him in many respects, both philosophical and aesthetic. To some eyes he will therefore appear as a barbarian, who rejects the tried and true; to others, he will seem prophetic.

From his earliest years as poet Moore realized the common ground between poet and psychiatrist, each a scholar of the soul and of the human personality. He showed a lively interest in almost all the sciences: striking and original sonnets are to be found with subject matter from astronomy, geology, botany, physics, chemistry, engineering, and, above all, psychology. He composes intellectual sonnets analyzing mind, soul and heart. He studies fear, hope, depression, passion, sex, sexual mores, and various illusions, those of alcoholism and drugs being conspicuous. With a psychologist's insight, he examines childhood and old age. With a doctor's realism, he broods on morbidity and death.

Moore's relation to social thinking proves of special interest, inasmuch as few writers so non-political as he possess so critical an awareness of the forces molding society. In an age accustomed to thinking of our social destiny as primarily political, it is heartening to consider a writer who so cogently presents other aspects of our organized living. Once more Moore's attitude reflects his profession as doctor and psychiatrist, for he is deeply concerned with public health and the public welfare, physical and mental. His revolt from the South was largely occasioned by his sociological views. A visit to Germany in the year of Hitlerian revolution and to China in the year of political liberation from Japan, not to dwell upon his ethnological studies aided by his life in the South Seas during the Second World War, gave additional strength to his social imagination, confirming and enriching a tendency long prominent in his poetry. Moore has led and participated in several movements of real importance to our society, chiefly in respect to public sanity and health. He has fought the obscurantist idealist, North and South, in more battles than one. This point of view is also reflected in his singularly vital poetry.

The enlightened physician has not only a responsible attitude toward society but entertains a peculiar and valuable variation of the pervasive ideas of comedy and tragedy. To the aesthetic detachment of the poet he adds the compound of sympathy and aloofness almost of necessity forced as an ideal and to some extent as an actuality upon the medical profession. Hence his comedy, of which the sonnets possess much, is reticent and urbane, his tragedy controlled and austere. His amused smile is no indication of a want of robust humor, his emotional control no mark of lack of emotion. In each case he appears not only a superior artist but a faithful physician to mankind and in a peculiar degree the modern, urbane man and thinker. The colors are not just pale; they are, in fact, well chosen and expressive. His wit is resilent, his pathos sincere.

Moore, in short, is a singularly provocative poet, highly unusual, though of uncommonly disputable merit as an artist. As a man he is indisputably worthy of the legends that surround him. There is also so much worthy of study in his work, that a formal judgment of it either for better or worse cannot wisely be made in haste. Criticism has not yet, I think, discovered where to place him. But of certain conclusions we may be sure: he is partly Southern, greatly fascinating, largely modern; he is the chief fugitive from the Fugitives, the chief spokesman for the imaginative power in modern science. Though surely not the best of poets, he is assuredly the most lyrical of physicians. He is a by no means minor witness to the poetical vitality of the American South. A culture has gone far that can propel a writer to such distances as Moore has traversed.

Index

Charleston, S. C., 126, 140
Charles Town, W. Va., 388 n.
Chambers of Commerce, in South, 23
Chaucer, Geoffrey, 321, 372, 429
Chekhov, Anton, 326
" Chicago Critics," 5, 9
Chirico, Georgio de, 372
Church, Margaret, 294
Classicism, 300, 326
Clay, Henry, 17
Clemens, Samuel L., *see* Twain, Mark
Coleman, Elliott, 174, 179
Coleridge, Samuel Taylor, 44
Collected Essays of John Peale Bishop, The,
   295, 302, 371
Collected Poems of John Peale Bishop,
   The, 369 n., 373–74
Collected Stories of William Faulkner, The,
   153
Collectivism, 23
Columbus, Miss., 109
Columbia University, 307, 394
Commager, Henry Steele, 172
Commentary, 155 n.
Commercialization, 103–105, 213
Communism—*see* Marxism
Concreteness, sense of, 3 ff.
Confederate States Army, 22 ff., 68, 112–
   26, 212, 239, 264, 410–11
" Confessions of Jereboam O. Beauchamp,
   The," 226
Connelly, Mark, 86 n.
Conquistadors, 371
Conrad, Joseph, 6
Conservatism, 45, 70, 87, 284, 326, 428
Contempo, 401
Cooke, John Esten, 112
Cords of Vanity, The, 256
Costain, Thomas B., 227
Counter-Statement, 379
Cowley, Abraham, 361
Cowley, Malcolm, 95, 96 n., 100, 115, 156,
   158 n., 307
Crane, Hart, 369
Crane, Stephen, 264–65, 326
Cranford, 308
Cream of the Jest, The, 252 ff.
Criterion, 368
Criticism, biographical, 419–20
Criticism, cultural, 421–22
Criticism, formalist, 416
Crockett, David, 402
Cultural criticism—*see* Criticism, cultural
Culture, folk, 88–94, 107, 111
Culture, urban, 100–107, 210, 215, 310
Cummings, E. E., 369, 371, 376–77, 428
Curtain of Green, A, 307

Dabney, Virginius, 398
Dali, Salvador, 372, 385–86
Dante, 251, 260, 361–62, 366
Davidson, Donald, 38, 83–88, 91 ff., 101,
   283, 291, 296, 303–304, 354 ff., 392–
   412, 423
Davis, Jefferson, 121
Death, attitude toward, 7, 120, 298–99,
   335, 345–46, 349, 357–58
Decision, 369 n.
Deliverance, The, 148
Delta region, of Mississippi, 306
Delta Wedding, 307
Destinations, 360
Determinism, 205, 230–34, 322, 333
Deutsch, Babette, 369 n.
Dewey, John, 11, 49, 431
Dial, 369 n.
Dickinson, Emily, 372, 390
Dillon, George, 86 n.
Divided We Stand, 395
Divine Comedy, The, 251, 260, 361–62,
   366
Dr. Martino and Other Stories, 307
Donne, John, 268, 372, 374, 420, 429
Dos Passos, John, 291, 299
Dostoevsky, Fyodor, 233, 249, 264, 334
Doubleday, Page, and Company, 100
Dowson, Ernest, 372
Dreiser, Theodore, 213, 233, 262, 271,
   316, 322, 396, 411
Dryden, John, 372, 374, 379, 429

Education, 397–99
Eliot, Thomas Stearns, 4, 13, 26, 28, 264,
   363, 368–74, 385–86, 389, 422, 428 ff.
Elizabethan Age, The, 48, 217, 372, 376
Emerson, Ralph Waldo, 98, 412
Empson, William, 4, 417
Enlightenment, 18th Century, 21
Environmentalism, 98–99
Ethos, 103
Eureka, 40–41
Evil, concept of, 297–98
Exegesis, method of, 417–18
Explicator, 369 n.
Expressionism, 431
Episode In Palmetto, 137
Erasmus, 342

Faculty psychology, 44–45
Fadiman, Clifton, 295
Family, attitude toward, 118, 266–68,
   280 ff., 295
Family Reunion, The, 13
Farewell To Arms, A, 274
Fathers, The, 48, 113–17
Faulkner, William, 3, 7 ff., 29, 83–88,

8/1/89
Gift

444   INDEX